Verse Saints' Lives
Written in the French of England

Saint Giles
by Guillaume de Berneville

Saint George
by Simund de Freine

Saint Faith of Agen
by Simon de Walsingham

Saint Mary Magdalene
by Guillaume Le Clerc de Normandie

MEDIEVAL AND RENAISSANCE
TEXTS AND STUDIES

VOLUME 431

THE FRENCH OF ENGLAND TRANSLATION SERIES
(FRETS)

VOLUME 5

Verse Saints' Lives
Written in the French of England

Saint Giles
by Guillaume de Berneville

Saint George
by Simund de Freine

Saint Faith of Agen
by Simon de Walsingham

Saint Mary Magdalene
by Guillaume Le Clerc de Normandie

Translated, with Notes and Introduction by
Delbert W. Russell

FRETS Series Editors
Thelma Fenster and
Jocelyn Wogan-Browne

Tempe, Arizona
2012

Published with the assistance of Fordham University.

THE ARIZONA CENTER FOR
MEDIEVAL &
RENAISSANCE
STUDIES

Published by ACMRS (Arizona Center for Medieval and Renaissance Studies)
Tempe, Arizona
© 2012 Arizona Board of Regents for Arizona State University.
All Rights Reserved.

Library of Congress Cataloging-in-Publication Data

Verse Saints' lives written in the French of England / translated, with notes and
introduction by Delbert W. Russell ; FRETS series editors, Thelma Fenster and Jocelyn
Wogan-Browne.
    pages cm. -- (Medieval and renaissance texts and studies ; volume 431) (The French
of England translation series (FRETS) ; volume 5)
  Includes bibliographical references and index.
  ISBN 978-0-86698-479-9 (alk. paper)
  1. Christian poetry, French--Translations into English. 2. Christian poetry, French--
England--History and criticism. 3. Christian saints--Poetry. 4. Aegidius, Saint, Abbot.
5. George, Saint, d. 303. 6. Foy, Saint, ca. 290-303. 7. Mary Magdalene, Saint.
I. Russell, Delbert W. II. Wogan-Browne, Jocelyn. III. Fenster, Thelma S. IV. Guillaume,
de Berneville, 12th cent. Vie de saint Gilles. English.
  PQ1325.L4V47 2012
  841'.108038270092--dc23

2012034173

Front Cover:
Sybil and Robert Fitzwalter with two monks from Conques, returning to England to
found the Priory of St. Faith at Horsham (Scene 8 in medieval cycle of wall paintings at
St. Faith's Priory, Horsham) ©*Crown Copyright. English Heritage. Used with permission.*

∞
This book is made to last. It is set in Adobe Caslon Pro,
smyth-sewn and printed on acid-free paper to library specifications.
Printed in the United States of America

Table of Contents

Series Editors' Preface	ix
Acknowledgments	xi
Abbreviations	xiii
Introduction	xv

Saint Giles, Hermit and Abbot — 1

The Cult of St. Giles in Medieval Europe	1
Creation of the Legend	2
The *Vita sancti Aegidii* and Vernacular Translations	4
La Vie de saint Gilles by Guillaume de Berneville	5
The Author	5
Manuscript	6
Guillaume's Reworking of His Latin Source	7
A Well-Read Canon	10
Feudal Obligations and Life in Religion	16
Versification and Style	19

Saint George, Soldier Martyr — 23

Historical Basis for the Legend	23
Medieval French Translations of the Legend of Saint George	26
La Vie de saint Georges by Simund de Freine	27
The Author	27
Manuscript	28
Simund's Treatment of his Latin Sources	29
Narrative Treatment and Techniques	32
Compelling Speech-Acts and Witticisms	34
Concrete Figures of Speech	36
Conclusion	39

Saint Faith of Agen, Virgin Martyr — 41
Historical Basis of the Legend — 41
Conques and the Occitan *Chanson de sainte Foy* — 43
Conques and the Northwards Diffusion of the Cult — 44
The Cult of Saint Faith in Medieval England — 45
La Vie sainte Fey, virgine e martire by Simon de Walsingham — 50
    Manuscript — 51
    Monastic Author and Patron — 51
    Simon's Treatment of the Latin Sources — 53
    The Prologue: Time Present — 54
    The *Passio*: Early Martyrdoms — 56
    Translatio to Conques: Expanding the Gift — 58

Saint Mary Magdalene — 61
Mary Magdalene in the Medieval West — 61
From Medieval Latin to Versions in French Prose and Verse — 63
Le Romanz de sainte Marie Magdalene (Guillaume Le Clerc de Normandie) — 66
    Manuscripts — 66
    Author — 66
    Guillaume's Treatment of the Latin Source — 67
    Remaining in *medias res* — 68
    Family Values — 69
    Pilgrimage — 71

Note on Translations, Manuscripts, and Editions — 75

Suggested Further Reading — 77
Primary Sources — 77
    1. Editions of French Texts — 77
    2. Latin Sources of the French Lives — 78
Secondary Sources — 79
    3. Studies of Individual Saints' Lives — 79
    4. Editions and Translations of Medieval Texts Cited — 82
    5. General Cultural, Historical, Literary Studies — 84

Texts
I.   *The Life of Saint Giles*, by Guillaume de Berneville — 87
II. *The Passion of Saint George*, by Simund de Freine — 143

III. *The Life of Saint Faith, Virgin Martyr*, by Simon de Walsingham, Monk of St. Edmunds Abbey, Bury	165
IV. *The Romance of Mary Magdalene*, by Guillaume Le Clerc de Normandie	187

Appendix 199

Guillaume de Berneville, *La Vie de saint Gilles*	199
Storm at Sea, followed by Clear Sailing (vv. 771–95, 876–912)	199
The Miracle of the Eucharist (vv. 2976–3015)	205
Spirited Conversation (vv. 3112–46)	209
Simund de Freine, *La Vie de saint Georges* (vv. 1527–1600)	212
Dacien Explores His Own Anger	212
Simon of Walsingham, *La Vie sainte Foy*	217
First Interrogation of St. Faith by Dacien (vv. 265–300)	217
Faith on her Bed of Torture (vv. 379–412, 523–96)	219
Guillaume le Clerc de Normandie, *Le Romanz de Marie Magdalene*	223
Storm at Sea and Premature Birth (vv. 231–308)	223

Index of Proper Names 227

Series Editors' Preface

In recent decades, saints' lives have attracted increasing attention as one of the most fascinating and important narrative forms of the Middle Ages. They now regularly find their way into undergraduate and graduate classes as well as into the exchanges and writings of scholars. Saints' lives composed in the French of England from the twelfth to the fourteenth centuries form a rich and varied body of hagiographic writing, exceptionally so in the late twelfth century; yet many texts remain to be translated.

We are therefore pleased to present this volume of translations with introductions and commentaries by Delbert Russell. Here four important saints' lives, each very different from the others, find their first full modern English versions. Among his other scholarly interests, Professor Russell is a leading editor of saints' lives in the French of England: in addition to the prose apostolic legendary extant in the famous trilingual manuscript Harley 2253 and other copies (*Le légendier apostolique anglo-normand*, Montreal and Paris, 1989), he has provided the Anglo-Norman Text Society with editions of the life of St. Laurent (*La Vie de saint Laurent*, ANTS 34, 1976), the life of St. Richard of Chichester (*La Vie de seint Richard, evesque de Cycestre*, ANTS 51, 1995), and the life of St. Francis (*La Vye de seynt Fraunceys*, ANTS 59–60, 2002).

The four lives in this volume comprise a varied set of saints: St. Giles is an abbot credited with confessing the emperor Charlemagne's secret sin; St. George is the well-known soldier saint; St. Faith, a young girl tortured at the command of a pagan tyrant by fire on a brass bed, is also both subject and patroness of one of the most notorious relic thefts of the Middle Ages; and Mary Magdalene, often a repentant prostitute figure, is here the guardian of fecundity and the helper of lay nobility in their family lives. Many medieval texts are anonymous, but in the case of these four saints' lives, we know the names and occupations of their authors and can therefore, as Professor Russell shows, reasonably infer more about their production context and potential audiences than is often the case.

In his introduction to this collection, Professor Russell treats the cults of each of these saints, the French of England versions of their lives, and the achievements of their authors. All FRETS volumes include passages of original text, and here we have made the formal innovation of presenting Professor Russell's detailed and informative analyses of these passages and the art of their composers alongside the text samples themselves in the volume's appendix. Together with the translations of the whole of each of these rich and richly varied lives, we hope that the opportunities of close appreciation provided by the appendix of texts and commentaries will draw still more readers to this remarkable literature.

Thelma Fenster
Jocelyn Wogan-Browne

Acknowledgments

Work on this project has been generously supported, both directly and indirectly, by funds from the Social Sciences and Humanities Research Council of Canada, and from the Faculty of Arts of the University of Waterloo, to whom I owe a debt of gratitude for their long-standing administrative and financial support: in particular, my thanks to Selena Santini, Valérie Miller, Kathleen St. Laurent, and Xing Liao.

In preparing these translations, I have relied on the inter-library loans librarians at the University of Waterloo, who have provided timely access to scholarly materials from across North America, and I am grateful to them for their indispensible services offered behind the scenes. My thanks to Roy Rukkila, Leslie MacCoul, and Todd Halvorsen, from the Arizona Center for Medieval and Renaissance Studies, for their expert work in bringing this volume to press; my thanks as well to Professor David Park of the Courtauld Institute, and Lucinda Walker of English Heritage for their help in locating photographs of the Horsham St. Faith medieval wall paintings.

This volume of translations owes its greatest debt, of course, to Jocelyn Wogan-Browne and Thelma Fenster, who first conceived the idea of such an anthology of saints' lives as part of a French of England Translation series. As general editors, their detailed responses to my draft versions have been a true collaboration as my critical approach to these texts evolved, and their comments have led to a sharper critical focus and more effective translations. My thanks as well, to my students in courses at Waterloo and to those of Professor Wogan-Browne at Fordham, for their responses to earlier versions of some of these translations.

Electronic editions of the medieval French originals of the lives translated here are also accessible online, as part of the electronic Campsey project, on the MARGOT website at the University of Waterloo (http://margot.uwaterloo.ca; see also the Note on Translations, Manuscripts, and Editions, below, 75–76). The creation and maintenance of this electronic resource continues to rely on the generous technical collaboration of Professor Frank Tompa, from the David Cheriton School of Computer Science, University of Waterloo, who has created and maintained the software and advised me on data structures. I have also benefited enormously from a number of humanist colleagues associated with the MARGOT project: my thanks in particular to Christine McWebb, Diane Jakacki,

Laurie Postlewate, and Helen Swift, and graduate students Joan Smeaton, Mark Finkelstein, Tara Hargraves, Carl Hayes, and Fabienne Beduneau.

Finally, my gratitude to my wife, Ruth, and members of my extended family for their forbearance as they have patiently listened to my digressions on hagiographical subjects over the years: this book is dedicated to them.

Abbreviations

AASS — *Acta Sanctorum* [...]. Antwerp: 1643–1864. Rev. ed. J. Carnandet et al., 60 vols. Paris, 1863–

ANC — M. Domenica Legge. *Anglo-Norman in the Cloisters: The Influence of the Orders upon Anglo-Norman Literature*. Edinburgh: Edinburgh University Press, 1950.

AND — *Anglo-Norman Dictionary*. Ed. Louise W. Stone, William Rothwell, et al. London: Modern Humanities Research Association, 1977–1992; 2nd ed., ed. Stewart Gregory, William Rothwell, and David Trotter. Vols A–C, D–E currently available; London: Modern Humanities Research Association, 2005; online at www.anglo-norman.net (unless otherwise noted, references are to the online edition).

ANL — M. Domenica Legge. *Anglo-Norman Literature and its Background*. Oxford: Oxford University Press, 1963; repr. 1971.

ANTS — Anglo-Norman Text Society

Baker — A. T. Baker, ed. "Vie anglo-normande de sainte Foy par Simon de Walsingham." *Romania* 66 (1940–1941): 49–84.

BHL — *Bibliotheca Hagiographica Latina antiquae et mediae aetatis*. Subsidia hagiographica 6. 2 vols. Brussels: Société des Bollandistes, 1898–1899; *Bibliotheca Hagiographica Latina antiquae et mediae aetatis: Novum Supplementum*. Subsidia hagiographica 70. Brussels: Société des Bollandistes, 1986.

CCHL — "Vita sanctae Mariae Magdalenae." In *Catalogus Codicum Hagiographicorum Latinorum antiquiorum saeculo XVI qui asservantur in Bibliotheca Nationali Parisiensi*, 3:524–30. Subsidia hagiographica 2. 3 vols. Brussels: Société des Bollandistes, 1889–1893.

CFMA — Classiques français du Moyen Âge

Dean — *Anglo-Norman Literature: A Guide to Texts and Manuscripts*. Ed. Ruth J. Dean, with the collaboration of Maureen B. M. Boulton. ANTS Occasional Publications Series 3. London: Anglo-Norman Text Society, 1999.

DLF	*Dictionnaire des lettres françaises: Le Moyen Âge.* Ed. Robert Bossuat, Louis Pichard, and Guy Raynaud de Lage. Paris: Fayard, 1964. Rev. ed. Geneviève Hasenohr and Michel Zink. Paris: Fayard, 1992.
Farmer	David Hugh Farmer. *The Oxford Dictionary of Saints.* Oxford: Oxford University Press, 1978; 5th ed. 2003 (online edition at http://www.oxfordreference.com.)
Gdf	F. Godefroy, ed. *Dictionnaire de l'ancienne langue française.* 10 vols. Paris: Champion, 1880–1902.
Jones	E[thel] C. Jones. *Saint Gilles: Essai d'histoire littéraire.* Paris: Champion, 1914.
Laurent, *SGilles*	Guillaume de Berneville. *La Vie de saint Gilles: Texte du XIIe siècle, publié d'après le manuscrit de la Bibliothèque Laurentienne de Florence.* Ed. Françoise Laurent. Champion Classiques, série Moyen Âge, editions bilingues 6. Paris: Champion, 2003.
ODNB	*Oxford Dictionary of National Biography.* Oxford University Press, online version (www.oxforddnb.com/view).
OED	*The Oxford English Dictionary.* 2nd ed. Ed. J. Simpson and E. Weiner. Oxford: Oxford University Press, 1989; online edition at http://www.oed.com.
Paris & Bos	Gaston Paris and Alphonse Bos, eds. *La Vie de saint Gilles par Guillaume de Berneville: Poème du XIIe siècle publié d'après le manuscrit unique de Florence.* SATF 16. Paris: Firmin-Didot, 1881; repr. New York and London: Johnson Reprint, 1966.
Pilgrim's Guide	*The Pilgrim's Guide to Santiago de Compostela: A Gazetteer.* Ed. Annie Shaver-Crandell and Paula Gerson, with Alison Stones. London: Harvey Miller, 1995.
Sheingorn, *Book*	Pamela Sheingorn, trans., intro. and notes. *The Book of Sainte Foy.* Philadephia: University of Pennsylvania Press, 1995.
T-L	A. Tobler and E. Lommatzsch, eds. *Altfranzösisches Wörterbuch.* Berlin and Wiesbaden: Steiner, 1925- .
Weiss	Franz-Karl Weiss. "Der 'Romanz de sainte Marie Magdaleine' von Guillaume, le Clerc de Normandie, und sein Quellenkreis." Diss. Westfälischen Wilhelms-Universität zu Münster (Westf.), 1968.
Wogan-Browne, *Saints' Lives*	Jocelyn Wogan-Browne. *Saints' Lives and Women's Literary Culture c. 1150–1300: Virginity and Its Authorizations.* Oxford: Oxford University Press, 2001.

Introduction

Saints' legends composed in the French of England are among the earliest and most notable of French vernacular texts in the literary histories of both England and northern France. They include the *Vie de saint Alexis*, beautifully illustrated in its earliest extant form for the famous psalter associated with Christina of Markyate;[1] the *Voyage de saint Brendan*, made for Henry I's queen, in which Brendan and his monks voyage westward from Ireland, looking for the earthly paradise;[2] and the lives of St. Catherine and Edward the Confessor by the nun(s) of Barking, two of the earliest French texts written by women (possibly earlier than, if not coeval with, Marie de France). Saints' lives continued to be among the most popular texts throughout the Middle Ages and beyond, in both Latin and the vernaculars: they constitute a rich genre with many narrative forms. The verse lives translated here vividly demonstrate this variety as well as some of hagiography's many strategies for reaching out to and shaping the lives of its audiences.

The *Vie de saint Gilles* (ca. 1170–1190), by Guillaume de Berneville, recounts the life and religious vocation of Giles from his birth to his death from natural causes. It traces the spiritual development of a young nobleman who renounces his power and wealth to embrace the ascetic life of a hermit, then later is made abbot of the monastery founded in his name. His spiritual growth occurs in the context of the responsibilities and pastimes of feudal lordship which are often in conflict with his religious vocation. Giles initially is drawn to the asocial eremitical life—his chief companion is a large doe—but he dies as the leader of a monastic community and one engaged to an extent with lay society. The life also addresses the doctrinal issue of confession, required of all, even the emperor Charlemagne, who seeks the aid of Giles for the remission of his secret and unspeakable sin.

The *Vie de saint Georges* (ca. 1186–1198) by Simund de Freine is not, strictly speaking, a life, but rather a passion narrative (*passio* being an early term for an account of martyrdom). Simund's *Saint Georges* is focussed on the dramatic

---

[1] The manuscript illuminations and online edition with English translation of the text are available at the St. Albans Psalter website, http://www.abdn.ac.uk/~lib399/english/

[2] See http://saintbrendan.d-t-x.com/ for a modern illuminated edition of the *Voyage de saint Brendan* with facing-page French translation, based on Ian Short and Brian Merrilees, eds., *Le Voyage de Saint Brendan*, Champion Classiques: Moyen Âge, éditions bilingues 19 (Paris: Champon, 2006).

conflict, expressed in both words and physical torture, between the Christian soldier and his pagan ruler. The narrative of the saint's martyrdom reflects the militant Christian crusader ethos in western Europe at the time of the third Crusade.

The *Vie de seinte Fey* (ca. 1200–1210), by Simon de Walsingham, is the lyrical and graphic passion of a young girl, St. Faith, child martyr of the southern French city of Agen, together with an account of the later medieval theft of her relics from Agen by a competing monastery at Conques. In recasting the story of St. Faith in French from the Latin life and related texts concerning the saint and her cult in France, Simon also, as he explains in a substantial prologue, translates her narrative for its value for himself and his contemporaries at Bury St. Edmunds abbey.

The *Romanz de sainte Marie Magdalene* (ca. the first third of the thirteenth century) by Guillaume le Clerc de Normandie uses the figure of the penitent prostitute saint Mary Magdalene, her preaching, and her special ability to ensure fecundity and the nurture of children as the material of a hagiographical pilgrim romance. This Christian adaptation of an earlier Latin romance is selected here for its striking demonstration of saintly intervention in the lives of the married. The *Romanz* provides a dramatic exposition of the saint's miraculous support for a mother and child left for dead on a desert island, a virtual tour of the Holy Land, and practical details for pilgrims taking sea voyages.

In the Middle Ages, especially in the earlier centuries, anonymous writing is more the rule than texts bearing the names of their authors. The lives in this anthology are therefore unusual in that their authors' names and professional status are known. A further bonus is that we know where they lived: all four can be associated with particular religious establishments in medieval England. Guillaume de Berneville, an Augustinian canon regular, was probably from the small monastic foundation of Barnwell Priory, Cambridge. Simund de Freine was a secular canon at Hereford cathedral, an important intellectual centre in the late twelfth century, in the west of England, near the Welsh border.[3] Simon de Walsingham, a native of Norfolk, was a monk at Bury St. Edmunds Abbey in Suffolk, in the east of England. Bury was also a major intellectual centre, and one of the wealthiest and most influential Benedictine monasteries in Europe at the time. In contrast to these three writers living and working in specific religious foundations, Guillaume Le Clerc de Normandie was not in religious orders: he was an independent writer using his training as a secular clerk to live by his pen

---

[3] A regular canon (usually also a priest) was a cleric who lived in community with other canons, following a rule (a *regula*, usually St. Augustine's Rule). In contrast, a secular canon did not live in community, under a monastic rule, but "in the world" (*in seculo*), and was a member of a chapter of clerics and priests serving a cathedral or a collegiate church under the supervision of a bishop.

and had a wife and children to support. Some of his works were for ecclesiastical patrons in the diocese of Lichfield-and-Coventry, in the West Midlands.

In composing these lives, each writer reworked the received material of the saint's legend for a particular public, in a specific social milieu and time. In order to situate the author and his public in their historical context, the discussion below comments, in turn, on the cultural background in which of each of these narratives was produced. The first step is to note briefly the evolution of the historical tradition of the saint in question, as well as the nature of the Latin sources on which each of these vernacular texts is based. Next we assess each vernacular writer's handling of his source material, which then allows us to evaluate the contribution his vernacular life makes to our understanding of the saint, and to the general evolution of the saint's legend.

1. Saint Giles, Hermit and Abbot

The Cult of St. Giles in Medieval Europe

The cult of St. Giles began in Provence and quickly spread to all of western Europe. The earliest documented references to Giles date from the early tenth century. They state that a Benedictine monastery in the south of France, formerly dedicated to St. Peter and founded as early as the seventh century, was placed under new patronage, that of Saint Giles. The monastery was strategically located south of Nîmes, on the site of a Roman settlement in the Rhone delta, overlooking the Petit Rhone River. Here, the shrine of the saint (and the town of St-Gilles-du-Gard which grew up around it) attracted pilgrims in its own right. It was also one of the most popular stops for pilgrims travelling elsewhere, since established pilgrimage routes to the three most popular destinations, Santiago de Compostela, Rome, and Jerusalem, all passed through St-Gilles.[1]

The rise of the cult was also helped by the economic importance of the site: the town of St-Gilles was a major port in the twelfth century, and a centre of trade between West and East, used by rival merchants from Genoa and Pisa. It was the main Mediterranean port of the counts of Toulouse, who were patrons of both the abbey and the town of St-Gilles, and was also one of the principal ports used by the early crusaders on their way to the Holy Land. But the town declined economically in the second half of the thirteenth century, as the prosperity of the counts of Toulouse waned during the suppression of the Albigensians (who were persecuted as religious heretics).[2] The port of St-Gilles lost its importance after the construction in 1240 of a rival port at nearby Aigues Mortes. The new port was built by Louis IX of France for his departure on the seventh crusade in

---

[1] St-Gilles is the first place mentioned in the description of the four routes through France in the twelfth-century pilgrim's guide to Santiago de Compostela. The route through St-Gilles begins at Arles. The powers of the saint and of his golden shrine are described in detail. See *Pilgrim's Guide*, 65, 75–77.

[2] Launched by Pope Innocent III, the so-called Albigensian crusade (1209–29) was a violent suppression of Cathars in southern France, begun with a massacre at Béziers in 1209; Raymond of Toulouse signed a treaty with France in 1229. Hostilities, however, continued well into mid-century.

1248, and again for the eighth crusade in 1270. Although the shrine of St-Gilles continued as a pilgrimage site until the end of the Middle Ages, its ability to attract pilgrim donations never recovered from the economic decline begun in the mid-thirteenth century.[3]

By the beginning of the thirteenth century the cult of Giles was widespread throughout Britain, Belgium, northern France, Germany, Bohemia, and Spain. It is attested in northern France and England by texts and foundations from the early eleventh century.[4] In Britain alone there were almost two hundred churches and hospitals dedicated to St. Giles, the best-known today being St. Giles in Edinburgh, and St. Giles, Cripplegate, London. In northern France the number of foundations was equally large, and the town of Saint-Gilles in Normandy was an important pilgrimage site. The stained glass depictions of the life of St. Giles in the cathedrals of Chartres and Amiens are just two examples of the numerous artistic representations of his legend in the Middle Ages. The widespread popularity of the legend is also attested by a reference to St. Giles in the *Chanson de Roland*, as well as in later epic texts.[5] In the twelfth-century pilgrim's guide to Santiago de Compostela, St. Giles, the pious confessor and abbot, is praised as the most prompt of all the saints to come to the aid of the poor and afflicted. His magnificent golden shrine in the monastery at St-Gilles-du-Gard, now lost (but described in detail in the *Pilgrim's Guide*, 75–77), demonstrates the immense status and popularity of the saint as a mediator of divine power on earth in the twelfth and early thirteenth centuries.

Creation of the Legend

The *Vita sancti Aegidii*,[6] the earliest known version of the life of St. Giles, is the source of all later versions. But it is clear that the *vita*, which presents Giles as a contemporary of both Caesarius of Arles (d. 542) and of a King Charles of

---

[3] For a general overview of the cult, see s.v. "Giles," in Farmer. See also Jean Nougaret, "Saint-Gilles-du-Gard," *Encyclopedia of the Middle Ages*, ed. André Vauchez, trans. Adrian Walford (Cambridge: James Clarke & Co., 2001); orig. *Encyclopédie du Moyen Age* (Paris: Editions du Cerf, 1997); e-reference edition, distributed by Oxford University Press (http://www.oxfordreference.com).

[4] Fulbert of Chartres (d. 1028) composed an office for St. Giles; the church of St. Giles, Cripplegate, London, was dedicated in 1090. The office and other texts can be read in the *Analecta Hymnica Medii Aevi Online* by searching under "Aegidius."

[5] See Françoise Laurent, *La Vie de saint Gilles* (Paris: Champion, 2003), xxviii–xxxi.

[6] The most accessible edition, with facing-page French translation, is Laurent, *SGilles*, 244–71. A more complete edition is in Jones, 2–9, 95–111. First published in AASS, Sept. I, 299–303. See also E. M. Treharne, *The Old English Life of St Nicholas*

France (either Charles Martel, d. 741, or Charlemagne, d. 814) is not historically accurate. The historical elements that lie behind the legend are assessed by Stilting, the Bollandist editor of the *Vita* published in the *Acta Sanctorum*,[7] and by Gaston Paris and Alphonse Bos, first editors of Guillaume's *Vie*.[8] Both examine medieval chronicles as well as documents from the cartulary of the monastery of St-Gilles to establish the historical origins of the legend. They conclude that the earlier monastery of St. Peter in the Flavian valley was given by a King Flavius to Giles to be refounded, about a decade before it was placed under papal control in 685, and that Giles died c. 720.[9]

Ethel Jones, however, argues that the medieval documents from the cartulary of St-Gilles used by Stilting and Paris to arrive at these dates were forgeries created at the monastery itself,[10] in the context of the long dispute (from 879 to 1091) between the bishops of Nîmes and the papacy over the control of the abbey. Jones also proposes that the *Vita sancti Aegidii* was produced in the first quarter of the tenth century by the monks of St-Gilles to support the monastery's claims. It would have been created about the same time as the earliest documentary evidence of the monastery being under the patronage of St. Giles, in the years 923 and 925.[11] The *Vita sancti Aegidii* presents the bishop of Nîmes as a witness of the foundation of the monastery, which it claims was built and richly endowed by King Flavius as a gift to Giles, who later placed the foundation under the direct supervision of the pope to guarantee its rights and privileges. The abbey's independence from episcopal control, confirmed by the pope during the lifetime of Giles, is proven, and made visible, according to the *vita*, by a gift from the pope, namely the physical doors of the abbey church which were miraculously conveyed by sea from Rome to St-Gilles.

The miraculous doors notwithstanding, the abbey needed written documents to protect its legendary claim of papal privilege. A manuscript created at St-Gilles shortly after 1132 includes both authentic and forged papal documents, and, as Amy Remensnyder shows, this manuscript's reworking of written

---

with the Old English Life of St Giles, Leeds Texts and Monographs, New Series 15 (Leeds: School of English, 1997), 198–206 for another edition of the *Vita sancti Aegidii*.

[7] AASS, Sept. I, 299–303.

[8] Paris & Bos, xlvi–lxxii.

[9] See AASS, Sept. I, 299–303. The arguments of Paris and Bos are summarized in Laurent, *SGilles*, xvii–xxvii.

[10] See Jones, 18–35. On the frequency of such forgeries see Giles Constable, "Forgery and Plagiarism in the Middle Ages," *Archiv für Diplomatik* 29 (1983): 1–41; repr. in idem, *Culture and Spirituality in Medieval Europe* (Aldershot: Variorum, 1996), no. I. The *Gesta Johannis VIII*, which Paris believed to be authentic, is now known to be the work of Pierre Guillaume, librarian-monk of St-Gilles, who also composed a book of miracles of St. Giles in 1121.

[11] Jones, 33–35. See also Laurent, *SGilles*, xxii–xxvii, which gives a summary of Jones' arguments.

documents to complement Giles' *vita* was used to counter continuing threats to the abbey's liberty from the bishops of Nîmes, the counts of Toulouse, and the abbey of Cluny.[12]

There is no documentary evidence of the origin of the cult earlier than the tenth century. Although some modern scholars still perpetuate the view that Giles flourished in the seventh century,[13] all are unanimous in viewing the account of his life in the *Vita sancti Aegidii* as legendary rather than historical.

The *Vita sancti Aegidii* and Vernacular Translations

The *Vita sancti Aegidii*, then, was written in the first quarter of the tenth century, probably by a monk of the abbey of St-Gilles.[14] From the eleventh to the fourteenth centuries a further ten redactions in Latin were derived from this first *vita*, including the version in the influential thirteenth-century "Golden Legend"—the Latin *Legenda aurea*, composed 1260–1275 by Jacopo de Voragine, bishop of Genoa.[15]

The first vernacular translation of the *vita* is in Old English (ca. 1170–90), in a version which remains relatively close to the Latin source.[16] Guillaume de Berneville's *Vie de s. Gilles*, the earliest French vernacular reworking (which is also derived from the *Vita sancti Aegidii*, but which adds considerably to its source text), is datable to the last third of the twelfth century. Guillaume's *Vie* was followed by eight later vernacularizations, dating from the end of the thirteenth century (in French, English, and Italian, some in very abbreviated form, and none derived from Guillaume's *Vie*).[17] Versions in English include the short verse life of Giles in the *South English Legendary* (attributed to Robert of Gloucester,

---

[12] See Amy Remensnyder, *Remembering the Past: Monastic Foundation Legends in Medieval Southern France* (Ithaca and London: Cornell University Press, 1995), 215–45.

[13] See, for example, the entry in Farmer, above, n. 3.

[14] Jones, 2. For an edition of the *Vita sancti Aegidii* (BHL 93, 94), see above, n. 6.

[15] See Jones, 1–9. See also *Jacobi a Voragine Legenda aurea*, ed. Th. Graesse, 3rd ed. (Breslau: Koebner, 1890; repr. Osnabruck: Otto Zeller, 1965); also, *The Golden Legend: Readings on the Saints*, trans. William Granger Ryan, 2 vols. (Princeton: Princeton University Press, 1993). The *Legenda aurea* was widely translated into the vernaculars.

[16] Treharne, *The Old English Life*, 130; the Old English *Life of St Giles*, with English translation, is 125–73.

[17] Jones, 62–70. See, for example, the transcription in Jones, 137–47, of the prose *Vie de s. Gilles* attributed to Jean Beleth, ca. 1285.

ca. 1280),[18] and the poem by John Lydgate (1370–1451).[19] There are many short vernacular prose redactions of the life of Giles included in legendaries derived from the *Legenda aurea*, such as the fourteenth-century *Légende dorée* by Jean de Vignay, which was used in turn by William Caxton in his *Golden Legend*.[20]

La Vie de saint Gilles by Guillaume de Berneville

The Author

Although Guillaume de Berneville tells readers his name (vv. 1039, 3765), and that he is a canon (v. 3761), little else is known about him. The language he uses in the *Vie* marks Guillaume as living and writing in England,[21] but he was perhaps originally from Normandy. Gaston Paris and Alphonse Bos suggest that Guillaume may have been from the commune of Besneville, in the department of La Manche. Berneville may, however, indicate the place in England where Guillaume lived and wrote, and Domenica Legge argues in favour of the proposal that Guillaume was a canon at Barnwell Priory, Cambridge, and suggests that his *Vie* may have been written in connection with the new church dedicated to St. Giles and St. Andrew built at Barnwell in 1190.[22]

The identification of Guillaume de Berneville as William of Barnwell is discussed at greater length by John Frankis, who analyzes two annotations in Anglo-Norman verse written in the same hand in a twelfth-century manuscript collection of Anglo-Saxon homilies.[23] In the margin of the manuscript (Cambridge, CUL, Ii.1.33) the annotator first writes four lines of French verse from a life of St. Andrew (source unknown), and in a later marginal annotation quotes three

---

[18] "St. Giles," in *The South English Legendary*, ed. Charlotte D'Evelyn and Anna Mill, EETS 236 (Oxford: Oxford University Press, 1952; repr. 1967), 2:384–89; on the attribution to Robert of Gloucester, see O. S. Pickering, "*South English Legendary* Style in Robert of Gloucester's *Chronicle*," *Medium Aevum* 70 (2001): 1–18.

[19] Jones, 63, suggests that Lydgate knew Guillaume's *Vie*; this is refuted by John Frankis, "Languages and Cultures in Contact: Vernacular Lives of St Giles and Anglo-Norman Annotations in an Anglo-Saxon Manuscript," *Leeds Studies in English*, n. s. 38 (2007): 101–33, at 131, n. 52.

[20] Jones, 62–70.

[21] See Laurent, *SGilles*, xii–xvii.

[22] See Laurent, *SGilles*, xii–xiv. Legge notes that this identification was first proposed by Ezio Levi, "Troveri ed Abbazie," *Archivio storico italiano* 83 (1925): 66, cited in Legge, *ANC*, 58–61; see also *ANL*, 254–57.

[23] See Frankis, "Languages and Cultures in Contact," 128–29, n. 35: "The commonest medieval form of 'Barnwell' is *Bernewelle*" and William may simply have seen "the common French place-name element *-ville* as an appropriate substitute for *welle* in a text in the French language."

extracts (vv. 89–90, 305–8, 547–48) from the *Vie de s. Gilles*. Frankis notes that saints Andrew and Giles are unusual joint patrons, with only one medieval foundation in England dedicated to both saints, namely the priory of St. Giles and St. Andrew at Barnwell, Cambridge. In this case the saints were linked by historical accident: the house of Augustinian canons dedicated to St. Giles, founded in 1092 in Cambridge, was moved in 1112 to a site better suited to its needs, and the new location chosen happened to be a former hermitage dedicated to St. Andrew; the refounded Priory at Barnwell was dedicated to both saints.[24] The annotator's knowledge of both the life of Giles by Guillaume de Berneville and a French verse life of Andrew suggests that he may also have had a direct connection with the Priory of St. Andrew and St. Giles at Barnwell. The reader (and annotator) of this Anglo-Saxon manuscript would have been a cleric, and may also have been one of Guillaume's fellow canons.

Manuscript

The complete text of the *Vie de saint Gilles* is extant in only one manuscript:

1. MS Florence, Biblioteca Medicea Laurenziana, Conv. soppr. 99; vellum, 258 × 180 mm. In two parts: fols. 1–146; fols. 147–162. The first part was written in England in the first half of the thirteenth century. The *Vie de s. Gilles* (fols. 111 va–145 ra) is preceded in part one of the manuscript by the Sermons of Maurice de Sully (fols. 1–98r) and the *Evangile de Nicodeme*, by Chrestien (fols. 99r–110r), and followed by a fragment of the *Vie de saint Jean Baptiste* (fols. 144–146). The second part of the manuscript (fols. 146–162) is in a smaller hand than the first part, and was written on the Continent. It contains part of a continental French verse translation of the *Elucidarium* of Honorius of Autun.

2. A second manuscript preserves a short fragment or excerpt of 95 lines:[25]

MS London, BL, Harley 912, fols. 183v–184r. The manuscript is datable to the end of the thirteenth century (Dean 529), or the mid-fifteenth century (Brandin). The fragment corresponds to vv. 2974–3057, dealing with the heavenly letter about Charlemagne's sin.[26]

---

[24] Frankis, "Languages and Cultures in Contact," 121–22, notes that the original site of St. Giles beside the castle in Cambridge lacked running water. The new site had water supplied from both springs and a river.

[25] See Dean §529.

[26] See L. Brandin, "Un fragment de la *Vie de saint Gilles* en vers français," *Romania* 33 (1904): 94–98. Also Laurent, *SGilles*, 273–76.

Guillaume's Reworking of his Latin Source

While the general arc of Giles' life as presented in the *Vita sancti Aegidii* is preserved by Guillaume, his poetic expansions of the *Vie* profoundly reshape the narrative. He demonstrates a wide knowledge of medieval society and draws on a range of motifs, including many originally hagiographic motifs that are now best known from their use in secular vernacular works, ranging from the epic to courtly romance.[27] Guillaume's skilful use of these motifs shows that in medieval society the secular and the sacred are interdependent, not mutually exclusive.[28] Guillaume's reworking of the legend is also influenced by the nature of religious life in the second half of the twelfth century. The marked rise in the popularity of hermits and anchorites and the early success of the Augustinian movement among the English elite in the twelfth century were symptomatic of wider social debate over the best form of religious life.[29] Guillame's participation in these debates in the *Vie de s. Gilles* is discussed below.

The interdependence of the secular and the sacred is not explicitly announced by Guillaume in the prologue to the *Vie s. Gilles* (vv. 1–17), nor does he exploit the conventional rhetorical strategy of vernacular writers in which hagiography is positioned in contrast to secular works. A famous example of the latter is the prologue to the *Vie seint Edmund le rei*,[30] in which Denis Piramus

---

[27] See Laurent, *SGilles*, xvi–xvii; and Frankis, "Languages and Cultures in Contact," 116–24: "*La Vie de Saint Gilles* is the work of an exceptionally gifted poet in its inventive adaptation of its source and in its connections with French secular verse from the *Chanson de Roland* to late twelfth-century romances . . ." (124).

[28] Cf. Giles Constable, *The Reformation of the Twelfth Century* (Cambridge: Cambridge University Press, 1996). Referring to the twelfth century, he states: "It is distinctly modern and western to think of human beings as having a basically secular nature, to which a body of thoughts or attitudes called religion may or may not be added. [. . .] No one at the time questioned that man was a spiritual being and naturally religious" (297).

[29] On the twelfth-century revival of the eremitic life, see Ann K. Warren, *Anchorites and Their Patrons in Medieval England* (Berkeley and London: University of California Press, 1985). See also Colin Morris, *The Papal Monarchy: The Western Church from 1050–1250* (Oxford: Oxford University Press, 1989), 250, who, citing Giles Constable, notes that public debate after 1125 centred on the proper form of religious life: the main areas of conflict were between the new Cistercian order and the black monks; between monks and regular canons, such as the Augustinians; and between secular canons and the new reformed monastic orders.

[30] Denis Piramus, *La Vie seint Edmund le rei: Poème anglo-normand du XIIe siècle*, ed. Hilding Kjellman (Göteborg: Elander, 1935; repr. Geneva: Slatkine, 1974). Another variation of this opposition between hagiography and secular works is found in the *Vie seinte Osith* (vv. 87–102, available online, http://margot.uwaterloo.ca, Electronic Campsey, part of the MARGOT site).

praises his *Edmund* at the expense of the *Lais* of "dame Marie"[31] and the romance *Partonopeu de Blois*,[32] among other secular works.

But as Ian Short argues, Denis does not establish a simple opposition between hagiography and secular works: instead he affirms the superiority of vernacular hagiography or history's truthfulness, based on written (and hence "verifiable") Latin sources, compared to secular works based only on "unverifiable" oral traditions and the creative imagination of the poet.[33] The first line of Guillaume's prologue (*D'un dulz escrit orrez la sume,* "Here you will hear the details of an uplifting story") subtly evokes this same distinction between "written and verifiable" and "imaginative and rhetorical," but here they are combined, not juxtaposed: his poem is both historically "verifiable" (since based on a written source, the *escrit*), and an imaginative reconstruction of this history, the rhetorical and persuasive nature of which is implicit in the adjective *dulz,* "sweet, uplifting" qualifying *escrit,* "history, written record."[34]

It is indeed Guillaume's poetic imagination that is the most remarkable aspect of the *Vie de s. Gilles,* for he portrays the saint's religious vocation both from the perspective of the external witness who sees the saint in action, and from the point of view of the protagonist's inner doubts and aspirations. The *Vie* introduces dialogues and monologues which show Giles questioning his own motivations, and debating with others the place of his vocation within medieval feudal society. This differs from the model of hagiography found in the *Vie de s. Alexis*[35] (the earliest fully developed literary saint's life written in northern French) in which the ascetic religious vocation of the protagonist is seen primarily from the outside. There is no introspection by Alexis; there is no self-doubt on the nature of his asceticism or his vocation, no debate between himself and other members of his society. The poet gives voice only to the incomprehension of the saint's parents and spouse in response to his disappearance from their lives. Their reactions eloquently express the incompatibility of the intergenerational aspirations held by Alexis' parents (maintaining the family's lineage, or the continuity

---

[31] *Lais de Marie de France,* ed. K. Warnke, trans. L. Harf-Lancner, Lettres gothiques (Paris: Livre de Poche, 1990); *The Lais of Marie de France,* trans. and intro. G. Burgess and K. Busby (Harmondsworth: Penguin, 1986).

[32] See *Partonopeus de Blois*: an Electronic Edition by Penny Eley, Penny Simons, et al., at http://www.hrionline.ac.uk/partonopeus/

[33] See Ian Short, "Denis Piramus and the Truth of Marie's *Lais,*" *Cultura Neolatina* 67 (2007): 319–40, for a new edition of the prologue (339–40), and a far-ranging analysis of medieval theorizing of the relationship between hagiography and secular works.

[34] See Mary Carruthers, "Sweetness," *Speculum* 81 (2006): 999–1013 for a discussion of the complex meanings conveyed by *dulcis* "when used to make a positive judgement about the effects of works of art" (999).

[35] *La Vie de saint Alexis,* ed. C. Storey (Oxford: Blackwell, 1968); online edition at the St Albans Psalter website, http://www.abdn.ac.uk/~lib399/english/

of genealogical capital), and Alexis' religious vocation (replacing his biological lineage with a spiritual lineage).[36] This same conflict is also found in the *Vie de s. Gilles*, but Guillaume allows his protagonist to articulate repeatedly his self-awareness and the self-doubts created by his choice of a spiritual family at the expense of his worldly family.

Guillaume also presents Giles' holiness as an apprenticeship, evolving as Giles proceeds through life.[37] In this regard, Giles is like the heroes of contemporary secular romances, such as Chrétien de Troyes' *Yvain*.[38] Chrétien's protagonist must practise his chivalric valour out of an inner strength of character, not out of mere superficial courtliness coupled with physical prowess. Yvain passes through the disintegration of the self and madness before he can rebuild, step by step, his identity and reputation, first as the "Chevalier au lion," and then as Yvain. So too Giles gains increasingly sophisticated levels of spiritual understanding as he moves through each stage of his life. He first moves from a childish practice of charity to an adult renunciation of his family's inheritance. Giles next embraces the life of a religious, first as a hermit, alone except for his companion doe, then as abbot of the monastic community founded for him by King Flovent.[39] As abbot, Giles lives apart from the other members of his community, in a separate building,[40] but he increasingly interacts with the monks. For example, Giles asks permission from his monks to accept the French king Charlemagne's invitation to travel to Orleans to hear the king's confession. Upon his return to his monastery in Provence Giles extends his pastoral role to ensure the future material and spiritual well-being of his religious community.

The stages of Giles's religious vocation as represented by Guillaume reflect important aspects of contemporary twelfth-century monasticism. Throughout the Middle Ages religious reforms repeatedly invoked a return to a simpler life, either

---

[36] See N. Vine Durling, "Hagiography and Lineage: The Example of the Old French *Vie de Saint Alexis*," *Romance Philology* 40 (1987): 451–69 for a discussion of this conflict as the essential paradigm of hagiography.

[37] See F. Laurent, *Plaire et édifier: les récits hagiographiques composés en Angleterre aux XIIe et XIIIe siècle* (Paris: Champion, 1998), 475–576, for a detailed analysis of the *Vie*, and of Giles as a reflection of the changes in religious thought evident in the last half of the twelfth century.

[38] Chrétien de Troyes, *Le Chevalier au lion (Yvain)*, ed. M. Roques (Paris: Champion, 1982).

[39] Flovent is introduced in the narrative (vv. 1541–82) immediately after the description of the living arrangements established between Giles and the doe. Giles' hermitage is in the region ruled by Flovent, who is king of Toulouse, Gascony, Provence, and Burgundy, which he rules as a vassal of Charles, king of France.

[40] The existence of hermitages within or beside monasteries was well known; see Giles Constable, "Eremitical Forms of Monastic Life," in *Istituzioni monastiche e istituzioni canonicali in occidente (1123–1215)* (Milan: Centro di Studi Medioevali, Vita e Pensiero, 1980), 239–64, at 254–55.

through eremitism, a life of individual holiness in isolation from society, or by creating a more "apostolic" communal monastic life.[41] As noted above, new forms of religious life proliferated in the twelfth century, including both hermits and anchorites,[42] and new religious orders were established, the most notable being the Cistercians and the houses of Augustinian canons. The social structures of religious life in this period were very complex, but, in broad terms, the Cistercians sought to implement a strict interpretation of the sixth-century Rule of St. Benedict, while the Augustinians claimed the authority of an early church father, modelling their monastic life on the writings of St. Augustine (354–430).[43] At the end of the eleventh century Pope Urban II, writing in support of the Augustinian order, characterized monasticism as having always comprised two broad branches, each with different roles: monks abandoned earthly things for the contemplative life, while canons redeemed the world through their engagement with it.[44] Guillaume de Berneville, as an Augustinian canon, would have been part of the reform movement committed to a more active engagement with lay society than was customary in the older Benedictine monasteries. At the same time, he would also have known of the contemporary revival of eremitism, since the creation of houses of Augustinian canons was also loosely associated with a revival of the eremitical tradition, many of the new houses being reformed hermitages.[45]

A Well-Read Canon

It is axiomatic that a cleric translating a saint's *vita* would know the Bible and related patristic commentary, as well as liturgical works connected with the saint in question. In his representation of Giles' prayers (which he skilfully makes an

---

[41] On the complexity of twelfth-century religious life which combined both eremitism and cenobitism, see Constable, "Eremitical Forms of Monastic Life": he notes that "eremitism can not only be considered part of monasticism in the twelfth century but also be said to have interpenetrated it, so that no form of monastic life was entirely free from its influence" (241).

[42] On the twelfth-century revival of the eremitic life, see Warren, *Anchorites and Their Patrons*; Henrietta Leyser, *Hermits and the New Monasticism: A Study of Religious Communities in Western Europe 1000–1150* (London: Macmillan, 1984).

[43] See R. W. Southern, *Western Society and the Church in the Middle Ages* (Harmondsworth: Penguin, 1970, repr. 1976), 240–50; Janet Burton, *Monastic and Religious Orders in Britain 1000–1300* (Cambridge: Cambridge University Press, 1994), 42–56; J. C. Dickinson, *The Origins of the Austin Canons and their Introduction into England* (London: S.P.C.K., 1950).

[44] Southern, *Western Society and the Church*, 244, notes: "The monks therefore played the part of Mary, the canons that of Martha in the church." See also Morris, *The Papal Monarchy*, 74–78. The papal bull was written in 1092.

[45] See Burton, *Monastic and Religious Orders*, 50–51; Morris, *The Papal Monarchy*, 74–78; Dickinson, *The Origins of the Austin Canons*, 143.

integral part of the narrative structure), Guillaume shows that he was also well versed in doctrine (see, for example, his handling of the Eucharist, below, 203–7). That Guillaume would draw on the literary and theological resources available to him in his Latin sources is to be expected in his vernacularization of a saint's life. But, in addition to his skilful exploitation of Latin sources, Guillaume also demonstrates that he has read widely in secular vernacular works. As a result the *Vie de s. Gilles* resonates with literary motifs drawn from both Latin hagiography and contemporary vernacular religious and secular writing. A striking example is the numinous animal motif, equally popular in hagiography and secular romance, in which an animal becomes a messenger from the spiritual world.[46] Guillaume exploits this image in the central episodes describing Giles' hermitage and its subsequent discovery by King Flovent and the bishop of Nîmes.

In the *Vie de s. Gilles* the numinous animal first erupts into the narrative in response to Giles' prayer for divine direction after he has established his new hermitage (v. 1499): a beautiful, large, sleek wild doe miraculously makes her way into his hidden shelter and lies down at his feet, offering him her milk. She leaves her shelter in the hermitage every day to pasture in the wilds, but returns faithfully at dinnertime to nourish Giles (who twice refers to the hind as his nurse, vv. 1613, 2067). Both the miraculous doe's appearance (first mentioned at v. 1507) and her disappearance from the narrative are equally abrupt, since she is not mentioned after King Flovent's discovery of the hermitage; Guillaume even feels obliged to comment on this dropped narrative thread ("I have read nothing further regarding the doe which had served Giles for such a long time; and, having found nothing else in my source, I will not write more about her" vv. 2249–52). This serves to underline the symbolic role of the strikingly beautiful hind, which not only links Giles to the spiritual world of divine providence, but also brings the social world of the royal court and the aristocratic hunt into contact with the hermit, and leads to the next stage in Giles' spiritual development.

The deer as messenger from the spiritual realm is a well-known motif: as Amy Remensnyder notes, from at least the second century onwards, the deer is accorded Christological value, an interpretation derived from the classical tradition in which the deer is seen as the natural enemy of the snake.[47] In medieval secular romance, the deer leads protagonists to their adventure and their desire.[48] In many monastic foundation legends, the deer delineates the boundaries of a

---

[46] See Remensnyder, *Remembering Kings Past*, 57–65.

[47] See Remensnyder, *Remembering Kings Past*, 61.

[48] See Marcelle Thiébaux, *The Stag of Love: The Chase in Medieval Literature* (Ithaca and London: Cornell University Press, 1974); Remensnyder, *Remembering Kings Past*, 61. There is an underlying allusion to Psalm 41:1. Also, *Physiologus* 45, "On the Stag," trans. M. J. Curley (Chicago: University of Chicago Press, 2009), 58–60.

sacred site,[49] or, as a hunted animal, leads its pursuers to such sites, as happens in the *Vie de s. Gilles*. Here the motif also serves to establish relationships of lordship (both King Flovent and the bishop of Nîmes bow to Giles's authority), as well as monastic boundaries (the deer effectively reveals Giles' hermitage as the sacred site on which a new monastery will be built), and spiritual identity (Giles and the doe as Christ figures).[50]

The royal hunt which takes place at the midpoint of the *Vie de s. Gilles* (vv. 1541–1915) skilfully exploits the motif and heightens the drama over three successive attempts to capture the miraculous doe, "the most beautiful I have seen," "no other deer like her" (vv. 1674–78). The different breeds of the eager hunting dogs are described; during the hunt we see and hear the tumultuous activity of both men and dogs, the evasive tactics of the doe, and the frustrations of the hunters, followed by their redoubled preparations to catch their prey the next day. The motivations of all involved in the hunt are expressively represented: young servants invited to join the hunt boast; the king subtly chides the master huntsman when he bursts into hall while the court is dining, and recruits the bishop as an expert adviser on the possibly magical or sacred nature of the elusive hind.

Guillaume's use of the numinous deer motif can be appreciated still further when it is compared to that of two other vernacular texts from the last half of the twelfth century.[51] In the *Vie seinte Osith* a white stag miraculously entices King Sighere to pursue it, distracting the king from the intended forcible consummation of his marriage to Osith. The king pursues the stag at length before it disappears into the sea, only to find on his return that Osith has taken the veil. The frustrated king nevertheless accedes to his wife's wishes and grants her land for a convent. In this adaptation (developed in the space of a hundred lines), the writer focuses on the excitement and titillation experienced by the dogs and hunters, as well as on the frustration of the king's physical desire. Marie de France devotes about fifty lines to the same motif in the lai *Guigemar*: while hunting, the protagonist is wounded in the thigh by his own rebounding arrow, shot at an unusual white doe. The dying doe speaks, telling Guigemar what he must do before he can be healed of his wound (in effect telling him of his psychological need for emotional growth).

The *Vie de s. Gilles* develops the motif more extensively than either the *Vie seinte Osith* or *Guigemar*, and includes the perspectives of both the hunted (Giles and the doe) and the hunters (King Flovent and his court). Guillaume's highly

---

[49] As in the refounding of the abbey at Mozac, near Clermont (cf. Remensnyder, *Remembering Kings Past*, 60–61).

[50] See Remensnyder, *Remembering Kings Past*, 63–65.

[51] *Osith*, vv. 536–627; see edition, and critical articles on *Osith*, in *PLL: Papers on Language & Literature* 41 (2005): 297–445, available online at the Margot Project website (http://margot.uwaterloo.ca); *Guigemar* (vv. 76–122), in *Lais de Marie de France*, trans. Harf-Lancner, 30–33.

sophisticated inflexion of this theme is a densely symbolic series of actions, a nexus of connections between the secular world of the court and the sacred space of the hermitage with its numinous animal.

The dramatic scenes of the royal hunt become a turning point in the evolution of Giles from hermit to abbot. The secular activity of the hunt is the noblest courtly pleasure, one learned by King Flovent, we are told expressly, in his cultured education in the French style (vv. 1548–64). The hunt takes place at Advent, the liturgical period (embracing four Sundays) which marks a time of waiting and anticipation of the birth of Christ. Advent is also specified in the *Vie* as the hunting season for does (*bisses chascer*, v. 1567), reminding the audience of the deer as a symbol of Christ. The four Sundays of Advent spent in the anticipation of Christmas are parallel to the series of frustrated hunts which precede the anticipated discovery of the doe's hiding place (and the revelation of the holy Giles).

Before his encounter with the doe King Flovent is also aware, from the reports of his huntsman, of the deer's probable otherworldly nature, and he invokes the aid of the sacred for pursuing his prey. In response to the hunters' belief that the hind is mocking them, the king first signs himself with the cross, then summons the bishop of Nîmes to ask his advice. The doe may be magic, the king says (v. 1780), or we may be lucky and discover a holy hermit in our woods (vv. 1807–14). To be fully prepared for the potential encounter with the other world, the king will not leave for the hunt until the bishop has celebrated mass for him (vv. 1829–32). The Advent season of the hunt, the symbolic nature of the deer, and the king's recourse to religious preparations all serve to underline the interpenetration of the sacred within the secular festival of the royal hunt.

The pursuit of the magnificent hind also allows the secular world to erupt into Giles' eremitical life, leading to his return to living in community. Giles, not the hind, becomes the object of the hunt, and his wound (deflected from the doe, in that Giles, rather than the doe, is struck by the arrow)[52] becomes the ultimate divine gift which allows him to internalize his asceticism (he keeps his wound secret, and unhealed, as an act of spiritual discipline, and in imitation of the Passion, vv. 2083–2103, 2135–41, 2151–54). Nursing his wound (rather than being nursed by the doe), Giles reluctantly returns to social life. Guillaume rearranges and modifies details of the *vita* to make this a gradual process: it begins with Giles' acceptance of Charlemagne's invitation to help him confess, and is completed only at the end of the *Vie* when Giles fully accepts the role of pastor to his fellow monks (see below, 134).

---

[52] Giles as unintended victim inevitably evokes the scene from *Guigemar*. Giles and his doe represent divine love and suffering (shown in the sacrifice of Christ), rather than Marie's examination of human love and suffering (which Guigemar must find to be healed); in *Guigemar* the deer, symbol of Christ, dies for him, while in *Gilles* the protagonist accepts the wound meant for the deer/Christ.

Studies of the *Vie de s. Gilles* have noted other literary motifs which have direct parallels in secular vernacular texts. For example, Guillaume's detailed list of luxury goods carried by the merchants, vv. 846–55 (see also below, 97), is reminiscent of the poetic description of luxury fabrics in *Erec et Enide* by Chrétien de Troyes.[53] As Madeleine Jeay reminds us, however, the rhetorical technique of enumerative lists is a very old literary tradition, well known from its use in classical antiquity and in the Bible.[54] Lists accentuate both the poetry and the reality of the objects described, and Guillaume's frequent and effective listings are part of this literary tradition. Similarly, in his use of rustic proverbs, introduced by the phrase *Li vileins dit* (vv. 89–90, 305–8, 547–48), Guillaume is following a well-established convention of twelfth-century narrative poems and romances.[55] While such proverbs express commonly held beliefs,[56] Guillaume uses them ironically, suggesting popular prejudice (Giles' childish piety and his early renunciation of his wealth are condemned by these proverbs, but Guillaume implies that Giles should be praised).[57]

Some of Guillaume's extended literary motifs are reminiscent of both monastic and secular courtly texts. In the detailed scenes leading up to Giles' departure from Athens, the rhetorical trope of the *planctus* (the lament of the barons and the chamberlain after they discover Giles has left Athens, vv. 661–762) is a vernacular motif first used in the *Vie de s. Alexis*, and widely present in both the epic and troubadour love lyrics.[58] The farewell feast in Athens (vv. 579–600) also evokes the biblical Last Supper and the scene at the garden of Gethsemane. At the feast Giles gives the impression of acceding to his feudal duties as outlined by

---

[53] *Erec et Enide*, ed. M. Roques, CFMA 80 (Paris: Champion, 1973), vv. 1573–1610; see Frankis, "Languages and Cultures in Contact," 117–18, and n. 56. See also note to translation, v. 848.

[54] See Madeleine Jeay, *Le Commerce des mots: L'usage des listes dans la littérature médiévale (XIIe–XVe siècles)* (Geneva: Droz, 2006), 22–55. The seafaring passages (discussed below in "Versification and Style") are prominent examples of this technique, but shorter lists include the desert animals, vv. 1232–38; the trees at the hermitage, vv. 1921–28; or articles of monastic furnishings, vv. 2254–63; see also Frankis, "Languages and Cultures in Contact," 118–21.

[55] Frankis, "Languages and Cultures in Contact," 107–11, at 110; cf. Chrétien's *Erec et Enide*, in which the opening line is: *Li vilains dit en son respit* ("the peasant proverb says").

[56] The medieval *arts poétiques* recommended, for example, that a text begin with a proverb, or general truth (see Edmond Faral, *Les arts poétiques du XIIe et du XIIIe siècle: Recherches et documents sur la technique littéraire du moyen âge* [Paris: Champion, 1923], 55).

[57] See Frankis, "Languages and Cultures in Contact," 110–11.

[58] Laurent, *SGilles*, xl–xli; Laurent, *Plaire et édifier*, 555–59.

his barons, leading his vassals to drink too well and later fall asleep while Giles is praying, allowing him to flee the city.[59]

Guillaume also occasionally makes specific allusions to well-known vernacular texts. The most obvious (below, 127) is a reference to the *Chanson de Roland*, when Guillaume's Charlemagne is told by Giles: "God showed his great love for you, when at the mountain pass of Roncesval he changed night into day to avenge the death of Roland."[60] Some nod to the *Chanson de Roland* is almost to be expected, however, since the use of Charlemagne as a protagonist inevitably invokes *chansons de geste* (commonly held in English monastic libraries), and the *Roland* text (vv. 2095–98, mentioned above) also includes a reference to Saint Giles, depicted as Bishop Turpin's companion. Guillaume also offers some parallels to Béroul's *Tristan*.[61] He adapts the motif of the unintended act induced by drinking drugged wine (*vin herbé*, vv. 613–16), and that of the ambiguous promise (which is both true and false, *la vraie fausse parole*) by which Giles leads his barons to believe he will marry a suitable noblewoman when in fact he is pledging his love to the Virgin (vv. 351–62).

Guillaume's remarkably detailed description of seafaring (analysed in Appendix 1.1) is also a common literary topos, the earliest known example being Wace's description of Arthur's voyage to Mont St. Michel (*Brut*, vv. 11193–238).[62] Denis Piramus, a contemporary of Guillaume, also uses seafaring terminology to good effect in the *Vie Seint Edmund le Rei* (vv. 1375–84, 1449–80). Although the seafaring passages in the *Vie de s. Gilles* (vv. 771–806, 876–906) are no doubt inspired by Wace's *Brut*, as Frankis notes, Guillaume's treatment of the theme is equally skilful, and more lexically detailed than Wace's.[63]

Guillaume's open and extensive embrace of secular motifs, an unusual rhetorical strategy in hagiography, has been explained in various ways. In his analysis, Frankis argues that Guillaume chooses to use all of the literary riches available to him, and that he is a talented writer with "an apparent delight in the potentialities of language."[64] Françoise Laurent's detailed study of the *Vie de s.*

---

[59] Although his action seems to be in bad faith, Giles believes he is justified in creating his spiritual inheritance at the expense of his biological inheritance. That this point of view was also difficult for medieval audiences to accept is shown by the fact that later rewritings of the *Vie de s. Alexis* tended to humanize the characters, expanding on motivations and providing a name for Alexis' wife. See Alison Elliott, *The* Vie de saint Alexis *in the Twelfth and Thirteenth Centuries: An Edition and Commentary* (Chapel Hill: University of North Carolina Press, 1983).

[60] Vv. 2892–94 underline the reference by citing a famous half-line, *as porz passant* (*Roland*, vv. 1071, 1766).

[61] Beroul, *The Romance of Tristan*, ed. A. Ewert, vol. 1 (Oxford: Blackwell, 1939; repr. 1970), vol. 2 (Oxford: Blackwell, 1970).

[62] *Le Roman de Brut de Wace*, ed. I. A. Arnold, 2 vols. (Paris: SATF, 1938–1940).

[63] Frankis, "Languages and Cultures in Contact," 117, and 131 n. 54.

[64] Frankis, "Languages and Cultures in Contact," 116–17.

Gilles, as noted above, suggests that Guillaume chooses to use the techniques of secular works to charm and convince his readers of the humanity of the saint, in a sophisticated deployment of the *prodesse et delectare* topos. The image of the saint is meant to underline his humanity, rather than emphasizing the hieratic qualities of earlier saints. Guillaume's richly ambivalent text both seduces its public by its literary sophistication and demands that the reader go beyond the surface brilliance to understand the underlying religious meaning.[65]

It would be wrong, however, to infer from the views of Frankis and Laurent that Guillaume saw secular literary techniques as different from those of hagiography. I suggest instead that Guillaume, as an Augustinian canon, is consciously proposing that life in religion and life in the world are inextricably connected and interdependent. Through its protagonist's evolving spirituality, the *Vie de s. Gilles* argues that the quest for a spiritual life must also include engagement with the lay world, rather than a flight from it. That is, the secular world needs to be accommodated within the spiritual life. The mutual dependence of lay and religious is figured explicitly by Guillaume in King Flovent's and Giles' discussions about establishing the monastery. The king will richly endow the physical buildings and even supervise their construction, but Giles is asked to assume the cure of souls (*la cure d'ames*) and a pastoral role (vv. 2211–15). This is a characteristically medieval patronage exchange: material capital is used to secure spiritual capital (which in turn needs material capital to survive). Such alliances between crown and church were characteristic in the active royal patronage of Augustinian foundations in twelfth-century England (discussed below). The image of monasticism which Guillaume presents as the end point of Giles' evolving spiritual development, is, I suggest, the Augustinian model, with its concern for pastoral work, which expanded throughout the twelfth century, and of which the Priory of St. Giles in Cambridge (and later, of St. Giles and St. Andrew in Barnwell), was one of the earliest examples in England.[66]

Feudal Obligations and Life in Religion

The Augustinian ideal of a religious life engaged with lay society, evoked above, is the end point of Giles' spiritual development. Abbot Giles has moved beyond his initial need to flee the world in search of spiritual perfection to his final position as a spiritual leader who ministers to his religious foundation's material and

---

[65] Laurent, *Plaire et édifier*, 575–76, suggests that Guillaume is like Bernard of Clairvaux in his sermons on the Song of Songs, demanding that the reader delve beneath the surface; "Le message religieux est bien là, subtilement sécrété, et Guillaume de Berneville amène, sans didactisme et sans glose, son lecteur et son public à 'la douceur de la moralité'" (576).

[66] See Burton, *Monastic and Religious Orders in Britain*, 42–56, at 45; Southern, *Western Society and the Church*, 240–50.

spiritual needs within feudal society. Guillaume's account of Giles at the end of his life emphasizes his social obligations in terms remarkably complementary to those used to describe Giles' flight from feudal lordship at the beginning of his adult life. These scenes at the beginning and end of the narrative serve to frame the question of the proper relationship between secular obligations and life in religion as a wider social debate.

At the beginning of the *Vie* Guillaume highlights the gulf that the young Giles perceives between feudal social obligations and a religious vocation. In his impassioned reply to his father about his missing cloak (an implicit rejection of the need to preserve his wealth, vv. 175–238), Giles expresses his need to practice Christian charity in terms which recall feudal obligations: he stresses the *duty of service* to God, the *obligation* of mankind to repay the sacrifice of Christ, in order to be claimed among the righteous on the Day of Judgement, to be part of the household of the just, seated on the right hand of their Lord.

Later, when Giles is in the process of giving away his inheritance, his barons advise him against the folly (in worldly terms) of his charity, and on the social and moral need to deal with his feudal obligations (vv. 281–340). They utter a long litany of Giles' moral duties: his need to respect his inheritance, to provide for his vassals, to protect his domains from war and devastation, to honour his family, to marry and produce an heir, and to follow the advice of his barons, for "they are your liegemen, and you are their lord" (v. 335). Although expressed in secular terms, these are reminiscent of the arguments that Giles had earlier given his father about duty, service, and safeguarding one's inheritance, with regard to spiritual obligations. In this scene the barons ask that these feudal social obligations be respected "for the love of God" (v. 281), and in frustration they challenge Giles, stating, "If you dare not accept your responsibilities as a landholder, go take refuge in the woods, and become a monk in a monastery, for you will be of use for nothing else!" (vv. 327–30), words which the audience will appreciate as both ironic and proleptic.

This dismissal of the eremitical or monastic life as a useless dereliction of social duty wittily encapsulates a lack of comprehension of the religious life among lay feudal lords. Giles' understanding of his religious calling shares the same (but opposite) view at the beginning of his religious life. At this point he feels compelled to flee the temptations and distractions of the secular world of wealth and feudal obligations in order to safeguard his quest for spiritual purity.

When it is known that Giles has fled from his social responsibilities, the sense of loss is acutely expressed by the words of the chamberlain (vv. 691–700), "What will now become of your knights, your young noblemen and your squires, who rightfully expected to receive largesse and fiefdoms from you? . . . they are now disconcerted, reduced to becoming poor beggars." The loss is felt by the whole city, "burghers . . . noblemen and peasants" (vv. 757–58). Guillaume's portrayal of this loss as sincerely and deeply felt gives legitimacy to these social concerns, and the wider perception that the religious life is incompatible with feudal lordship.

At the end of his life, however, Giles realizes that the potential conflict is resolved when religious life engages with lay society. Abbot Giles embraces the material and social duties of lordship when he is divinely led to secure confirmation of his monastery's rights and privileges. He now pays close attention to precisely the sorts of obligations which he had refused to fulfill for his secular vassals when he was in Athens. Although the Latin *vita* includes the act of procuring the written and sealed confirmation of the abbey's independence from any future "lay person ignorant of religion and the church,"[67] it is Guillaume who invents Giles' explicit list of rights and privileges. He now states that he would be irresponsible "if this monastery were not guaranteed, confirmed, and dedicated and its rights and privileges assured" so that they will not in the future lose "their rights and privileges, nor their tilled fields or their pastures, their woodlots or their arable lands, their crop revenues or their fisheries, or anything with which the king has endowed them" (vv. 3312–21).

It is not only the material life of his monastery that concerns Giles, of course, and we see him progressively involved in ministering spiritually to his fellow monks. Upon his return from visiting Charlemagne's court, Giles greets each monk with a kiss, and engages each of them directly in conversation about his needs (vv. 3252–57). He seeks the monks' blessing before going to Rome, and after his return, his imminent death becomes a communal event. Giles both blesses (vv. 3706–10) and asks blessing from each of the monks (vv. 3541–46); he gives them advice on how to elect their new master (vv. 3523–36), urges them to be charitable among themselves and attentive to the poor (vv. 3535–36), and tells them to welcome the pilgrims who will come to his shrine (vv. 3547–52).

The image of Abbot Giles at the end of the *Vie* is of a man who has become fully committed to his community's material and spiritual needs. Giles' role in Charlemagne's confession and in performing the sacrament of the Eucharist is symbolic of his wider pastoral work. This image of a reinvigorated communal religious life engaged with lay society corresponds (not surprisingly, since it is written by an Augustinian canon) with the Augustinian renewal of religious life. In recognizing Abbot Giles' social and religious utility, Charlemagne's and King Flovent's roles in the *Vie* reflect changing perceptions of the role of monastic life in feudal society in twelfth-century England. For example, strong royal support for religious reform came from Henry I (1100–1135) and his first wife, Matilda, who were early patrons of houses of regular canons in England, during what has been called the "heyday of Augustinian foundations"; the regular canons were

---

[67] "ne alicujus laïcae personae, ecclesiasticae religionis ignarae, quandoque subderetur" ("pour qu'il ne soit jamais soumis à un laïc ignorant de la religion et de l'Église"): *Vita s. Aegidii*, §22 (Laurent, *SGilles*, 268).

expected to "function in a wider context of social and pastoral concern than existing monasteries."[68]

But while in the *Vie de s. Gilles* the new monastery is richly endowed by King Flovent, the Augustinian priory of St. Giles and St. Andrew at Barnwell would have been a more modest foundation. Although early Augustinian houses in England were notable for their close connection with royal patronage, such benefactions also appealed to lesser magnates who wanted the prestige "of a religious house where they would be honoured as founders and patrons, and buried with decency in the midst of their family."[69] R. W. Southern cites as examples Oseney Abbey on the outskirts of Oxford, and the priory of St. Giles in Cambridge, both founded by county sheriffs. Following its relocation to Barnwell in 1112, the priory of St. Giles and St. Andrew flourished in the period 1150–1200.[70] Its period of ascendancy corresponds precisely with the time when Guillaume de Berneville was writing this imaginative reconstruction of the life of Giles, reflecting a late twelfth-century Augustinian ideal view of the proper form of religious life.

Versification and Style

Detailed analyses of Guillaume's virtuoso mastery accompany the passages in Appendix I below, chosen to exemplify his range. More generally it can be said that his poetic effects are often based on striking images, and, as noted earlier (above, 7–8, 10–11, 15–16), his use of literary conventions is wide-ranging, borrowing motifs and themes from all genres, and his lexical range is remarkable. His colourful descriptions and evocative lists of *realia*, his lively dialogues and monologues, are all deployed with an unerring sense of the dramatic possibilities of his poem, and the narrative structure of the whole is carefully elaborated for poetic effect.

Here it is worth noting that many other aspects of the *Vie de s. Gilles* could also be fruitfully examined: all repay the closest attention to language and form. Françoise Laurent[71] mentions, for example, Guillaume's skilfully coherent narrative structure, which provides motivations for actions, and often uses prolepsis to foreshadow future events (paradoxically creating narrative suspense thereby). When Giles is pressed by his barons to marry, for example, he promises to reveal his plans for marriage "between now and the feast of St. Martin" (v. 359): the choice of the feast-day deadline reminds the audience that Giles' first charitable act imitated St. Martin's cutting his cloak in two to give half to a beggar; the

---

[68] Burton, *Monastic and Religious Orders*, 45–46.

[69] See Burton, *Monastic and Religious Orders*, 51; Southern, *Western Society and the Church*, 245.

[70] See Southern, *Western Society and the Church*, 245–47; Dickinson, *Origins of the Austin Canons*, 115, 135.

[71] Both in her Introduction, *SGilles*, xi–liv, and in *Plaire et Édifier*, 475–576.

fact that St. Martin was a hermit who attracted followers, leading him to found the first monastery in Gaul, also suggests to the audience that this too will be Giles' destiny.[72] Guillaume re-orders narrative events from the Latin source to focus on the development of Giles' spirituality: for example, he reduces the number of miracles from twelve to nine, and arranges them in the narrative so that each successive miracle shows an increase in Giles' power. In an exemplary display, Giles is shown participating in all seven sacraments of the church which lay people were expected to know about: baptism, confirmation, ordination, confession and penitence, the Eucharist, marriage (by sublimation to the Virgin), and anointing of the sick (chrism). Guillaume's exploration of eremitical life, seen in the island hermit, then in the hill hermit, and finally in the grotto of Giles, with its suggestion of the rich cultural topography and high medieval valuation of eremitism, can also sustain closer analysis,[73] including further study of the parallels with the *Voyage de s. Brendan*.

Another aspect which could be further studied are the vestimentary codes and the alimentary themes which reappear throughout the narrative. Giles first gives away his cloak; his father buys him another one made of better fabric; Giles gives all his possessions away, and leaves with just the clothes on his back; "what will he wear, what will he eat?" is the response his departure elicits from his household; Giles then meets merchants of luxury fabrics and foodstuffs, and sails off with them to meet a hermit; Giles insistently asks the hermit what he eats, and how he lives with nothing; when the huntsman comes to court, the theme of clothing is explicitly noted; when Giles is discovered by Flovent and the bishop of Nîmes he is dressed in rags, but refuses new clothing; when the monastery is endowed, the liturgical vestments are described in detail, and so on. Underlying these details are implicit questions on what is materially necessary for life, and comments on the nature of dress and human social displays and hierarchy.

The broad area of the theological and doctrinal questions raised in the *Vie de s. Gilles* also calls out for further study: in particular, the idea and practice of asceticism, an area which modern sensibilities tend to discount as simply masochistic. The image of Giles leaving his wound untended as an act of self-discipline is similar to known historical ascetic practices of the period. Archbishop Thomas Becket's secret practice of self-mortification, for example, was discovered by his intimates only when they were preparing his body for burial.[74]

---

[72] See also the comments, above (in the section "Feudal Obligations and Life in Religion"), on the ironic proleptic retort of Giles' barons: "go take refuge in the woods, or become a monk in a monastery" (vv. 328–29).

[73] Explored to some extent by Frankis, "Languages and Cultures in Contact," 118–23.

[74] Guernes de Pont-Sainte-Maxence, *La Vie de s. Thomas le martyr*, vv. 5778–5822 (Electronic Campsey Project: http://margot.uwaterloo.ca). Becket's clothing is described in detail: this included a hair shirt; his body was covered in vermin, and he had scourged himself three times on the day he was assassinated.

Guillaume's text is never innocently straightforward, but always multi-layered in meaning: the prayers offered by Giles are unlikely to be merely clichéd statements of doctrine, and repay exploration for their specific doctrinal and thematic relevance and functions in the text. At the narrative level, the power relationships between Giles and Charlemagne, or Giles and the pope, seen in the giving and receiving of gifts, are also significant: Giles refuses the king's offered gifts from his royal treasury, while he accepts the carved doors from the pope. Charlemagne and the pope both request the same gift from Giles, namely that they be granted confraternity in his monastery.

In summary, Guillaume de Berneville is a talented poet whose work engages artistically with the intellectual and social questions of his time. His only known work, the *Vie de s. Gilles*, combines the best of didactic historical writing and imaginative poetic composition in its exploration of the proper form of religious life. Guillaume's impressive mastery of literary techniques and philosophical concepts is never employed just as an end in itself, as a stylistic exercise, but serves to express his profound understanding of human nature. This achievement places him among the most accomplished of vernacular writers of French in the twelfth century.

2. Saint George, Soldier Martyr

Historical Basis for the Legend

George (d. ca. 303) was initially revered only for his spectacular martyrdom. The story of George and the dragon, now the most widely known part of the legend in the West, was a later medieval addition.[1] There are no historical documents regarding the life of George, but there is ample evidence of the growth of his cult from the early fourth century, and an accretion of legendary accounts which are frequently in conflict.[2] According to the earliest traditions, George, who spent his adult life as a soldier in Cappadocia, was martyred (and his body placed in a shrine) at Lydda (modern-day Lod in Israel), which was also his birthplace according to some traditions, and where there is evidence of his cult from the early fourth century. His fame spread quickly, and not long after his death George had already become the most popular saint of both the Eastern and Western Church. In the English-speaking world he is now best known as the patron saint of England.

George's legend, as shaped in its complex manuscript tradition, can be divided into two main groups: the oldest form of the legend, declared to be apocryphal

---

[1] The Acts of George (who was known as "megalomartyros" in the East) "survive in Greek, Latin, Armenian, Coptic, Syriac, Ethiopian and Turkish" (Farmer, 166). Yvette Guilcher, ed., *Deux versions de* "la Vie de saint Georges", CFMA 138 (Paris: Champion, 2001), 40–50 gives the most recent resumé of the history of the legend. See also the study of this text by Duncan Robertson, *The Medieval Saints' Lives: Spiritual Renewal and Old French Literature* (Lexington, KY: French Forum, 1995), 40–53. The standard study of the manuscript tradition is John E. Matzke, "Contributions to the History of the Legend of Saint George, with Special Reference to the Sources of the French, German and Anglo-Saxon Metrical Versions," *PMLA* 17 (1902): 464–535, 18 (1903): 99–171. Matzke analyzes manuscript filiations and proposes a classification of the complex manuscript history.

[2] See David Howell, "St. George as Intercessor," *Byzantion* 39 (1969): 121–36, at 121–23, on the early growth of the cult of George at Lydda, and its quick spread in the East. See also A. Kazhdan and N. P. Ševčenko, "George," in *Oxford Dictionary of Byzantium*, ed. A. Kazhdan, 3 vols. (New York: Oxford University Press, 1991), 2:834–35; Christopher Walter, "The Origins of the Cult of St. George," *Revue des Études Byzantines* 53 (1995); 295–326.

at the end of the fifth century; and the shorter, more acceptable "canonical" version, which circulated from the eighth century.[3]

The apocryphal legend, described by some modern critics as an encyclopedia of tortures, is a passion narrative in which the protagonist is subjected to a series of four martyrdoms lasting seven years in all (he is resuscitated three times, and enters heaven after the fourth death by torture).[4] The fantastic elements of this narrative have caused it to be compared with the eastern tradition of the "Tales of A Thousand and One Nights," and George himself has been compared to the superheroes of modern animated cartoons.[5] By contrast, the "canonical" version reduced the passion narrative to a single death, and placed the persecution of George in the time of the historical Roman emperor Diocletian, rather than in the era of the mythical Persian king Dacien. The pre-dragon versions of George's story, when they did not follow faithfully one or the other narrative line, added to or deleted from one or the other source to make a composite version.

The completely new and independent motif of the battle against the dragon arose during the twelfth century. As it grew in popularity, this incident was more and more frequently accepted as George's original legend. Often used as a prologue to the narrative of George's passion, the story of George and the dragon

---

[3] The decree of Pope Gelasius at Rome in 494 included the legend of George among the apocryphal works; see Matzke, "Contributions to the History of the Legend of Saint George," *PMLA* 17 (1902): 464. Robertson, *The Medieval Saints' Lives*, 44–45 cites an extract from the decree, and comments on its "pontifical ambiguity."

[4] See Guilcher, *Deux versions*, 40–46. The oldest text is a fragmentary Greek manuscript from the fifth century, of which two ninth-century Latin adaptations are known, the codex Gallicanus and the codex Sangallensis. For the relationships between the textual families, see Matzke, *Oeuvres de Simund de Freine* (Paris: SATF, 1909; repr. New York: Johnson Reprint, 1968), lxxxiii–lxxxviii. For the codex Gallicanus see Wilhelm Arndt, "Passio Sancti Georgii," in *Berichte über die Verhandlungen der königlich sächsischen Gesellschaft der Wissenschaften zu Leipzig, philologisch-historische Classe*, 26 (1874): 43–70; Guilcher, *Deux versions*, 125–31, gives a transcription of BnF, MS latin 5256, a later version of the codex Gallicanus. For the codex Sangallensis, see F. Zarncke, "Eine zweite Redaction der Georgslegende aus dem 9. Jahrhunderte," in *Berichte über die Verhandlungen der königlich sächsischen Gesellschaft der Wissenschaften zu Leipzig, philologisch-historische Classe*, 27 (1875): 257–77.

[5] See Hippolyte Delehaye, *Les Légendes grecques des saints militaires* (Paris: Picard, 1909; repr. New York: Arno Press, 1975) 55, 69. His view is endorsed and expanded by Robertson, *The Medieval Saints' Lives*, 39–40; and by Yvette Guilcher-Pellat, "La Légende de Saint Georges: du *Mégalomartyr* au *Tropaïophoros*," in *Miscellanea Mediaevalia: Mélanges offerts à Philippe Ménard*, ed. J. Claude Faucon, Alain Labbé, and Danielle Quéruel, 2 vols. (Paris: Champion, 1998), 1:601–15, at 602, 604. Sarah Kay, "The Sublime Body of the Martyr: Violence in Early Romance Saints' Lives," in *Violence in Medieval Society*, ed. Richard W. Kaeuper (Woodbridge: Boydell Press, 2000), 3–20, at 13 refers to the "Tom and Jerry plot" of *St. George*. Her study is a subtle Lacanian analysis of the enjoyment of sexualized violence used to propound ideology and generate vernacular texts.

may have arisen from the conjunction of the ideals of militant Western Christian crusaders and the unfamiliar Christian iconographical tradition they encountered in the East. From the eleventh century onward, the Eastern Church showed George defeating the devil, figured metaphorically as a dragon. Crusader knights returning to the West brought back a literal interpretation of this allegory, in a version which featured a chivalrous George defeating a physically menacing dragon, and this new creation was added to the existing passion legend.[6]

The cult of St. George was known in England from the seventh and eighth centuries, but it was the timely "rediscovery" of the soldier-saint during the Crusades which led to his wider popularity.[7] George was said to have appeared in a vision to the Christian crusaders during their siege of Antioch, and was seen as instrumental in their defeat of the Saracens in the first Crusade (at the end of the eleventh century).[8] Richard I of England (reigned 1189–99) placed himself and his army under St. George's patronage during the third Crusade (1189–93), and in 1191 the crusader army stayed for six weeks in Lydda, site of the church sacred to St. George. In the fourteenth century Edward III (1327–77) created the Order of the Garter under the patronage of St. George (a chivalric honour which would continue to be closely associated with the royal chapel eventually built at Windsor Castle during the reigns of Edward IV and Henry VII and dedicated to St. George). During the Hundred Years' War Henry V claimed St. George as the patron of England at the Battle of Agincourt in 1415, and the same year Archbishop Chichele made the feast of St. George (April 23) one of the principal feasts of the liturgical year in England.

In addition to these consistent claims that George was the patron saint of England, George's popularity as the personification of chivalry and saintly martyrdom extended throughout the West, with the result that by the late medieval period he was also held as patron saint by Portugal and Catalonia and by the cities of Venice and Genoa.

---

[6] Guilcher-Pellat, "La Légende de Saint Georges," analyzes the steps by which this process of narrativization of allegorical images likely happened. Robertson, *The Medieval Saints' Lives*, 51–52 suggests a more complex influence of images of dragons and serpents from other literary sources.

[7] See Farmer, *s.v.* George, for a succinct treatment of the development of the cult in England. For an illustrated account, see Samantha Riches, *St. George: Hero, Martyr and Myth* (Stroud: Sutton, 2000).

[8] For a detailed discussion of contemporary accounts of George's intervention during the Crusades see Matzke, "Contributions to the History of the Legend of Saint George," *PMLA* 18 (1903): 125, 150–57, and Robertson, *The Medieval Saints' Lives*, 45–46.

Medieval French Translations of the Legend of Saint George

A large number of French prose translations of the Latin legends of St. George are extant in thirteenth- and fourteenth-century legendaries. They include prose translations based on the apocryphal, canonical, and composite forms of the *passio*. Many translations followed the version in the influential Latin *Legenda aurea* (c. 1260–1275), which included the new dragon-slaying incident.[9]

In contrast, extant medieval French metrical translations of the Latin legend are limited to five only, including the poem by Simund de Freine, which is translated below. The following list serves to demonstrate the importance of Simund's *Vie* as the both the earliest and the longest medieval French poem recounting the legend:

1) the *Vie de saint Georges*[10] by Simund de Freine, dated to the end of the twelfth century, comprising 1711 heptasyllabic lines (MS Paris, BNF, fr. 902);

2) a late twelfth-century anonymous life, 478 octosyllables (MS Tours, Bibl. mun., 927;[11] although copied at Tours, this manuscript has insular connections: it contains the only copy of the *Jeu d'Adam*,[12] and also includes pieces by Wace);[13]

---

[9] See Matzke, "Contributions to the History of the Legend of Saint George," *PMLA* 17 (1902): 492–535; also discussed briefly by Guilcher, *Deux versions*, 137–40.

[10] The conventional title, *Vie de saint Georges*, was invented by John E. Matzke, ed., *Les Oeuvres de Simund de Freine*, 61–117. The manuscript opening rubric is in Latin only: *Passio beati Georgii militis et martiris*, "Passion of blessed George, soldier and martyr." Nowhere in Simund's text does he refer to his narrative as a *Vie*. In the prologue Simund calls his work *cest romanz*, "this work in the French vernacular" (v. 5); the term here is limited to the linguistic sense, not the narrative form, in contrast to the use of this term *romanz* when it is applied to Guillaume le Clerc's reworking of the legend of Mary Magdalene, where it means both the romance language of the text and the narrative form.

[11] Ed. Guilcher, *Deux versions*, 81–94; this supersedes V. Luzarche, ed., *Vie de la Vierge Marie de Maistre Wace* [. . .] *suivie de la Vie de saint Georges* (Tours: J. Bouserez, 1861).

[12] See Dean, §716.

[13] See Wace, *La Vie de sainte Marguerite*, ed. Hans-Erich Keller (Tübingen: Niemeyer, 1990), 21–23, 26–27 for details of the manuscript, which also contains Wace, *Conception Nostre Dame*.

3) a fourteenth-century anonymous life which includes the dragon incident, of 538 octosyllables (MS Amsterdam, Bibliotheca Philosophica Hermetica, BPH 58; formerly MS Cheltenham, Sir Thomas Phillipps, no. 3668); [14]

4) a fourteenth-century verse epitome, 42 lines, mainly hexameters (MS Paris, BNF, nouv. acq. fr. 4412); [15]

5) an Occitan verse version, which follows the legend as recounted in the *Legenda aurea*, 801 octosyllables (MS Paris, BNF, fr. 14973). [16]

La Vie de saint Georges by Simund de Freine

The Author

Simund's family was connected with Sutton Freen, Herefordshire, and his professional life remained centered on Hereford. He held the position of canon at Hereford by ca. 1190, and his use of the title *magister* indicates he was university-educated. Works by him are extant in both Latin and French.[17] He gives his name in acrostic form (one letter at the beginning of each of the opening lines) in his two known works in vernacular verse, the *Roman de philosophie* and the *Vie de saint Georges*.[18] These two works were probably composed near the end of the twelfth century, perhaps under the patronage of William de Vere, bishop of

---

[14] Ed. Guilcher, *Deux versions*, 95–105; this supersedes Matzke, "Contributions to the History of the Legend of Saint George," *PMLA* 18 (1903): 158–71.

[15] Ed. Holger Petersen, "Une Vie inédite de saint Georges en vers français du moyen âge," *Neuphilologische Mitteilungen* 27 (1926): 1–7.

[16] Ed. C. Chabaneau, "Vie de saint Georges," *Revue des langues romanes* 29 (1886): 246–54; 31 (1887): 139–55.

[17] See Jocelyn Wogan-Browne, "Freine, Simund de [Simon de Fraxino] (*d*. before 1228?), poet," *ODNB* [www.oxforddnb.com/view/article/25570]; see also John Frankis, "Toward a Regional Context for Lawman's *Brut*: Literary Activity in the Dioceses of Worcester and Hereford in the Twelfth Century," in *Layamon: Contexts, Languages, and Interpretations*, ed. Rosamund Allen, Lucy Perry, and Jane Roberts (London: King's College, 2002), 53–78, at 63–65 for discussion of Simund's work and the literary milieu in which he wrote.

[18] Both works are in Matzke, ed., *Oeuvres de Simund de Freine* (1909). The acrostic signature is "SIMUND DE FREINE ME FIST" in each work. The presence of the acrostic signature is announced explicitly in the final lines of the *Roman de philosophie* (*Icil ki cest romanz fist / Sun nun en cest romanz mist. / Mis est en vint premers vers, / Ceo puet veër ki est clers*, "He who wrote this vernacular work put his name in it. It is in the first twenty lines, and can be seen by anyone who is a clerk [i.e. who can read]," vv. 1655–58).

Hereford (1186–98).[19] The vernacular works were likely written before his two Latin poems (datable to 1194–97), addressed to Gerald of Wales. Simund died before 1228.

Simund's poems addressed to Gerald of Wales defend the high reputation of the cathedral school at Hereford as a centre of learning (Roger of Hereford, who compiled an astronomical table based on the meridian of Hereford in 1178, was a well-known astronomer; Gerald of Wales called Hereford a place of joy for philosophers). Simund's interest in philosophy can be seen in the *Roman de philosophie*, an adaptation of Boethius's *Consolation of Philosophy*, containing 1658 lines of heptasyllabic couplets. The major theme of Simund's text, the vanity of worldly wealth, is reflected in the alternate title, the *Roman de fortune*, which is used in some manuscript copies of the work.

Simund's *Vie de saint Georges* may have been written in support of the third Crusade (1189–92), preached by Baldwin, archbishop of Canterbury (1184–90), whose preaching tour of Wales, begun in March 1188, is reputed to have persuaded three thousand persons to join the Crusade.[20]

Manuscript

As noted above, Simund de Freine's *Vie de saint Georges* is extant in one manuscript only, Paris, BNF, fr. 902, fols. 108va–117vb. The manuscript is a small volume of 162 folios, with two columns of 46 lines per page, written in England, and datable to the second half of the thirteenth century.[21]

All the works in the volume are religious in nature. *Saint Georges* is preceded in the manuscript by Robert Grosseteste's *Chasteau d'amour*, and followed by the *Vie de saint Nicolas* by Wace.[22] Other well-known Anglo-Norman works in this manuscript, to cite only a few, include a verse translation of the Old Testament (fols. 1–95),[23] the *Seinte Resureccion* play (fols. 97–98),[24] and Beneit of St. Albans'

---

[19] See Julia Barrow, "William de Vere, a Twelfth-Century Bishop and Literary Patron," *Viator* 18 (1987): 175–89.

[20] For a brief mention of the influence of this preaching tour in Wales, see Christopher Holdsworth, "Baldwin (*c.* 1125–1190)," *ODNB* [www.oxforddnb.com/view/article/1164, accessed 29 March 2006].

[21] Pierre Nobel, ed., *Poème anglo-normand sur l'Ancien Testament*, 2 vols., Nouvelle Bibliothèque du Moyen Âge 37 (Paris: Champion, 1996), 2:16–17 gives an up-to-date summary of details on the manuscript.

[22] J. Murray, ed., *Le Château d'amour de Robert Grosseteste, évêque de Lincoln* (Paris: Champion, 1918); Einar Ronsjö, ed., *La Vie de saint Nicolas par Wace*, Études romanes de Lund 5 (Lund: Gleerup, 1942). See also Dean §§ 622 and 537.1.

[23] Nobel, ed., *Poème anglo-normand sur l'Ancien Testament*. See also Dean §462.

[24] T. Atkinson Jenkins, J. M. Manly, Mildred K. Pope, and Jean G. Wright, eds., *La Seinte Resureccion from the Paris and Canterbury MSS*, ANTS 4 (Oxford: Anglo-Norman Text Society, 1943). See also Dean §717.

Vie de saint Thomas [Becket] (fols. 129vb–35ra).[25] Simund's *Vie de saint Georges* is preserved, then, in a manuscript collection of Anglo-Norman metrical religious and clerical texts of an impressive variety, including biblical translation, religious drama, and lives of both contemporary English saints (Thomas Becket, Hugh of Lincoln) and those of the early Christian era (George, Nicholas), along with other moral and didactic works. Created presumably for an Anglo-Norman patron, the manuscript is broadly reflective of the varied Anglo-Norman clerical and intellectual culture of the twelfth and thirteenth centuries. By the seventeenth century the manuscript had passed to France, where it was owned by Colbert, before becoming part of the collections of the Bibliothèque Nationale.

Simund's Treatment of his Latin Sources

In Simund's reworking of the legend the emphasis in the narrative remains, as it does in the Latin sources, on the extended conflict between George and Dacien, the emperor whose gods are represented almost solely by Apollo (a second god, Tervagant, is mentioned only once, v. 589). The site of the conflict is the eastern city of Milette, in Cappadocia, the native country of George.

In his prologue, however, Simund frames the conflict differently, by using one brief anachronistic reference, saying that George would not recant his religion for the faith of Mohammed (*Rien ne vout vers Deu mesprendre / E en Mahon ne vout crere*, (*lit.*) "he did not wish to sin against God by believing in Mohammed," vv. 10–11). Simund stresses George's loyalty and steadfastness (vv. 16–17) and his fierce defence of his religion (*Fer fut pur sa lei defendre* v. 9), and evokes his willingness to die (four times, vv. 12, 14, 18, 20) rather than recant (*reneër* v. 13). By placing this self-sacrifice in defence of his religion in the context of George's unwillingness to believe in Mohammed it appears that, despite the fact that the narrative is clearly focused on the Roman persecutions of Christians, the implied audience that Simund is targeting is really those who might be encouraged to defend their Christian faith by going on a crusade to free Jerusalem from the Saracens.

In his analysis of Simund's use of both the earliest apocryphal texts and the later canonical Latin tradition, Matzke also makes a connection with the crusaders. The direct source for the body of Simund's narrative remains unknown, but his *Vie de s. Georges* follows the major lines of the earliest apocryphal texts, recounting the series of four martyrdoms of George before his ascension to heaven. But Simund also uses a slightly different ordering of the episodes than is found in the apocryphal texts, his *Vie* at times being close to the ordering found in the later canonical Latin textual tradition. Because of this difference, and because of its unique combination of details from the different variant Latin texts, Matzke

---

[25] Börje Schlyter, ed., *La Vie de Thomas Becket par Beneit*, Études romanes de Lund 4 (Lund: Gleerup; Copenhagen: Munksgaard, 1941). See also Dean §509.

proposes that Simund's text is based on an apocryphal version newly imported to the West at the time of the crusades, and now lost.[26]

Many of the variants unique to Simund's text (such as the number of kings who respond to Dacien's invitation to meet at Milette, or other details of the torture implements and methods) are likely to be derived, then, from unknown Latin sources. Sometimes this is signalled directly in the text, for example, by Simund's identification of Dacien as the emperor of Rome (vv. 24–26, citing his written source), which follows neither the standard earliest legend naming Dacien as emperor of Persia, nor the later canonical versions which name the tyrant as Diocletian (Roman emperor 284–305, well known historically for his persecution of Christians at the beginning of the fourth century). Dacien was traditionally known as the proconsul of Diocletian, and was responsible for a number of martyrdoms, including those of Saint Faith and her companions. As will be seen in our discussion of this latter saint, below, in contrast to Simund, the author of the *Vie sainte Fey* clearly distinguishes between the two tyrants, and Dacien is explicitly named as provost of Diocletian and Maximian, emperors of Rome (vv. 111–13).[27]

What is most striking to the modern reader, however, is that Simund chose a version of the legend which seems to revel in physical details of the fourfold tortures and death of the protagonist. This attention to repetitive violence has usually been viewed pejoratively by modern critics.[28] Duncan Robertson, for example, discusses the degeneration of the passion genre into "an apparently endless series of cartoon-like presentations pitting an insentient super-martyr against a parodically raging tyrant. [. . .] The more the tortures are multiplied and detailed, the more unreal and seemingly pornographic the literature becomes."[29]

Although a negative reaction from modern readers to the explicit violence in these texts seems almost inevitable, some critics have sought a more nuanced understanding of the role of violence, either through applying modern theories of psychoanalysis, or by expanding our knowledge of the sociocultural contexts of these texts. Sarah Kay, for example, moves beyond the common pejorative view in her subtle analysis of the psychological function of physical violence in medieval French hagiography.[30] She evokes both the medieval audience's enjoyment of this "pious pornography," and the modern reader's sense of complicity "with

---

[26] Matzke, *Oeuvres*, lxxviii–lxxxviii.

[27] See the *Life of Saint Faith*, note to vv. 111–18, below. Dacien, provost of Diocletian and Maximian, also figures, for example, in the legend of Vincent of Saragossa (see the *Legenda aurea* version). It is also perhaps possible that Simund's source has confused Dacien with Decius, Roman emperor 249–51, persecutor of the martyr Lawrence; see D. W. Russell, ed., *La Vie de saint Laurent*, Anglo-Norman Texts 34 (London: ANTS, 1976), 63–64, 76.

[28] See above, 24 n. 5.

[29] Robertson, *Medieval Saints' Lives*, 68–73, at 69.

[30] See Kay, "The Sublime Body," 3–20.

the prurient sadism of these tales," but then provides an analysis, using concepts of Jacques Lacan and Slavoj Žižek, to show that these texts create a space "where appalling violence is both indulged and denied, [. . .] the space of the sublime in which, while the miraculous is manifested and doctrine propounded, at the same time the thrill of enjoyment is elicited."[31]

The historical and cultural context of medieval views of the body and physical violence has also recently been studied by Caroline Bynum. She has shown that fascination with the horror of torture and fragmentation was common among medieval theologians, and directly connected with the belief that at resurrection on the Day of Judgement the body would be reassembled.[32]

Medieval society was of necessity accustomed to seeing and experiencing direct physical violence, both in the waging of war and in the continuous knightly training for war. Chivalry itself was closely associated with hand-to-hand physical violence as a guarantor of honour and status.[33] Crusader knights (and all of medieval society) would identify directly with the physical brutality involved in man-to-man armed combat, and those preparing to leave for the third Crusade would surely have heard reports of the extreme bloodshed in Jerusalem during the first Crusade. Would they not see the repetitive deaths and reassembling of the parts of George as examples of the faithful courageously overcoming the fear of physical dismemberment and death, as well as confirmation of the prevalent twelfth-century theological teachings on the afterlife?

George's triple resuscitation on earth serves explicitly to allay anxiety about corporeal wholeness in paradise: the description of the tortures inflicted emphasizes the attempt to destroy the body physically, but despite Dacien's best efforts to disperse the remains of his victim in unrecoverable parts and unreachable places, by divine intervention George is three times reconstituted on earth in his physical body to resume his opposition to the tyrant. Crusaders who might perish and have their bodies scattered unknown on distant battlefields could presumably take heart from George's example.

---

[31] Kay, "The Sublime Body," 4–5, 20.

[32] Caroline Walker Bynum, *Fragmentation and Redemption: Essays on Gender and the Human Body in Medieval Religion* (New York: Zone Books, 1991), 12–13, 268–97. She cites the monk Guibert of Nogent and Abbess Herrad of Hohenbourg as examples of twelfth-century writers who show that the medieval view of bodies as "the mediators between earth and heaven" is more complex than we might imagine, and has much in common with late twentieth-century debates on the nature of identity and the body; she also discusses the *Legenda aurea* as evidence that the fascination with torture was common. See also eadem, *The Resurrection of the Body in Western Christianity, 200–1336* (New York: Columbia University Press, 1995).

[33] See Richard W. Kaeuper, "Chivalry and the 'Civilizing Process'," in *Violence in Medieval Society*, ed. idem, 21–35. This collection of essays discusses the evolution of medieval social and legal views on violence in both the public and private spheres.

This threefold divine resurrection of George is repeated proof on earth of "the victory of intactness over division."[34] In contrast, George's fourth death by decapitation is followed by his soul's immediate entrance into paradise. It is left to the faithful carefully to reassemble his body and bury it by night in a church. Although body and soul will remain separated until the resurrection, God's love for George is shown by the miracles effected by divine power through the body of the saint at his tomb. In Simund's late-twelfth-century rewriting of the life, the treatment of the body as holy object is dealt with very briefly (vv. 1673–85), and there is no division of the parts as relics for shrines elsewhere, a custom which is common toward the end of the thirteenth century (in the *Vies* of Edmund Rich, archbishop of Canterbury, and Richard, bishop of Chichester, for example, written in the last third of the thirteenth century, parts of the saint's body are given as relics to separate locations before burial).[35] In the *Vie de s. Georges*, however, there is not yet an expression of the belief that any one body part may be a powerful representative of the whole.

Narrative Treatment and Techniques

The *Vie de saint Georges*, like Simund's other known vernacular work, the *Roman de philosophie*, is written in heptasyllabic verse couplets, as opposed to the octosyllabic verse almost routinely used in both saints' lives and secular romance.[36] As a vernacular hagiographer turning Latin prose material into French verse, Simund makes choices over how best to adapt his material to render his narrative compelling for his audience. One obvious strategy he uses is to place in the foreground the divine prophecy to George (drawn from his Latin sources), announced at the

---

[34] Bynum, *Fragmentation and Redemption*, 290.

[35] See A. T. Baker, ed., "La Vie de saint Edmond, archevêque de Cantorbéry," *Romania* 55 (1929): 332–81: Edmund explicitly leaves his heart (and viscera) at the abbey of Soisy (vv. 1649–50), while his body is buried at Pontigny (with much discussion of why Pontigny is chosen, vv. 1669–1936); and D. W. Russell, ed., *La Vie seint Richard, evesque de Cycestre* by Pierre d'Abernon of Fetcham, Anglo-Norman Texts 51 (London: ANTS, 1995): Richard bequeaths his viscera to the chapel dedicated to Edmund at Dover (vv. 1614–37), while his body is buried at Chichester (vv. 1638–97). Bynum, *Fragmentation and Redemption*, 270 notes: "Despite worries about fragmentation, however, division of the body was widely and enthusiastically practiced in the thirteenth century." She analyzes the ambivalence and inconsistency of this practice (272–80).

[36] Syllable count in French poetry composed in England is not the same as that in Continental French, and we will not repeat here the various points of what is a perennial discussion. For a summary of the issues, and recent bibliographical references, see *The History of Saint Edward the King by Matthew Paris*, trans. Thelma Fenster and Jocelyn Wogan-Browne, FRETS 1 (Tempe, Arizona: Arizona Center for Medieval and Renaissance Studies, 2008), 32–33, and n. 116. Sample text from Simund's *George*, together with a detailed analysis, will be found in Appendix 1.2 below.

end of his first day of torture: "Do not be afraid if you are beaten and wounded, you will die three times for my sake, defending my law. Three times by my power you will come back to life from death. The fourth time you will die, you will remain with me on my right hand in celestial paradise" (vv. 482–93).

This divine promise effectively becomes a "narrative engine," since it announces and justifies the narrative framework, in which many actions or events occur in repetitive groups of three or four. For example, before George's first death (v. 517), he is subjected to four different tortures; before his second death (v. 687) he confronts three main challenges, from Magnacius, Anastasius, and Dacien's new tortures; before his third death (v. 1143) George again performs three main actions: his conversion of an impoverished woman, his debate with Dacien, and his confrontation with Apollo.

The audience is encouraged, then, to anticipate the repetition of incidents before the final inevitable victory of the saint. To meet this narrative expectation, Simund chooses incidents and arguments reworking the conventional hagiographic topoi that clearly appealed to his medieval audience, in part, perhaps, because of their very familiarity, but also because of the skill of his stylisation of these elements.

Three specific conventional topics developed by Simund are also used to great effect by earlier and contemporary hagiographers writing in French. Simund's description of hell, vv. 1391–1526, given in the context of the resuscitation of long-dead people, is also a topos treated at greater length in the *St. Brendan*, a text composed probably a half-century before Simund's *Vie* (to cite just one famous example).[37] The scene where Dacien's queen Alexandrine converts (vv. 1216–65), followed by Dacien's sense of personal loss as he orders her execution (vv. 1266–95), unexpectedly gives depth to the character of the tyrant, as the audience is drawn into a deeper understanding of Dacien's helpless frustration. This topos is found in the roughly contemporary *Life of St Catherine* by Clemence of Barking, which also develops pathos in its tyrant figure, Maximien: he expresses his deep regret at losing the trust and love of his queen, even as, like Dacien, he orders that his queen be executed because she has converted to Christianity.[38] In *George*, another conventional topos is the physical description of Apollo (vv. 1018–51) when George forces him to show himself to the people who witness his expulsion from the idol (although it is not in the standard Latin legend).[39]

---

[37] See Benedeit, *Le Voyage de saint Brendan*, ed. and trans. Short and Merrilees, vv. 1317–1438.

[38] See Jocelyn Wogan-Browne and Glyn Burgess, trans. and intro., *Virgin Lives and Holy Deaths: Two Exemplary Biographies for Anglo-Norman Women: The Life of St Catherine. The Life of St Lawrence*, Everyman Library (London: J. M. Dent; Rutland, VT: Charles E. Tuttle, 1996), 36–37 (vv. 2155–2256).

[39] The prose legend of St. Bartholomew has a similar scene: the saint forces the demon Astaroth to confess publicly how he tricks those who worship idols, and then

Simund also uses familiar biblical stories to illustrate his points, beyond what is found in the Latin source text. These include both well-known miracles of Jesus from the New Testament (the changing of water to wine at Cana [John 2:1–11] and raising Lazarus from the dead [John 11:1–45], vv. 1409–14), and the torture scene involving animals (vv. 1198–1215). This latter is a reworking of the biblical narrative of Daniel in the lions' den (later explicitly mentioned at v. 1412). Medieval audiences would have known the allusion to Daniel, and recognized the resonances Simund's variations on such narratives add to the figure of George as holy wonder-worker.

Compelling Speech-Acts and Witticisms

Despite the "narrative engine" which generates and justifies the repetition of incidents, and the development of topoi which would not fail to be of interest to his audience, Simund's *Vie*, like modern opera, still risks being viewed as an improbable sequence of extreme events culminating in the ascension of the saint into paradise (or, in the case of opera, the tragic death of the hero or heroine).[40] But far from being a clichéd repetition of conventional topoi, Simund's *Vie* is transformed into a compelling narrative by his remarkable skill in creating direct discourse to bring alive his treatment of Christian doctrine.[41] Thus, where the Latin text uses the mere listing of numerous and exaggerated tortures for rhetorical effect, the vernacular text creates new dialogues which combine logical argument and verbal inventiveness.[42]

The development of George and Dacien's initial debate exemplifies Simund's lively resumé of Christian doctrine: it is a catechism of spirited questions and

---

an angel makes Astaroth show himself in all his physical deformities to the assembled witnesses before he is banished. Cf. "S. Barthélemy," ll. 155–60, 251–56, in Delbert W. Russell, ed., *Légendier apostolique anglo-normand* (Montreal: Presses de l'Université de Montréal; Paris: Vrin, 1989), 102–3.

[40] Much of nineteenth-century literary criticism saw medieval hagiography as a purely predictable accumulation of conventional clichés, repeated in life after life. Similarly, the implausibility of opera plots has been lampooned by twentieth-century comedian-musicians such as Anna Russell and Victor Borge.

[41] Vernacular hagiography traditionally both abridges its sources to sharpen narrative focus and amplifies its Latin sources to create debate in direct discourse and to heighten the drama inherent in the conflict between martyrs and their torturers. See, for example, Robertson, *Medieval Saints' Lives*, 47–53 on the techniques used by Simund in the *Vie de saint Georges*; and Laurent, *Plaire et édifier*, on the techniques of hagiographic vernacularization in general.

[42] Robertson, *Medieval Saints' Lives*, 51 refers to the text as a "chivalric duel between saint and emperor, in words and deeds. [. . .] The passion genre has evolved, strangely as it might seem, into a discourse of urbanity, virtuosity, sophistication; the pathos of the martyrdom has become transformed into an exercise of wit."

answers. In response to George's opening verbal attacks on his gods and their wooden images, Dacien proceeds to a detailed rational refutation of Christian doctrine (vv. 263–316). Simund allows Dacien's arguments to be both eloquent and convincing in their demonstration of Christian doctrine's logical absurdities. The Trinity is demonstrably nonsense, he argues:

> everyone can plainly see that a father and a son cannot be one person. So tell me, then, according to your religion how can God be three in one? (vv. 267–74).

Dacien is equally incredulous about the nativity in the stable and the virgin birth:

> Your God [. . .] when he was hungry could he eat straw? [. . .] Who is such a fool that he accepts that any virgin [. . .] could bear a child unless she had first been made love to by a man? (vv. 295–308).

George responds to these arguments, point by point, with rhetorical verve: he uses the metaphor of sunlight passing through stained glass windows while the windows remain whole as an explanation of the virgin birth, and makes the child in the manger an example of humility and poverty. Although the most striking image of his argument is a medieval commonplace (the sunlight through glass analogy is repeated in Rutebeuf's *Miracle de Théophile*, for example),[43] George's reponse is articulate and assured, and the debate is a draw, forcing Dacien to resort to the threatened tortures as his only response.

Simund also increases the complexity of the strategies used in the conflict. Somewhat surprisingly, to gain advantage both protagonists use the "bait and switch" technique, a universal mainstay of street performers and confidence men. George pretends to be swayed by Dacien's arguments (vv. 317–24), but refuses Dacien's kiss, then launches into his debate response (vv. 339–422). He also later pretends to be willing to sacrifice to Apollo (vv. 940–55), in order to gather a large crowd at the temple to witness the exposure and banishment of Apollo. Similarly, Dacien offers to become a Christian if George can resuscitate the bodies of Joel and his companions (vv. 1369–89), but in the event reneges on this promise.

---

[43] Rutebeuf, *Le Miracle de Théophile, miracle du XIIIe siècle*, ed. G. Frank, CFMA 49 (Paris: Champion, 1925; 2nd ed. 1949), vv. 492–97; see also Andrew Breeze, "The Blessed Virgin and the Sunbeam Through Glass," *Celtica* 23 (1999): 19–29, who traces the origin of the Latin text to North Africa in the fifth and sixth centuries. The image gained wide circulation when it was included in an Advent reading of the Sarum Breviary, and was well known in the circles of Anselm (23–25).

Concrete Figures of Speech

Throughout his text, Simund shows himself to be a master of the concrete image used to express more cogently abstract ideas found in the Latin sources.[44] The following examples will serve to illustrate this technique.

In the opening scene where Dacien displays his instruments of torture and announces his persecution of Christians, the fear inspired in his audience is stated simply in Latin: *prae timore avertebantur* "they were turned away, dissuaded by fear."[45] Simund expands: "Everyone looked carefully about on all sides, seeking to protect himself, like a hare does when it sees a hound" (vv. 65–66).

George's renunciation of worldly wealth is developed in detail in the vernacular version in an interior monologue (vv. 98–158) not present in the Latin sources. He tells himself that earthly possessions come and go like the waxing and the waning moon (vv. 105–8).[46] He also remarks that it is unwise to plan to repent of one's sins late in life, noting that "it is madness to trust to this, for old sticks do not bend in the wind, you cannot use an old dried-out stick to bind up a bunch of faggots, you need a young green switch. I will begin without delay to serve God, before I am surprised by death" (vv. 133–40). The idea that a person becomes increasingly inflexible with advancing age is firmly anchored in an image from medieval daily life, the seasonal gathering and binding of faggots as fuel for winter fires. The faggots should be old and dried, but the binding must be done with a young and pliable switch.

George's interior monologue also includes wordplay which will be typical of the debate and interrogation scenes created by Simund. A striking example can be seen in the puns used by George as he concludes his thought: "I have called him emperor (*emperur*), but it is better to call him degrader (*empeirur*), for he degrades (*empire*) the law of God who gave him his empire (*empire*)" (vv. 145–48).

Subtly sustained wordplay, developed in three widely separated scenes, can be seen in Simund's treatment of the kiss of reconciliation offered by Dacien to George. Medieval society continued to follow Roman tradition in which a kiss given and received in public had strong legal and juridical meaning.[47] A kiss on

---

[44] For discussion of such figures as a contemporary trend, see Antonia Gransden, "Realistic Observation in Twelfth Century England," in eadem, *Legends, Traditions and History in Medieval England* (London: Hambledon Press, 1992), 175–97. Gransden's discussion is chiefly concerned with Simund's colleague, Gerald of Wales, but Simund's use of natural analogy is equally striking, whether to be attributed to the influence of new Arabic science and changing twelfth-century views of nature at Hereford or to a didactic acuteness about the value of vivid and graspable similes.

[45] In the Codex Gallicanus: Arndt, "Passio Georgii martyris," 49.

[46] This same image of the waxing and waning moon is used by Simund in the *Roman de philosophie*, vv. 115–24.

[47] For a succinct account of the symbolism of the kiss in Roman and medieval society, see Hanna Vollrath, "The Kiss of Peace," in *Peace Treaties and International Law in*

the mouth in public was not erotic, but rather performative body language which confirmed the acceptance of binding obligations, including those in written contracts. In medieval feudal society, for example, bonds of vassalage were sealed with a kiss. At a more general level, the kiss was a symbol of the obligation to live in peace with fellow members of the group as well as a sign of acceptance into a group or elite. So too, the public kiss at baptism signified reception into the Christian community, and a public kiss between adult Christians signified their sharing in the spiritual gift of the peace of Christ. Medieval society was highly attuned to the political symbolism of the public kiss, and to the hierarchy of rank denoted by kisses to various parts of the body.[48] Clearly, "a kiss was *not* just a kiss,"[49] and seen against this background, Simund's deployment of the kiss between George and Dacien takes on added meaning.

In the Latin sources Dacien proposes a kiss to George only once, but Simund expands it into a series of three scenes.[50] In the first scene added by Simund, Dacien exclaims joyfully: "Dear friend, since you accept this god, with all my heart I wish to embrace you with a kiss and bring you to make your peace with Apollo!" (vv. 321–24). In effect, Dacien wants formally to welcome George into the pagan community (and legally bind him in the "peace of Apollo," as opposed to the peace of Christ). George rebuffs this offer, saying duplicitously, "I will reserve your kiss for later" (v. 326).

The second scene in which Dacien proposes a kiss to George is based on the Latin source, but Simund adds the narrator's explicit acknowledgement that George is being deceitful: "Dacien was overjoyed at the news, but he would later greatly regret it. He wanted to give George a kiss, but George was not pleased by

---

European History, ed. Randall Lesaffer (Cambridge: Cambridge University Press, 2004), 162–83. For a more detailed account of medieval kissing practices, see Yannick Carré, *Le baiser sur la bouche au moyen âge: rites, symboles, mentalités à travers les textes et les images, XIe-XVe siècle* (Paris: Léopard d'Or, 1992).

[48] See Vollrath, "The Kiss of Peace," who states, "Kisses, then, were ever-present in medieval communication. The 'normal' kiss was a kiss exchanged by men, and if the men were of equal rank it was given on the mouth" (172). This can be seen in the *Life of Saint Giles* in this volume, where the kiss is used in a number of instances in the classic fashion: Giles and the hermit he meets on the island kiss on parting (vv. 1018–19), Charlemagne greets Giles with seven kisses (on eyes, mouth, and chin, vv. 2633–34), and Giles kisses his brethren on his return to the monastery (v. 3252).

[49] Cf. the song "As Time Goes By" by Herman Hupfeld. Created for the 1931 Broadway musical "Everybody's Welcome," the song was made famous in the 1942 movie *Casablanca*: the first lines of the refrain are "You must remember this, A kiss is just a kiss."

[50] The kiss is proposed in the Latin source at the point where George announces he will sacrifice to Apollo (Simund's second scene, vv. 946–52); cf. Arndt, *Passio Sancti Georgii*: "Tunc laetus factus est totus imperator et coepit osculare capud eius. Sanctus vero Georgius non permisit osculare capud suum dicens . . ." (62 [§16]).

this sign of acceptance. Dacien truly believed that George was about to do fully what he wanted him to do, but George had something completely different in mind" (vv. 946–52).

In a third scene, added by Simund, the kiss that might reconcile the two opponents is finally shown to be an impossibility. Here Simund evokes the image of the kiss at the end of his long description of Apollo's physical attributes. The vocabulary of courtly love is often used by hagiographers to express the positive relationship between virgin martyrs and their bridegroom Christ (as will be seen, for example, in the Life of Faith, below), but Simund here uses courtly terms contrastively, underlining moral with physical repulsiveness: "His foul breath smelled like sulfur thrown on flames; his was not at all the sweet mouth that gives a lover's kisses" (vv. 1048–51). It is no wonder that George has resisted Dacien's embrace and that of his god.

The gamesmanship involved in George and Dacien's conflict is also evoked in an image Simund adds from chess (vv. 1096–1107). Simund has Dacien characterize what he sees as George's deceitful moves as similar to those of the bishop piece in chess, thus aligning George with the church in the mind of his audience, while Dacien sees himself as the victim pawn or rook pieces of the game.

Occasionally Simund invents a concrete image which seems simply comic. For example, Alexandrine, in her debate with her husband, remarks that her husband, in choosing Apollo rather than George's God, is like someone choosing to sit on a thistle to rest himself while travelling through a meadow (vv. 1246–58). Indeed, why torture yourself by such a foolish and wilful act? At the same time, of course, this image humanizes the character of Alexandrine, showing her gentle chiding of her husband as a stark contrast to his own brutal order that she be executed by the sword.

Simund's treatment of George's third death (vv. 1122–43) is an example of the manner in which, throughout his poem, he both abridges his Latin source by cutting selected details, and expands the images and dialogues in scenes which he retains. Here he reduces the list of tortures found in his Latin source, keeping just one, the candle torture.[51] Simund adds a series of gruesome comparisons, having his narrator say that from the heat of candles George's "body began to melt. His body vanished, like snow in sunshine. Hot grease flowed from every

---

[51] Cf. Arndt, "Passio Sancti Georgii," 60 (§15). The list of tortures (beatings, fire, iron nails) omitted by Simund is: "Et extenso eum fustibus carminare precepit, et cassidem igneam super capud eius poni precepit, et ungulis ferreis radi corpus eius, et defecerunt ministri eius operantes in eum et in nullis tormentis prevalebant ei." This is followed directly by the candle torture: "Iterum iussit candelas subponi per latera eius, et tribulatus est. Ardebat enim corpus eius sicut cera et exclamavit ad dominum voce magna, emisit spiritum." (Then he ordered lit candles to be placed under both sides of his body, and he was tortured. His body burned like wax, and he cried out to God in a loud voice, and died.) (alluding to Matthew 27:50, Mark 15:37, Luke 23:46).

part of his body. No meat grilled over charcoal ever burned as quickly" (vv. 1129–35). Simund ends this scene with the rhetorical device of *occupatio*, as he tells his listeners that he is cutting short the enumeration ("But why should I go into more detail? Suffice it to say that his body was subjected to every indignity!"). Simund has, of course, brought greater detail to his description of a single torture than is found in his Latin source. By emphasizing one detailed atrocity at the expense of a summary catalogue of tortures in his Latin sources, Simund once again addresses twelfth-century anxieties about the resurrection of fragmented and, in this case, melted and burned, bodies.

Conclusion

Simund's vernacular reworking of the soldier martyr's legendary passion can be seen to have been shaped to respond to contemporary social and cultural pressures, in subtle and skilful vernacular verse. A reading of the *Vie de s. Georges* in this light suggests further areas for exploration. For example, apart from the dramatic physical and mental conflict between Dacien and George, Simund's representation of the divine powers operating through George also raises questions. To what extent are the miracles of provision and healing given to humble widows inflected by the crusader ethos? Was this in response to anxieties about loss and widowhood in families left behind by crusading soldiers? How are we to view the Christianization of fertility in the miracle of the thrones returned to flowering fruit trees? How far does Simund address his work to audience needs for a spectacular affirmation of Christian power in response to the crusaders' loss of Jerusalem in 1187? Or does an increased awareness of the East brought back to the West by previous crusaders also lead Simund to portray Dacien as a more human enemy, a more equal opponent to George, who shares his debating skill? A rival who is fascinated by George's power, and who is sensitive to his own defeat and loss? (Whose defeat, in fact, also requires his own awareness of it?)

In short, far from being a cartoon-like depiction of good and evil, the *Vie de s. Georges* is a sophisticated poetic creation in which Simund, who is versed in both learned and vernacular intellectual traditions, examines and responds to contemporary questions central to twelfth-century society.

3. Saint Faith of Agen, Virgin Martyr

Historical Basis of the Legend

The extraordinary, bejewelled and hieratic gold reliquary statue of St. Faith still gazes impassively at modern pilgrims to Conques, in the Aveyron, in France. Conques' medieval church remains intact, and, as Pamela Sheingorn notes, continues to draw crowds of tourists, just as it attracted countless pilgrims in the eleventh and twelfth centuries.[1] The reliquary statue of St. Faith is no doubt still the best-known manifestation of her cult. But the long and complex development of the various texts relating to St. Faith allows us to see the protean nature of hagiographic narrative, and gives insights into the assumptions and conventions of the European preoccupation with saints.

Faith, a child from Agen, is believed to have been martyred at the end of the third or the beginning of the fourth century. The legend which recounted this event, however, was largely a medieval creation. The earliest extant reference to the martyrdom of Saint Faith (*Sancta Fides*) is found in a late sixth-century manuscript copy of the martyrology of Jerome (d. 420), where 6 October is recorded as the saint's feast day.[2] Her later legend is recounted by three distinct medieval Latin narratives.

The first, the *Passio*, concentrates on her martyrdom. This version's oldest extant traces are a brief summary in Florus of Lyons' mid-ninth-century *Martyrology*,[3] and the earliest manuscript copies of the *Passio* date only to the

---

[1] Pamela Sheingorn, *The Book of Sainte Foy* (Philadephia: University of Pennsylvania Press, 1995), 1–31, at 4, 12, 16.

[2] For the most current scholarly views on the historical and documentary evidence relating to Saint Faith, see Sheingorn, *Book*, 1–31; also Kathleen Ashley and Pamela Sheingorn, *Writing Faith: Text, Sign and History in the Miracles of Sainte Foy* (Chicago: University of Chicago Press, 1999), 1–21. Our account of the historical and textual background draws extensively from these two studies. As Sheingorn notes with reference to *The Book of Sainte Foy,* her compilation of the *Passio*, the *Translatio*, and the *Liber miraculorum* (along with their translations into English) is similar to the medieval *libellus*, or dossier, compiled for the canonization of a saint.

[3] See Ashley and Sheingorn, *Writing Faith*, 3–8 for a concise presentation of the textual history of the *Passio*, the *Translatio*, and the *Liber miraculorum*, with details of the manuscripts and their classification in the *Bibliotheca Hagiographica Latina*.

tenth century.[4] In this earliest known version Faith's passion is associated with that of Caprais, a young man who followed her example and was martyred beside her. It is likely that the *Passio* was written at Agen in the Carolingian period in response to reforms requiring written documentation for all saints' cults.[5] Saint Faith's popularity and her cult's vigorous spread from the ninth century onward led to the proliferation of medieval copies of the *Passio*.[6]

A major element in Faith's legend is the dramatic removal of her relics in the ninth century from Agen to Conques, one of the most spectacular examples of medieval "furta sacra" (holy thefts), in the competition between monasteries for saints' relics.[7] Whether or not the theft actually occurred is unknown, but the monastery at Conques was very persuasive in making its claim to possess Faith's relics. This was done in part through the *Translatio*, composed in the period 1020–1060, a narrative account of the theft by a monk from Conques, sent to Agen for that purpose. The theft was reputed to have happened on the feast of the Epiphany (6 January), probably in 866. The prose *Translatio* text was put into Latin verse shortly after 1060. Also about 1050 the *Passio* was rewritten, in both prose (BHL 2929–30) and verse (BHL 2938).

Saints' lives routinely include accounts of the saint's miracles, both in life and after death. Posthumous miracles were often compiled in books kept at saints' shrines, and sometimes stand as independent texts, or are appended as a sequel to the account of the saint's life. Such accounts were important in attracting pilgrims seeking their own miracles at the saint's shrine.

The development of St. Faith's cult at Conques demonstrates this process at work. One early collection of the miracles attributed to her, Bernard of Angers' *Liber miraculorum sancte Fidis*, was particularly influential in spreading the

---

[4] These are Montpellier, Bibliothèque de l'Ecole de Médecine, MS H 152, fols. 231v–237r, which is datable to the end of the ninth century or early tenth century; and Paris, BnF, MS. latin 5301, fols. 328r–329v (on a tenth-century bifolium inserted in a manuscript datable to the end of the eleventh century). These two versions are classified in the *Bibliotheca Hagiographica Latina* as BHL 2934 and BHL 2936a, respectively. A collated version is published by Auguste Bouillet and L. Servières, *Sainte Foy, Vierge et Martyre* (Rodez, France: E. Carrère, 1900), 707–11. BHL 2928 (for 6 Oct., Faith only), in AASS, Oct., III, 288–89, is just part of BHL 2930 (for 20 Oct., Faith and Caprais), in AASS, Oct., VIII, 823–25; an edition is published in Ernest Hoepffner and Prosper Alfaric, eds., *La Chanson de sainte Foy*, 2: *Traduction française et Sources latines, Introduction et Commentaire historiques* (Paris: Belles Lettres, 1926), 179–97.

[5] Ashley and Sheingorn, *Writing Faith*, 4–5.

[6] The Bollandists list six major versions of the *Passio*, with variants (BHL 2928–2938). The *Translatio* is BHL 2939–2941. BHL 2942–2965 gives eight versions of the miracle collection.

[7] See Patrick J. Geary, *Furta Sacra: Thefts of Relics in the Central Middle Ages* (Princeton: Princeton University Press, 1978; rev. ed. 1990), 58–62. A Conques cartulary first claims to possess Faith's relics in the year 883.

cult and in establishing the belief that Conques possessed her relics.[8] Bernard of Angers visited Conques three times between 1013 and 1020 to investigate the reliability of the miracle stories he had heard in the north of France, and he turned his journeys and investigations into a polished account of Faith's miracles for his educated northern French ecclesiastical colleagues. Following Bernard's death sometime after 1020, the work of recording miracles was carried on by the monks of Conques themselves, who by about 1050 had added two further books of miracles. Numerous copies of this miracle collection are also extant and it circulated in England as elsewhere.[9]

Although Faith shares many of her miracle stories with other saints, she is particularly known for vengeance miracles, for appreciating gifts of jewellery as tokens of gratitude, and for trickster-like joking miracles—*joca sanctorum*.[10]

Conques and the Occitan *Chanson de sainte Foy*

Despite the immense popularity of the cult in medieval Europe, only two French vernacular verse versions of the life of Saint Faith are known. The first, which has had most modern attention, is the *Chanson de Ste Foy* (to use the nineteenth-century title). Composed in the Occitan dialect of southern France, the *Chanson* is generally dated ca. 1070, predating the earliest *chansons de geste*, and roughly

---

[8] For the miracle collection itself see Sheingorn, *Book*, 39–261. For an analysis of the cultural role of these texts see Ashley and Sheingorn, *Writing Faith*, 136–47.

[9] Ashley and Sheingorn, *Writing Faith*, 7–8 summarize the findings of Luca Robertini, ed., *Liber miraculorum sancte Fidis: Edizione critica e commento* (Spoleto: Centro italiano di studi sull'alto medioevo, 1994). Robertini suggests that the earliest fragmentary manuscript of miracles, Conques, Bibliothèque de l'Abbaye, MS 1, dated about 1050–1075, is probably part of the earliest version of all four books of miracles. He also suggests that a now lost *libellus*, containing a selection of miracles, the *Passio, Translatio,* and liturgical texts, was created between 1070 and 1080 and used as an instrument for promulgating the cult. Descended from this lost *libellus* are manuscripts such as the one now in four parts (Orléans, Bibliothèque municipale 296; Leiden, Bibliothèque universitaire Voss. lat. O.60; Paris, BnF, nouv. acq. lat. 443; Vatican, Reg. lat. 467) which contains the only known copy of the Occitan poem on Saint Faith (*La Chanson de sainte Foy*), and the English manuscript, London, British Library, Arundel 91, dated 1100–1125, containing the *Passio,* Bernard of Angers' introductory letter, and a selection of miracles. Another type of descendant of the lost *libellus* is the Sélestat manuscript, Bibliothèque Humaniste MS. lat. 22 (the most complete extant compilation of texts dealing with St. Faith; cf. Sheingorn, *Book*, 27).

[10] See further Benedicta Ward, *Miracles and the Medieval Mind: Theory, Record, and Event, 1000–1215* (Philadelphia: University of Pennsylvania Press, 1982), 212–13.

contemporary with the northern French vernacular *Vie de saint Alexis*.[11] The legend of Faith in this early text includes Caprais witnessing Faith's martyrdom and seeing a vision of her angelic visitors (vv. 353–72), but does not include Caprais' own martyrdom. There is a brief account of the recovery of Faith's relics by Dulcidius, and the creation of Faith's tomb in Agen (vv. 422–31). Then follows an account of their removal by stealth to Conques (vv. 432–36), and the foundation miracle of Conques (vv. 441–44). The final part of the poem leaves Faith's story to recount the divine vengeance later wreaked on Maximien and Diocletian (vv. 454–593, based on a text by Lactantius). This Occitan text is generally believed to be closely associated with the monastery at Conques, where it was perhaps used in dramatic performance in the abbey church.[12]

Conques and the Northwards Diffusion of the Cult

The shrine at Conques quickly grew in importance as a pilgrimage site and became the centre for the northward diffusion of the cult. Faith's shrine at Conques was established, as noted above, on a theft of relics. In the late ninth century it was decided to remove the monastery from Conques to a better site at Figeac, but one faction within the monastery refused to leave Conques, and an intense rivalry grew between the two foundations, both seeking to attract patronage. The monks who remained at Conques saw the need to acquire potent new relics, and this led them to make the claim that they possessed those of St. Faith (through theft from Agen sanctioned by the saint).[13] To support this claim Faith's reliquary statue was fashioned at Conques in the last quarter of the ninth century. Sometime after the foundation miracle of Faith's shrine there (the healing of

---

[11] The *Chanson de sainte Foy* (593 lines, in 55 mono-rhymed laisses of unequal length) has attracted critical attention because of its early date, and the nature and function of the text has been much debated. The first edition of the *Chanson de sainte Foy* was by J. Leite de Vasconcellos, *Romania* 31 (1902): 177–200; the major critical edition is by E. Hoepffner and P. Alfaric, *La Chanson de sainte Foy:* 1, *Fac-similé du manuscrit et texte critique, Introduction et Commentaire philologiques;* 2, *Traduction française et Sources latines, Introduction et Commentaire historiques* (Paris: Belles Lettres, 1926). English translation by R. L. Clark, in Sheingorn, *Book*, 275–84.

[12] See Robert Lafont, ed. and trans., *La Chanson de sainte Foi* (Geneva: Droz, 1998), 20–35 for a discussion of the poem as sung liturgical dance created specifically for the abbey church.

[13] Sheingorn, *Book*, 8. See also Geary, *Furta sacra*, 70–76 on the rivalry between the two convents and on the politics of relic thefts. Geary reports that the monks of Conques initially tried to steal the relics of Saint Vincent of Saragossa, but failed. It is probable that the monks of Conques then stole Faith's relics only as an afterthought during their theft of a second Saint Vincent (of Pompijac) from a site near Agen. Eventually, however, the cult of Faith eclipsed that of Vincent, and he was expunged from the *Translatio*.

Guibert's eyes, dated to about 983) the reliquary statue was renovated, with the addition of a crown, ecclesiastical garments, and a throne for the gold-covered wooden statue.[14] From this date on, the monastery began to receive important gifts from pilgrim patrons from all over Europe.

The cult's popularity expanded greatly in the eleventh century, attracting large numbers of pilgrims and crusaders, since Conques was both a convenient stop for those on their way east to Jerusalem or Rome, as well as a stop for pilgrims on one of the main routes west to Saint James' shrine in Santiago de Compostela. The press of pilgrims led to the building of a larger abbey church, begun about 1050 and finished before 1120. St. Faith had indeed become an important patroness for the monks who had so expeditiously appropriated her to Conques.

The Cult of Saint Faith in Medieval England

The second, and only northern French, vernacular life of St. Faith was composed in England, where the popularity of Faith's cult is attested by numerous foundations in her honour. Her feast was celebrated in some fifteen English Benedictine abbeys, and was included in the widespread Sarum liturgical use. Twenty-three medieval churches were dedicated to her, as well as chapels in St. Paul's Cathedral and Westminster Abbey in London.[15] Versions of her legend were composed in Middle English, and appear in the *South English Legendary*, in Osbern Bokenham's *Legendys of Hooly Wummen*, and in Caxton's *Golden Legend*.[16]

Dramatic evidence of the manner in which Faith's cult was spread throughout Europe by pilgrims who had travelled to Conques has been revealed by architectural and archaeological discoveries at an early cult centre in England. In the Norfolk village of Horsham, a priory dedicated to Faith was founded by Robert and Sybil Fitzwalter ca. 1105.[17] Fortuitously, the medieval wall paintings of the refectory have survived, and these recount how the priory came to be established

---

[14] Sheingorn, *Book*, 16: the golden head is of an "adult male and came from an imperial portrait bust, probably of the fifth century, which must have been a royal donation."

[15] Farmer, 146–47. Alison Binns, *Dedications of Monastic Houses in England and Wales, 1066–1216* (Woodbridge: Boydell Press, 1989), 19, 99, 115 lists two monastic houses dedicated to Saint Faith: the priory of Horsham St. Faith, and a priory at Newton Longville, Buckinghamshire, a cell of the Abbey of St. Faith at Longueville, Normandy. The parish church of Newton Longville is dedicated to St. Faith.

[16] Cf. Charlotte D'Evelyn and Frances A. Foster, "Individual Saints' Legends," in *A Manual of Writings in Middle English: 1050–1500*, ed. Albert E. Hartung, II (Hamden, CT: Archon, 1970), Bibliography, §102 (587).

[17] Wogan-Browne, *Saints' Lives*, 70, notes that Sybil was the heiress of Ralph de Cheney, and from a family of higher rank than the Fitzwalters. She gave her marriage portion of land to the priory and was probably the major patron.

by Robert and Sybil after their return from pilgrimage to Rome. On the way home, the Fitzwalters were held prisoner by brigands in the south of France, following their visit to the monastery of St. Giles (on whom see 5–6 above), but upon praying to St. Faith for deliverance they were miraculously freed. Visiting the abbey at Conques in thanksgiving, they vowed to found a daughter cell of Conques in their native country. To help with the new foundation, two monks from Conques travelled back to Norfolk with them.

The priory of Horsham St. Faith is a few miles north of Norwich. Of the original priory buildings, the cloister walls and the refectory remain.[18] When the refectory was converted to a private dwelling in the sixteenth century the medieval refectory wall paintings were covered by new interior walls. Then, in 1924, a roof fire led to the discovery of a large Crucifixion painting on the hidden wall, and more extensive paintings were later discovered in 1969 (see Fig. 1). These paintings have been described as "the most impressive surviving scheme of mid-thirteenth-century wall painting in England," and the painting style has been characterized as similar, but superior, to that of Matthew Paris, monk of St. Albans.[19]

The sequence of wall paintings runs the width of the east wall of the medieval refectory, presenting the history of the foundation in nine scenes, each two

---

[18] Horsham St. Faith's charter was confirmed by Henry I, the priory consecrated by the bishop of Norwich sometime before 1119, and the foundation charter was confirmed by the pope in 1163. Established for twelve monks and a prior, it remained an alien priory until 1390 when it was granted denization. At its most prosperous period at the end of the thirteenth century it had possessions in seventy-seven Norfolk parishes, but it never expanded beyond its original twelve monks. At its dissolution in 1534 there remained only the prior and six monks in the community. On Horsham St. Faith priory see Julian Eve, *A History of Horsham St. Faith, Norfolk* (Norwich: J. R. Eve, 1992, rev. 1994); David Sherlock, "Discoveries at Horsham St. Faith Priory, 1970–73," *Norfolk Archaeology* 36 (1976): 202–23; Donovan Purcell, "The Priory of Horsham St. Faith and its Wallpaintings," *Norfolk Archaeology* 35 (1974): 469–73; Walter R. Rudd, "The Priory of Horsham St. Faith," *Norfolk Archaeology* 23 (1929): 68–73; J. B. Cox, "The Priory of St. Faith, Horsham," in *The Victoria History of the County of Norfolk*, ed. William Page (Folkestone: Dawson for University of London Institute of Historical Research, 1906; repr. 1975), 2:346–49.

[19] David Park, "Wall Painting," in *Age of Chivalry: Art in Plantagenet England 1200–1400*, ed. Jonathan Alexander and Paul Binski (London: Royal Academy of Arts, in association with Weidenfeld and Nicolson, 1987), 125–30, 313. Park states: "Compared with a celebrated sheet of drawings by Matthew Paris (Cambridge, Corpus Christi College, MS 26, f. vii) the similarities are obvious, yet the marked surety of the drawing of St Faith sets it off as even higher in quality" (127). He also comments that the style of the paintings is matched by their technique: "to elaborate incised drawing and final gilding of details can be added unlooked-for complexities such as a lead white ground, and layers of glazes added to the secco painting" (127).

III. *Saint Faith of Agen, Virgin Martyr* 47

Figure 1. Refectory wall of St. Faith's Pirory, Horsham, with cycle of medieval paintings relating the foundation narrative. ©*Crown Copyright. English Heritage. Used with permission.*

Figure 2. Foundation Cycle of Horsham St. Faith Priory, Scene Six: Crowned Faith opens prison door for Robert and Sybil. ©*Crown Copyright. English Heritage. Used with permission.*

feet high. The first scene is now hidden by a reconstructed north wall. The second scene, also mostly destroyed, shows traces of a ship, probably showing the voyage of Robert and Sybil from Rome to southern France. The third scene shows their capture while travelling on horseback. The fourth scene has them imprisoned in an octagonal tower, the fifth shows them praying for deliverance in a church, and the sixth shows them back in their prison, but with the crowned St. Faith holding open the door (see Fig. 2). In the seventh scene they kneel before the abbot of Conques, and in the eighth, they are on a ship, with two monks, returning to Norfolk (see front cover image). The final scene shows the priory church's construction, "and is full of action and interest as an illustration of late thirteenth-century building techniques."[20]

During the restoration of these paintings in late 1970, two more figures were discovered. They are part of the large Crucifixion scene which dominates the east wall of the refectory, above the sequence relating the foundation story. In the Crucifixion, Christ and the Virgin and St. John at either side of the cross are double life-size. Of the two additional figures, one is male and the other a crowned female (see Fig. 3). The identity of the female figure is open to question,

---

[20] Purcell, "Horsham St. Faith and its Wallpaintings," 472.

Figure 3. Large-scale frontal portrait of crowned St. Faith, medieval refectory wall painting at St. Faith's Priory, Horsham. ©*Crown Copyright. English Heritage. Used with permission.*

but the most recent view is that she represents St. Faith.[21] She is described in the following terms by David Park: "daunting in her uncompromising frontality, her broad face, staring eyes with solid black pupils, small pursed mouth and heavy chin, some of these features the last residues of earlier Byzantine influences."[22]

La Vie sainte Fey, virgine e martire by Simon de Walsingham

The evidence of the wall paintings shows Horsham St. Faith to have been a major site of Faith's cult in England, and to have close ties to Conques itself. However, it was not at Horsham, but at nearby Bury St. Edmunds Abbey, in Suffolk, that the *Vie sainte Fey*, the only known northern French version of the legend, was composed in the early thirteenth century.[23] In the belief (widely shared at the time) that French texts copied in English manuscripts frequently suffered corruption at the hands of careless scribes, Simon's first modern editor, A. T. Baker, freely corrected the text in his edition of the life to create a more regular octosyllabic work. Baker also compared the *Vie sainte Fey* unfavourably with the *Chanson de sainte Foy*, considering Simon less skilled than the author of the *Chanson*, writing a century earlier.[24] But recent studies refute this view, and critics such as Jocelyn Wogan-Browne argue convincingly that Simon de Walsingham is consciously working in a complex literary tradition that he shapes to his own ends. In the *Vie sainte Fey*, Simon is conscious of the stylistic possibilities of the vernacular, which he exploits most obviously in wordplay, in lexical and syntactic patterning, and in his choice of vocabulary.[25]

---

[21] Both Eve, *History of Horsham St. Faith*, 20, and Purcell, "Horsham St. Faith and its Wallpaintings," 472–73 state that the figure may be either Faith or Margaret of Scotland (mother of Matilda, wife of Henry I; Margaret was canonized in 1250); Park, *Age of Chivalry*, 313 says the figure "is almost certainly identifiable as St. Faith herself."

[22] Park, "Wall Painting," in *Age of Chivalry*, 127.

[23] Edited by A. T. Baker, "*Vie Anglo-Normande de Sainte Foy* par Simon de Walsingham," *Romania* 66 (1940–1941): 49–84. The manuscript text is available electronically, at the Campsey Project, www.margot.uwaterloo.ca. Cf. also Brigitte Cazelles, "The Life of St. Faith," in eadem, *The Lady as Saint: A Collection of French Hagiographic Romances of the Thirteenth Century* (Philadelphia: University of Pennsylvania Press, 1991), 182–203 (a translation of vv. 1–894). For a detailed analysis of the historical, cultural, and literary aspects of the text see Wogan-Browne, *Saints' Lives*, 69–79.

[24] Baker, "Vie," 58.

[25] Wogan-Browne, *Saints' Lives*, 69–79.

Manuscript

La Vie sainte Fey is found in a single manuscript, London, British Library, MS. Additional 70513, fols. 146 vb–156 vb.[26] This is the well-known Campsey collection of verse saints' lives, the only known manuscript collection composed solely of verse saints' lives in French. It contains thirteen lives, and the major part of it was copied in England in the last quarter of the thirteenth century. It was owned in the fourteenth century by a female convent at Campsey Ash, Suffolk, and was used for mealtime reading. The lives included are of Edward the Confessor by a nun of Barking, of Thomas Becket by Guernes de Pont Sainte-Maxence, of Catherine of Alexandria by Clemence of Barking, all dating from the last third of the twelfth century; the early thirteenth-century lives of Osith, Faith, Modwenna, Audrey, and Mary Magdalene by Guillaume le Clerc de Normandie; the lives of Edmund Archbishop by Matthew Paris, and Richard Bishop of Chichester by Pierre d'Abernon from the third quarter of the thirteenth century. The first quire of the manuscript, written in a different, slightly later hand, contains three lives by Bozon from the early fourteenth century: Elizabeth of Hungary, Paul the hermit, and Panuce (Paphnutius).

Of the thirteen lives in this collection, seven are known only from this manuscript, and three are composed by women. An unusually high proportion of the lives are of women saints (seven of thirteen), and there is a strong focus on Insular saints (also seven of thirteen), while others were written by Anglo-Norman writers for Insular patrons.[27]

Monastic Author and Patron

According to the prologue to the Life, Simon de Walsingham, a monk at Bury St. Edmunds Abbey, who was born on St. Faith's feast day, was asked to write a French version of the saint's life. It is likely that this life was connected with Bury's renovations to Faith's chapel in the abbey church under Abbot Samson: these were completed in the last year or two of the twelfth or in the first decade

---

[26] For a detailed description of the manuscript see Delbert Russell, "The Campsey Collection of Old French Saints' Lives: A Re-Examination of its Structure and Provenance," *Scriptorium* 57 (2003): 51–83, + colour plates 4–7. The electronic text of the manuscript is available online; see the Campsey project at http://margot.uwaterloo.ca.

[27] See Russell, "The Campsey Collection," 74–83 for summary details on these lives: items 6, 8, and 13 are by women; items 1, 5, 8–11, and 13 are lives of women. See also W. MacBain, "Anglo-Norman Women Hagiographers," in *Anglo-Norman Anniversary Essays*, OP series 2, ed. Ian Short (London: ANTS, 1993), 235–50; Jocelyn Wogan-Browne, "Powers of Record, Powers of Example: Hagiography and Women's History," in *Gendering the Master Narrative: Women and Power in the Middle Ages*, ed. Mary C. Erler and Maryanne Kowaleski (Ithaca and London: Cornell University Press, 2003), 71–93.

of the thirteenth century.[28] Little is known of Simon, apart from his name and his affiliation with Bury St. Edmunds. He states that he is "a servant" of St. Mary at St. Edmunds (v. 102). This suggests that as a monk he was assigned a duty which he performed at the parish church dedicated to St. Mary situated within the precincts of the Abbey.[29] He was literate, since his vernacular life is based on Latin sources, but he was not university-educated. Simon was aligned, however, with the learned faction (which included all the Masters in the abbey, among them Thomas of Walsingham who may have been Simon's kinsman) in supporting the election in 1213 of Hugh of Northwold as abbot to succeed Samson.[30]

---

[28] Legge, *ANC*, 10–11 states that the building celebrations could not have taken place before 1200, and Samson died in 1211, so she suggests the period 1205–1210; Legge later puts the date as "a little before 1216" (*ANL*, 257). However, renovations to St. Faith's chapel are mentioned in Jocelin de Brakelonde's chronicle, in the entry for 1198 (Greenway and Sayers, *Chronicle*, 85; Jane, *Chronicle*, 151; Arnold, *Memorials*, 1: 297), and these renovations are noted as well in the *Sacristarum gesta* of the Abbey (Arnold, *Memorials*, 2: 291–92). The sacrist Hugh was in charge of this work, and Hugh was no longer in that office in 1200. These turn-of-the-century renovations may have been the impetus for the new vernacular life, or it may have been later renovations—the tower of the abbey collapsed in 1210, for example, but we have no detailed chronicle references to Samson's rebuilding at this date, since Jocelin of Brakelond's chronicle ends in 1202, a decade before the end of Samson's life. The tower was directly adjacent to the chapel of St. Faith.

[29] Legge, *ANC*, 10.

[30] R. M. Thomson, ed. and trans., *The Chronicle of the Election of Hugh, Abbot of Bury St. Edmunds and later Bishop of Ely* (Oxford: Oxford University Press, 1974), xxx-vi. The disputed election exacerbated the division between the learned and unlearned members of the monastery, as we learn from the *Chronicle* of Jocelin of Brakelond and the text which relates the controversy in 1212–1215 over the election. Thomson analyzes the composition of the two rival factions; they were divided along many lines—learned against unlearned, younger against older—but the strongest grouping seemed to be geographical: those from East Anglia (which included Suffolk and Norfolk) versus those from outside this region (xxxii–xlvii). Among the *Magistri* during Samson's abbacy were Samson himself and Thomas of Walsingham. In the party from St. Edmund's Abbey that went to Rome in 1214 seeking papal support against the king were three men from Bury St. Edmunds with the surname "of Walsingham": the two monks, Master Thomas and his kinsman Simon, and the clerk Stephen, son of Roger of Walsingham (36–37). Another Master, Alan of Walsingham, is later referred to in the *Electio Hugonis* text as a member of the faction supporting Hugh. The blood relationship of these men is unspecified, and the kinship between Master Thomas and Simon remains vague—the Latin term used is *cognatum eius*, which can mean a kinsman on either the mother or father's side of the family. The suggestion that Thomas was the cousin of Simon seems to derive from the speculation by Legge that the phrase "nurri de sun pais" might be an oblique way of claiming cousinhood (Legge, *ANC*, 11).

The request that Simon write the *Vie* was made, according to the Life's prologue, by a learned fellow monk. Baker's suggestion that this refers to Simon's kinsman, Thomas of Walsingham, has often been accepted by later critics.[31] It is clear, however, that Simon is referring to Abbot Samson, for he comments that his earthly patron is a learned monk and fellow countryman (Simon says that he was "born and raised in the same region," *nurri de son pais*, v. 84), and he playfully remarks on his patron's short physical but tall moral stature (*Grant en science e en resun / Ke est de stature petiz*, lit. "Tall in learning and good sense, but short of stature," vv. 80–81). These are all details found in the contemporary biography of Abbot Samson by his chaplain, Jocelin of Brakelond. His *Chronicle* describes Samson as "below average height," and the pages of his biography portray the impeccable moral integrity of this learned and eloquent man. He spoke French, Latin, and English, but he remained a proud Norfolkman, since when he preached to the people in English he used "the dialect of Norfolk where he was born and bred."[32] Thomson has pointed out the importance, in both the internal and external politics of Bury St. Edmunds, of the county of Norfolk, seen both as the principal area of St. Edmund's cult and the region of which the saint was most protective. Simon, from Walsingham in Norfolk, is also staking his claim to this power and protection of Edmund by the mention of this shared regional identity.[33]

Simon's Treatment of the Latin Sources

Simon comments that he was sent his Latin source by *danz Benjamin* (vv. 443–44). Earlier scholars have suggested that Benjamin may have been a monk at Horsham.[34] Although Simon would certainly have known of the priory of St. Faith at Horsham (about twenty-five miles from his birthplace at Walsingham), we know of no special connection between Simon and the priory.[35] It is possible that a large and learned monastery such as Bury St. Edmunds would have had its

---

[31] Baker, "Vie," 50; Legge, *ANC*, 11; eadem, *ANL*, 257–58; Thomson, *Chronicle of the Election of Hugh*, 32–43; Wogan-Browne, *Saints' Lives*, 69. See also Wogan-Browne, "Powers of Record, Powers of Example," 84–86 on the complex nexus of noble familial relationships often involved in political-religious matters at Bury St. Edmunds.

[32] L. C. Jane, ed. and trans., *The Chronicle of Jocelin of Brakelond, Monk of St. Edmundsbury: A Picture of Monastic and Social Life in the XIIth Century* (New York: Cooper Square Publishers, 1966), 62, 64.

[33] Thomson, *Chronicle of the Election of Hugh*, xl–xlvii.

[34] Baker, "Vie," 53.

[35] The *Chronicle* of Jocelin of Brakelond shows that there were collegial contacts between the Abbey of Bury St. Edmunds and the priory at Horsham. For example, Bertrand, prior of Horsham St. Faith, was nominated by Bury monks in February 1182, under royal constraint, as one of three external candidates for the abbacy of Bury, in the process which led to the election of Samson (Jane, *Chronicle*, 33–36).

own Latin texts relating to Faith, dating from the time that the abbey chapel to St. Faith was first built.[36]

Simon was familiar with the *Passio*, the *Translatio*, liturgical offices for St. Faith, and the *Liber miraculorum sancte Fidis*. His poem of 1242 flexible octosyllabic lines, however, includes only the traditional narrative of the *Passio* and the *Translatio*. As Baker points out, Simon uses both the prose and metrical versions of the *Passio*, as well as *lectiones* of the Sarum use (an abbreviated version of the *Passio*), and perhaps echoes of liturgical responses.[37] Simon mentions the *Liber miraculorum*, but defers vernacularization of it to a later time, focussing instead on the removal of Faith's relics from Agen to Conques as recounted in the *Translatio*, and presenting this as another example of the saint's intervention: "You will hear further details of her miracles when I have more leisure to recount them, but I cannot do so now for I wish to inform you of another matter relating to her good deeds" (vv. 968–72).

In his reworking of the narrative material Simon also adds a detailed prologue (vv. 1–111, see 50–51 above and 164–66 below) which situates the genesis of his *Vie* in the context of his contemporaries at St. Edmund's Abbey. Simon thus allows his audience to view St. Faith's role and power in three distinct historical periods, as a drama in three acts: the time present of Simon's writing in the early thirteenth century; the period of the original martyrdom in the early fourth century; and the period of the establishment of the shrine at Conques, following its appropriation of the relics in the ninth century.

The Prologue: Time Present

Simon's prologue borrows images and themes from the traditional narrative of St. Faith in order to involve his audience in the work which he is about to perform, and which they are about to hear. He links his audience (*Seignurs*, "Lords," v.1) of fellow monks (or of mixed lay and clerical lords), his author, and the saint by repeated wordplay on *fey*. *Fey* is both "faith" and "Faith," the proper name: those who are already confirmed in the faith know that they can only be saved by faith (or Faith), and therefore will be happy to increase their faith by hearing

---

[36] R. M. Thomson, "The Library of Bury St Edmunds Abbey in the Eleventh and Twelfth Centuries," *Speculum* 47 (1972): 617–45 analyzes the library at Bury, but his study does not deal with service books and hagiography. He states: "Patristics and the works of classical and late antique authors account for most of the library before c. 1150, according to the available evidence. The remainder consists of service-books and hagiography, with which I am not primarily concerned, the works of medieval theologians and biblical scholars—Bede, the Carolingians and contemporaries—and some (mainly medical) science" (633–34).

[37] Baker, "Vie," 55–57. He cites v. 20 ("Bele de vis, de fei plus bele") as a possible liturgical phrase.

of St. Faith. By listening to the recitation in song and story of Faith's virtues, the community of believers will be strengthened in their faith, and saved. This reference to a sung recitation may suggest a liturgical context for the audition of the text (*Devez plus voluntiers oir / De seinte Fey chanter e lire*, "You should all the more willingly hear the story of St. Faith [or, "holy faith"] sung and read," vv. 12–13). At the same time Simon solicits the faith of his audience in himself as a writer (*si jeo ne ment*, "(*lit.*) if I am not lying," v. 3, implying "of course I am not lying, so you must believe me"), and casts his audience as representative of the whole community of the faithful (*Veuz e juvenes, petit ne grant*, "old and young, of high or low estate," v. 6, all will be saved by their faith). The traditional image of St. Faith associated with the famous golden and bejewelled reliquary at Conques is also linked verbally with the double meaning of *fey*, since her holy name (*Fey*) and her holy life (*fey*, the virtue) are said to be as unified and well-matched as a jewel on a golden ring (vv. 23–27).

In a replica of the literary and linguistic humility expressed in Latin by the narrators of the *Passio* and the *Translatio*, Simon as narrator professes inadequacy in the vernacular.[38] He asks forgiveness for any errors in the *romanz*, using (as with *fey*) a double meaning for the term: his narrative and also his French (vv. 34–38). His potential for error comes from his presumption in taking on the task since, he claims, he is both unlearned in Latin (*Jeo qui ne sui guere lettré*, v. 37, implying he might make errors in understanding his source), and unskilled in the vernacular (*Et povrement enromancé*, v. 38, and hence might misspeak himself in French). The pejorative view of Simon's work taken by his first modern editor, A. T. Baker, may have been the result of reading the prologue as a literal statement of inadequacy, rather than as a version of the humility topos in which Simon exploits hagiography's conventions with a conscious attention to the effects of language.

To linguistic and cultural modesty, Simon adds the humility of the penitent: he is but a weak sinner, in thought, in deed, and in word. This leads him to beg the indulgence of his audience on devotional grounds: another motive for his work is his personal devotion to St. Faith. Devotion to Faith as a motive for writing is taken from the Latin sources,[39] but Simon adds a stronger personal connection: because he was born on her feast day he owes Faith a special reverence. He develops the contrast between Faith's heavenly birth into eternal joy

---

[38] Sheingorn, *Book*, 34, 263–64. The narrator of the *Passio* refers to his "stammering style" and says his talent is "feeble and barren." The narrator of the *Translatio* claims himself to be "lowest of all," to "have no lively style of elegant, rhetorical writing." Wogan-Browne, *Saints' Lives,* 78, suggests that this claim to have only a child-like linguistic simplicity is an attempt by the narrator to align himself with the child-like integrity of Saint Faith.

[39] Sheingorn, *Book*, 33, 264. The narrator of the *Translatio* twice asserts he is writing "more out of devotion than ability" (264).

and his own earthly birth into pain and suffering (vv. 56–74), with the repetition of words such as *peine,* "pain, suffering" (vv. 55, 56, 60), *travail,* "suffering, labour" (vv. 57, 58, 63, 66), linked to *nasqui,* "I was born" (vv. 56, 60, 72). Part of the narrator's suffering is the struggle of writing this translation (*En cest travailz peines,* "the painful struggle of this translation," v. 63), and vv. 72–73 perhaps cast translation as the labour of giving birth (*Ke jeo nasqui a cest labur; / Pur ceo començai cest escrit* "the very day that I was born into the toil of this earthly life ... I began writing this work").

Simon's audience would have frequently heard variations on such rhetorical topoi. His veiled reference, mentioned earlier, to Abbot Samson as the patron who requested the *Vie* draws on a different level of insider information. Composition by monks usually requires the permission or command of a monastic superior, and the convention is used here with a mixture of seriousness and joking that relies on insider knowledge of Samson's physical attributes and of Norfolk's importance in Faith's cult. But at the same time Simon is also using the topos of writing out of love for the community (vv. 88–89).[40] This community includes the present and the future: all who wish to hear it, or may later possess the work (guests of the monastic house where it was composed, and performed, and later patrons, or owners of the work in manuscript copies, such as the female convent at Campsey). And it includes learned and lay—those who have no Latin will have no choice but to listen to the vernacular version. In return, Simon de Walsingham, monk at St. Edmunds, claims his own reward, announcing his name, and requesting that all members of his community hold him in their prayers, so that they all may enter the kingdom of the Father (thus returning to the theme of the common salvation of the faithful which began the prologue). "Now," he intones, "I will relate briefly to you the details I have learned from the Latin regarding the passion of St. Faith, and how Jesus took her to himself in heaven." Faith, he has shown, serves as both model and assurance of salvation for the community of the faithful.

The *Passio*: Early Martyrdoms

Although Christian martyrdom was no longer a direct model for religious life in the late twelfth and early thirteenth centuries, clerical male fantasy of virginal sacrifice and the valorization of virginity as a metaphor for female holiness was

---

[40] See Duncan Robertson, "Writing in the Textual Community: Clemence of Barking's Life of St. Catherine," *French Forum* 21 (1996): 5–28; Simon Gaunt, *Gender and Genre in Medieval French Literature* (Cambridge: Cambridge University Press, 1995), 213–33.

particularly strong, and legends of virgin martyrs remained the most popular hagiographic narrative type.[41]

In his reworking of Faith's legend Simon remains close to the narrative structure of the Latin texts, but he consistently introduces emotive language in details which reveal his knowledge (shared by his audience) of Faith's "second life" after her martyrdom as a mediator between God and those who invoke her patronage.

Dacien's character, for example, is given more substance and colour than is found in the Latin sources, when he is first introduced (vv. 172–84); he is ungodly (*un Deu enemi*), and cruel, "extremely wicked and arrogant, choleric, evil, and given to excess" (*Mut esteit feus e orguillius, / Colorus, purvers, (e) surfaitus*, v. 175–76). He is a traitor (*traitre*), guided by the devil (*le maufé*, v. 181, *le diable*, v. 183). During his later debate with Faith, despite his anger and distress (*Irus esteit e [mut] marri*, v. 302), he treacherously feigns goodwill (*Par felunie . . . Respundi deboneirement*, vv. 302–4), and he is repeatedly called *fel*, or *felun* "evil man" (vv. 267, 282, 349, 773). In a scene similar to that found in *St. George* (vv. 1543–46), the intellectual and theological defeat of Dacien is presented in a strikingly concrete image: Dacien is physically perturbed by his anger: *De irë e de maltalent / Se torst cume fet la serpent / Kant del venin li bat al quer / E si ne se pot pas desenfler*, "His body was distorted with anger and rage like a serpent unable to prevent itself from puffing up with venom when it is poised to strike," vv. 803–6).

Descriptions of Saint Faith oppose her to Dacien as the beloved of God (*la Deu amye*, vv. 87, 157, 265, 287, 331, 363, 501, 811). She is "a glorious, precious gem/woman" (*Fey la gloriuse*, vv. 207, 213; *femme precieuse*, v. 208; *gemme precieuse*, v. 214), whose brilliance shines all the brighter the more Dacien tries to extinguish it (vv. 205–22). When Faith announces her name to Dacien she uses expanded wordplay on *fey* (vv. 275–80). In their dialogues, Simon expands Faith's replies to incorporate standard elements of Christian doctrine (e.g. the virgin birth and the Passion, vv. 252–54, 372–77, and the standard Christian denunciation of idols derived from biblical sources: "they have mouths but cannot speak . . ." vv. 341–46).

Simon's representation of Faith, then, is constantly inflected by awareness of Faith as a young virgin martyr and as an authoritative speaker for the heavenly realm to which her sanctity gives access. This double perspective needs to be borne in mind when considering the famous scene of Faith's martyrdom, as she is stripped and tied to a brass bed set over flames (vv. 381–412, see Appendix

---

[41] Wogan-Browne, *Saints' Lives* offers a detailed study of medieval social authorizations and literary representations of virginity; chap. 2, "Virginity and the Gift" (57–90), deals with the *Vie sainte Fey*. See also Emma Campbell, *Medieval Saints' Lives: The Gift, Kinship and Community in Old French Hagiography* (Cambridge: D. S. Brewer, 2008) which includes discussion of community in the Campsey MS, and the life of Faith. On the prevalence of the virgin martyr model in the twelfth century, see Wogan-Browne and Burgess, *Virgin Lives and Holy Deaths*, xi–xix.

3 ii). It complicates the question of the kind of figure Faith is here and how the narrative's internal and external audiences view her. The fact that the scene is told twice, once in the third person and again through the eyes of Caprais, Faith's disciple, who watches her torture from the hillside where he has taken refuge (vv. 523–96; Appendix 3 ii), adds to the complexity of the question. Unsurprisingly, there has been considerable discussion of the eroticism and voyeurism attached to Faith's martyrdom in Simon's (and to some extent the Latin) narrative. Simon's pervasive gem metaphors, in the Prologue and elsewhere, as discussed above, suggest that the erotics—and multiple significations—of treasure are what is at stake; modern models of pornography and sadism (which are sometimes applied to medieval saints' lives)[42] do not fully address what is happening in this martyrdom scene (see further Appendix 3 ii, Commentary).

Indeed one assumption of Faith's *passio* is that an act of exchange lies at the heart of it: Faith's gift of herself is rewarded by God's transmutation of her into a bejewelled and crowned citizen of heaven. Hoarding treasure is usually frowned on in medieval literature: gems and jewels are too important a means of display and gifting, and of the symbolic affirmation of relationships and affinities, not to be circulated. Simon's martyrdom narrative shows the repeated exchange of the powerful treasure stored up in the virginal Faith as a gift between males. As her martyrdom is recorded and reworked in Latin, the vernacular Faith's gift of her virginity to Jesus becomes a gift to Caprais, then a gift from Caprais to Primus and Felicianus, as well as a gift between each writer and his audience. Wogan-Browne argues that despite this homosocial chain of exchanges in the vernacular text's creation, Faith's own agency as giver of the gift of her power is paramount. It is her "foundational gift [of herself] to Christ that enables the further circulations of value."[43] These were not, and need not have been, confined to male participants, given that, in a further circulation, the extant copy of the text appears in the Campsey collection of saints' lives (noted above, 48), a manuscript probably produced for a female patron, and certainly owned by a female convent.[44]

Translatio to Conques: Expanding the Gift

The saint's agency as giver of herself and her power is made more evident in the last section of the *Vie sainte Fey*. Initially, however, it is God, not Faith (v. 851–58), who preserves the martyrs' bodies in secret burial in Agen until the period of Christian persecution has passed and the relics are moved to a place of honour by

---

[42] See above, 24 n. 5, 30 n. 28.
[43] Wogan-Browne, *Saints' Lives*, 77.
[44] Wogan-Browne, *Saints' Lives*, 69–70, and Russell, "The Campsey Collection," 63–71.

III. Saint Faith of Agen, Virgin Martyr　　　　　　　　　　　　　　　　　　　　　　　　　59

Agen's bishop (vv. 870–94).[45] Miracles happen at her shrine in the church dedicated to her in Agen (vv. 895–922). The miracles performed by Jesus (vv. 907–8, 915–16) in Faith's honour attract people from far and wide (vv. 918–19) to Agen, but then the city suddenly loses its treasure.

In rewriting Faith's post-mortem life Simon omits some details of her patronage of Agen (such as the belief that Faith herself had demanded to be placed in a tomb there, or the marble mausoleum built for her with the story of her passion inscribed on it),[46] while he increases Faith's direct complicity in changing her client community. The translation to Conques is announced abruptly (vv. 923–30), by stating that Agen is "stripped of this honour [i.e. Faith's relics]" (v. 924). The verb *despuillier* (strip) is used earlier to denote the stripping of Faith before she is placed on the brass bed (vv. 385–86) and to express the divine wish not to rob Agen of the bodies of the martyrs which have brought honour to the place of their death (vv. 855–56). Now the same verb is used to state that Agen is in fact robbed of both the honour and the treasure of the relics (*Despuiliée de cel honur*, v. 924; *E del cel tresor despoliez*, v. 1144).

The narrator of the *Vie* offers no reason for the relic theft beyond the assertion that Agen's loss is a gain for Conques, made at Faith's own wish and pleasure (vv. 927–30). Faith's agency in her own translation is further expanded in vv. 961–72, where it is asserted that she "loved the companionship" of Conques, and wanted to "honour" it with her presence. Not only does Faith herself conceive the idea of switching her client community to Conques, but her wish is transmitted to the monks at Conques by frequent visions admonishing them to translate Faith's relics there (vv. 980–84).[47]

As noted earlier, Simon seems to rely in his prologue on his audience understanding that when he evokes the saint as a precious jewel it is a reference to the famous gem-studded golden reliquary at Conques (which would have been seen in person by Horsham St. Faith's founders, Sybil and Robert Fitzwalter). Yet the reliquary is not described in Simon's rewriting, and he reduces details of the translation of Faith's relics both at Agen and Conques. Of the shrine at Agen, Simon writes that, unable to open the marble tomb, Arinisdus breaks the marble at its base (vv. 1078–79) to make a hole through which he removes the body and places it in a wicker container (*une bele esceppe*, v. 1085). This suggests that the Agen tomb was a marble image of the saint containing her bones. The *Passio* describes it as beautiful, and as demanded by the saint herself, while the

---

[45] The *Vie sainte Fey* addresses the same anxiety about fragmentation of the saints' bodies as seen in the *Vie de saint Georges*.

[46] Sheingorn, *Book*, 37. The *Passio* states: "she was entombed so beautifully that afterward everyone agreed that she had demanded it herself for her own benefit." Details of the inscription and tomb are in the *Translatio*, 265–66.

[47] Simon says the visions are noted in his Latin source (*L'estorie nus cunte e dist*, v. 977). See note to v. 977.

Translatio notes that the story of her passion is carved in letters on her marble mausoleum.[48] The wicker vessel (*cele escheppe,* vv. 1188, 1195; *la ceppe,* v. 1200) in which her body is carried from Agen, and which effects miracles when it is venerated and touched or kissed (vv. 1187, 1195, 1200), is an addition by Simon (the Latin text refers only to the blind man at Figeac touching the veil covering her body). Simon completely omits the Latin narrative of the later attempt to translate the relics to a new shrine at Conques and the decision to make a reliquary "of gleaming red gold and scintillating gems."[49] The *Vie sainte Fey* refers only to the triumphal arrival of the virgin martyr, whose body is brought into Conques in a sung procession of monks who have gone out to meet Arinisdus carrying the relics. They place the body "in a beautiful and appropriate setting" (*E en beau liu e avenant / Mistrent icel cors bonuré,* vv. 1220–21), and the narrative ends with a prayer for intercession by Faith on behalf of the narrator and his audience.

As mentioned above (51), Simon defers discussion of the well-known book of miracles of Faith at Conques (vv. 969–72), and treats instead the story of the miraculous theft of the relics from Agen as proof of Faith's expansion of her gift of power to Conques. Given that the Horsham St. Faith priory was established due to a miraculous rescue of the founders while on pilgrimage to Conques, is it possible that Simon's statement deferring a more ample discussion of the miracles (vv. 968–69) means that he was planning, and may have written, a second vernacular work relating Horsham's foundation miracle, incorporated into a treatment of the *Liber miraculorum* along with a description of her jewelled reliquary?

Whether we have only the first part of Simon's work on St. Faith, or whether the extant text in the Campsey manuscript is all he ever composed, the positive assessments of his work that have replaced Baker's pejorative view seem more productive. In the last century, researchers have increased our understanding of medieval society in general and of the monastery of Bury St. Edmunds in particular. This affords a more detailed sense of the cultural milieu in which Simon de Walsingham was writing, so that although much remains unclear, more is now known about Simon and his fellow monks at Bury St. Edmunds than about any of the other medieval hagiographers translated in this anthology. When the *Vie sainte Fey* is viewed in this context, it can be argued that the confidence shown at the end of the twelfth century by Abbot Samson, the leader of Bury St. Edmunds monastery, in the skill of Simon de Walsingham as an effective writer of vernacular verse, was fully justified.

---

[48] Sheingorn, *Book,* 37, 265.
[49] Sheingorn, *Book,* 272.

4. Saint Mary Magdalene

Mary Magdalene in the Medieval West

In terms of her ability to engage both lay and clerical people alike, the figure of Mary Magdalene is one of the most powerful of all saints, and her cult and its texts have, understandably, a complex and varied history. Before examining the immediate sources of the particular "romance" version of her life composed by Guillaume Le Clerc in the early thirteenth century, it is worth understanding something of the development of the Magdalen legend in medieval culture, where she is so often second only to the Virgin Mary in her prominence in medieval people's hopes and fears.

The medieval view of Mary Magdalene in the Western church conflated three separate women from the New Testament. The single identity of these biblical women was explicitly mentioned as early as the sixth century, in the writings of Gregory the Great (pope, 590–604), and universally accepted by later medieval writers.[1] Mary of Magdala, from whom Jesus cast out seven devils, was present at the crucifixion; she was the first to see the risen Jesus, and she reported the news of the resurrection to his disciples, making her the "apostle to the apostles."[2] She was easily confused, or identified, with Mary of Bethany, who, along with her sister Martha, witnessed Jesus raise their brother Lazarus from the dead. Mary of Bethany had anointed Jesus' feet with perfume, and the act was understandably assimilated with the unnamed repentant sinner (mentioned in the gospel of Luke), who bathed the feet of Jesus with her tears and anointed them with oil at the house of Simon the Pharisee in Bethany.[3]

---

[1] Victor Saxer, *Le Culte de Marie Madeleine en occident, des origines à la fin du moyen âge*. Cahiers d'Archéologie et d'Histoire 3 (Paris: Clavreuil, and Auxerre: Publications de la Société des Fouilles Archéologiques et des Monuments Historiques de l'Yonne, 1959), 3–4. Among the writers cited by Saxer are Bede, Anselm, Bernard of Clairvaux, and Bonaventure.

[2] For the multiple references to Mary Magdalene and Mary of Bethany, see Matthew 27:55–61, 28:1–10; Mark 15:40–41, 47, 16:1–11; Luke 8:2, 10:38–42, 24:1–11; John 11:1–46, 12:1–8, 19:25, 20:1–18. For a recent general study, see Susan Haskins, *Mary Magdalen: Myth and Metaphor* (London: Harper Collins, 1994).

[3] Luke 7:36–50; Matthew 26:6–13; Mark 14:3–9.

But in some ways the most striking development in the Magdalen's cult was the unblushing medieval appropriation of the saint from the Holy Land to Europe, and the creation of an entire post-Gospel life for her there, based in southern and central France. By the ninth century the western medieval legend of Mary Magdalene was extended to incorporate a period of eremitical penance in the desert preceding her death, a motif borrowed directly from the legend of another penitent sinner, St. Mary the Egyptian.

Mary Magdalene's cult was widespread in northern Europe at the beginning of the tenth century, at which time the Western church followed the Eastern tradition that her tomb was in Ephesus.[4] This changed dramatically in the mid-eleventh century when one French abbey suddenly became dominant through its claim to possess the relics of the saint. Vézelay, in Burgundy, quickly established its prominence as the centre of her cult when the pope sanctioned the abbey's claim to possess the Magdalen's relics, making it a new centre for pilgrimage.[5] Vézelay's influence and wealth grew rapidly during this period. The abbey was on the pilgrimage route to Compostela, and its importance is described in the well-known mid-twelfth-century pilgrim's guide (falsely) attributed to Aimeri Picaud.[6] An indication of the abbey's influence as a religious centre is seen in the choice of Vézelay by Bernard of Clairvaux as the site where he began to preach the Second Crusade, at Easter 1146, in the presence of Louis VII and Eleanor of Aquitaine, among hundreds of other potential crusaders. A few decades later, in 1190, the Third Crusade was also launched from Vézelay, with armies led by

---

[4] Elisabeth Pinto-Mathieu, *Marie-Madeleine dans la littérature du Moyen Âge* (Paris: Beauchesne, 1997), viii–ix, cites Saxer, *Le Culte*, who lists thirty-three sites in England, northern France, and Germany where the cult of Mary Magdalene was active in the early tenth century. The site of the tomb at Ephesus was noted by Gregory of Tours in the sixth century, and various later pilgrims confirmed visiting the tomb: the English pilgrim Willibald saw her tomb in Ephesus in the eighth century (cited in Farmer, 270), and Pinto-Mathieu cites a Russian pilgrim named Daniel who visited the tomb in Ephesus in 1106.

[5] Saxer, *Le Culte de Marie Madeleine*, 65–74. The papal bull of 27 April 1050 from Leo IX (under the influence of Abbot Geoffrey) adds Mary Magdalene as one of the official patrons of the abbey. A bull in March 1058 from Stephen IX confirms the presence of the tomb of Mary Magdalene at Vézelay, and the Magdalene quickly becomes the sole patron of the abbey.

[6] Aimeri Picaud, *Guide du pèlerin de Saint Jacques (c. 1130–40)*; ed. and trans. J. Vielliard (Mâcon: Protat frères, 1950), cited in Pinto-Mathieu, *Marie-Madeleine*, 111. Shaver-Crandell and Gerson, *The Pilgrim's Guide,* effectively refute the attribution of the guide to Aimeri Picaud. St-Gilles, Conques, and Vézelay are each on separate pilgrim routes in France leading to Santiago (the opening lines of the guide list the four pilgrim routes to Santiago: *Pilgrim's Guide*, 65; the shrine to Mary Magdalene at Vézelay is described, 78–79).

Philip Augustus and Richard Lionheart, after Richard formally took his crusader's vow at the abbey.[7]

During Vézelay's ascendancy the legend acquired important additions. Mary Magdalen's apostolic mission in Provence (used to explain her presence in the south of France) was elaborated at this time, together with a miracle story concerning the prince of Marseille, and an account of the Magdalen's holy death after a lengthy period of asceticism at an undisclosed site near Aix-en-Provence. Hagiographers at Vézelay also created the story of her relics' translation from Provence to their abbey in central France.

In the thirteenth century, however, Vézelay's influence waned, and in an ironic twist, in December 1279 the monks at Saint-Maximin in Provence "discovered" the previously overlooked tomb of Mary Magdalene at their monastery, replete with a textual attestation of authenticity. A refinement of the legend propagated by Vézelay in the mid-twelfth century had introduced the identification of the grotto of Sainte-Baume in Provence as the place where the Magdalen died. This new localization allowed the subsequent claim by the monks of Saint-Maximin to be seen as legitimate by the papacy,[8] and the newly discovered tomb in Provence replaced Vézelay as the centre of pilgrimage during the fourteenth century.

The medieval conflation of three biblical persons in the figure of Mary Magdalene was vigorously disputed and deconstructed by the Renaissance humanist Lefèvre d'Étaples in 1517, and the authenticity of the Provençal apostolate of the Magdalen continued to be debated among French theologians and historians from the sixteenth through the twentieth centuries, before it was conclusively shown to be a medieval creation.[9]

From Medieval Latin to Versions in French Prose and Verse

The active development of the Mary Magdalene legend during the medieval period was both created by, and reflected in, the numerous Latin texts written to support and explain the various claims made with respect to the possession of the relics of the saint, and their efficacy. The *Bibliotheca Hagiographica Latina*, now the standard analytical bibliographic classification of medieval Latin hagiography, lists some seventy-five Latin texts devoted to the life and miracles of the Magdalen, including sermons, lives, and accounts of miracles.[10]

---

[7] Pinto-Mathieu, *Marie-Madeleine*, x; Legge, *ANL*, 266.
[8] Saxer, *Le Culte*, 241.
[9] Saxer, *Le Culte*, 4–8; Pinto-Mathieu, *Marie-Madeleine*, v, xiv.
[10] See *BHL*, nos. 5439–5513 (804–11). The *BHL* is published by the Bollandist order (re-established in Brussels in the early 19th century), which has continued the historical

There was a corresponding proliferation of French texts derived from the Latin sources. All the known medieval French adaptations have recently become readily available, with the publication of an omnibus critical edition of twenty-eight separate versions, extant in roughly one hundred manuscripts.[11] The editors state that it is difficult to establish a firm relative chronology for the composition of the different texts, but there was a continuous development of medieval French versions from the late twelfth or early thirteenth century until the end of the Middle Ages.[12] Nine medieval French versions predate the enormously popular medieval Latin legendary, the *Legenda aurea* of Jacopo de Voragine (dated to ca. 1267), which in turn is the direct source of fourteen French versions.[13]

Most medieval French versions are in prose (twenty-three of twenty-eight items in the omnibus edition), and are mainly transmitted in legendaries similar to the *Legenda aurea* (more or less lengthy compilations, often organized by the liturgical year or by type of saint). The earliest French prose life of the Magdalen, however, datable to the early thirteenth century, circulated as an independent text.[14] Manuscript Nantes, Musée Dobré 5, in which this prose life is found, is well known as having some of the earliest examples of French prose.[15] This prose life is also generally considered to be the earliest known French life of the Magdalen, although whether it preceded the verse versions, discussed below, remains debatable.[16]

In general, throughout the medieval period, the authors of the prose lives of Mary Magdalene pick and choose from among the same narrative segments: these include the life of the Magdalen before the events related in the Gospels, the miracle of Marseille, the eremitical retreat, the translation of her relics,

---

and philological work of the seventeenth-century Bollandists, Jesuit scholars who published the monumental *Acta Sanctorum*, critical editions of all known Latin saints' lives. For a brief history of the Bollandists, see their website: http://www.kbr.be/~socboll/index.html.

[11] See *Vies médiévales de Marie-Madeleine*, ed. Olivier Collet and Sylviane Messerli, Textes vernaculaires du Moyen Âge 3 (Turnhout: Brepols, 2008). This is the first critical edition for the majority of these texts.

[12] Collet and Messerli, *Vies médiévales*, 16.

[13] See also *DLF*, 1359 (*s.v. Sainte Marie-Madelaine*) for a brief discussion of the medieval French texts. Vernacular texts in Occitan are also known; see Paul Meyer, "Légendes pieuses en provençal," in *Histoire littéraire de la France*, vol. 32 (Paris: Imprimerie Nationale, 1898; repr. Nendeln Kraus: 1972), 90–100.

[14] See Collet and Messerli, *Vies médiévales*, item 1 (49–88); this now supersedes the first edition, C. Corcoran et al., "De la Madeleine, Vie anonyme," *Zeitschrift für Romanische Philologie* 98 (1982): 20–42.

[15] See Collet and Messerli, *Vies médiévales*, 49, 51. MS Nantes, Musée Dobré, 5 was probably written in the first decades of the thirteenth century.

[16] The verse life by Guillaume le Clerc de Normandie is datable to 1210–1240, making it contemporary with the first prose life.

IV. Saint Mary Magdalene

and posthumous miracles. The only constant, in all the vernacular versions, both prose and verse, is the inclusion of the miracle of Marseille segment, which Collet and Messerli call the heart of the legend, although they note that its treatment varies enormously within the vernacular tradition.[17]

One of the most striking examples of this variation in treatment is found in the earliest French verse life, discussed in more detail below. As with the production of prose versions, French verse reworkings of the Magdalen's legend continue in the medieval period from the early thirteenth to the mid-fourteenth centuries, but in contrast to the plethora of French prose lives, there are only five known medieval French verse lives of Mary Magdalene (of which two are extant only in fragments).[18] The *Romanz* by Guillaume le Clerc de Normandie is the earliest known verse life, datable, as noted above, to the period 1210–1240.[19] It was followed in the first third of the fourteenth century by the short verse life written by Nicholas Bozon,[20] and then, probably in the early or mid-fourteenth century, by an anonymous verse life, extant in two Continental manuscripts.[21] Four of the verse lives were written in England, and it is to the earliest of these lives, translated below, that we now turn.

---

[17] Collet and Messerli, *Vies médiévales*, 19.

[18] For the fragments see Collet and Messerli, *Vies médiévales*, items 27 and 28 (641–45, 647–50), and Dean, §§577, 578. The fragments may possibly be the earliest French verse lives of the Magdalen, but there is insufficient evidence to judge. Both fragments are in unusual verse forms that are also used by well-known lives of Thomas Becket, dated 1171–74 and 1184. Dean dates the manuscript of item 28 as late twelfth / early thirteenth century.

[19] Collet and Messerli, *Vies médiévales*, item 5 (131–61). See also Dean §579. Among the earlier editions, see Franz Karl Weiss, "Der 'Romanz de sainte Marie Magdaleine' von Guillaume le Clerc de Normandie und sein Quellenkreis," diss., Universität Münster, 1968, an edition of both manuscripts, with Latin source text and parallel text of a French prose version. For an electronic edition see the Campsey Project, www.margot.uwaterloo.ca.

[20] Collet and Messerli, *Vies médiévales*, item 13 (357–73). See also Dean, §582, and M. Amelia Klenke, ed. and trans., *Three Saints' Lives by Nicholas Bozon*, Franciscan Institute Publications, History Series 1 (St. Bonaventure, NY: The Franciscan Institute, 1947), 1–25.

[21] Collet and Messerli, *Vies médiévales*, item 8 (237–94); they state this may be a copy of an Anglo-Norman work (15, 244).

Le Romanz de sainte Marie Magdalene

Manuscripts

The *Romanz de sainte Marie Magdalene* by Guillaume le Clerc de Normandie is extant in two manuscripts:

MS Paris, BnF, fr. 19525, fols. 67ra–72va;[22]

MS London, British Library, Additional 70513, fols. 50va–55va.[23]

Author

Guillaume, born in Normandy, was a married clerk who probably lived most of his life in England. He supported his family by writing religious didactic works, and those of his patrons who are named are from the diocese of Coventry and Lichfield.[24] His *Bestiaire divin* (1210/11), written for Radulphus (possibly Ralph of Maidstone, treasurer of Lichfield by 1215, and bishop of Hereford in 1234), survives in some twenty manuscript copies. *Le Besant de Dieu*, his second major work, for which no patron is mentioned, is datable to 1226–27 from historical allusions. His *Vie de Tobie* was written for William, prior of Kenilworth in Arden (1214–27), in the diocese of Coventry and Lichfield, and *Les treis moz* (1227–38) was written for Alexander Stavensby, bishop of Lichfield and Coventry (1224–38). No date more specific than the first third of the thirteenth century can be given for his *Joies Nostre Dame* and the *Romanz de sainte Marie Madeleine*.

---

[22] The life is in the second part of MS Paris, BnF, fr. 19525, which was from the workshop of William de Brailles, Oxford, and is dated c. 1230–50 on art-historical grounds; see Nigel Morgan, *Early Gothic Manuscripts*, 2 vols. (London: Harvey Miller, 1982), 1:36, n. 35, and François Avril and Patricia Stirnemann, *Manuscrits enluminés d'origine insulaire, VIIe–XXe siècles* (Paris: Bibliothèque nationale, 1987), 67–68.

[23] The Campsey manuscript; for details see Russell, "The Campsey Collection."

[24] See *ANL*, 207–8, 224–25, 228, 266–67, and Tony Hunt, "William the Clerk (*fl. c.* 1200–*c.* 1240)," *ODNB*, www.oxforddnb.com/view/article/29475 (see sub-entry on William the Clerk [Guillaume le Clerc] from Normandy [*fl.* 1210/11–1227x38], not the same poet as William the Clerk [*fl. c.* 1200–*c.* 1240], author of the *Roman de Fergus*). See also Pierre Ruelle, ed., *Le Besant de Dieu* de Guillaume le clerc de Normandie (Brussels: Université de Bruxelles, 1973), 7–18, and "Guillaume le Clerc de Normandie," in *DLF*, 628.

Guillaume's Treatment of the Latin Source

Guillaume, an immigrant to England from Normandy, writes in octosyllabic couplets, which he uses with ease. Guillaume creates dramatically effective scenes in the vernacular through his use of concrete and varied vocabulary, and through his sense of realistic dialogue, coupled with rhetorical asides directed at his audience that heighten the pathos. The syntax of his verse is supple, and both rhyme and rhythm are used for rhetorical effect. The passage "Storm at Sea and Difficult Birth" (see Appendix 4 below) is an example of his vernacular style. Moreover, Guillaume's deployment of the vernacular's stylistic resources subserve a particular vision and adaptation of the Latin source's potential.

The major narrative action of Guillaume's source is shared with the backstory of Shakespeare's *Pericles*: storm and death at sea during childbirth, forced abandonment of the seemingly dead mother and child, and later reunion of husband, wife, and child. This story was itself adapted from an episode in the late classical popular Latin romance *Apollonius of Tyre*, dating from the fifth and sixth centuries.[25] This Latin romance was retold and reworked from the early Middle Ages through to the seventeenth century, Shakespeare's being now the best-known version. In the thirteenth century this romance plot formed the most popular version of Mary Magdalene's legend and often supplanted the longer text as the life of the saint.[26]

The immediate source of Guillaume's *Romanz* is the Latin text known from its incipit as *Postquam Dominus*.[27] Guillaume's *Romanz* expands slightly on the immediate Latin source text, itself a skilful remodeling of the episode from *Apollonius of Tyre* to make it a polished narrative perfectly adapted to its use as a

---

[25] Chapters 24–26 (of 51) recount the episode of the voyage and seeming death during childbirth; see Elizabeth Archibald, *Apollonius of Tyre: Medieval and Renaissance Themes and Variations: Including the Text of the* Historia Apollonius Regis Tyri *with an English Translation* (Cambridge: D.S. Brewer, 1991), 137–41. For the most recent study of the Latin text see G. A. A. Kortekaas, *The Story of Apollonius, King of Tyre: A Study of its Greek Origin and an Edition of the Two Oldest Latin Recensions* (Leiden and Boston: Brill, 2004). Collet and Messerli reject the influence of *Apollonius of Tyre* on Guillaume, and argue that motifs from folklore and biblical reminiscences are the basis for the story (*Vies médiévales*, 19–20).

[26] See Pinto-Mathieu, *Marie-Madeleine*, 89–148 for a detailed discussion of the development of the legend from the eleventh through thirteenth centuries in France. The popularity of the detailed version of the miracle of Marseille is shown by the fact that the *Legenda aurea* version of the legend of Mary Magdalene includes the complete Latin text relating this incident, but only a shortened version of the penitential life.

[27] BHL 5457, the seventh *vita* in the listing for Mary Magdalene. For the Latin text, from Paris BnF Latin 803, a 15th-c. manuscript, see *Catalogus Codicum Hagiographicorum Latinorum [. . .] in Bibliotheca Nationali Parisiensi* (Brussels: Société des Bollandistes, 1893), 3:525–39.

Christian saint's legend.[28] But the choice of not altering source material is if anything the rarer procedure in medieval narrative, and, as we argue below, Guillaume's acceptance of the Latin narrative's outlines is itself very significant in context.

Guillaume's treatment of the legend thus uses a Latin source which focuses on the interrelations of the saint and the prince of Marseille and his wife. As we have seen, narratives of Mary Magdalene's apostolic mission were well established: despite or perhaps because of this, Guillaume makes only brief allusion to the conversion of Gaul to Christianity on the return of the prince and his family to Marseille. Guillaume does not include the traditional extension whereby the legend embraced Mary's later eremitical life in Provence and the translation of her relics from Provence to Vézelay. This is a striking omission since the translation narrative was central to Vézelay's claims as a centre for pilgrimage. This omission is an artistic choice by Guillaume, who prefers to keep the central focus of his *Romanz* on the detailed development of the episode in which Mary and the prince and his wife meet and interact, followed by the storm at sea, the birth, the pilgrimage to Jerusalem, and the reunion of the family on the deserted island.

Remaining in *medias res*

The Latin source, as noted above, is usually viewed as one episode in the legend of Mary Magdalene. Although the text does present a completely developed narrative, preceded by a brief introduction of Mary's apostolic mission in Gaul and ending with the mass conversion of Gaul, it is not a typical saint's life. There is no discussion of the early life, nor of the saint's death (and no martyrdom), and no "second life" of miracle-working after the death of the saint. Guillaume's reworking of his Latin source retains this sense of the narrative being in some sense *in medias res* since he also does not present either the earlier or later life of Mary Magdalene or that of the prince of Marseille and his family. Although some Latin versions of the legend present the initial voyage of Mary Magdalene and her companions as an act of persecution on the part of the Jews (in which Mary and company are cast adrift in a boat to die), the source version used by Guillaume makes the trip to Marseille part of the general dispersal of the apostles on their missions across the world (vv. 7–8), and Guillaume does not develop the persecutory motif as a framework for his narrative. Nor does he attempt to place his vernacular version in a wider hagiographical context, and in fact the *Romanz* remains remarkably free from a vernacular authorial framing presence, most obvious in the lack of a prologue or any mention of the genesis of the work or its possible audience. The epilogue, in which Guillaume names himself, is also very brief in its invocation of divine intercession on behalf of narrator and audience.

---

[28] Pinto-Mathieu, *Marie-Madeleine*, 142, 145, 147, argues that every episode is explained or modified to demonstrate the workings of Providence.

Guillaume's lack of prologue is a marked contrast with Simon de Walsingham, who, as discussed above, develops his prologue at length to serve a number of rhetorical and literary aims: explaining the genesis of his text, giving details of his monastic community and patron, his own personal connection with the saint, as well as the relevance of his work to his audience. It also contrasts with Simund de Freine's prologue in the *Vie de saint Georges*, which, although less ambitious than that of Simon de Walsingham, stands out for its technical virtuosity in spelling out the name of the writer in acrostic form, while invoking the moral merit of his work for his audience, and placing George's defence of his religion in the context of the crusaders' conflict with Islam. And although the *Vie de s. Gilles*, as noted above, has only a minimal prologue, unlike the *Romanz*, the author of the *Vie* does briefly introduce the subject about to be treated before launching into the narrative.

In many ways Guillaume's *Romanz* presents a trajectory directly opposite to that found in the works of Simon de Walsingham and Simund de Freine. The role of the pagan tyrant in this tale is played by the prince of Marseille who is converted to Christianity, and benefits from a miraculous intervention which makes his marriage fecund and perpetuates his dynastic power. The saint in question is not a virgin martyr, but a repentant sinner, associated with family life, who has a mission to preach to the pagans. For a large part of the narrative Mary Magdalene remains in the background while the adventures of the prince and his wife are brought into the foreground. There is no attempt to make Christians recant their belief by the use of torture, but rather active proselytizing, and the intervention of fate in the form of a storm at sea and an accident of childbirth which tests the faith of the new convert. The narrative reaffirms the resumption of secular dynastic family life on earth, not the birth of a saint into eternal life. It is, in fact, the vicissitudes of life on earth and the confirmation by the living of the truth of the Christian mysteries that Guillaume develops in his reworking of the Latin text of this hagiographical romance.

Family Values

There are subtle references to a sense of family belonging in the opening lines of the *Romanz*. Guillaume, following the Latin legend, presents Mary Magdalene as the leader of a band of believers, similar to a medieval episcopal or seigneurial household, a group which in Latin was routinely referred to as the *familia* of the lord in question. Those who travel with Mary Magdalene (vv. 9–27) include her sister and brother, Martha and Lazarus. Awareness of the importance of family is evident in the depiction of another member of the group, Marcilla. Her biblical blessing of the physical maternity (both womb and suckling breasts) of Mary, mother of Jesus, is explicitly noted (vv. 17–20; only the beginning words are given in the Latin source).[29] The man blind from birth cured by Jesus (John 9:1–38), and Maximinus, one of the "seventy," along with "others who believed in our Lord" (vv. 25–26), complete the *familia* of this apostle to the Apostles. Mary and her followers are also perceived as a group by the prince's wife; when she sends food secretly to the proselytizers, it is for Mary "and (*lit.*) her company" (*A lui e a sa compaignie,* v. 77). The prince also refers to them as a collective group ("these people," *cele gent,* v. 143), and in his epilogue the narrator and author, Guillaume, refers to the conversion of the region by Mary Magdalene and "her (*lit.*) household" (*maisnee,* v. 718).

The pagan protagonists are also introduced by reference to their family relationships. Initially we see the standard hagiographic theme of the evil ruler who is feared by his wife (her fear causes her to send her aid secretly to Mary Magdalene, v. 90). Although castigated by Mary Magdalene as a wicked tyrant and a gluttonous drunkard (vv. 99–109), the prince is made more sympathetic by his frustration at remaining childless (vv. 60–69): he has come to the temple to pray to his gods that his wife may conceive; his lack of a son or daughter has left him "sad and dejected, full of doubts and sorrow" (*forment marris / E mult tristes e mult confus,* vv. 68–69).

What begins as a standard conflict between Christian witness and pagan ruler is suddenly reversed, however, when the prince and his wife discuss the apparition of Mary. They begin the first of what will be a series of realistic companionable conjugal discussions, of the type: "Did you see what I just saw?" "Yes! What do you think we should do?" (vv. 115–20). Guillaume adds details not in the Latin source: his wife confesses she hasn't told her husband of the two previous visions because she was afraid of his anger (v. 121–27), and after proposing that they ask Mary for help in their attempt to have offspring, she adds, "If the lady were to make it possible that, through her God, we could have a son or daughter to be our heir, then I would gladly support her preaching" (vv. 132–36). The prince's equally realistic response is that of a compliant husband, not of a truculent ruler: "Wife, you have spoken well!" (v. 137). Rather than rebelling against the advice of the Magdalene, they immediately obey her and set their plan in action: the conflict between pagan and Christian saint has disappeared from the narrative.

Guillaume's knowledge of married life can also be seen in the surprisingly modern discussion of conjugal responsibilities presented by the prince's wife (vv. 171–80) in response to his proposal to set off to Jerusalem to visit Christ's empty tomb. Guillaume expands his Latin source's litany of actions which should be shared as a couple, borrowing from biblical parallels to do so.[30] In the husband's overly protective response, the vernacular version reduces details in the Latin source on the wife's role as guardian of their possessions while her husband is

---

[29] See the note to the translation of vv. 1–29, below.
[30] See note to vv. 173–80.

away (v. 182), and increases both the husband's wish that she be pampered ("Instead, in your painted chamber I will have you waited upon, and bathed, for you must not do any physical labour," vv. 186–88), and the wife's impassioned rebuttal ("I will never see the child born if I remain behind without you for the sake of a bath or any other physical comfort!" vv. 190–92).

The scene of family reunion (vv. 557–668) in the Latin source is also expanded by Guillaume, who adds the prince's detailed expression of thanks for the saintly nourishing of his son (vv. 609–12). His happiness upon finding his son alive would be made complete, he remarks, if his wife also were given back to him: "Then there would be no man on earth richer than I would be, and I would serve you always, if we could go back to Marseille together and see you again" (vv. 622–26). The dialogue between the reawakened wife and her husband is also touchingly realistic:

> When the good man heard her speak, he called out to her, "My dear, are you alive?"
> "'Yes!" she replied, "indeed I am! I am alive and well, thanks be to God and Mary Magdalene . . ." (vv. 633–38).

These scenes of family interaction are usually found in the Latin source, but Guillaume is always careful to express them in lively and realistic vernacular language, in both direct speech and narrative description.

Pilgrimage

The *Romanz* also presents the prince of Marseille as an early pilgrim, the first to wear the cross as a pilgrim's badge ("And Mary Magdalene graciously gave him the first cross ever worn by a pilgrim. In short, she put a cross on his shoulder as a sign, and she commended him to God and blessed him with the sign of the Cross. She marked him with the Cross so that the devil could never tempt him, nor make him forsake his pilgrimage": *E la curteise Magdaleine / Li dona la croiz premeraine, / Ke unkes portast pelerin. / Sur s'espaule, ceo est la fin, / Lui mist une croiz a enseigne; / A Deu le comande, sil seigne. / La dame pur ceo le croiza, / Ke li malfé nel peust ja / Tempter ne faire repentir / De sun veage parfurnir,* vv. 205–14). This scene in the Latin text also includes Mary's admonition that Saint Peter, the leader of the apostles, will be able to confirm in person in Jerusalem what she has preached in Marseille; in the vernacular version this detail is reserved for the prince's arrival at his destination.

Pilgrimage to Jerusalem was begun as early as the second century, and at the time that Guillaume was composing his *Romanz* pilgrims' guides to Jerusalem (and the two other major sites, Rome and Compostela) were well known.[31] The *Romanz*, following the Latin text, incorporates some of the usefulness of such guides, noting, for example, the very practical considerations that must be taken into account by pilgrims about to set off to a distant land (no doubt in order to make more credible the view that the prince of Marseille was one of the earliest pilgrims to travel to Jerusalem).

First there are monetary considerations. One of the reasons the prince wants his wife to remain in Marseille is that he expects her to protect their property in his absence (the vernacular reduces this concern, extensively expressed in Latin, to one line: *Ceo que nus avum guarderez* "You will keep safe what we have," v. 182).[32] When his wife refuses to remain in Marseille, the prince formally entrusts his property and revenues to Mary Magdalene's keeping (vv. 191–201). He next gathers sufficient gold and silver to pay for the voyage (vv. 202–4, 479) and to cover emergency expenses. As we see later, money (and the helmsman's desire for profit, vv. 364–72) is needed to procure the ship's delay and to pay for the trip in the tender to the island so the prince can bury his wife and leave his child in Mary Magdalene's care, rather than allowing them to be thrown into the sea. Similarly, on the return trip from Syria to Marseille, the prince makes an agreement on the fare (*sun covenant*, v. 545), and again bribes the captain to delay the ship and take him to the island where he had left his wife and child (vv. 561–66). When he and his wife come back aboard ship the prince "paid his wife's passage, which he considered money well spent" (*puis ad paié sa veiture / K'il teneit a bien empleié*, vv. 678–79).

The prince's status as the first pilgrim to wear the cross as a badge is confirmed by St. Peter, who greets him as he disembarks from the ship, and who questions him on his place of origin and his motivation. St. Peter also declares that Mary Magdalene has been a wise advisor, and promises to personally instruct the prince in Christian doctrine, and to lead him to the pilgrimage sites. In a foreshadowing of what is to come, the saint also remarks that the prince's sorrow for his wife will be turned to joy when Jesus chooses.

The *Romanz* also expands the enumeration of pilgrimage sites in and around Jerusalem beyond the Latin text's vague reference ("ad alia plura loca duxit eum") to include the Sepulchre, Solomon's temple, Bethlehem, the mount of Calvary, and the river Jordan. "The whole country" is visited during a period of two years (vv. 519–31).

---

[31] On pilgrimage to Jerusalem see John Wilkinson (with Joyce Hill and W. F. Ryan), *Jerusalem Pilgrimage 1099–1185*, Hakluyt Society 2nd ser. 167 (London: Hakluyt Society, 1988); see also Nicole Chareyron, *Pèlerins de Jerusalem au Moyen âge* (Paris: Imago, 2000), [English translation] *Pilgrims to Jerusalem in the Middle Ages*, trans. W. Donald Wilson (New York: Columbia University Press, 2005). On pilgrimage to Compostela see Shaver-Crandell and Gerson, *Pilgrim's Guide*.

[32] See also the note to v. 182, below.

Later in the narrative the prince's wife tells him that Mary Magdalene has carried her in spirit beside him throughout his two-year pilgrimage. This act by Mary Magdalene not only allows the mother to benefit from the planned pilgrimage, it also affirms the wife's initial description of her role in marriage, to be a partner with her husband in all things and at all times. The prince confirms their joint conjugal partnership when he expresses the wish that they return together to Marseille, so that they and all their people may honour and serve God and Mary Magdalene (vv. 653–61). The prince of Marseille has been confirmed in his faith by St. Peter, the leader of the apostles, while his wife has been confirmed in the same faith by seeing and hearing all that her husband has seen, through the agency of Mary Magdalene, the "apostle to the Apostles." Although the pilgrimage ostensibly serves to confirm the protagonists' Christian faith, the narrative also asserts that in marriage both wife and husband share equally their rights and duties in all spheres of human activity.

If the abbot of Kenilworth had commissioned Guillaume's life of the Magdalen with a view to intensifying relations between his monastery and lay patrons, he chose well: this vividly written text must have spoken eloquently to any lay audiences who heard it read aloud.

5. Note on Translations, Manuscripts, and Editions

The French verse texts have been translated into prose, aiming to provide an accurate and idiomatic English rendering, while remaining attentive to tonal and stylistic effects in the original French. When necessary for clarity, proper names are inserted without comment in the translation to replace subject pronouns whose antecedents are ambiguous in the French text.

The names of the writers themselves also raise the question of translation, and the relationship between French and English in medieval Britain: should they be called Simon of Freen, Simon of Walsingham, William of Barnwell, and William the Clerk of Normandy? Or should their names be left in French, and if so, with medieval or modern spelling? The acrostic signature of the poet Simund de Freine (given in two separate poems) provides evidence of Simund's own preferred spelling of his name, which has been kept here. For the other names, however, we use the normalized modern spelling. Simon de Walsingham's name is written only once in the text (as *Symon*); Guillaume de Berneville's name is written twice only, as *Gwillame(s) de Bernevile*. Guillaume Le Clerc's name is given only as *Williame* (in abbreviated form) in both manuscripts of the Magdalene text, but the more common forms *Guillame*, or *Guillem*, appear numerous times in manuscripts of his other works."[1]

The poems by Guillaume de Berneville, Simund de Freine, and Simon de Walsingham that are translated below are each extant in only one manuscript, while the poem by Guillaume Le Clerc de Normandie is extant in two manuscripts.

The *Life of Saint Giles* is based on the critical edition of the *Vie de s. Gilles* by Françoise Laurent (2003), with reference to the edition of Gaston Paris and Alphonse Bos (1881). The *Passion of Saint George* is based on Matzke's highly interventionist edition (1909) of the *Vie de s. Georges*, supplemented by reference to the manuscript. Passages where the translation follows the manuscript reading, and not the edited text, are discussed in the Notes.

The *Life of Saint Faith* and the *Romance of Mary Magdalene* are based on the electronic texts available on the website of the Electronic Campsey Project

---

[1] Cf. *Le Besant de Dieu*, ed. P. Ruelle (Brussels: Editions de l'Université de Bruxelles, 1973), 8.

(http://margot.uwaterloo.ca). Significant differences between the electronic text and Baker's edition of *S. Foy* are discussed in the Notes. The *Romance of Mary Magdalene* uses P (Ms. Paris, BNF, f. fr. 19525) as the base manuscript, but incorporates lines from W (Ms. London, BL, Additional 70513) that are not found in P. Significant differences in P and W are discussed in the Notes to the translation. Reference is also made to the edition by Franz-Karl Weiss (1968), which also uses P as base manuscript, and incorporates all lines from W not found in P. The edition of the *Marie Madeleine* by Collet and Messerli was published after the completion of our translation.

Suggested Further Reading

Primary Sources

1. Editions of French Texts

i. Guillaume de Berneville

Guillaume de Berneville. *La Vie de saint Gilles: Poème du XIIe siècle, publié d'après le manuscrit unique de Florence*. Ed. Gaston Paris and Alphonse Bos. Paris: SATF, 1881; repr. New York and London: Johnson Reprint, 1966.

———. *La Vie de saint Gilles: Texte du XIIe siècle, publié d'après le manuscrit de la Bibliothèque Laurentienne de Florence*. Ed. and trans. Françoise Laurent. Champion Classiques, série Moyen Âge, editions bilingues 6. Paris: Champion, 2003.

———. "Un Fragment de la Vie de saint Gilles en vers français." Ed. Louis Brandin. *Romania* 33 (1904): 94–98.

ii. Simund de Freine

Simund de Freine. "Vie de Saint Georges." In *Les Oeuvres de Simund de Freine*, ed. John E. Matzke, 61–117. Paris: SATF, 1909; repr. New York: Johnson Reprint, 1968.

———. "Roman de Philosophie." In *Les Oeuvres de Simund de Freine*, ed. Matzke, 1–60.

iii. Simon de Walsingham

Simon de Walsingham. "*Vie Anglo-Normande de Sainte Foy* par Simon de Walsingham." Ed. A.T. Baker. *Romania* 66 (1940–1941): 49–84.

———. Electronic Campsey Project (electronic edition): http://margot.uwaterloo.ca/campsey/CmpBrowserFrame_e.html.

iv. Guillaume le Clerc de Normandie

Guillaume le Clerc de Normandie. "5. Vie de Marie-Madeleine." In *Vies médiévales de Marie-Madeleine*, ed. Olivier Collet and Sylviane Messerli, 131–61. Textes vernaculaires du Moyen Âge 3. Turnhout: Brepols, 2008.

———. "Guillaume, le clerc de Normandie, insbesondere seine Magdalenenlegende." Ed. Adolf Schmidt. *Romanische Studien* 4 (1879–80): 493–542, at 523–36.

———. "La Vie de Madeleine: Gedicht des Guillaume le Clerc, nach der Pariser Hs." Ed. Robert Reinsch. *Archiv für das Studium der Neueren Sprachen und Literaturen* 64 (1880): 85–94.

———. "Der 'Romanz de sainte Marie Magdaleine' von Guillaume le Clerc de Normandie und sein Quellenkreis." Ed. Franz-Karl Weiss. Diss. Westfälischen Wilhelms-Universität Münster, 1968.

———. Electronic Campsey Project (electronic edition): http://margot.uwaterloo.ca/campsey/CmpBrowserFrame_e.html.

2. Latin Sources of the French Lives

i. St. Giles

"Vita sancti Aegidii." In *La Vie de saint Gilles: Texte du XIIe siècle, publié d'après le manuscrit de la Bibliothèque Laurentienne de Florence*, ed. Laurent, 244–71.

———. In E. C. Jones, *Saint Gilles: Essai d'histoire littéraire*, 95–111. Paris: Champion, 1914.

———. AASS. Sept. I, 299–303.

———. In E. M. Treharne, *The Old English Life of St Nicholas with the Old English Life of St Giles*, 198–206. Leeds Texts and Monographs, New Series 15. Leeds: School of English, 1997.

ii. St. George

"Passio Sancti Georgii." Ed. Wilhelm Arndt. *Berichte über die Verhandlungen der königlich sächsischen Gesellschaft der Wissenschaften zu Leipzig, philologisch-historische Classe*, 26 (1874): 43–70 [codex Gallicanus].

———. Ed. F. Zarncke. "Eine zweite Redaction der Georgslegende aus dem 9. Jahrhunderte." *Berichte über die Verhandlungen der königlich sächsischen Gesellschaft der Wissenschaften zu Leipzig, philologisch-historische Classe*, 27 (1875): 257–77 [codex Sangallensis].

iii. St. Faith

Liber miraculorum sancte Fidis: Edizione critica e commento. Ed. Luca Robertini. Spoleto: Centro italiano di studi sull'alto medioevo, 1994.

Passio sanctorum Fidis et Caprasii. AASS. Oct. 6, III, 288–89 (Fides only); Oct. 20, VIII, 823–25 (Fides and Caprasius).

———. In *La Chanson de sainte Foy*, ed. P. Alfaric and E. Hoepffner, 2:179–97. 2 vols. Paris: Belles Lettres; Oxford: Oxford University Press, 1926. [both prose and metrical versions of the *Passio*].

"*Passio*: The Passion of Sainte Foy"; "*Translatio*: The Translation of Sainte Foy, Virgin and Martyr, to the Conques Monastery." In Pamela Sheingorn, *The Book of Sainte Foy*, 33–38, 263–74. Philadelphia: University of Pennsylvania Press, 1995.

iv. St. Mary Magdalene

"Vita s. Mariae Magdalenae" (*BHL* 5457: Postquam Dominus noster). In *Catalogus Codicum Hagiographicorum Latinorum [. . .] in Bibliotheca Nationali Parisiensi*, 3:525–30. Subsidia hagiographica 2. 3 vols. Brussels: Société des Bollandistes, 1889–93.

———. In "Der 'Romanz de sainte Marie Magdaleine' von Guillaume le Clerc de Normandie und sein Quellenkreis," ed. Weiss, 83–146.

Secondary Sources

3. Studies of Individual Saints' Lives

i. La Vie de saint Gilles

Frankis, John. "Languages and Cultures in Contact: Vernacular Lives of St Giles and Anglo-Norman Annotations in an Anglo-Saxon Manuscript." *Leeds Studies in English*, n. s. 38 (2007): 101–33.

Jones, E[thel] C. *Saint Gilles: Essai d'histoire littéraire*. Paris: Champion, 1914.

Labie-Leurquin, A.-F. "Guillaume de Berneville ou de Barneville." In *DLF*, 608–9.

Laurent, Françoise. "Une oeuvre exemplaire: la *Vie de saint Gilles*." Part 5 in *Plaire et édifier: Les récits hagiographiques composés en Angleterre aux XIIe et XIIIe siècles*, 475–575. Paris: Champion, 1998.

Levi, Ezio. "Troveri ed Abbazie." *Archivio storico italiano* 83 (1925): 45–81.

Grisward, Joel. "A propos du thème descriptif de la tempête chez Wace et chez Thomas d'Angleterre." In *Mélanges de langue et de littérature du Moyen Âge et de la Renaissance offerts à Jean Frappier, professeur à la Sorbonne, par ses collègues, ses élèves et ses amis*, 1: 375–89. 2 vols. Publications romanes et françaises 112. Geneva: Droz, 1970.

Rembry, Ernest. *Saint Gilles, sa vie, ses reliques, son culte en Belgique et dans le nord de la France: Essai d'hagiographie*. 2 vols. Bruges: Gaillard, 1881.

Treharne, E. M. *The Old English Life of St Nicholas with the Old English Life of St Giles*. Leeds Texts and Monographs, New Series 15. Leeds: University of Leeds, 1997.

ii. La Vie de saint Georges

Barrow, Julia. "William de Vere, a Twelfth-Century Bishop and Literary Patron." *Viator* 18 (1987): 175–89.

Chabaneau, C., ed. "Vie de saint Georges." *Revue des langues romanes* 29 (1886): 246–54; 31 (1887): 139–55.

Guilcher, Yvette, ed. *Deux versions de* la Vie de saint Georges. CFMA 138. Paris: Champion, 2001.

Guilcher-Pellat, Yvette. "La Légende de Saint Georges: du *Mégalomartyr* au *Tropaïophoros*." In *Miscellanea Mediaevalia: Mélanges offerts à Philippe Ménard*, ed. J. Claude Faucon, Alain Labbé, and Danielle Quéruel, 1: 601–11. 2 vols. Paris: Champion, 1998.

Holdsworth, Christopher. "Baldwin (*c.* 1125–1190)." In *Oxford Dictionary of National Biography*, http://www.oxforddnb.com/view/article/1164.

Kaeuper, Richard W. "Chivalry and the 'Civilizing Process'." In *Violence in Medieval Society*, ed. idem, 21–35. Woodbridge: Boydell Press, 2000.

Kay, Sarah. "The Sublime Body of the Martyr: Violence in Early Romance Saints' Lives." In *Violence in Medieval Society*, ed. Kaeuper, 3–20.

Labie-Leurquin, A-F. "Simon de Freine." In *DLF*, 1392–93.

Matzke, John E. "Contributions to the History of the Legend of Saint George, with Special Reference to the Sources of the French, German and Anglo-Saxon Metrical Versions. " *PMLA* 17 (1902): 464–535; 18 (1903): 99–171.

———. "The Legend of Saint George: Its Development into a *Roman d'aventure*." *PMLA* 19 (1904): 449–78.

Petersen, Holger, ed. "Une Vie inédite de saint Georges en vers français du moyen âge." *Neuphilologische Mitteilungen* 27 (1926): 1–7.

Riches, Samantha. *St. George: Hero, Martyr and Myth*. Stroud: Sutton, 2000.

Robertson, Duncan. "The Passions of the Martyrs." In *The Medieval Saints' Lives: Spiritual Renewal and Old French Literature*, 29–75. Lexington, KY: French Forum, 1995.

Wogan-Browne, Jocelyn. "Freine, Simund de [Simon de Fraxino] (*d.* before 1228?), poet." In *Oxford Dictionary of National Biography*, www.oxforddnb.com/view/article/25570.

iii. La Vie de sainte Foy (Fey)

Arnold, Thomas, ed. *Jocelini de Brakelonda Cronica* [Chronicle of Jocelin de Brakelonde]. In *Memorials of St. Edmund's Abbey*, 1:209–336. Rolls Series 96. 3 vols. London: Public Record Office, 1890; repr. 1965.

———. *Gesta Sacristarum*. In *Memorials of St. Edmund's Abbey*, 2:289–96.

Ashley, Kathleen, and Pamela Sheingorn. *Writing Faith: Text, Sign and History in the Miracles of Sainte Foy*. Chicago: University of Chicago Press, 1999.

Baker, A. T., ed. "*Vie Anglo-Normande de Sainte Foy* par Simon de Walsingham." *Romania* 66 (1940–1941): 49–84.

Bouillet, Auguste, and L. Servières. *Sainte Foy, Vierge et Martyre*. Rodez, France: E. Carrère, 1900.

Campbell, Emma. "Sacrificial Spectacle and Interpassive Vision in the Anglo-Norman Life of Saint Faith." In *Troubled Vision: Gender, Sexuality, and Sight in Medieval Text and Image*, ed. eadem and Robert Mills, 97–115. New York: Palgrave, 2004.

Cazelles, Brigitte. "The Life of St. Faith." In *The Lady as Saint: A Collection of French Hagiographic Romances of the Thirteenth Century*, 182–203. Philadelphia: University of Pennsylvania Press, 1991.

Cox, J. C. "The Priory of St. Faith, Horsham." In *The Victoria History of the County of Norfolk*, ed. William Page, 2:346–49. 2 vols. Westminster: Constable, 1906; repr. London: University of London, Institute of Historical Research, 1975.

———. "The Religious Houses of Suffolk." In *The Victoria History of the County of Suffolk*, ed. William Page, 2:53–72. 2 vols. Westminster: Constable, 1911; repr. London: University of London, Institute of Historical Research, 1975.

Eve, Julian. *A History of Horsham St. Faith, Norfolk*. Norwich: J. R. Eve, 1992, rev. ed. 1994.

Greenway, Diana, and Jane Sayers, trans. Jocelin of Brakelond, *Chronicle of the Abbey of Bury St Edmunds*. Oxford: Oxford University Press, 1989.

Jane, L. C., ed., and trans. *The Chronicle of Jocelin of Brakelond, Monk of St. Edmundsbury: A Picture of Monastic and Social Life in the XIIth Century*. New York: Cooper Square Publishers, 1966.

Hoepffner, E., and Alfaric, P., eds. *La Chanson de sainte Foy: 1. Fac-similé du manuscrit et texte critique, Introduction et Commentaire philologiques; 2. Traduction française et Sources latines, Introduction et Commentaire historiques*. Paris: Belles Lettres, 1926.

Lafont, Robert, ed., and trans. *La Chanson de sainte Foi*. Geneva: Droz, 1998.

Park, David. "Wall Painting." In *Age of Chivalry: Art in Plantagenet England 1200–1400*, ed. Jonathan Alexander and Paul Binski, 125–30, 313. London: Royal Academy of Arts, Weidenfeld and Nicolson, 1987.

Purcell, Donovan. "The Priory of Horsham St. Faith and its Wall Paintings." *Norfolk Archaeology* 35 (1974): 469–73.

Rudd, Walter R. "The Priory of Horsham St. Faith." *Norfolk Archaeology* 23 (1929): 68–73.

Sheingorn, Pamela. *The Book of Sainte Foy*. Philadephia: University of Pennsylvania Press, 1995.

Sherlock, David. "Discoveries at Horsham St. Faith Priory, 1970–73." *Norfolk Archaeology* 36 (1976): 202–23.

Thomson, R. M. "The Library of Bury St Edmunds Abbey in the Eleventh and Twelfth Centuries." *Speculum* 47 (1972): 617–45.

———, ed. and trans. *The Chronicle of the Election of Hugh, Abbot of Bury St. Edmunds and later Bishop of Ely*. Oxford: Oxford University Press, 1974.

Wogan-Browne, Jocelyn. "Powers of Record, Powers of Example: Hagiography and Women's History." In *Gendering the Master Narrative: Women and Power in the Middle Ages*, ed. Mary C. Erler and Maryanne Kowaleski, 71–93. Ithaca and London: Cornell University Press, 2003.

———. "Virginity and the Gift." In eadem, *Saints' Lives and Women's Literary Culture c. 1150–1300: Virginity and its Authorizations*, 57–90. Oxford: Oxford University Press, 2001.

iv. Le Romanz de Marie Madeleine

Haskins, Susan. *Mary Magdalen: Myth and Metaphor.* London: Harper Collins, 1994.
Hunt, Tony. "William the Norman clerk (*fl.* 1210/11–1227x38)," sub-entry in "William the Clerk (*fl. c.* 1200–c. 1240)." In *Oxford Dictionary of National Biography*, www.oxforddnb.com/view/article/29475.
Karl, Ludwig. "Die Episode aus der Vie de Madeleine." *Zeitschrift für Romanische Philologie* 34 (1910): 362–67.
———. "Notice sur l'unique manuscrit français de la bibliothèque du duc de Portland à Welbeck." *Revue des langues romanes* 54 (1911): 210–29.
Labie-Leurquin, A.-F. "Guillaume le Clerc de Normandie." In *DLF*, 628.
Pinto-Mathieu, Elisabeth. *Marie-Madeleine dans la littérature du Moyen Âge.* Paris: Beauchesne, 1997.
Saxer, Victor. *Le Culte de Marie Madeleine en occident, des origines à la fin du moyen âge.* Cahiers d'Archéologie et d'Histoire 3. Paris: Clavreuil; Auxerre: Publications de la Société des Fouilles Archéologiques et des Monuments Historiques de l'Yonne, 1959.
Vies médiévales de Marie-Madeleine. Ed. Olivier Collet and Sylviane Messerli. Textes vernaculaires du Moyen Âge 3. Turnhout: Brepols, 2008.

4. Editions and Translations of Medieval Texts Cited

Benedeit. *Le Voyage de Saint Brendan.* Ed., trans. [French] and intro. Ian Short and Brian Merrilees. Paris: Champion, 2006.
———. *The Voyage of Saint Brendan: Representative Versions of the Legend in English Translation.* Trans. and intro. W. R. S. Barron and Glyn S. Burgess. Exeter: University of Exeter Press, 2002.
Beroul. *The Romance of Tristan.* Ed. A. Ewert. Vol 1. Oxford: Blackwell, 1939; repr. 1970, Vol. 2. Oxford: Blackwell, 1970.
———. *The Romance of Tristan.* Trans. and intro. Alan S. Federik. Harmondsworth: Penguin Classic, 1978.
Chanson de Roland. Ed., trans. [French], and intro. Ian Short. Lettres gothiques. Paris: Livre de Poche, 1990.
———. *The Song of Roland.* Trans. [English] and intro. Glyn S. Burgess. Harmondsworth: Penguin Classic, 1990.
Chrétien de Troyes. *Le Chevalier au lion (Yvain).* Ed. M. Roques. Paris: Champion, 1982.
———. *Erec et Enide.* Ed. M. Roques. Paris: Champion, 1973.

———. *Arthurian Romances*. Trans. and intro. William W. Kibler and Carleton W. Carroll. Harmondsworth: Penguin Classic, 1991.
Clemence of Barking. "The Life of St Catherine." In Jocelyn Wogan-Browne and Glyn Burgess, trans. and intro., *Virgin Lives and Holy Deaths: Two Exemplary Biographies for Anglo-Norman Women: The Life of St Catherine, The Life of St Lawrence*, 3–44. Everyman Library. London: J. M. Dent; Rutland, VT: Charles E. Tuttle, 1996.
Denis Piramus. *La Vie seint Edmund le rei: Poème anglo-normand du XIIe siècle*. Ed. Hilding Kjellman. Göteborg: Elander, 1935; repr. Geneva: Slatkine, 1974.
Geffrei Gaimar. *Estoire des Engleis. History of the English*. Ed., trans. [English] and intro. Ian Short. Oxford: Oxford University Press, 2009.
Guernes de Pont-Sainte-Maxence. *La Vie de saint Thomas le martyr*. Ed. E. Walberg. Lund: Gleerup; Oxford: Oxford University Press; Paris: Champion, 1922.
———. *Garnier's Becket*. Trans. [English] Janet Shirley. London: Phillimore, 1975.
———. *La Vie de saint Thomas de Canterbury*. Ed. and trans. [French] Jacques T. E. Thomas. Louvain and Paris: Peeters, 2002.
———. *La vie del martir seint Thomas Becket*. Electronic text (Electronic Campsey Project: http://margot.uwaterloo.ca).
"Life of St. Lawrence." In *Virgin Lives and Holy Deaths*, trans. Wogan-Browne and Burgess, 45–59.
"Life of St Osith." See "Vie seinte Osith, virge e martire."
Marie de France. *Lais de Marie de France*. Ed. K. Warnke, trans. [French] and intro. L. Harf-Lancner. Lettres gothiques. Paris: Livre de Poche, 1990.
———. *The Lais of Marie de France*. Trans. [English] and intro. Glyn S. Burgess and Keith Busby. London: Penguin Books, 1999.
Matthew Paris. *The History of Saint Edward the King by Matthew Paris*. Trans. and intro. Thelma Fenster and Jocelyn Wogan-Browne. FRETS 1. Tempe: Arizona Center for Medieval and Renaissance Studies, 2008.
Partonopeus de Blois: an Electronic Edition by Penny Eley, Penny Simons, et al., at http://www.hrionline.ac.uk/partonopeus/
Rutebeuf. *Le Miracle de Théophile, miracle du XIIIe siècle*. Ed. G. Frank. CFMA 49. Paris: Champion, 1925; 2nd ed. 1949.
"Saint Barthélemy." In *Légendier apostolique anglo-normand*, ed. Delbert W. Russell, 92–106. Montreal: Presses de l'Université de Montréal; Paris: Vrin, 1989.
Thomas. *Le Roman de Tristan*. Ed. F. Lecoy, trans. [French] and intro. Emmanuèle Baumgartner and Ian Short. Paris: Champion, 2003.
———. *Thomas of Britain: Tristan*. Trans. [facing-page English and medieval French] and intro. Stewart Gregory. New York: Garland, 1991.
Vie de saint Alexis. Ed. C. Storey. Oxford: Blackwell, 1968.

———. Online edition, the St Albans Psalter, http://www.abdn.ac.uk/~lib399/english/ [includes English trans.].
"Vie de saint Edmond, archevêque de Cantorbéry, La." Ed. A. T. Baker. *Romania* 55 (1929): 332–81.
Vie de saint Laurent, La. Ed. D. W. Russell. Anglo-Norman Texts 34. London: ANTS, 1976. See also "Life of St. Lawrence."
Vie seint Richard, evesque de Cycestre, La, by Pierre d'Abernon of Fetcham. Ed. D. W. Russell. Anglo-Norman Texts 51. London: ANTS, 1995.
"Vie seinte Osith, virge e martire, La." Ed. D. W. Russell [French with facing-page English trans. by Jane Zatta, rev. and annot. Jocelyn Wogan-Browne]. *Papers on Language & Literature* 41 (2005): 339–444. Online at the Electronic Campsey Project: http://margot.uwaterloo.ca. See also "Life of St. Osith."
Wace. *Le Roman de Brut de Wace.* Ed. I. A. Arnold. 2 vols. Paris: SATF, 1938–40.
———. *Wace's Roman de Brut, A History of the British.* Ed. and trans. [English] Judith Weiss. Exeter: Exeter University Press, 1999.
———. *Wace, Le Roman de Brut: The French Book of Brutus.* Trans. A. W. Glowka. MRTS 279. Tempe: ACMRS, 2005.

5. General Cultural, Historical, Literary Studies

Apollonius of Tyre: Medieval and Renaissance Themes and Variations, Including the Text of the Historia Apollonius Regis Tyri *with an English Translation.* Ed. and trans. Elizabeth Archibald. Cambridge: D.S. Brewer, 1991.
Binns, Alison. *Dedications of Monastic Houses in England and Wales, 1066–1216.* Woodbridge: Boydell Press, 1989.
Burton, Janet. *Monastic and Religious Orders in Britain 1000–1300.* Cambridge: Cambridge University Press, 1994.
Bynum, Caroline Walker. *Fragmentation and Redemption: Essays on Gender and the Human Body in Medieval Religion.* New York: Zone Books, 1991.
———. *The Resurrection of the Body in Western Christianity, 200–1336.* New York: Columbia University Press, 1995.
Campbell, Emma. *Medieval Saints' Lives: The Gift, Kinship and Community in Old French Hagiography.* Cambridge: D. S. Brewer, 2008.
Carré, Yannick. *Le baiser sur la bouche au moyen âge: rites, symboles, mentalités à travers les textes et les images, XIe–XVe siècle.* Paris: Léopard d'Or, 1992.
Chareyron, Nicole. *Pilgrims to Jerusalem in the Middle Ages.* Trans. W. Donald Wilson. New York: Columbia University Press, 2005; orig. *Pèlerins de Jerusalem au Moyen âge.* Paris: Imago, 2000.
Dictionnaire des lettres françaises: Le Moyen Age. Ed. Robert Bossuat, Louis Pichard, and Guy Raynaud de Lage. Paris: Fayard, 1964. Rev. ed. Geneviève Hasenohr and Michel Zink. Paris: Fayard, 1992.

Durling, Nancy Vine. "Hagiography and Lineage: The Example of the Old French 'Vie de Saint Alexis'." *Romance Philology* 40 (1987): 451–69.
Farmer, David Hugh. *The Oxford Dictionary of Saints*. Oxford: Clarendon Press, 1978, repr. 1979. Also in *Oxford Reference Online*.
Gaunt, Simon. *Gender and Genre in Medieval French Literature*. Cambridge: Cambridge University Press, 1995.
Geary, Patrick J. *Furta Sacra: Thefts of Relics in the Central Middle Ages*. Princeton: Princeton University Press, 1978, rev. ed. 1990.
Jacobus de Voragine. *Legenda aurea*. Ed. Th. Graesse. 3rd ed. Breslau: Koebner, 1890; repr. Osnabruck: Otto Zeller, 1965.
———. *The Golden Legend: Readings on the Saints*. Trans. William Granger Ryan. 2 vols. Princeton: Princeton University Press, 1993.
———. *Jacques de Voragine, La Legende dorée*. Trans. [French] J.-B. M. Roze. 2 vols. Paris: Garnier-Flammarion, 1967.
Knowles, David. *Medieval Religious Houses, England and Wales*. Rev. ed. with R. Neville Hadcock. London: Longman, 1971.
Kowaleski, Maryanne. "The French of England: A Maritime *lingua franca*?" In *Language and Culture*, ed. Wogan-Browne et al., 103–17.
Laurent, Françoise. *Plaire et édifier: Les récits hagiographiques composés en Angleterre aux XIIe et XIIIe siècles*. Paris: Champion, 1998.
Legge, M. Domenica. *Anglo-Norman in the Cloisters: The Influence of the Orders upon Anglo-Norman Literature*. Edinburgh: Edinburgh University Press, 1950.
———. *Anglo-Norman Literature and its Background*. Oxford: Oxford University Press, 1971.
Leyser, Henrietta. *Hermits and the New Monasticism: A Study of Religious Communities in Western Europe, 1000–1150*. London: Macmillan, 1984.
Morris, Colin. *The Papal Monarchy: The Western Church from 1050 to 1250*. Oxford: Oxford University Press, 1989.
Pilgrim's Guide to Santiago de Compostela: A Gazetteer. Ed. Annie Shaver-Crandell and Paula Gerson, with Alison Stones. London: Harvey Miller, 1995.
Robertson, Duncan. *The Medieval Saints' Lives: Spiritual Renewal and Old French Literature*. Lexington, KY: French Forum Publishers, 1995.
Russell, Delbert. "The Campsey Collection of Old French Saints' Lives: A Re-Examination of its Structure and Provenance." *Scriptorium* 57 (2003): 51–83, + colour plates 4–7.
Short, Ian. "Denis Piramus and the Truth of Marie's *Lais*." *Cultura Neolatina* 67 (2007): 319–40.
Southern, R. W. *Western Society and the Church in the Middle Ages*. Harmondsworth: Penguin, 1970, repr. 1976.
Thiébaux, Marcelle. *The Stag of Love: The Chase in Medieval Literature*. Ithaca and London: Cornell University Press, 1974.

Vollrath, Hanna. "The Kiss of Peace." In *Peace Treaties and International Law in European History*, ed. Randall Lesaffer, 162–83. Cambridge: Cambridge University Press, 2004.

Ward, Benedicta. *Miracles and the Medieval Mind: Theory, Record, and Event, 1000–1215*. Philadephia: University of Pennsylvania Press, 1982.

Ward, Robin. "The Shipmaster at Sea—Seamanship." In *The World of the Medieval Shipmaster: Law, Business and the Sea c. 1350–c. 1450*, 157–78. Rochester: Boydell Press, 2009.

Wilkinson, John, with Joyce Hill and W. F. Ryan. *Jerusalem Pilgrimage 1099–1185*. Hakluyt Society, 2nd ser. 167. London: Hakluyt Society, 1988.

Wogan-Browne, Jocelyn. *Saints' Lives and Women's Literary Culture c. 1150–1300: Virginity and its Authorizations*. Oxford: Oxford University Press, 2001.

———, et al., eds. *Language and Culture in Medieval Britain: The French of England c. 1100–c. 1500*. York: York Medieval Press, 2009.

I.
Guillaume de Berneville

The Life of Saint Giles

Here you will hear the details of an uplifting story preserved in the written record. In it I will tell you of the life of a holy man who, for the love of his dear Lord, endured hunger and cold and many hardships. In addition, he spent many years living only on wild plants, which he ate in the silent company of animals. He was born to a family of great nobility, rich in land and possessions, but he placed little value on his property and his noble rank, an attitude which he demonstrated once and for all when he abandoned his property and his friends to become a poor beggar. He secretly fled from his homeland, under cover of night, so that neither friends nor family knew of his going. From that day forward he lived a holy life devoted completely to the expression of his great faith.

He was Greek, and his name was Giles. He was not a lowborn child, from the family of a minor noble or a peasant, but was the son of princes and kings; all his ancestors were Greek. Giles was born and educated in the city of Athens. His father was Theodorus, a wealthy man of property, and his mother was called Pelagia. In all Greece and beyond, from that distant land to here, there was no woman her equal in chaste virtue and in charity. Together his parents were an admirable couple, who were praised during their lifetime; both lived good lives, serving and praising God; night and day their greatest effort was spent in the service of God (1–36).

God gave them an infant son whose birth filled them with happiness. His parents were overjoyed. They baptized him with great rejoicing and with affection named him Giles, and his parents confirmed him in the faith. When he reached the age of seven Giles was robust and tall, and his father sent him to school, where even as a child Giles took a keen interest in theology. Early in his life he devoted himself to the service of God, and scrupulously followed the straight and narrow path of faith until his death. He was well versed in theological learning and God granted him great wisdom; his character and actions were marked by his great honesty and goodness (37–54).

The child Giles was very handsome, a flower among the other noble youths from the region where he was born. His hair was blond and curly, his complexion as white as milk, his eyes smiling, his nose well-formed, his teeth sparkling white and his lips beautifully shaped. His chin was beardless; his handsome hands had white fingers, his torso was long and slender, his hips were broad: Nature had never created a more beautiful child.[1] His father loved him above all else and his mother held him in great affection. They provided him with fine clothing, but he gave the best of his garments to the poor. He was not interested in clothes; his sole joy was in loving God. He scorned gold and silver, war horses, palfreys and mules, sumptuous clothing and good accoutrements. Of his own accord he would go to church to hear mass and to pray to God, then from the church he would go directly to school. In short, this sums up his life: what more can I tell you? His life was completely devoted to the spiritual. The young nobles of his age, sons of the barons from his city, often blamed him for not wanting to join in their games.

"Look," they said to their companions, "see how Giles wants to play at being the little saint! The rustic proverb, 'young saint, old devil' warns against this.[2] Giles will not always be like this; he will one day be very fierce and cruel." But what they said was not at all true, and they wouldn't get what they were hoping. Giles was neither cruel nor wicked, and it was only a short time before God effected a great miracle through his young servant (55–98).

And so it happened one day, when the child Giles was on his way to the school where he studied, that he saw on a city street a miserable wretch lying by a stable door on a dung heap, lamenting, pale and sickly; the man had lain there for more than a year. All his limbs were deformed and horribly misshapen; he asked passersby for alms, but they gave him nothing. As soon as Giles saw him,

---

[1] 55–66 **The child Giles . . . beautiful child** *Li emfes Gires . . . plus bele ren ne fist Nature*: a standard medieval description of physical beauty, usually also the outward sign of inner virtue; cf. Paris & Bos, *Vie de s. Gilles*, xxxviii.

[2] 89 **The rustic proverb . . . warns against this** *Li vileins dit en repruver*: the word *vileins* "peasant" refers to the well-known collection of proverbs commonly called *Li Proverbes au vilain*. The phrase *li vileins dit* is generic (lit. "the peasant says"), meaning "rustic proverb" or "the old saying." *Repruver* can mean either "reproach" or "proverb," and the translation suggests both meanings. Using a proverb introduced by the phrase *li vileins dit* is a literary convention found in many medieval narrative poems; see John Frankis, "Languages and Cultures in Contact: Vernacular Lives of St. Giles and Anglo-Norman Annotations in an Anglo-Saxon Manuscript," *Leeds Studies in English*, n. s. 38 (2007): 101–33, at 107–11, and nn. 127–128. The standard modern references for these proverbs are J. Morawski, *Proverbes français antérieurs au XVe siècle* (Paris: Champion, 1925), and E. Schulze-Busacker, *Proverbes et expressions proverbiales dans la littérature narrative du Moyen Âge français: Recueil et analyse* (Paris: Champion, 1985). Cf. Morawski, *Proverbes*, no. 509, Schulze-Busacker, *Proverbes*, 86.

he ran up to him with his childish steps, asking what was the matter and why he was lamenting.

"Sir," he replied, "I can't bear it any longer! I can no longer remain silent. I am dying of hunger and perishing from cold: God grant that my life may end soon! I have lived too long, my life is now nothing but pain: I pray God that I die before the day is out. Death is all I wish for, and I will gladly welcome it. I can't go on living: my death is close, I can feel it!" (99–124).

Giles listened to the man speaking wildly in this fashion, and it brought tears to his eyes; he had neither gold nor silver with him, so he offered the man some of his own clothing. On the spot he took off the cloak he was wearing and put it on the beggar, helping him into the sleeves. The beggar put the cloak on his back: his body shuddered, his bones creaked and he cried out and stretched out his limbs, and then he quickly rose to his feet. Hear now how gracious is the generosity[3] of God: the invalid who was formerly stricken with infirmity is now standing on his own two feet! Before Giles left, the man approached the child as if to embrace him, and Giles fled. The beggar ran after him, crying out:

"This child should be praised by everyone. It is clear that he has done a great deed, since through him God has healed a cripple; for this I give thanks to both him and God!" (125–47).

At once a large crowd of men and women, more than a hundred in all, gathered around him. There was a great crush of people milling about, but Giles had already left. Slipping behind now one, now another person in the crowd, he returned to his house, dejected and sad, and threw himself down on a bench with his head bowed, lost in thought. He was sorry and regretted that so many people had seen him and witnessed how completely the cripple was healed.

His father was in the city and heard the news on the street as word spread throughout of the miracle cure of the cripple performed by his son Giles, but he did not know if it was true or not. As quickly as he could, he returned home and saw his son seated on a bench, and started to question him:

"My dear son, I am sorry to see you looking pale: what is troubling you? Has someone angered you? Where is your cloak? Why are you not wearing it?"

"Father," he replied, "I have given it away, where it is being put to good use. I gave it this morning to a sick man on the street, who was in great distress, dying of cold and in a pitiful state. There was nothing else I could do! I took my cloak from my back and gave it to the man who asked me for it, for the love of God, creator of us all. For us God let himself be sold to the Jews and hanged on the cross. And we, alas, what have we done for him? Alas, dear father, I believe we will be judged harshly for this on Judgement Day, when all the angels will tremble in fear. When even the archangels are afraid, as well as the beloved of our Lord, the apostles and the martyrs, where will sinners be able to conceal them-

---

[3] 137 **gracious is the generosity of God** *cum Deus est curteis*: "gracious generosity" is an attempt to express the sense of *curteis* qualifying God; cf. notes to vv. 353, 1300.

selves, for they will find no woods, no city, no hut or house to shield them? Indeed, they will not be able to hide, but will be forced to come forward; the Lord's voice will fill them with fear, saying: 'Sinners, see here the cross and the nails, and the blood which flowed down my side. See here the crown and the lance, and contemplate your own disbelief. You have sinned against me: for you, I was put to death, I allowed myself to be crucified, to be scorned and vilely beaten. Tell me, what have you suffered for me? Show me now, openly and clearly. If you have served me well, you will be well rewarded, here and now!' (148–214).

Those who can show nothing, he will have sent from him, to be placed in hell, into that vileness from which they will nevermore return. They are damned eternally to the deep pit of Baratrum.[4] And whoever lies there in that foul mud will never rise again. But Father, those who will sit on God's right hand can rejoice! In truth, to them he will say, 'My people, approach and receive your heavenly reward, which your ancestors condemned you to lose, but which you have rightfully regained. You will be given abundant joy, and you will live with me forever. You will no longer fear torment, but all will dwell instead in my household.' Great will be the rejoicing of all those to whom his kingdom will be granted! May it please God, through his mercy, to place us on his right hand, and grant us eternal life!" (215–38).[5]

His father heard him speak, and marvelled at his son's words, amazed that a child of his age could have become so wise in such a short time. The fact that he had given away his cloak was quickly forgiven, and his father was not at all concerned that his son praised God, but loved him all the more dearly for it. He bought him a new cloak, one that was better made, of a more expensive fabric. Giles, however, did not value it, since he would gladly have given this cloak also to another pauper, had he dared (239–52).

It was not long after this that Giles lost his wealthy parents; both his mother and father died, and he had neither brother nor sister. He alone inherited the property and titles, along with the dependent knights and all the household. Giles accepted his inheritance, but God knew well his true feelings. Giles cared little for his title and his property: all his possessions he dedicated to God. He wished, I firmly believe, to make God his heir. He was left with a large inheritance: castles and towns, vineyards and meadows, gold and silver, rich raiments of silk,[6] palfreys, mules and fine horses, and vessels of gold and silver. But he gave it away generously: he did not spend it on loose living, on prostitutes or

---

[4] 220 **to the deep pit of Baratrum** *el parfund puz de Baratrum*: Laurent, *SGilles*, 15, notes that Greek *barathron* "abyss," used here to name the pit of hell, is also a name used in *Fierabras* (v. 4301) for a "divinité des mahométans," cf. Gdf. 1: 578c, T-L 1: 833.29.

[5] Cf. Matthew 25:31–46.

[6] 267 **rich raiments of silk** *pailles, cendals*: cf. Laurent, *SGilles*, 17, who notes that *paile* denotes a rare fabric, richly decorated, such as silk brocaded with gold, while *cendal* was a light silk, like taffeta.

jongleurs;[7] instead he built abbeys for the poor, hospitals for the infirm,[8] the sick and the crippled, the lepers and the disfigured: with all these he shared his wealth (253–77).

His barons were seriously worried by this behaviour. They confronted him with their reprimands, and said repeatedly to him:

"Sire, for the love of God, do not waste your inheritance in this fashion, do not be so generous, keep some reserves for yourself as a landholder! Your faithful advisors are right when they say that you will shortly have nothing left. How can your wealth last if you continue endlessly to give it away? You do not seem to care if any of it remains! You have greatly impoverished your people, and gone against the advice of your barons. If you do not behave differently, all your men will leave you. You will do well to pay heed to our counsel, and act wisely: do as we advise you, and take as wife the daughter of a baron, or of a count or a king. You should be completely ashamed of yourself because you have acted so thoughtlessly! What has become of your great wealth? Where is your gold and silver? You have spent your wealth badly: those who have received it are not even grateful to you for giving it to them. This proves the old saying: 'A fool and his riches soon part company!'[9] My lord, change your thinking: take a noblewoman as your wife, who will give you children, to whom you will pass on your inheritance. For if your land remains without an heir, we will all perish by war, and if the land is lost, you will have committed a great sin, for you are well able to protect it. Your ancestors who ruled before you were worthy lords; take care that you do not prove to be less worthy, take care, sire, that it not be said of you: 'the fiefdom has passed to a very weak heir.' You seem to be an intelligent man, yet you are bent on destroying your inheritance. Your beautiful face and fine physique will mean nothing if your character is not based on an inner goodness. If you dare not accept your responsibilities as a landholder, go take refuge in the woods, and become a monk in a monastery, for you will be of use for nothing else. But cease this constant refrain, and sing a new tune: believe your barons who are here, follow their advice: they are your liegemen, and you are their lord; that is why they are an-

---

[7] 271–72 **spend it on loose living** *nel donout mie as lecheürs*: the text says he did not give his money to scoundrels (*lecheürs*), whores or jongleurs; this translation attempts to convey that this is a rejection of a life style, as well as a refusal of spending. This is also an allusion to the parable of the prodigal son (Luke 15:11–13).

[8] For the history of an important medieval hospital dedicated to St Giles, see Carole Rawcliffe, *Medicine for the Soul: The Life, Death, and Resurrection of an English Medieval Hospital, St. Giles, Norwich, c. 1249–1550* (Stroud: Sutton, 1999).

[9] 306-8 **This proves the old saying . . . part company** *Pur ço di li vileins verté*: (lit. "For this reason the peasant speaks the truth") . . . *ne sunt pas lunges cumpaignun*: Frankis, "Languages and Cultures in Contact," 108, translates the proverb "As for the miser and the wastrel, they aren't long companions." This proverb is not cited in Morawski, *Proverbes*, but nos. 1082, 1496, 2088 are similar in meaning; cf. Laurent, *SGilles*, 21.

gered and troubled that you are behaving so foolishly. They are much concerned. Abandon this foolishness and follow good sense; you will do well to be guided by their judgement!" (278–340).

Giles listened as his barons spoke, and he began to think how he would respond to them. He sighed deeply as he bent his head in thought. Hear now his reply.

"My lords," he said, "what you say is wise. I have thought deeply about something I want to confess to you now, which I dared not reveal earlier. I dearly love a young maiden, still a pure and untouched virgin, a most beautiful, courteous young woman, from a very noble family.[10] If I could have her love I would ask for no other riches. I wish to devote myself to winning her love, but I ask that you keep this secret. Between now and the feast of St. Martin[11] you will be told all of my plans with respect to where I wish to go and the spouse I wish to win. I would request that you agree to wait until then, for it is not a long time. Be assured, as long as I am hale and hearty, I will be able to inform you fully of my plans well before the appointed date!" (341–69).

They were all pleased and relieved to hear this request, and granted Giles the delay, and spent the night with him, feasting and celebrating because of their great joy. Early the next day the barons took their leave and returned to their own houses. Giles remained, in order to pray to his dear friend that she protect him from the pitfalls set by the devil, who was always there, around him night and day, thinking to trick him. But he had given himself to a Lord who does not let sinners perish if they want to serve him faithfully. Before the agreed-upon day arrived, Giles had a marvellous experience, in which God showed him that he was concerned that Giles had forgotten his prayers in favour of following the advice of his barons (370–90).

One day Giles went to church to hear divine office. At the end of the service he bowed before the altar as he left. A sick man approached him, who looked deformed and repulsive. It was no wonder he was complaining, for he had been bitten and poisoned by the venom of a very dangerous snake. He had barely escaped with his life; his hands and feet were swollen, it was obvious that he was in a bad state. He had heard the talk, circulated throughout the region, that God accomplished miracles through Giles. Throwing himself at Giles' feet, the wretch cried out for his pity:

"My lord, for the love of God, the Son of Mary, have mercy on this sufferer: I have been stricken by a serpent. Take pity on me, my lord, for the love of the

---

[10] 353 **courteous** *curteise*: this adjective is often used to qualify the divine; cf. notes to vv. 137, 1300.

[11] 359 **the feast of St. Martin** *le seint Martin*: 11 November. As Laurent, *SGilles*, 23, notes, St. Martin of Tours (the first hermit in Gaul) will guide Giles in his life as a hermit (v. 1456), and the feast of St. Martin marks the beginning of the annual liturgical cycle of the proper of the saints.

Sovereign King. If you will pray to your Lord I will be healed of this suffering. Have pity on me, my lord, see how I am in great pain. Make me healthy again, for I know for certain that you have the power to do it!" (391–418).

Giles heard the pleas of the unfortunate man, and tears came to his eyes; he replied softly to him:

"My friend, you have heard wrong: please understand that I do not have the power to restore your health, but be assured that I would be happy if my prayer helped you. Do not worry, wait a moment while I pray to God on your behalf" (419–28).

Quietly weeping, Giles held out both hands toward heaven:

"Oh Lord," he said, "gentle King, in your pity advise me. I do not know what to say to this wretch who weeps and asks for your mercy. I see that he is near death, and he thinks he will have solace from me. I do not have the power to comfort him, but you can show him your goodness. Show it to this sufferer, and make known to this people that you hold everything in your hand, and that you can restore the sick. Show this man your goodness; give him back, sweet Lord, his health, if it be your will and if it is right to do so" (429–45).

When he had finished his prayer, he came outside to the sick man; in front of the large crowd which was there, the sick man stood up at his approach. His hands and feet were no longer swollen; he was completely healed of the swelling and felt no pain or injury. He had found an excellent doctor to cure him! We should indeed serve a Lord such as this, who performs such miracles through his servant. Those who had come there to witness the scene saw that he was completely healed; they cried out with one voice:

"Saint Giles, have pity on us; pray to God, your dear friend, that he defend us against the devil. Your actions have shown today that God is with you, and you with him. You can be of great help to us in securing his aid!" (446–65).

Everyone wished to fall at his feet; Giles was very troubled when he heard them:

"Good people," he cried, "for the love of God! what you have seen here did not happen because of me! I tell you, and be assured this is the truth, this man was healed by his faith. Praise God, not me, for on my word of honour, I have no more power than you to give a man health. Abandon this foolish idea, and pray to Saint Mary that she, as a merciful and compassionate mother, intercede on your behalf with God" (466–80).

Not wishing to stay longer at the scene of this event, Giles set out for home and quickly came to his own house. He was both annoyed and overjoyed: he was very happy that God had shown his love for him so completely, but at the same time he was very troubled by the fact that the people honoured him so greatly. Nothing would persuade him to remain there, for so many people already knew about him. All throughout the length and breadth of Greece the word about Giles spread: that God performs great miracles through him, making the crippled to walk and the dumb to speak. In the city where he lives there are so many infirm that a person can not go anywhere without seeing someone who has lost an arm, or who is blind: never had there been seen so many sick, suffering from fevers and gangrenous infections. They assembled at his doorstep, and cried out in one voice:

"Saint Giles, have pity on us, see our great need! Have mercy on us, poor miserable wretches, who have come here from distant countries to ask for your compassion: you have the power to restore our health, we will not leave here until we are healed!" (481–510).

Giles listened to their cries and pleas, and he was saddened. Tearfully, he lamented to himself:

"Oh Lord, true and good King, glorious Father, what can I do? I now know well, from what I see, that I am nothing in your sight, when you allow people from distant lands to come here looking for my help![12] The worst among them, the most evil among them, is more worthy than I am: but your goodness is shown according to your power, you restore health at the pleasure of your divine will. This is not my concern, I am a miserable sinner, and if I have done anything for good, in deed, in speech, or in prayer, I beseech you that my recompense be given in heaven.[13] My Lord, I beg and pray that my reward be given later, for I do not seek people's praise; my heart is elsewhere. Worldly praise quickly passes: there are those who love it too much, but I do not embrace it, preferring to avoid it, and to distance myself from it: 'he who sits too close to the sparks quickly finds holes burned in his cloak'; and 'if you huddle close to the fire day and night, it is not surprising that you are burned.'[14] I am in the midst of a fire, and fear that my sin is deceiving me; but I plan to withdraw so that I will not be tempted. The proverb says 'The eye goes where it wishes; what the eye does not see, the heart

---

[12] 518–19 **I am nothing..., when you allow people from distant lands** *ke nen as meis cure de mei, quant la gent de luintaine terre*: the addition of "you allow" after "when" makes evident the causal link in Giles' mind between God's lack of concern for him and the presence of the supplicants at his door.

[13] 530–31 **recompense be given in heaven** *aillurs te pri le gueredun*: the adv. *aillurs* is used in both these verses to refer to a time after this earthly life, translated here as "in heaven" and "later."

[14] 539–42 **'he who sits . . . you are burned'** "*ki est veisin a l'estencele / tost ad parcee la gunele*"; / "*ki le fu hante e jur e nuit / n'est merveille se il se quit*": these two proverbs are not introduced by the usual phrase *li vileins dit*; nor are they cited in Morawski or Schulze-Busacker, but similar ones are Morawski no. 2088, Schulze-Busacker no. 2372, and Schulze-Busacker no. 2088; cf. Laurent, *SGilles*, 33.

does not covet.'[15] The great riches which are mine[16] would quickly win me over if I remained here for long, and I would become an object of scorn as a result. Lord God and Father, what should I do? Teach me what I should do, show me what path I should follow so that I may come to you. Rome, where the apostles lived, is the head of Christianity; I think if I were there I would learn what is right, and would hear the truth; with the counsel of the pope I would know the path forward."

With this he ended his reflexion, upon the decision that he was determined to follow: very soon he would abandon his extensive lands and his great feudal lordship. May his Lord now protect him, for it is because of his love for God that he undertakes this great task! (511–69).

He left his palace and went straight to the sick: he had seen many kinds of afflictions among those suffering illness. He prayed that God would restore their health, and they who had long been stricken were healed of their infirmities.

Daylight was fading, and night fell; Giles went away filled with happiness, and ordered his servants to prepare a great meal, with abundant food and drink. They were quick to obey his orders, and prepared a great feast. Giles sat down to dine, taking care to appear very happy. His men, who had formerly seen him lost in his pensive mood, were now very pleased. Wine was brought in great quantity, all the cellars were opened, and indeed, the wine they served was of excellent quality and his men drank it joyfully. Everyone was happy and full of good cheer, but their joy and happiness would soon turn to great sadness, for they would shortly hear news to cause them many tears—news, indeed, that would be the source of many cries of sorrow and pain, and that would lead many to tear out their hair (570–600).

When it was time to retire for the night the squires went to their lodgings. Giles remained behind, and went to lie down in the room where his bed was prepared; there were a number of his men who went with him to attend him and help him remove his boots and leggings. When he was in bed they left the room, and from that moment on they never saw him again. It would have been better had they fasted the whole day long rather than lose their lord this night; they kept watch over him badly, they who would never see his like again. The servants who lay down in his chamber quickly fell asleep: they had drunk too much spiced wine, which had gone to their heads. But regardless of who was sleeping and who

---

[15] 547–48 **The proverb says . . . covet**' *Li vileins dit: ". . . dolt"*: see Frankis, "Languages and Cultures in Contact," 108–9, who silently emends to *L'oil [va] u vult*. It is possible to construe *la oil u vult*, with adv. *la* "there," equivalent to Mod. Fr. *là l'oeil, où il veut*, lit. "there [is] the eye, where it wishes [to be]." Cf. Morawski, nos. 39, 976, 1140, 1835, Schulze-Busacker, nos. 1766, 1767.

[16] 549 **The great riches which are mine** *La grant richesse ke jo vai* (lit. "which I see"): Giles refers here to his inherited wealth, which he equates earlier, in v. 543, with the comfortable fire he must also flee.

was not, Giles spent the whole time in prayer; all night long he could not sleep, for he was anxious to fulfill his plan.

Once those with him had fallen asleep, Giles arose and quietly left the room where he lay, so that his chamberlain did not notice him leaving. He chose not to take any clothing, apart from what was essential, for if he burdened himself down with clothes it would be harder to walk. The night was pitch black: he arrived at the outer wall, right at the base of the tower, but he was afraid he would be seen by the watchman on the tower who was sounding his horn, his fife, flute, and shawm. But because of the fog and the darkness the sentinels did not notice him, so he passed through without being seen, except by his Lord who guided him. May God now protect him, for love of whom he has abandoned everything! (601–40).

Giles set out on his way, leaving behind his lands and his friends: he took no gold or silver with him, no horse, or mule or palfrey. He wore no fur cloak of miniver, but poor and inexpensive clothing; God who is the source of all riches would provide for his needs. He travelled all night, and, not surprisingly, he was exhausted, since he was unaccustomed to travelling on foot. Nonetheless, he pushed himself on, for he feared that his barons would follow him in an attempt to stop him. And they did just that: they sent couriers and spies to several regions, who looked high and low, both on foot and on horseback. In my view, this was all in vain, for they would never again set their eyes on him (641–60).

The following day, at first light, the chamberlain went up to Giles' room, for it was his lord's habit to go to church in the early morning. He intended to help him into his hose, and went toward the bed looking for them, but he didn't find them, for they weren't there. He felt about with his hand, but found only the blankets. The chamberlain now realized that his master had left, and he fell back in a faint on the bed. When he came to his senses, he began to wail, wringing his hands and tearing at his hair:

"Alas!", he cried, "Giles, sweet lord, I am sure that I have lost you! What will I say to your friends who left you in my care? I have watched over you badly. My anguish is twofold: first on your account, then on my own, and I am very fearful. I am filled with great misgivings because of your relatives. I don't know where I can flee. I can only await my inevitable death here, for I have no defence against the fact that by my foolish behaviour they have lost an important member of their family. Cursed be the hour when this wine was made, and my body which drank so much of it! What will now become of your knights, your young noblemen and your squires, who rightfully expected to receive largesse and fiefdoms from you? But you have dashed their hopes, for you have left no heir capable of granting them even one square foot of land: let them go elsewhere to win a feudal domain, for I believe they have failed to do so with you, and they are now disconcerted, reduced to becoming poor beggars, and I, more than anyone, have lost everything!"

With these words he fell prostrate to the floor (661–702).

The others in the castle were awakened by the loud lamentations and cries of grief uttered by the chamberlain. They rose hastily, and all came into the chamber asking the whereabouts of their lord. And the chamberlain told them, crying:

"He has gone, but I do not know when he left!"

They set out searching for him throughout the city, but they did not find him; all their efforts were in vain, for he could not be found. When they realized that they would not find him they returned to the hall. Their grief was fierce, and deep beyond measure; everyone was immersed in his own pain. Anyone who was there that day in the great hall would have seen the bitter anguish of those who could be heard crying out and weeping, wringing their hands and tearing at their hair. They mourned all day long, weeping and lamenting for their lord, declaring through their tears:

"Noble and valiant lord, your great goodness, your intelligence, and your beauty are for naught! What good has come from your sweet youth? Your clear white complexion and rose-coloured cheeks will be burned by the sun and frozen by cold! How will you fare on foot? Who will offer you a single penny? Where will you find food and clothing, meals during the day, and lodging at night? What a waste of your youthful beauty! There was never anyone of your age, son of a count or a king, blessed with such qualities as you had! What does all this matter, now that everything has turned to grief? You will never rejoice a single day of your life. We who are left here after your departure will no longer shave our beards or cut our hair, but will instead wear only garments of mourning: we have lost our lord. What will become of us, miserable wretches that we are! Cursed be death, which leaves us in the land of the living! We live only in grief now that we have lost you!"

All day long they made these plaintive and mournful cries.

The news spread throughout the city that God's servant had fled, and the townspeople, the nobility, and the peasants all expressed great sorrow: knights and burghers wept, noblemen and peasants cried out in anguish; there was no one in the town who was not moved by pity to tears. But they wept to no avail, it seems to me, since Giles was quickly distancing himself from the region (703–62).

Giles travelled without stopping, taking the road straight toward the great sea, but he didn't go directly to the harbour, for he was afraid that he would be recognized. He continued his journey night and day, enduring hunger and thirst and fatigue, over mountains and through valleys, plains, and woodlands, until he reached the seashore. Once there he sat down, for he was exhausted; he prayed to God and Saint Nicholas that he be sent a vessel of some kind, a fishing boat or a merchant barge, a warship or a smaller boat,[17] that could carry him across

---

[17] 774 **a vessel of some kind, a fishing boat or a merchant barge, a warship or a smaller boat** *buce u kenar, nef u batel*: the four types of vessel are very specific, and not easily rendered in translation; Laurent, *SGilles*, 47, proposes fishing boat for *buce*, and a transport ship for *kenar*; the *AND* gives *buce* "buss, store-ship" (citing four sources), and

the sea. He looked far out to sea, and saw a ship in peril, buffeted by the storm, fighting against the enormous waves and disappearing into the deep troughs, for the sea was very rough, the waves crashing and raging like a wild beast. The ship was at the mercy of the waves, pushed along at the whim of the storm which was fierce, with lightning and thunder and rain driven by the wind. Battered by the wild seas, and buffeted by the gales, the ship almost split open: it would be thrust skyward on the crest of one wave, then pitched down into the deep trough before the next wave, pushed up by one, dropped down by the next, so that it almost broke apart completely! (763–92).

Giles saw the ship foundering in the tumultuous, turbulent, swelling seas and he feared greatly for the sailors. He prayed that our Lord bring them safely to harbour: the fierce wind dropped, and the churning waves became as calm as a sea of glass; the tempest moved off, and a favourable wind arose. Much relieved, the sailors went to the capstan and raised the sail, and the ship came directly to shore; it beached safely, without harm or damage. The sailors emerged from the vessel, looked around and saw Giles, who was still in the midst of his prayer for them. They gently questioned him, asking where he was born, and what had brought him there. They knew for certain that it was through his love that God had spared them that day.

"Sire," they said, "please speak to us, for we know that we have been saved by you, through your prayer and your words. Tell us what country you come from, who you are, where you wish to go, and what you are seeking!" (793–820).

Giles, who did not wish to be untruthful, told them he was a Christian, a Greek, he said, an errant sinner born in Greece:

"To expiate my sins I have had to leave my homeland. I must go to Rome, but I have no means of paying my fare. I beseech you in the name of God, take me to your country; if you do this it will be a great act of charity, for I have wandered far from home, and I have been here too long, but I have no gold or silver, not even a penny or a farthing"[18] (821–35).

"Good sir," replied the sailors, "even if you had a thousand marks of silver we would accept no payment from you! But if you wish to come with us, we all will gladly be at your service!" (836–40).

He responded with a low bow of thanks, then asked where they were from. They confided in him that some of them were born and raised in Provence, and that many of them were merchants coming with their merchandise. They were

---

kenar "Norse warship" (citing Gaimair, *Estoire des Engleis*, vv. 2438, 2507); the context of Gaimar, *Estoire des Engleis* v. 384, shows that Gaimar also uses *kenart* to indicate a transport ship. A *batel* is a small boat, or tender, used to disembark from a ship to land.

[18] 835 **not even a penny or a farthing** *n'ai une maille ne dener*, lit. "I have neither maille nor denier." Terms from the pre-decimal English monetary system are used instead to suggest the small value of the coins in question; a *maille* was half a *dener* (a farthing is only one-fourth of a penny).

transporting brocades from Russia, fine silken taffetas and samites, rich oriental fabrics and beautiful rich cloaks and crimson-coloured murreys, flowered silken diasper, rich purple cloth, costly oriental fabrics, and fine textiles from Alexandria in hues of red and azure, and Greek green; they had sugar, cinnamon and licorice, galingale and scammony.[19]

"There is no rich spice in all the lands beyond Christendom[20] that we do not have. But we cannot make the sea crossing. We are attempting to return to our country but this storm is preventing us. It has beaten us back repeatedly, and we almost drowned. We know full well that God saved us through your prayers. Stay with us if you want to travel to the region of Rome; if you choose to come with us, we will be eager to help."

"My lords," he responded, "I thank you, and I tell you truly that my heart is set on going there, if God grants that I may do so."

They all were overjoyed and happy that Giles had agreed to travel with them (856–75).

The day was fair, the sun shone brightly, the sea and wind were calm. They quickly went to the ship, very pleased to have fine weather. They weighed the anchors in preparation for leaving; they hurried to ready the ship to set off, for they were eager to make the sea crossing. The wind was in the right quarter, and the sea calm, and there was no need to adjust their tackle; during the night there was no need to nail down the point of the sail to keep their course, nor did they need to lower the stunsail, nor trim the mainsail. It was not necessary to man the hauling ropes, the sheets, or sheet-rings, nor was it necessary to tie a bowline, the sea was so completely calm.[21] There was no need to strike sail, to add sail, or to

---

[19] 848–55 **brocades from Russia, fine silken taffetas and samites . . . beautiful rich cloaks and crimson-coloured murreys, . . . scammony** *pailles de Russie, / cendaus, samiz et mutabez, / e bels ciclatuns e morez, . . . escamonie*: samite is a richer silk fabric than *cendal* "taffeta" (cf. note to v. 267, above); Laurent, *SGilles*, 53, states that *ciclatun* is a long coat, worn by men and women, made of silk or other expensive fabric; *mutabet* is a rich fabric of eastern origin. The *AND* gives *muré* as derived from the mulberry colour of the fabric; at this period *diasper* (mod. Fr. *diaprer*, adj. *diapré*) referred to a flowered silk cloth; galingale is an aromatic made from the root of various plants; scammony, also herbal, is an irritant or a stimulant, as well as a laxative. On this early mention of Russia as a source of luxury goods, see Frankis, "Languages and Cultures in Contact," 117–18. On the affective appeal of luxury fabrics in literature see also E. Jane Burns, *Courtly Love Undressed: Reading Through Clothes in Medieval French Culture* (Philadelphia: University of Pennsylvania Press, 2002), 179–211.

[20] 856 **beyond Christendom** *en paienie*: lit. "in pagan lands."

[21] 885–90 **During the night . . . the sea was so completely calm** *ne n'i out la nuit lof cloé, . . . tute fud queie la marine*: for the discussion of these technical nautical terms see below (Appendices, 199–203). The terms refer to manoeuvres to both increase the surface area and change the angle of the sails, as well as to actions to lower or reduce the sails. The *boesline* "bowline," for example, ran from the luff (or weather edge) of the sail

tie fast the rudder.[22] The sail stay was strong, and the guy-lines were firmly fixed against the wind, and on the leeward side the rigging and the braces were strong. No ship had better runner-ties on the sail, the sails were sturdy and the ship stout, and they travelled quickly with a good wind. They sailed all night by the light of the moon, with the sail hauled up to the crow's nest; there was no need to change the rigging during the night, nor the next day. They continued their voyage across the open sea, for he whom God loves travels thus (876–906).

Giles, who was extremely tired, fell asleep sitting close to the helmsman next to the capstan. The sailors were not slow to man the rigging, for they had a long journey ahead of them. They sailed on for four days as fast as they could, and saw nothing but sea and sky. On the fifth day, as dawn broke and the sun rose quickly in the sky, the ship sailed along under wind-filled sails, travelling rapidly without much effort on the part of the crew. The man at the helm thought he saw land, but he didn't know which country it was. They saw an island off the bow, but they didn't know its position. They changed course toward it, approached the island under full sail, and found an excellent harbour. They launched their tender, and prepared their ship to remain at anchor: they erected an awning under the sail, then went ashore to repair their rigging. They dried their lines, wet with sea water. The captain left first, followed closely by Giles. The land was flat and even, and higher up they found a spring; watercress grew in the bed of the stream which flowed from it. Looking at the sand nearby they found the footprints of a man who had come there to get water; both immediately followed the tracks and came upon the man, praying in front of the door to his dwelling. He was a short, slight man with a long beard and grey hair. He was very thin and unhealthy-looking, weathered by the sun and hard work. He raised his head and saw them approaching; at first he wanted to flee, then changed his mind. He raised his hand to mark himself with the sign of the cross, and greeted them from a distance, asking how they had come there, where they were from, and where they were headed (907–57).

The captain of the ship replied:

---

to the bowsprit, to maintain the angle of the main sail forward against the wind, while the leeward edge of the main sail is held back by a brace and a sheet. On the technicalities of sailing, see Robin Ward, *The World of the Medieval Shipmaster: Law, Business and the Sea, c. 1350–c. 1450* (Woodbridge: Boydell Press, 2009), ch. 7: "The Shipmaster at Sea—Seamanship," 157–78, at 162–65; also Laurent, *SGilles*, 55–59; Frankis, "Languages and Cultures in Contact," 117.

[22] 891–92 **There was no need to strike sail, to add sail, or to tie fast the rudder** *ne lur estut pas estricher, / ne tendre tref ne helenger*: the *AND* suggests this should read *hel enger*; *hel* "helm, rudder" is of English origin, as is *estricher* "strike sail"; the meaning of *enger* is unknown. Perhaps the noun "hanger" (ME "strap, hanger") is used here as a verb: "strap, tie down with a strap."

"Kind sir," he said, "we are merchants who have had many misadventures; however, all is now well, and we have sailed for four days with a strong and favourable wind. Our crew have landed here in order to discover which country this is, but they have found nothing: no huts or houses, no men or women, apart from you."

"My lords," he replied, "what you say is true. No one chooses to live here: the landscape is austere and isolated, with frequent storms and rains; for this reason it is uninhabitable."

Giles looked at him closely, and took him aside and began to ask him about his life:

"Tell me the truth: how long have you lived here? How do you manage to live, when there is nothing here to eat? How can you live without bread? I do not see a single grain of wheat from which you could provide for yourself by ploughing and sowing!" (958–84).

"Brother," he responded, "I am well provided for, I have enough, I lack nothing. It is now more than two years since I came here, and I have seen no one except you. Here I do my penitence with fasting and abstinence. I eat no bread, but I am hale and hearty. Sometimes I find a fish under a rock in the sand. What more can I tell you? I have enough, and want for nothing. On this island I am far removed from others; the devil tries me often, and I have struggled mightily against him, but our Lord is my shield. I cannot leave this island, surrounded on all sides by the sea. I live chastely, out of necessity, and I have no occasion to sin. I may have very wicked thoughts, but thanks to God, I do not put them into action. I see and hear no evil; in God I rejoice, in him I am glad. Here no one causes me trouble, and I fear neither storms nor tempests. I hear of no quarrels or conflicts here, and here I shall remain during my life, and after my death. I have fled the world to live in this place, which I have just described to you" (985–1014).

In this simple fashion he described his existence and his way of life. Giles stood and listened, and then embraced and kissed the man, who returned his kiss, for in this way good people acknowledge each other, and these two recognized themselves as kindred spirits.[23] Giles was the first to speak:

"Sir," he said, "I beseech you that I may also seek blessing through your good works and your prayers."

---

[23] 1018–21 **embraced and kissed ... as kindred spirits** *enbrace le, puis le beisat ... cil dui se sunt entretrové*: the kiss is not erotic, but a formal sign of becoming a member of a particular group; in this case Giles is espousing the eremitical vocation, and his doing so is formally accepted by the hermit. This agreement is made explicit in the following lines, vv. 1023–28. The verbs *s'ajuster* (v. 1020) and *s'entretrover* (v. 1020), often used to describe the joining together of military combatants or of lovers, are here used to emphasize the union of like minds, and the joining together of physical forces. See below, *The Life of St. George*, for further discussion of the kiss as symbol of a legally binding agreement; also above, 36–38.

"Brother," he responded, "I grant your request, and ask in return that you do not forget me, but keep me in your prayers."

On both sides, each one agreed to the other's request. Then Giles and the captain took their leave of the hermit (1015–30).

They went swiftly back to the ship, for the wind was favourable. They raised their anchors from the shingle beach, and pushed the ship away from the rocks, and set out onto the open sea. They travelled quickly toward their own country, for the ship was well rigged; they crossed the salt-water sea at great speed. Guillaume of Berneville reports that in three days time they came to the beautiful and large city of Marseille. They brought the ship in to the quay, and Giles took leave of his companions, who escorted him at some length as he started on his way.

He left them and came into Marseille, but he knew no one in the city; he was like a stranger in a foreign country. He looked throughout the city for a lodging, but now that he was obliged to beg, he knew very little about how to set about doing this. Formerly a rich man, he now found himself a beggar, so it is little wonder that he was in a quandary! But his Lord directed him to a burgher who gave him lodging and willingly supplied his needs while he was in the city. Meanwhile, the sailors had a favourable wind and happily went on their way to their own country (1031–58).

Giles remained in Marseille, although the city was not to his liking, and he did not plan to stay there long. He had heard reports of a bishop named Caesarius, whom the inhabitants of Gascony and Provence respected highly for his great piety, for he loved God sincerely. The seat of his diocese was the city of Arles.[24] Giles had been told of this bishop, and he wanted to go directly to Arles to learn from him. He took his leave from his host, and after travelling through woods and plains he came the next day to the city, much wearied and exhausted. He was given shelter by a widow named Theocrita, who welcomed him into her house and prepared him a meal. From down on the floor, in a remote corner, he heard someone complaining bitterly of illness. He asked who was hidden away in the corner and complaining.

"Good sir," replied Theocrita, "it is my mother who lies there.[25] It is now more than twelve years since she has stepped outside. She has long lived in this state, without ever being able to find help. If you know of anything that can help her I will give you as much of my possessions as you would like. For pity's sake try to help her; if she could receive relief through you, it would reflect greatly on your honour and renown. For the love of God I beg you to try to help her!" (1059–98).

---

[24] 1068 **Arles** *Arrelais*: the form in the *Vie* is cited by Paris & Bos as evidence that Guillaume was not familiar with the geography of the Midi, since he did not recognize the Latin name for the city known in the vernacular as *Arles*. For the real-life Caesarius see W. Klingshirn, *Caesarius of Arles* (Cambridge: Cambridge University Press, 1984).

[25] 1086 **mother** *mere*: in the *Vita* it is Theocrita's daughter, not her mother, who is ill.

"Lady," he responded, "truly, I know nothing about medicine. May our Lord grant her health, for the power to do so is his, and if you accept my advice, you will look for no other doctor. Even if I could be of help to her, I would not take your payment: but I cannot, nor do I know anything about this illness. But show her to me, and I will look at her; in my view, certainly, my looking at her will do her no harm. Let us go together to her."

"Good sir," said Theocrita, "she has languished so long that everyone is repulsed by the sight of her. Nonetheless, if you would consent to see her it would be an act of charity and kindness" (1099–1116).

Giles came up to the bed where the wretched woman lay. As soon as he saw her he was moved by pity, and devoutly implored God:

"Oh Lord, glorious King, you are full of goodness and strength: you mete out justice to the wicked, and deflate and bring low the proud. Foolish is he who struggles against you! Her own arrogance and pride have been the cause of this miserable woman's misfortune! Glorious God, I beseech you to forgive her foolishness. Lord, may you not find it necessary to avenge yourself on us according to our misdeeds. You are merciful and holy; do not permit the devil to pervert your justice. For her and for other wretches you suffered great hunger and cold, and you were poor and a beggar. You paid dearly to redeem us, but not with wealth or money: your blood was shed there for us, and your body hung on a cross. This unhappy woman who languishes here deeply repents her countless sins. Continuously, night and day, the devil loiters near her, for he would willingly draw her away with him. But I pray you, glorious King, grant her life long enough to repent of her folly!" (1117–1150).

When he had ended his prayer, he called the woman by name, raised his hand and blessed her with the sign of the cross, and she stood up, healthy and rejoicing. From her colour it did not appear that she had been bedridden a single day. Theocrita was amazed that her mother was healed in this fashion: she trembled and shook with fear because it seemed such a great miracle. She went out of her house and recounted the miracle to those she found in the street. People came from all around to witness it. But you can be assured of one thing: Giles would have preferred to be at Blois,[26] for the embarrassment the townspeople caused him (1151–68).

He was disturbed a great deal by the prolonged praise given him by these strangers. This miracle was related to the bishop of the city, who, when he learned of it, rejoiced and gave thanks to Our Lord. He asked how the miracle had happened, for he wanted to know all about it. The people said:

---

[26] 1167 **Blois** *Bleis*: the final word in this line (referring to the French city on the Loire river) seems to be used only to create a rhyme with *burgeis* "townspeople" (the final word in v. 1168). The meaning is that Giles would have preferred to be anywhere but there, since he did not wish to be praised for what God had done.

"A holy man came to us last night seeking shelter. We don't know where he is from, but we assuredly know that he is beloved of God."

The bishop spoke not a word in response, but had his archdeacon Aurelius summoned, who was in his house in the city. Urged by the messenger to come quickly, Aurelius came before the bishop.

"My lord," said the bishop, "have you not heard? I believe that God has come among us; he has sent us his servant who has performed a great miracle. He came late yesterday and lodged in the house of Theocrita. Her mother who had long been bedridden is now healthier than she ever was. This man is still there, I believe, and I would very much like to speak with him. Go to him, and have him brought to us so we can hear all about him, what sort of man he is and what region he comes from. Go quickly, without delay!"

"Willingly, my good lord," replied Aurelius (1170–1203).

The archdeacon came to the house where Giles had stayed, but did not find him, for he was not there: he had gone elsewhere in the city. Aurelius went looking throughout the city and found him in a church, offering prayers and doing penance. The archdeacon greeted him, asking about his travels, and in which country he had been born. Giles responded truthfully to all his queries. Aurelius accompanied him to the bishop, who gave him a fine lodging for the night. When the bishop had learned the facts of Giles' story, he held him in high esteem and honour. I believe he kept him at his court for two whole years. During the two years Giles spent there, God worked many miracles through him; I cannot begin to count the number of weak and crippled who were healed by him. Word of his deeds spread far and wide, which concerned Giles: he decided to live henceforth in Provence, and he crossed the Rhone in a boat (1204–28).

Between the Rhone and Montpellier the countryside is vast, filled with scrub woodlands and large deserts. There are many wild beasts, bears, lions, bucks and does, wild boars and sows, and fierce wild animals, elephants and horned beasts, vipers, tigers, tortoises, centaurs and hyenas,[27] and all manner of serpents. Giles had no fear whatsoever of these creatures, for he placed his trust completely in his good Lord. He entered the great woodlands and travelled along the shore of the Rhone. May God have pity on him, for he has abandoned everything for the love of God. If God does not protect him, he will starve, for he has nothing to eat;

---

[27] 1237 **centaurs and hyenas** *sagittaires e locerveres*: the centaur and other miraculous beasts are found in St. Jerome's life of Paul, the first hermit (PL 23. 23–24); the translation follows Frankis; see "Languages and Cultures in Contact," 118–20, for a discussion of this passage. See also Bozon's *Vie* of Paul the first hermit, vv. 95–98, 103–18, available online at http://margot.uwaterloo.ca/campsey/CmpBrowserFrame_e.html. Cf. Isaiah 13:21 (Vulgate).

The Life of Saint Giles   *105*

he has brought with him neither bread nor wine to make himself a meal in the morning, nor even enough food or provisions to feed a beetle! (1229–50).[28]

Giles penetrated into the forest of high branches and tall broom undergrowth. He saw neither cabin nor house, nor anyone to whom he could speak. He went so deep into the forest that he came upon a hermit who lived high up on a rock outcrop, which could be reached only with great difficulty. The rock spur was high and steep and to climb up it was perilous. The holy man who lived on the summit neither plowed nor tilled, for there was nothing but bare rock; nothing grew there, neither leeks nor chives, neither shallots nor onions, chervil, lettuce nor cress, nor anything that one could use for even as much as a single meal. Nonetheless he suffered neither hunger nor thirst, for God provided for him amply. He was much loved in that region, and sought after by people from many countries, who often came to see him, and he counselled them well. The sick from across the land came to him, seeking cures, and whoever asked him in good faith was healed, without fail (1250–78).

Giles went around the base of the cliff, disappointed that he could not find a path to the top. Then by chance he came upon stairs cut into the rock. He climbed up the steps and at the top found Veredemius (such was the hermit's name).[29] The latter came out of his house, for God had shown him earlier that one of his servants would come to him. When he saw Giles he knew who he was. He paid him the honour which was his due, leading him back into his shelter, and setting about making him welcome. Giles and Veredemius were together, high on this rock, with no pride or vanity on either side. Each loved the other as himself, and they rejoiced in one another's company, for they both led holy lives. One was Greek, the other French: our Lord is most gracious,[30] who has brought together in this way two men from such distant countries.

The whole countryside gains renown from these two men, and I will tell you why: under heaven there is no one so afflicted with leprosy, so crippled or maimed or stricken with gout, so palsied, so fevered, misshapen or hunchbacked, lacking an arm or blind or mute, that, if he were presented to one of these two, he would not be cured by their prayer. Two years and more, I believe, they lived together in holiness. Their life together was very saintly and pure, but one day an unexpected incident happened which caused them to part ways. But to this

---

[28] 1249 **not even enough . . . beetle** *ne tant que vaille un hanetun*: lit. "a beetle's worth of food and provisions."

[29] 1284 **Veredemius** *Veredemïus*: recorded in the *Acta Sanctorum* as a bishop of Avignon (feast 15 June), and as a hermit who lived near Uzès (probably the same person, feast 23 August); see Laurent, *SGilles*, 81, and Jones 45–46. No documentation on Veredemius is preserved before the *Vita sancti Aegidii*, but he continued to be a popular rural saint into the modern era.

[30] 1300 **gracious** *curteis*: again the adj. *curteis* qualifies God; cf. notes to vv. 137, 353.

day I have yet to hear of a reason as fitting as this for the separation of two such companions (1279–1318).

One day Giles rose early to take some exercise out in the countryside. Four men passed by, with a fifth man carried on a litter pulled by two horses;[31] the man was complaining bitterly that he had long languished in illness. Now good fortune shone on the four men transporting their companion, for they came upon Giles in the open countryside. They approached and addressed him; he bowed and responded in kind, and asked who they were. They replied,

"My lord, we have sought you from afar, from another country, and we will tell you the reason. See this wretched man in the litter who has been ill for more than seven years: he was formerly a rich landowner, and although he has spent everything on doctors, it is to no avail. Now he has come to you, and you must help him" (1319–40).

"My lords," responded Giles, "I assure you, you have come to the wrong person: it is not for me that you have come. My lords, you have made a great mistake; it seems that your travels have been in vain. If you wish that your companion be restored to health, you should look elsewhere. I am a poor man from a foreign country, and I came here to stay with the hermit who lives on this rock outcrop. I have been here for some time, living humbly with him. Anyone who in good faith asks his advice and help will be given it, without fail" (1341–54).

"Sir," they replied, "for pity's sake tell us the true story of the man who lives up there: what is his name?"

"He is called Veredemius."

"And what is your name?"

"I am called Giles."

"May Our Lord be praised that we have found you here, for we have been looking for you, thanks be to God!"

"And why have you been looking for me?"

"[. . .] for you."[32]

"I assure you that I have no skill in medicine, and cannot help your companion in any way."

"But you can pray to God on his behalf."

"That I can certainly do, but I am not sure that it will help him!"

"If you pray for him, we know for a certainty that God will do it, that he will be cured."

"Do you think so?"

"We know this to be the case!"

"Pray with me, then, that because of your good faith, God will quickly give him relief from his illness."

---

[31] 1322 **a litter**: this litter is explicitly mentioned later, v. 1334.
[32] 1363 **For you** *Pur tei*: the line is incomplete in the manuscript.

The Life of Saint Giles

Giles saw, and fully understood, that his attempt to send them away was useless; they were very determined (they all had prostrated themselves at his feet!) and would never stop pleading, no matter what he said to them, until he had done what they had asked of him (1355–81).

Much troubled in thought and filled with doubts, Giles withdrew a short distance from them; tears streamed down his face: with much fear and awe he called on God, his Lord, that he take true pity on him, and send him wise counsel.

"Lord, omnipotent King," he prayed, "you who have created everything out of the void, to which all things will return when it is your will that they do so; all things are subject to your will, you grant life to all according to your pleasure.[33] God of glory, most high King, do not scorn my plea! Do not look upon my sins or my wickedness, but show us your grace by restoring health to this unfortunate man. He has come here from another country and another region seeking his health, and asks that I help him. I now beseech you, God, that he not fail in his quest; I trust that his belief and his good faith will stand him in good stead. The illness has greatly weakened him; he has already been much chastened, and is repentant of his folly. Grant him a life long enough, with physical strength and health, that he may make penance for his sins against your will!" (1382–1414).

While Giles prayed, our Lord performed a miracle on his behalf, for the invalid was healed.

"Truly," his companions cried out, "may God be praised and thanked for his mercy!"

Then they took their leave of Giles and returned to their own country, but Giles remained troubled in thought. He thanked God, our Lord, who had done this miracle out of his love:

"Lord God," he prayed, "what am I to do? How am I to conduct my life? I have lived here with this man, Veredemius, who has done me great honour, and I would willingly stay much longer, for his way of life is much to my liking; it is very seemly, holy, and chaste. But when Veredemius hears of this miracle, he will wish to honour me even more and devote his goodness to me. If I look for earthly praise, all my efforts will have been in vain—it is not for this that I left my extensive lands and came here! God knows I am looking for just the opposite, and I will now look elsewhere for shelter, for I can no longer stay here. I will go out into this wilderness; if I cannot find peace there, I will never find it.[34] If I ask Veredemius' permission to leave, I will not be granted it without it causing him pain. I do not wish to trouble him or cause him greater suffering. For this reason it is better to part from him than to remain here as a source of upset. I plan to go to a region where no one will look for me. May God grant honour to Veredemius, for through his love of God he has been good to me!" (1415–54).

---

[33] Cf. Psalm 103: 29 (Vulgate).

[34] 1444 **I will never find it** *jo ne la querai dunc ja meis*: lit. "I will never again seek it."

With these words, he set out on his way. May Saint Martin guide him! He made his way through the wooded desert, looking for a hermitage where he might find relief from the demands of people looking for him. He continued travelling through the wasteland until he came to a deserted spot where he found a large cave, with a wide entrance. It had once been a pleasant place to shelter, but now was overgrown by brambles, thorns, and bushes. In front of the entrance was a small stream created by a spring flowing there, with sweet water running down through it. In the gravel bed of the stream grew brightly coloured cress. Giles saw this welcoming spot, and thanked our Lord; he was very pleased to have found it and would not have exchanged it for a whole county. He lay there all night, without eating or drinking. The next day, when it was light, he began to clear away the brush. The gravel bed of the stream passed inside this handsome cave; he made his sleeping quarters to one side of the cave, using branches which he had collected and brought in. He completed his shelter by gathering grass to cover the branches.

Giles spent three years in this deserted place, worshipping and serving and believing in God alone. During the three years he was there he neither saw nor heard another human being, nor did he eat bread or anything made from grains, nor did he eat meat or fish; instead, he lived all this time in the wild, eating only roots and water cress (1455–95).

But listen now to how our Lord provided for him in fine fashion. After Giles had built his shelter, he prayed to our Lord that he have pity on him, and send him guidance so that he would not be lacking in any way in his service to God.

My lords, listen now to this great miracle: there, while Giles was in his small house, worshipping God and praying inside his shelter, he saw a wild doe come directly up to his hermit's hut. It was a beautiful hind, and it came right to the entrance[35] of the cave, following a path which it had found. She slipped in among the branches,[36] without fear, and came right in to the cave. Her udder was large and full of milk, and she lay down at Giles' feet, as if to offer herself to him. Giles saw the doe lying at his feet, and he was greatly heartened, since he believed that God had sent her to him.[37] All the time that he was there in the desert he lived on the milk of the doe. And hear how the deer served him: by day she went to pasture in the wilds; when it was dinnertime, there was no need to go out to fetch the doe, for she always knew the right time and you can be sure that she was never late in coming directly back into the cave. She was a beautiful, large, sleek doe: there was never, nor will there ever be, a more magnificent one anywhere

---

[35] 1510 **came right to the entrance** *vint tut dreit a la venele*: the meaning of *venele* is normally "alley, small street," but here means "passageway" or "entrance."

[36] 1512 **slipped in among the branches** *entre les branches se musçat*: lit. "hid itself among, or between, the branches."

[37] 1519 **since he believed** *kar ben suschad*: the sense of this verb is usually "suspect"; cf. Laurent, *SGilles*, 95.

The Life of Saint Giles 109

in the whole country. To one side of the clearing by the cave Giles made a small stall for her, where she lay at night to avoid the cold, and every morning she left to go out to pasture. For many days, God's servant lived only with food such as I have described to you; drinking as much as he wanted, he suffered from neither illness nor hunger (1496–1540).

During the period I am speaking about, the king of Toulouse, Gascony, Provence, and Burgundy was named Flovent.[38] He was a strong and powerful king who paid a yearly tribute to Charles, then the king of France. Flovent was very courtly, having been educated in France. He was devoted to courtly pursuits, and he particularly loved his dogs and hunting birds, of which he owned many excellent specimens: goshawks, gyrfalcons, sparrowhawks; pointers, bloodhounds, and greyhounds.[39] His household was well stocked with game; he took many deer and fallow-deer, roebucks, does, and wild game; he didn't give up the chase until the hunting pack had brought down their prey. When the prey could not escape elsewhere it fled to the Rhone, which was close by; there the hunters took their game, sometimes three or four a day. The prime season for hunting deer is during Advent, close to Christmas, when everyone returns home (1541–67).

Flovent was at Montpellier and he summoned his vassals, of all estates, both great and small, to come to his court at Christmas, for, as he said, he wished to have a lavish and elegant feast. The summons was given on very short notice: his servants threw themselves into the task, each according to his duties, and they brought in many provisions in preparation for the king's feast. The master huntsman, whose task it was to do this, went each day into the wilds, and took his choice among the most beautiful does that he found in the woods (1568–82).

One day he rose early and went directly to the forest, taking two packs of hounds; even the less capable pack could capture two deer each day. He set the greyhounds on the scent, while he had the kennel-men hold back on leash the more excited dogs. He passed through the woods for some time without seeing a doe to his liking. He went up and down the forest trails until[40] [. . .] he was

---

[38] 1542 **Flovent** *Flovenz*: the protagonist of a lost *chanson de geste*, where he is the first king of France and nephew of Emperor Constantine of Rome; cf. Laurent, *SGilles*, 97.

[39] 1554 **pointers, bloodhounds, and greyhounds** *seüs e veautres e levrers*: the breeds used for hunting have evolved since the twelfth century, making it difficult to be precise with respect to the nomenclature, and this translation only approximates the different kinds of hunting dogs. A *seüs* was a hunting dog bred for its running ability and its skill in flushing game; a *veautre* was a dog bred for its strength, not speed, and was used for hunting bears and boars; a *levrer* was a dog bred for speed and used for hunting hares. Cf. Laurent, *SGilles*, 99. For details on the arts of falconry and hunting, along with training of hunting birds and dogs, see Armand Strubel and Chantal de Saulnier, *La Poétique de la chasse au Moyen Age: les livres de chasse du XIVe siècle* (Paris: PUF, 1994), 97–125.

[40] 1591–92 **up and down . . . until** *Tant est alez aval, amunt / par les destreiz qui el bois sunt*: the first part only of the compound conjunction *tant que* ("until") is expressed, and

overjoyed when he spotted the doe: he unleashed the whole pack and let them run in pursuit of it. May God protect the doe! If she doesn't escape more quickly she will find herself in a very bad pass![41] The hind heard the approaching pack of dogs, and began to flee into the forest: despite the doe's many ruses, the hunters kept the chase close. The dogs followed the scent, without being misled elsewhere in the forest, and stayed close to the deer, in hot pursuit through the undergrowth, baying with great excitement.[42] When the doe saw that the dogs were getting close, she retreated to her refuge, and entered the cave, terrified and covered in sweat. Giles saw her, and was saddened; with tears streaming down his face he begged God to protect the hind, his source of nourishment, from harm.[43] He sprinkled the deer with cold water until she had recovered her breath, then led her into his shelter, telling her to rest there. The dogs came chasing after the doe, followed by the hallooing hunters. The hind was unafraid and fearless, for the dogs had lost the scent; no dog could get closer to her than the distance of an arrrow's flight.[44] They searched around and about, examining and looking under every little bush and branch, until they all were worn out and exhausted. When they had lost the scent completely the hounds began to howl. The master-huntsman spurred his horse forward to join the howling dogs: he was amazed at their behaviour, wondering why they were baying in distress. He was infuriated and almost burst into a rage of frustration as he began to search for the deer, crying out hunting calls and blowing his hunting horn. As the day was short, dusk was already falling, and the dogs were tired of running; they had exhausted

---

the second part (*que*) is missing since there is a gap in the text after 1592; the lacuna is at least two lines, omitting the narrative of the hunter's initial sighting of the doe which feeds Giles.

[41] 1598 **she will find herself in a very bad pass!** *ja erent li merel mestreit*: Laurent gives *mestrer le merel* "jouer un mauvais jeu," and notes that a *merel* "a token, coin," was normally given by a seller to the purchaser as a proof of payment. The adj. *mestreit* (from *mestraire*) means "tricked, cheated." The *AND* refers to the game of merels, and translates this passage as "things will turn out badly!"

[42] 1608 **baying with great excitement** *tut esbaés* [Ms *esbae*] *pur le grant chalt*" Laurent's emendation is unnecessary (*esbaé* is the masc. nom. pl. form, so no final -s is needed). *Lit.* "open-mouthed because of the great heat." The great heat is caused by the dogs' excitement. This translation adds sound ("baying") to the open mouths of the running dogs. The meaning here is the literal sense of "open-mouthed," as opposed to the more usual figurative sense "amazed, dumbstruck." This translation transfers the phrase *le grant chalt* to qualify the pursuit, and adds sound to the open mouths of the dogs.

[43] 1613 **the hind, his source of nourishment** *sa nurice*: a periphrastic translation is substituted for the literal meaning of the only word used here to refer to the doe (*nurice* "wet-nurse").

[44] 1623 **than the distance of an arrow's flight** *de tant cum get d'un arc manier*: lit. "a shot from a hand bow" or "longbow," as opposed to a "crossbow."

themselves and found nothing. The master-huntsman called off his dogs and left (1583–1642).

He went straight back to Montpellier, where he found the king dining in the midst of his large court, surrounded by his noblemen. The valets who served the high table were dressed not in rough English woolens, but in cloaks lined with miniver and ermine, in mantles of silk and oriental fabrics.[45] The master-huntsman, dressed as he was, came up to the king, who saw him and said jokingly,

"Where have you been all this time? Is the day so short that you now hunt deer by night? You have ravaged the whole countryside; there is no prey that you have not caught. If you take all the game now, what will you hunt next year? 'He who eats all his seed grain in one year will do penance for this for the next seven years.' You really should leave some game to replenish the future forest stock!" (1643–64).

"My lord," he replied, "this is not a joking matter! Tomorrow you can yourself test your best dogs, which you value so highly; today I found them so worn out that they could not follow me one step further."

The king was astounded, and asked what prey had outrun the pack.

"My lord," he said, "it was a hind, the most beautiful I have seen since the day I was born. Indeed, I am disappointed, but I can say without shame that there is no other deer like her. She did not flee far, for I know the deep thicket where we left her, and tomorrow morning we will try again to find her there."

He remounted his horse and went to take off his hunting gear. He returned to his quarters, where his friends welcomed him. He ate a copious meal and afterwards drank mulled wine; when his bed was ready he retired and slept soundly all night long (1665–90).

Early next morning, just at the break of day, the watchman on the tower sounded his horn. The huntsman had not forgotten, and at this call of dawn he arose and summoned his kennel-men to take the dog pack and the hare-hounds, and their choice of the best hounds, to go directly into the forest. They left at once, without delay, and went into the woods. The dog-handlers came straight to the place where they had been the day before, and saw the doe pasturing; with their hunting horns they called the master of the hunt to come quickly. But their calls were unnecessary, for he was coming as fast as he could. And he was leading no small number of people with him! In the king's household, there was no servant who knew anything about the forest, who had not brought a dog with him. And all had bragged that even if they had to hunt both day and night they would continue the pursuit until this great doe had been captured (1691–1714).

They came to where the others were waiting and all dismounted. The sun was shining, the day was fine, and the youths were filled with impatience and said they could wait no longer: they set all the dogs loose at once. The hind heard

---

[45] 1650 **mantles of silk and oriental fabrics** *ciclatuns e osterins*: another example of clothing as a marker of social distinction; cf. note to v. 848.

the cry of the hounds, and was not slow to move off: as soon as she heard the tumult and saw the pack coming toward her, she raised her head, twitched her ears, and moved with miraculous speed. She circled the woods three times before coming back to the safety of her master who was waiting for her. He was overjoyed to see her, for he well knew that she was being hunted. He reproved and chastised her, saying that she had gone too far into the wilds: he would be badly off if she were captured. The hounds chasing after her came close to the cave, but stayed outside it, howling, barking and baying, just as they had done the day before. Their handlers were reduced to rage: they shouted and cried out their hunting calls to the hounds, striking and beating and urging them on. They surrounded the cave, and it was only by the merest chance that they did not find the doe. Night was falling, and they left, having failed to achieve their goal; they were completely frustrated and enraged (1715–47).

They returned to Montpellier and came before the king. Word for word, they recounted how the doe had eluded them, and they considered themselves to have been mocked by her. The king made the sign of the cross, and sent for the bishop from the city of Nîmes, who was a worthy and loyal man. The king loved and trusted him, for he was a pure and chaste man. The messenger came to him and said:

"My lord, the king sends you his greetings, with assurances of his friendship and support, and requests that you come without delay to his court, where he awaits you."

"Dear friend," he replied, "indeed, I will come as quickly as I can."

He asked for his palfrey and went to the king at his court, who rose up to meet him and paid him great honour.

"Sire," he declared, "I will tell you the reason I sent for you. Anyone who asks advice of good people never later regrets having done so. In my view, when you hear this, you will think it is a great miracle. My most skilled huntsmen have hunted for two days in these woods, and found a doe; I don't know if it is a magic creature, for on each of the two days they have lost it in the same fashion, and they don't know how it disappears. They don't know where to look for it, any more than if it had hidden itself somewhere in the earth, for each time it escapes the hounds somewhere in the woods below Septimania and all their efforts to find it are in vain. All their reports make me despair of ever taking it. I want to go on a hunt for it tomorrow, and neither forest nor plain will prevent me from discovering the truth of this matter.[46] Let the huntsmen and dog-handlers be ready at the break of dawn. There is not a single greyhound, no hound large or small, bloodhound, pointer, or foxhound that will stay behind, they will all come with me tomorrow: let everyone prepare himself for the hunt!" (1748–98).

---

[46] 1790–1 **neither forest nor plain will prevent me from discovering the truth of this matter** *ne la guarad ne bois ne plein / ke jo ne sache ke ço est*: lit. "the forest and plain will not protect it [the doe] so that I do not know the truth of this matter."

The king ordered his valets to bring their strong hounds:[47]

"Tomorrow we shall see which one is the swiftest!"

The youths welcomed this news, and were gladdened by the king's summons, and each one set about preparing what was necessary for the hunt. But their frenetic preparations would be for nothing, for their prey would skillfully escape from them![48]

"My lord bishop," cried the king, "come take some sport with me. I have frequently heard it said that holy religious men often take up dwellings in the forest! If God has favoured us with such a man who has taken shelter in our woods, we will all rejoice!"

The bishop replied:

"I accept, and since I see that this is your wish, I will go there with you."

Having asked permission to leave he returned to his lodging; God willing, he would join the hunt in the forest.

Early in the morning, at the break of dawn, King Flovent arose, and dressed and equipped himself to hunt in the woods. He sent for the bishop, asking for him to prepare himself quickly, and to come join him at court. The bishop was quick to do so, and arrived at court fully equipped, but the king would not set out until he had heard mass, which the bishop celebrated in a small chapel. After mass they ate a meal, then mounted their horses and went into the forest. They came to the place where the hunters had lost sight of the doe and where they had pursued it the day before, and the king dismounted. The king ordered his men to search the woods for the doe, and they found her in a clearing where she had been pasturing all morning. With their fingers they pointed out the doe to each other, and came back to the king to say that they had found the deer. The king sent his hunters to take up their positions, and ordered his archers to be at the ready. He sent in his excited dogs first, unleashing seven score to charge in together: the whole forest resounded and trembled. The doe heard the tumult echoing through the forest and saw the hounds rushing towards her. She ran for the safety of her shelter, with the hunters hallooing after her (1799–1852).

She fled with great speed down her well-known path toward her refuge. The king was stationed at a hunting blind, and saw the hind coming in his direction.

---

[47] 1800 **their strong hounds** *lur berserez*: the *AND* (s.v. *berselet*) cites Latin glosses *molosus* and *venaticus*, both suggesting that this is a strong hound.

[48] 1805–6 **But their frenetic preparations . . . escape from them** *meis pur neënt funt tel barete / kar li cors ert assez a erte*: the passage is problematic and the French text is cited from the edition of Paris & Bos. They do not emend, but suggest that one could correct *barete* to *barate*, and *a erte* to *a aate*; Laurent (*SGilles*, 114) emends, following this suggestion, and glosses *cors* as *la course*; I suggest that *cors* could also mean the body of the prey, in this case the doe; MS *a erte* = *aarte*, which is glossed "adroit, skilful" or "well-formed," "suitable, fine" in the *AND*, and these senses apply well to the nature of the hunted deer which will escape from them.

He immediately spurred on his horse, which went quickly in pursuit, and he came so close to the doe that he discovered where she was hiding. If the doe had not been as swift as she was, she would have come to grief, and she would have feared that she was about to be killed (1853–63).[49]

Giles heard this commotion, and the loud cries of the hunters, who were scattered throughout the woods, and he was filled with fear for his doe and prayed that God would protect her. He came out of his retreat to discover the whereabouts of the doe and stood in the shadow of a tree where no one noticed him. The doe came running up to him, for she had no other protector; she slipped through the narrow entrance to the shelter and disappeared inside. Close by was an archer who saw the deer disappear between the branches. The evil arrow he loosed that day was the worst he ever shot! Just as the doe passed the entrance, he let fly the arrow which struck straight into Giles' body, where he was standing outside his cave to see the doe. The blow he received was severe, and he suffered greatly because of the large wound, from which blood streamed down his body to his feet. He thanked our Lord, and quickly moved back; he did not attempt to stanch the wound, but instead let the blood flow from it freely (1864–92).

The king then put his hunting horn to his lips and blew long and loud, four times, to alert his men, who came quickly. The king stood next to the cave, and the dogs rushed up, along with the kennel-men and the huntsmen, eager to put their hounds to the test. For a good three leagues—this is no lie—you could have heard the forest echoing with their cries. They came up to the king, who had dismounted beneath a tree. He commanded them all to be silent, and called for the bishop to come to him. Together they withdrew to one side.

"My lord," he said, "in my view, the doe we are hunting has some special protection. I have discovered the entrance here through which she passed, but a man can scarcely squeeze through it. Let us go to see what sort of place it is to which the deer escapes" (1893–1915).

Both men went in that direction and pushed their way into the heart of the thicket sheltering Giles and his hind. With great effort and exertion they found their way in, and they discovered a place of great beauty. Trees, which had been planted all around it, each bearing fruit in its season, occupied the whole area: quince, pearmains,[50] peaches and figs, almonds and service-berries, and many other kinds of fruits which exude sweet fragrances. There in his shelter they found Giles, his face without colour, pale and livid. It is no wonder that he was distressed: blood was streaming down his body. His clothing was tattered and

---

[49] 1862–3 **she would have come to grief ... be killed** *oïe eüst dure nuvele / del quir perdre oüst grant poür*: the original passage uses more concrete images: "she would have heard bad news, she would have feared greatly that she would lose part of her hide."

[50] 1925 **quince, pearmains, peaches and figs** *coinz, permeines, pesches e fies*: Paris & Bos emend to *cooinz, permeins, pesches e fies*. The origin of *permein* is obscure; the *AND* glosses as "pearmain, variety of apple or pear."

The Life of Saint Giles

torn, hanging in pieces; he wore the same garments day and night, since he had nothing better. The doe lay at her master's feet, with no wish to go outside to find pasture. The bishop drew the king's attention to this scene:

"My lord, do you see what I see? We should not be surprised if our hunting pack failed yesterday! God, who makes the doe a servant to his servant, was protecting her.[51] We would be sinners to doubt this! Let us approach and greet him."

They advanced with cautious steps. Giles seemed not to notice, but the king came forward and said:

"My lord, we wish you no harm![52] If you have been sent here by God, speak to us, my lord, for pity's sake. Tell us, sire, about your way of life, what rule you follow,[53] and what God you serve. We have come to you in private, without fear, and we want to ask you who you are and where you were born. Tell us, sire, in the spirit of charity, how long have you lived here?" (1916–60).

Giles sat down, listened, and raised his head to look at them. When he heard them speak of God tears began to flow from his eyes. Out of joy and tenderness he completely forgot his suffering and no longer felt distressed.

"My lords," he responded, "may God protect you! If you would care to stay, food and lodging are prepared for you."

They sat down beside him, and asked him who he was and in what country he had been born; and he told them the whole truth. The king saw that Giles was bleeding heavily. He wanted to tear his tunic into strips to bandage the wound and stop the flow of blood, but Giles would not permit it: he preferred to let his blood flow out of his body.

He spoke gently to them:

"My lords, you ask me how I came to this wilderness, and what I live on? I will tell you my true story: I was born in Greece and educated in Athens. I left there because of my sins, and came to this region. I came into this wood looking for a good site, and found here, in this welcoming spot, all I could want of plants and water. I dwell here just as you see me, and I have always had enough plants and roots and milk. To feed me, God sent me this doe standing here. I don't know who wishes to take her away from me. This morning I went outside to see where she was, for I was greatly distressed on her account. She came fleeing

---

[51] 1943–44 **God . . . protecting her** *ben la deveit celui guarir / ki ci la feit sun serf servir*: "Whoever makes her the servant of his servant is the one who was protecting her."

[52] 1950 **we wish you no harm** *saf seies tu*: lit. "may you be safe, unharmed." The word *saf* has multiple resonances in this context, since it could mean that the king wishes Giles no harm, or that he wishes him health from his wounds. The sense is perhaps both: the king wishes Giles to feel reassured that he will not be harmed by him, and that he will also seek medical help for his wound.

[53] 1954 **what rule you follow** *quele lei tens*: lit. "what law you obey." Laurent, *SGilles*,125, translates as "quelle religion vous suivez." Here "rule" is used to suggest a monastic order.

straight to me and slipped into her hiding place. I don't know who shot the arrow which has given me this body wound,[54] but may God forgive him his sin. He did not know I was here. All this, and much more, I deserve. In the country where I was born I was named Giles; I was baptized with this name and it will never be changed. Now that I have told you the truth about myself, I would also like to know your names and who you are" (1961–2015).

The king replied:

"It is only right that we answer you candidly. This man is a consecrated bishop, and I am a rich, strong and powerful man, king of this country. All this land is under my rule, land and sea, woods and plains. I am truly sorry for the wound which severely afflicts you, but I will immediately have very good doctors come here to heal you. Bread and wine, meat and fish, clothes and other provisions—whatever you need—will be brought to you without delay!" (2016–30).

"My lord," said Giles, "I thank you, but be assured of one thing: no doctor will touch me; I will be healed when it pleases God. If it was his will that I be unafflicted I would not have received this wound. Our Lord is grateful to you for the help and provisions that you offer me, but none of that will be needed here: I have as much food as I wish, and at present I have no need for new clothing or other provisions. What I have is sufficient, nor am I even worthy of that, for I barely deserve my blessings, and am not thankful enough to God for them!" (2031–46).

The king and the bishop offered to share their possessions with him, but he did not wish to accept. Speaking among themselves, they marvelled that the holy man did not want to accept any of their aid, nor relief from his painful wound. They knelt before him to take their leave:

"Sir," they asked, "we beg you to remember us in your prayers. We will return here to see you, in secret and without ceremony, and no one will know about it except us."

"My lords," he responded, "mark that you do, for I wish to remain unknown except to you who have seen me, for if God had wished to conceal me it would have been difficult for you to find me. You, my lord king, I beseech you to come here no longer to hunt. Leave my nurse in peace!"

The king laughed. He said that he would no longer approach, pursue, or frighten the hind, and then he and the bishop immediately mounted their horses, and rode on until they had returned to their city. The king was overjoyed and set about in good spirits to celebrate with his people (2047–76).

Giles remained in the forest where his wound was growing worse and he cried out in pain. He felt very weak for he had lost a lot of blood, and he had no cloth large enough to bind his wound.

---

[54] 2005 **given me this body wound** *si m'ad aukes al cors blescé*: lit. "wounded me a little in the body." The adv. *aukes* "somewhat; a little," suggests that Giles is downplaying the seriousness of his wound. This use of litotes is an echo of *chanson de geste* humour.

"Oh God," he sighed, "King of creation, Lord, I worship and praise you; may you be thanked, Lord, for all that you have given me. I have commended myself to you: may your will be done regarding your servant. My wound is causing me suffering; I am weaker than normal. It is right that I feel unwell, so that I may suppress the demands of my flesh, for if my body dominated my spirit, it would later be very difficult to regain control of my impulses. 'Whoever places too great a burden on his shoulders realizes his folly when he starts to walk.'[55] I took on a great burden, but it will now be adjusted. I am weighed down by wicked weeds, that is, by pride and haughtiness. The pain I now feel is going to restrain me severely, but in my view I suffer very little. Lord God, Alpha and Omega, you who created me, who formed me in your own image, and saved us all: You became flesh in the womb of the Virgin who is so chaste and pure and beautiful, and you were born of her as a child, according to your wish and your pleasure, in the city of Bethlehem, close to Jerusalem. There you were sought out by the kings Gaspar, Melchior, and Balthasar.[56] They brought you gold and incense and each present had a separate meaning; the third present was precious myrrh which symbolizes mortal flesh.[57] You reigned and preached your holy name in the world according to your will. The Jews were filled with envy and betrayed you to martyrdom; with great perfidy they raised you on the cross, then you were laid in the tomb. On the third day you arose from death and went directly to hell to deliver your followers who had been condemned because of Adam. Then you ascended to heaven to your Father. Now you have your sweet mother beside you, who comforts the downtrodden, the sinners, and the wretched. As I know well that what I say is true, and truly believe it, I beseech you that I may never be healed of this

---

[55] 2095–96 **Whoever places too great . . . to walk** *Ki trop grant fes met sur sun col, / al departir se tent pur fol:* Laurent, *SGilles*, 133, notes that this is close to the proverb *Nus ne doit feis emprendre qu'il ne puisse porter* "no one should take on a burden that he cannot carry," citing Schulze-Busaker, *Proverbes,* no. 1407. In the following lines Giles calls his burdens of pride and haughtiness "wicked weeds," perhaps to suggest their persistent presence.

[56] 2113–14 **Gaspar, Melchior and Balthazar** *Jaspar / e Melchior e Baltasar*: the names of the Magi circulated in the West only after 1158, date of the supposed discovery of their tombs in Milan; their use here provides a *terminus post quem* for the dating of the *Vie de s. Gilles.* See Paris & Bos, xxv–xxvii; Laurent, *SGilles*, 135.

[57] 2115–18 **They brought you gold . . . mortal flesh** *or te porterent e encens / e en chascun out divers sens / li terz present fud mirre chier / a mortel charn signifier*: although there is no break in the rhyme, Laurent, following Paris & Bos, states that there are at least two lines missing after v. 2116, on the grounds that the usual symbolic meanings of gold and incense are not explicitly stated (only the meaning of the third gift is mentioned). The gifts of the Magi were seen as symbolically representing the triple nature of Christ, as God (incense), king (gold), and mortal man (myrrh). See Laurent, *SGilles*, 135, who cites H. Leclercq, "Épiphanie," *Dictionnaire d'archéologie chrétienne et de liturgie* 5 (1922): cols. 197–201.

pain. I do not seek a cure, for I never wish to leave here. It is for this reason that I left my friends and my great estates and my country, to come here in search of suffering. The king of this region now wants to provide me with clothing and provisions. My own parents were wealthy; they had ample furs and pelts, and rich raiments of purple and dark-coloured silks and taffetas,[58] so if I had wished to wear fine garments I would not have needed to leave Greece. But I care nothing for riches and find neither enjoyment nor pride in my wealth, but seek instead the suffering of my body."

All his life Giles remained steadfast in this: his wound remained unhealed until the day he died (2077–2154).

The king dearly loved Giles and came often to see him privately on visits that were not known to anyone in his kingdom. The king frequently urged Giles to accept something as a gift from him, but Giles refused completely, and would take no present, either large or small. The king beseeched him every day:

"Sir," he pleaded, "for the love of God accept some small gift from me. I will feel ill at ease, and will not return to see you unless you accept something from me, either silver or gold, for I have a great treasure of both. Hear my prayer, my lord: I have all manner of wealth; accept as much as you desire, from among my vessels and costly garments, my gold and silver. If you do not wish it for your own use, have it all shared among the poor, or given away wherever you like!" (2155–77).

When Giles heard him he was deeply saddened.

"In God's name," he replied, "dear lord king, believe me, and drop this request. The wealth you wish to give me you yourself could use in a worthwhile manner, and I will explain how. Take your vessels and your silver, and a part of your land, and found an abbey, placing in it monks to serve God, furnishing them with all they need to pray night and day for you and your people and the faith" (2178–90).

The king responded:

"I will gladly do this. If you grant me one thing, for which I plead and beg you, I will have the monastery built immediately, and I will grant it enough income from lands and woods, vineyards and meadows, and I will furnish it with all that is necessary for those who will reside there under monastic rule. Otherwise, be assured that I will provide it with nothing from my wealth, not a single Rouen penny![59] And I will tell you, in short, my one condition: if you accept to be their abbot, their leader, father, and master, I will quickly have the abbey built, the dormitory, the chapter house and good cellars, the guest house and refectory, all fine, well-furnished buildings!" (2191–2208).

---

[58] 2145–46 **rich raiments** ... *pailes, cendals purpres e bis*: the narrator is repeating the litany of earthly wealth given earlier; cf. note to v. 267.

[59] 2201 **not a single Rouen penny** *ne tant ki vaille un romesin*: a small coin from Rouen, with little value.

Giles listened. He heard one thing in this proposal which bothered him greatly: he feared accepting the burden of the cure of souls, while at the same time he understood with certainty that the king would do nothing unless he accepted the role of pastor.

"My lord," he said, "for the love of God I will do everything you ask, rather than prevent the abbey from being built, for the blame would fall on me if the monastery remained unfounded. Because you have placed the responsibility for this on me, I will tell you what causes me concern, and why this is so: I am not a strong man, I am weak and filled with doubts, and not suited to govern, and you must bear the ultimate responsibility."[60]

The king replied, giving assurances that Giles would be father and abbot of the community, and Giles agreed to this arrangement. As it was now growing late, the king departed, content with the agreement which had been reached (2209–31).

In the woods the preparations began, with stone, lime, and mortar; the foundations for two churches were laid. The larger, in which the convent was established, was dedicated to St. Peter and was built with strong pillars and a high tower, and granted land and endowments. When the church was ready the king installed a fine group of worthy men and wise clerics who read and sang exuberantly; the king attracted many men to be members of this community. Then the king summoned Giles before him, and placed the monastery under his direction; thus, against his will, and without having sought to purchase it by simony, Giles received the gift of the abbacy (2232–48).[61]

I have read nothing further regarding the doe which had served Giles for such a long time; and, having found nothing else in my source, I will not write more about her.

The king furnished the abbey well with an abundance of books, chasubles, albs and tunics, silken capes and dalmatics, shrines and crosses and candelabras, reliquaries and censers, basins, lamps and phials, monastic shirts, frocks,

---

[60] 2226 **you must bear . . . responsibility** *sur vus estot le feis turner*: the agreement is not explicitly stated, but we construe it to be that the king will supervise the building, while Giles will be the spiritual father of the flock (without the administrative responsibility for the buildings and the estates, usually part of the duties of an abbot). The king will continue to provide material support to the convent after it is built, and Giles will have the cure of souls.

[61] 2247–48 **against his will, . . . gift of the abbacy** *estre sun gré, senz simonie, / reçut le dun de l'abbeïe*: Laurent, *SGilles*, 143, notes that "simony," the name for the abuse of purchasing religious office, is derived from the name of Simon the Magician who attempted to buy the power of miracles from Peter (Acts 8:20). Common in the tenth and eleventh centuries, simony was widely condemned by the Gregorian reforms.

and cowls,[62] dossals, wall hangings and tapestries, ecclesiastical chairs and swivel-backed benches, oil and incense and worked-metal vessels. Once he had the monks well equipped, the king began the construction of another, much smaller, building in which the abbot was housed, next to the large monastery. Because of his infirmities the holy man lived apart from the others; Giles spent night and day in fasting and prayer, in vigils and self-mortification. He wished for no other distraction, taking great pleasure in this privation. The king returned there often for he gladly listened to Giles speak, and he came back as well to encourage the monks, for he greatly admired their way of life (2249–80).

One day the king went there with a small retinue of only three companions. Giles heard him coming and went out to meet him, emerging slowly from his dwelling. The king was overjoyed to see him. He dismounted in the courtyard and went over to embrace him.

"Giles," he cried, "I will tell you the reward I will give you for having come out to meet me despite your physical suffering. I will increase the size of this monastery such that no king that comes after me could ever add more to it in a single day than I now do. In a single grant I will extend the domains of the monastery by five leagues all around the site, both fields and woods, to be held without fees as an act of charity by me. This grant of land is so completely free of obligation that you will soon forget that it ever belonged to me!"

They went into the church together and, at the altar, the king confirmed his gift, for the benefits I have described to you had been put in writing in a charter. Whatever may happen later, either in time of war or peace, the abbey will never lose these lands (2281–2308).

Giles loved and served God, spending both night and day in prayer; he was completely without self-pride. God often came to him and performed fine miracles through him, so that he was much loved by the people of Provence, and by those from Gascony as well as Provence: all revered him. Well might they cherish and honour him, and they could indeed rejoice that God had sent them such a man, for they received from him wise counsel for their good health and well-being. His fame spread as far as Rome, where it was reported that a holy man lived in Provence. His reputation spread abroad: the news reached sweet France and King Charles, who was eager to hear it.[63] He wanted to know where and in what region the saint lived. They reported and confirmed that his home was on the Rhone, where his abbey was founded by King Flovent. The large community

---

[62] 2260 **monastic shirts, frocks and cowls** *estamines e frocs e colles*: the *estamine* was a woolen shirt worn under the *froc*, or tunic, covering the upper body; the *colle* was worn over the tunic or frock, and covered the head and shoulders. Cf. Laurent, *SGilles*, 143.

[63] 2326 **King Charles** *rei Charlun*: see above, 9, 15, 18, for Guillaume's treatment of this character. The identity of the king is vague in the *Vita sancti Aegidii*, but Guillaume identifies him as Charlemagne, and exploits the narrative riches associated with this famous ruler.

assembled there led a very holy life, supported by the king's gift of extensive lands and a great treasure of silver and gold.

The king of France listened to these words and in his heart decided that, whatever the cost, he would spare no expense until he had seen Giles himself.[64] No more was spoken on this subject, but the king could not forget the report, for he was very eager to speak with him. His mind was troubled; he sighed and lamented, filled with fear because of his sins. If he could, he wanted to bring Giles to his court, to confess his sins to the holy man. Charles ordered mules and horses to be shod, had a letter written and sealed, and equipped messengers who were both wise, clever, and eloquent speakers. They were richly appointed, bearing much gold and silver. They set out on the route to Provence and the king escorted them during their departure, urging them to make haste and return without delay. The messengers promised they would do so, and that they would return in good time, for they were confident that their horses were excellent. They travelled over summits, through plains and valleys, following the cart-road until they reached Montpellier (2309–64).

Exhausted from riding and their travels, they took lodging in well-appointed rooms in the city. When they had recovered from their exertions, they took their host aside and asked him politely:

"Good sir, do you know a man such as the one we are looking for in this region? A saintly abbot named Giles? We have come here from sweet France, our native land, to find him. Our lord Charlemagne longs day and night to see him, for so many good things are said of him by both rich and poor, by noblemen and peasants, that Charlemagne will not be content until he has seen him and spoken with him. Giles used to live in this region."

"By my faith," exclaimed their host, "it is true, the man you are seeking lives close by, not far from here. What you have heard of him is true, you will never see a better man. God is truly with him, and frequently does great miracles through him. Let me tell you what you must do: for the remainder of tonight you will sleep here; tomorrow, after you have eaten at leisure and been rested, you can go to him at your pleasure and I will find you a guide who knows well how to take you there, so that you will have no fear of losing your way" (2365–98).

The next morning, when they had eaten, they took leave of their host who accompanied them for some distance, pointing out the route. When he parted from them, he found a guide who led them to Giles' home.

They were welcomed with great joy in the abbey where Giles lived, and the monastery willingly granted them the charity of lodging which they sought. The

---

[64] 2341 **until he had seen Giles himself** *ke il nel veie*: the direct object of *veie* is third person singular masculine, and could refer either to Giles or to the convent. The following line, *ke mult coveite sun parler* "for he was very eager to speak with him" v. 2344, indicates that the reference is to Giles.

monk hosteler met them and led them to the guest room.[65] He was courteous and polite, asking if they had eaten, and when they responded that they had already amply dined, wine was brought for them. They then enquired of the hosteler:

"My lord," they said, "where is the abbot? We are both messengers and would like to speak with him; we carry letters and charters for him from our region. Charles, the king of St. Denis, has sent us here. Please arrange for us to speak with him."

"My lords," he replied, "if I am not mistaken, you will be able to speak with him at length. Please do not worry, but wait for me here" (2399–2426).

The hosteler went directly to the chapel where he found Abbot Giles praying; he bowed down and said: "*Benedicite.*" The abbot responded: "*Dominus.*"[66] They moved away from the altar, and the hosteler spoke:

"Sire, two messengers have come, both wealthy barons travelling in full regalia; they come on behalf of the king of France, who has sent them here to you."

"To me, brother?"

"Indeed, sir, to you."

"Have you offered them our hospitality?"

"They do not want for food or drink, but the king asks urgently to see you."

"He knows nothing of my infirmity; the king has never met me, I have never seen him, nor he me."

"Why is that a concern? Even if he has not seen you, he will have heard many reports of your life and deeds."

"Has anyone spoken ill of me to him?"

"By my faith, my lord, never, only of your good deeds."

"What deeds are those?"

"There are so many!"

"There is very little good in me, as God knows; I am astonished at these reports."

"Do you want to conceal what God wishes to reveal?"

"Has God been revealed in me?"

"*Crede michi*, yes!"[67]

"In what manner?"

"Through the sick and the lepers that God has cured through you."

---

[65] 2409 **hosteler** *l'ostelers*: the hosteler, or guest master, was responsible for receiving visitors to the monastery, and his duties made this an important monastic office.

[66] 2430–1 *Benedicite ... Dominus*: this is the traditional greeting and response between a Benedictine monk and his superior.

[67] 2456 *Crede michi*: "believe me" stated in Latin, perhaps to emphasize the veracity of the assertion, as well as to underline the parallel with the liturgical *Credo*, a profession of faith.

"Brother, even if I had not been born, God would nonetheless have accomplished his will. Let us freely accept, then, what God in his pleasure wishes to bring to pass. Send the messengers to me" (2427–62).

The hosteler went to find them and led them immediately to the abbot, who awaited them in the chapel. When Giles saw them, he spoke warmly to them and welcomed them in his native tongue.[68] The envoys greeted him in the name of the king and delivered their message to him. The abbot bowed to them, then took his seat in silence:

"My lord," they declared, "hear us speak, for we have been sent here to greet you. Through us, Charles, the king of St. Denis, sends you his greeting, and his friendship is at your service. He entreats you to come visit him at Orleans, where he awaits our return, and where he is attended by his large court.[69] Come to him, do not decline his invitation for whatever reason anyone might suggest to you for not coming. He is very eager to meet you, and fervently hopes you will come!" (2463–82).

"My lords," the abbot replied, "as God, creator of the world, is my witness, you have stated your message well, but I cannot give an immediate response to your request. But remain here with us and enjoy such hospitality as we can offer, and tomorrow we will discuss this with our brethren in chapter. I will explain to them that the emperor has sent for me, and if they willingly give me leave I shall be able to return with you. Tomorrow we will know their decision; you must stay here with us until then. Brother Hosteler, make the necessary arrangements."

What more is there to say? They received a welcome worthy of Saint Julian (2483–2500).[70]

Giles remained in the chapel. In prayer he called repeatedly upon God to give him holy counsel, for his mind was in great turmoil.

"Oh Lord," he cried, "glorious King, what is the meaning of this message, that such a wealthy prince has sent envoys here to seek me? Alas, I am most wretched: why could I not have remained unseen in the cave where I hid myself?

---

[68] 2467 **welcomed them in his native tongue** *i les welcume en sa language*: the use of *welcume* shows English influence on narrator Guillaume's French; Giles' native tongue, of course, was Greek.

[69] 2478 **attended by his large court** *grant assemblé i ad de gent*: lit. "where there is a large gathering of people."

[70] 2500 **they received a welcome worthy of Saint Julian** *Il unt ostel saint Julien*: the *Legenda aurea* notes that travellers invoked Saint Julian in order to find good lodgings; of the several holy Julians, two were examples of good hospitality: Julian, bishop of Le Mans, offered hospitality to Jesus in thanks for being cured of leprosy, and Julian the hosteler (*l'hospitalier*) offered lodging to the poor in penitence for having mistakenly killed his parents. See Laurent, *SGilles*, 150, and the entry on Saint Julian, in Jacques de Voragine, *La Légende dorée*, trans. J.-B. M. Roze (Paris: Garnier-Flammarion, 1967), 1: 168–73.

My sins have led to my being discovered: oh, woe is me, it is for my sins that this has happened! My troubles increase, and I am overcome with suffering. Of what possible use can I be at a royal court? I thought never again to be a courtier, for I had that role for too long. I thought I had now left that life behind, but by a trick of the devil it has come back to afflict me. I fear that my anxiety is making my wound worse: but may God's will be done, either through the bleeding of my wound, or my death!" (2501–24).

He remained deep in thought, feeling lost and without direction, not knowing which was the best choice in answer to the invitation of such a great man: to remain in his abbey, or to leave with the messengers.

All night he worried. At dawn, when the office of prime was rung, he went to the church to hear mass. When the service was finished a large group of the monks went to the chapter house. During their discussion of matters pertaining to the monastery the abbot explained the situation:

"Brothers, listen to me for a moment: I wish to discuss a matter with you, and to be guided by your advice. Charlemagne, the king of France, a prince of great power, has asked me to come to him, urging that I let none of my duties keep me from going. He wishes to speak to me, he informs me, on a matter of great importance to himself. But I am not at all comfortable with this request. Nonetheless, I would not travel a single league's distance without your permission, lest I be reproached later for doing so. Let each one of you now speak his mind and give his thoughts on this. The envoys have brought a letter; if you are all in agreement, remove the seals and show the letter to everyone" (2525–56).

When the convent heard the details of the request made by the wealthy prince, they lowered their heads in sadness and wept, hiding their tears within their hoods. There was a long period of silence before any response came from them. The prior[71] eased the tension by speaking:

"My lords," he stated, "your silence is wrong, since our lord abbot has spoken sincerely: he is not willing to undertake anything without your consent. And you need to act with great foresight: when a man such as the king of France has sent for him, I do not see how the abbot can delay his departure. By my oath of duty to you, I say in all sincerity, if we wish to live in peace we must obey the will of the wealthy princes on this earth, for if war should break out in our region we would need their protection. The king of France, in particular, can protect us from all other princes. Now tell me what you would wish to do, for I have told you my views!" (2557–79).

"My lord," came the reply, "you have spoken well, but we remain very fearful, and we will tell you why. Our lord abbot has not been in good health for some time; his heart is weak and fragile and he would not be capable of the rigours of travel. And we have no one else to support us. It would be better for

---

[71] The prior was second-in-command under the abbot of a Benedictine abbey.

us to die than to lose him and his protection, for without him this whole abbey would fall into ruin. That is why we are fearful. But let him go to court since the king has sent for him, and his cause is important. We pray only that he not forget us!" (2580–97).

Then one and all lamented; the monks who feared the loss of their abbot remained troubled in thought, but they granted him leave nonetheless, while urging and imploring him not to remain absent long. He assured them it would be only a brief period before he returned to them. You can be sure that many a tear was shed in chapter that day! (2598–2607).

The abbot ordered whatever preparations were necessary to be made and when all was ready he took leave of his brethren and set out on his route to France, to Saint Denis. But he did not have to travel as far as that, for the king was to be found closer to hand. He was at Orleans, where he awaited Giles, attended by a rich court and a large assembly of his people. Giles travelled without delay until he reached Orleans, where the king of France awaited his arrival. The envoys acted with courtesy: as they came close to the city in the region of Orleans they summoned a youth whom they sent ahead to the court. When the king heard the news he was gladdened and ordered his horse readied.[72] He came out of the city, spurring his horse on, waiting for neither peers nor companions. When he met Giles, he approached and greeted him, embracing him fervently seven times, bestowing kisses on his eyes, his mouth, and his chin.[73]

"My lord," he exclaimed, "please be assured that you are most welcome here among us. It would have been more logical, I believe, for me to have travelled to meet you, rather than your travelling to visit me!" (2608–38).

With those words they entered the city, under the expectant and watchful gaze of many knights and townspeople, peasants and courtiers. When Giles noticed this he was troubled and felt ashamed and unworthy. They rode up to the castle, where a crowd of people, gathered at the entrance to the hall, immediately surrounded the king, who took no notice. The king came over to hold the stirrup for the abbot, took him in his arms as he dismounted, and took him by his right hand; then the king and the abbot went up into the royal palace. They seated themselves apart from the others, on a fresh new tapestry. The king looked intently at the abbot's face, where the sort of life Giles led was readily apparent. The

---

[72] 2627 **ordered his horse readied** *il ad lues sun cheval mandé*: the uneven number of lines rhyming in [e] is seen, by Paris & Bos, followed by Laurent, as evidence of a line missing after v. 2627. It is possible, however, that the author used an unusual series of five identical rhymes, and that there is not a missing line, since there is no noticeable gap in the syntax or sense of the passage.

[73] 2632–34 **Greeted him . . . his chin** *si l'ad salué, / set feiz le beisë a randun, / les olz, la buche et le mentun*: on the signficance of these kisses, see the discussion of the *Vie de s. Georges*, above, 36–38.

king signalled to his chamberlain to prepare a room, well cleaned and spacious.[74] The two men remained alone, withdrawn from the press of people, in order to speak privately to each other. The king wasted no time in enquiring about Giles' identity, about his family, and what was his country.

Giles, who was incapable of duplicity, told him in detail how he came to live in a hermitage; how the wild doe nourished him for three years in the wilderness; how he was discovered, and how the king found him there, and in what manner he persuaded him to leave; and that the king founded an abbey for him in that region that was richly furnished and endowed with land, since the king granted it a large part of his kingdom. What more can I say? Suffice it to say that Giles told him everything about himself, except about his wound; the king never learned anything about this from Giles, but he later heard the truth from others (2639–83).

After hearing all that Giles related, the king could not keep from weeping and sighing deeply.

As day ended and night fell the king sent to his kitchen to learn if his meal was prepared, and the cooks responded that it was and that he could dine when he pleased. He had only a steward and butler come to serve them in private. The king asked for water to be brought, then they sat down to eat.[75] When Giles saw the food that was brought in, he sat looking at it for a long time in silence, staring at it: he no longer was accustomed to eating such a meal. Charles looked at him and asked:

"My dear lord, kind sir," exclaimed the king, "does this feast not meet with your pleasure?"

"Indeed, truly, it is very much to my liking," replied the abbot.

"For pity's sake, then, eat what has been brought to you, and partake, in the name of holy observance, of the food that is before you. Do you not find written in Holy Scripture that Our Lord commanded and required of his apostles, when they went out preaching, that they accept in the name of charity whatever was placed before them?" (2684–2715).[76]

Abbot Giles listened to what Charlemagne said and turned aside to smile to himself, then asked politely:

---

[74] 2660 **well cleaned and spacious** *e bel neer e delivrer*: "spacious" is used here to express the sense of the second verb, *delivrer* "clear out, free up space."

[75] 2692–95 **only a steward and butler ... asked for water** *un despenser e un butiller sulement / pur eus servir preveement. / Li reis feit l'eve demander*: the medieval butler (*butiller*, "bottler") was in charge of wine; water was for washing hands before the meal.

[76] 2709–15 **Do you not find ... in the name of charity whatever was placed before them** *Dunc ne trovez vus en escrit / ço k'um lur mettereit devant / receüssent par charité?*: cf. Jesus' injunction to his disciples to rely on charity as they go into the world to preach (Mark 6:7–11; Luke 9:1–5).

"My lord, how long have you been a preacher? You know how to deliver a good sermon!"

After they had eaten copiously and the abbot had expressed his thanks, the king and the abbot washed their hands, then sat down again and talked well into the night.

There, beside the fireplace, they prepared a bed for Giles—indeed, a finer bed could not have been found. When the bed was ready the king ordered wine, which the abbot drank first, then he offered it to the king. When both had drunk, the king, who was beside the abbot, stood up:

"My lord, it is time for bed. You must be tired from riding, and you will rise earlier than I."

"Yes, my lord, I believe I will; and tomorrow we will once more talk together."

"Indeed, yes, rest assured that I will speak again to you," came the king's reply.

He was eager for sleep, for they had sat together for a long time. The king took his leave from Giles and went to his chamber to lie down.

But rather than going to sleep, the abbot started to sing the service of matins, and it was almost dawn before he had finished. The chamberlain had fallen asleep before the end of the service. The abbot gathered up the straw which had been strewn about the floor and made it his bed (2716–56).

The king arose early, put on a linen shirt, and when he was shod and dressed entered the chamber where the abbot was, and saw that the holy man lay sleeping on the hard floor. The king was amazed at this, and wakened the chamberlain, and asked him what this meant, and why the abbot was lying there.

"My lord," explained the chamberlain, "because he was reciting verses all the time, he spent the whole night in prayer, in vigils and self-mortification. When he was ready to sleep, he gathered up this straw to serve as his bed on the hard floor; I have never seen anyone do this!"

"Be silent," interrupted the king, "don't wake him, let him sleep in peace!" (2757–76).

The abbot heard them talking, and at the sound he began to awaken. He opened his eyes and saw the king standing close beside him. Together they went into the chapel to celebrate a solemn and beautiful mass. Abbot Giles chanted the mass and the knights and barons who were nearby listened devoutly. At the end of the mass, while Giles removed his vestments, the king called an usher to empty the chapel, leaving him alone with the abbot.

With tears, and asking for mercy, the king made his confession. He never revealed to anyone what he confessed there in the chapel, all the while asking for mercy: he shed many tears on that day. The abbot was moved to great compassion, and began to comfort him:

"Leave your weeping. Our Lord's apostles, who were with him night and day, committed very great sins. You have heard often of how they sinned. Judas, who was his friend and ate and drank with him, betrayed and cheated him, and St. Peter denied him. One denied him, the other betrayed him; both were repugnant acts: one was saved by his faith, the other perished because of his doubts. Be assured that St. Peter remembered, and wept bitterly;[77] Jesus saw the repentance in his heart and pardoned him for what he had said. For this reason let us not despair, but now ask for God's mercy. God is a fountain of pity, he will forgive you for your sin. For this reason I urge you to confess everything, repent and beg for mercy. Have you anything else to say? Is there anything you should add?" (2777–2823).

The king bowed down before him, and remained silent for a long time. He would have said more, but dared not. He could not stop himself from sighing deeply as he said:

"My lord, may God have mercy on me, I have not yet confessed all my sins to you. You ask if there are more?"

"Yes."

"My sin will never be spoken, I will never tell it to any mortal man! Even though I be condemned to eternal damnation, it will never be confessed by me! In the name of God I beg your pity; pray for me to our Lord that he, in his sweet compassion, grant me pardon, if it be his will."

The abbot replied:

"Let us pray to him: may God, if it be his will, be merciful. For the sin that you have confessed, we will grant you your penance, whatever may or may not result from it" (2824–44).

They left the chapel where they had been for some time and went into the palace by the stairway crowded with knights. There were counts and barons, French, Normans, Bretons, and soldiers from many countries.[78] The king sat on a bench, and from the floor of the hall the crowd pressed forward around him as he washed his hands. When Charlemagne had washed, the water was carried to the abbot, and many rushed to assist him, and the man who succeeded in this was pleased. After they had washed in the hall, the king led the abbot by the hand up to the high table in the hall, where they took their seats.

It is not my intention to describe the meal to you, for that would be a distraction. After they had eaten everyone left to enjoy the pleasures of the city. The great hall was emptied of people, apart from the king and a few companions. Af-

---

[77] Cf. Matthew 26:75, Luke 22:62.

[78] 2852 **soldiers** *soldeiers*: knights who fought as paid warriors, receiving a *solde* "payment" for their service. The implication is that, since they did not fight as part of their feudal obligation, they were foreign to the court for which they waged war.

ter the meal the king and Giles went together into the chamber to talk. The abbot asked him if he had reconsidered his confession, and Charlemagne responded that he had not; he would sooner die unshriven than confess his sin to anyone.

"I am greatly saddened," replied the abbot, "that the devil has such power over you and your heart. If you were to die in this state, it would be a great misfortune and a cause for much sorrow. May God, if it pleases him, have pity on you, for although you have fought valiantly in battle and you have defeated many a king in combat, you are unable to mend your ways or to make your heart humble. If you win great territories and gain possessions in your wars, it is through God, and not by your own power. Do not be so arrogant! God showed his great love for you when he changed night into day at the mountain pass of Roncesval to avenge the death of Roland.[79] For all this you should offer many thanks to God. My dear lord, give up this sin!"

But Giles had spoken and laboured in vain, for the king cared not a fig for all the words of his sermon (2845–98).

The abbot stayed with the king for more than twenty days, I believe, and all the while begged him to confess his secret sin. It was for naught, Charlemagne did not wish to confess: not even the fear of dying moved him. The Sunday following Charlemagne's first confession the court was gathered at Orleans. The abbot rose early; when he was fully dressed he went to the episcopal church of Sainte-Croix to pray throughout the morning. Inside the church, close to the entrance, he heard a wretch who was tied to a pillar, weeping and wailing in great distress. The abbot asked him what was the matter and the man replied that he knew for a certainty that the devil had tempted him, and had entered his body, and that no exorcism had been able to cure him. When Giles saw him he took pity on him and prayed to Our Lord that he have mercy on him.

Hear now what the devil did! As soon as he knew that Giles was in the church he cried out and shouted like a demon:

"Giles, let me be! Have you come here to rob me? By brute force and forcible means you are casting me out of my place of shelter, which I have rightfully earned. Cursed be he who sent you here! If the king had followed my advice he would never have sent for you! I am hidden inside this body, and dare not come out for fear of you. Stop praying and let me escape, I do not want to come anywhere near you!" (2898–2938).

---

[79] 2892–94 **he changed night into day . . . Roland** *quant pur vus fist de noit le jur . . . Rollant*: a composite reference to the *Chanson de Roland*. The phrase *az porz passant* is a direct citation (vv. 1071, 1766) referring to Charlemagne "crossing the mountain passes" to come to the aid of Roland; Charlemagne exacts vengeance in laisse 180 (vv. 2458–2475), when God makes the sun stand still during Charlemagne's battle with the Saracens. This miracle is, in turn, an allusion to the biblical story of the sun standing still during battle (Joshua 10:13). See also Frankis, "Languages and Cultures in Contact," 123–24.

All the people were astounded by the devil's words. They heard him speak, but did not see him, so it is little wonder they were frightened. Giles heard the devil's voice and, making the sign of the Holy Cross to protect himself, slowly advanced toward him.

"Ah, wicked Satan," he cried, "you were foolish to enter this body, for you have violated the temple of God. Flee from this church, leave this wretch alone, relinquish his body!"[80]

The devil emerged from the wretch in front of more than a hundred people who saw him. All who saw this miracle fell down at the feet of the holy man, but he slipped away from the crowd. They rang the bells throughout the city, and I believe more than three thousand persons went to the church to seek Giles' intercession, but they were unsuccessful, for he had gone to put on his priestly vestments (2939–60).

The king of France arose and dressed and prepared himself elegantly. A more handsome man could not be found: he had all the regal bearing of an earthly prince. All the details of the miracle that Giles performed were told and retold to him. He went to the church of Sainte-Croix and found that the abbot, now robed in his priestly garments, had begun divine service.

The sacrifice that Giles made that day was very acceptable to God. Hear now how our Lord is full of great kindness! On that day he performed a great and most powerful miracle through his servant. During the *secreta* of the mass,[81] when the abbot held the body of our Lord, he thought of Charlemagne, and in piety he spoke sorrowfully to the communion host:

"O God, source of true understanding, king who is without beginning and who will be without end, who has always been and who will be always, who established and commanded that your body be a sacrifice for the ransom of our sins, great is the miracle of you and your body which I see before me.[82] You are whole in body in heaven above, and we have your body here below on earth. Lord, you are both there and here, yet you are not divided in two parts; you are

---

[80] 2949 **Flee from this church** *fui t'en de cest muster*: the author alludes to the body of the possessed man, since the body, as stated in the preceding line, is also the *temple Deu* (as expressed in Pauline theology; cf. 1 Corinthians 3:16; 6:19).

[81] 2976 ***Secreta* of the mass** *El segrei*: the Secret, or *Secreta*, is a prayer said in a low voice by the priest at the end of the Offertory, while the choir sings the Offertory. It is not a prayer meant to be heard by the congregation. In this scene Giles addresses his private prayer directly to the communion host, the body of Christ.

[82] 2987–88 **great is the miracle of you and your body** *mult est grant merveille de tei / e de tun cors*: this passage begins an elaboration of the doctrine of Transubstantiation, debated in an early form in the eleventh century, in which the communion host is held to be the literal body of Christ. See discussion of this scene above, 11, and below, 204–7. See also Gary Macy, *Treasures from the Storeroom: Medieval Religion and the Eucharist* (Collegeville, MN: Liturgical Press, 1999).

one God in your deity. You have ordained and commanded that we drink your blood and eat your flesh, yet forever your body remains whole; it can never be diminished even when it is consumed and eaten, for it forever remains whole. Your kingdom will never end, and whoever does not sincerely receive you through communion eats and drinks his own death;[83] this I believe and know to be true. I pray to you, Omnipotent Father, have pity on Charlemagne, who has laboured hard for you, who has conquered many kingdoms by his strength for the glory of Christendom. Overlook his folly! Jesus, son of St. Mary, tell me what I should do, what penitence I should demand of him when he refuses to confess his sin. But please, do not let the devil take him!" (2961–3015).

With these words he ended his prayer. Our Lord listened to him, and accepted his plea. While the abbot was performing the *secreta* an angel came down to him, bearing in his hand a small letter, but no mortal man except the worthy abbot saw him: he was clearly visible to Giles. Where the angel had descended, the whole chapel shone brilliantly, but the angel spoke not a word. He immediately placed the letter on the altar beside the host which the abbot had consecrated, and when the angel had placed it there he turned at once and left. The abbot gave no indication whatsoever that he had seen the letter, but in a spirit of rejoicing continued reciting the mass, for he was very pleased by this gift which the angel had brought him.

When the service was over, Abbot Giles picked up the letter so that it would not be seen by anyone else, and he read it through three times from beginning to end. Are you curious to hear what was in the letter?

"Good Abbot Giles, accept the greetings of Our Lord, and hear now the message that he sends you.[84] He has heard your prayer, and he is pleased and gratified that you have prayed on behalf of the king. Thanks to you he will be shown great mercy. He is pardoned for this sin, but hear his confession. He must be careful not to relapse, and must abandon completely his sinful ways, and sincerely make his penance. He need not fear that he will ever be reproached for this sin, for it has now been pardoned once and for all" (3016–54).

Then Giles looked at the letter and saw that Charlemagne's sin was written out in full, with no details lacking.[85] He looked again and saw at the top of the letter, written at the side,

"Giles, you may rejoice, for your Lord has granted that whatever you may ask, be assured that you will accomplish it. Whether your request is a great or a small matter, it will not be refused you. The Lord has looked into the depths of your heart and knows that you have abandoned your inheritance, your friends,

---

[83] 1 Corinthians 11:29.

[84] 3042 **hear now . . . he sends you** *sez ke te mande Nostre Sires*: lit. "know what Our Lord commands of you," or "sends to you."

[85] 3058 **with no details lacking** *ke nule ren n'i desesteit*: the audience, however, is never privy to this sin. See note to v. 3155.

and your great lands and domains. You went into a foreign country seeking suffering and poverty. For this you will receive a great recompense: you will be rewarded a hundredfold, for your inheritance will be in paradise. The celestial court rejoices because of you, and eagerly awaits your coming. They do not wish you to dwell longer here below, and in a short while you will leave this earth."

The letter ended there; nothing more was written. Overjoyed and happy because of what he had read, the abbot refolded the letter.

Charlemagne, who was waiting for Giles in the chapel, looked closely at him, and saw clearly from his demeanour that he had heard good news, for his face was smiling and radiant. The king went to Giles, took him by the hand, and they sat down together on a bench. The abbot admonished him briefly about making his confession:

"My lord," he advised, "in the name of the Most High God, consider your duty to yourself, and, for your own good, make your confession. Your death is fast approaching: you know neither the day nor the hour when the judge will come to assess both the righteous and the wicked. He will place his own on one side and call them his friends and they will be with him in paradise, in everlasting joy and happiness. And the others will despair, for they will be separated from him, and they will be damned to the pit of hell and forever tortured.[86] Sweet lord, take care now to avoid such companions! Admit the truth, and beg mercy for the sin that you have hidden so long. You are foolish and unreasonable when you choose not to confess your sin. Do you think you can hide anything from God? You can't even hide it from me!" (3055–3115).

"From you? Of course I can!"
"Indeed no, I swear you can't!"
"I can't? Why not?"
"Because I already know it!"
"My sin is not known by anyone in all of Christendom!"
"I'm a Christian, and I know it!"
"I cannot bring myself to believe you!"
"I will prove it to you!"
"You, how can you possibly know of my sin?"
"Do you see this?"
"I can see nothing."
"Nevertheless, I know the details of your sin."
"And how would you know that?"
"I have been told everything."
"I don't believe a word you say!"
"You don't believe me?"
"Indeed I don't!"

---

[86] Cf. Matthew 24:36, Mark 13:32, and Matthew 25:31–46.

"That is an even greater folly!"
"For what reason?"
"Because you must bring yourself to make your confession!"
"I will never do that, until the day I die!"
"Then it will be too late."
"I can do no more than that."
"Yes you can!"—"How?"—"By making your confession!"
"I assure you that I will never confess during my lifetime!"
"In this you are acting very thoughtlessly, when you think you can keep something secret from God, when even from me you cannot hide it!"
"By all the saints of heaven, I am astounded by what I hear!"
"Don't let this upset you, but listen to me for a moment and you will soon understand everything."
"I do not dare to contradict you, but if anyone else said these words I would call him a liar."
"And what would you say if I described your sin to you?"
"In that case I do not say that I would not believe you."
"Would you believe me if I told you what your sin was?"
"Indeed, yes, be assured that I would!"

With that, Giles brought out the letter and read it to the king from top to bottom (3116–46).

When Charles heard his sin described he was astounded, but he acknowledged that it was God who had revealed it to Giles.

"My lord," he pleaded, "for the love of God, have pity on what you have heard! I fully recognize and confess that I had the misfortune to commit this sin, this folly, that you have just heard.[87] In God's name, good sir, pray for me, call on God, the true King, to grant me a complete pardon, and I ask to make my confession to you. Pray for me in the future: the burden I bear is heavy, and you can lighten it if you will pray for me. I can tell you in all certainty that I no longer fear eternal torment, and as long as we both live, I will not agree to do penance for any man except you, even if I have to go to Provence to find you!"

The abbot replied:

---

[87] 3155–56 this sin ... which you have just heard *cest peché . . . / ke vus avez ici oïe*: the sin remains a secret of Charlemagne's confession to Giles. The sin that Charlemagne dares not speak was, according to medieval legend, an incestuous relationship between Charlemagne and his sister Gisèle, from which Charlemagne's nephew (or son) Roland is born. Cf. Laurent, *SGilles*, 147, who cites B. de Gaiffier, "La légende de Charlemagne, le péché de l'empereur et son pardon," in *Mélanges Clovis Brunel* (Paris: Société de l'Ecole des Chartres, 1955), 1: 496–503. See now S. Hafner, "Charlemagne's Unspeakable Sin," *Modern Language Notes* 32.2 (2002): 1–14; also E. Archibald, *Incest and the Medieval Imagination* (Oxford: Oxford University Press, 2001), 209 with n. 48.

"We accept these conditions, and we will be happy to return to see you, if necessary; we remain at your service."[88]

"I give you my thanks," responded the king, bowing deeply to the abbot (3147–76).

They climbed the stairs into the hall, rejoining the knights who were there. The king was light-hearted and happy, for he had shed a great burden. For the duration of his stay at court the king treated the abbot as an honoured and distinguished guest. Three days after this last conversation, so I have been told, the abbot came before the king, seeking his permission to take his leave; he wished to return to his abbey because his brethren deeply regretted his prolonged absence, for he had stayed at least a month.

"Sweet lord," replied the king, "will you not stay with us a while longer?"

"Please understand that that is not possible. I do not wish to prolong my stay; I must return to my monks."

Charlemagne, who was exhausted from his long day, retired to his bed.

The next day Abbot Giles rose at dawn, eager to start his journey. He went to the chapel to pray, and in good spirits celebrated mass. Charlemagne went to hear him say the mass, then he summoned his treasurer and had him prepare gold and silver, mules and horses, rich fabrics of silk, sendal, and taffeta, and fine vestments that he wished to present to the abbot. When the abbot had finished the service he came out of the chapel. The king called him aside:

"My lord, I realize that nothing will persuade you to remain here longer, that you wish to return to your home. I beseech you, for the love of God, take back to the brethren in your abbey the gifts that we will send them: you see here gold and silver, and many luxurious vestments as well. Greet everyone on my behalf, and tell them it is I who send this. Let them know as well that if I live a long life, they will receive other fine presents" (3177–3222).

"My lord," said the abbot, "my thanks, but I am unwilling to carry back these riches. I will not accept a single penny from you for all the treasure of Montpellier. Do not insist on this, say no more about it."

The king replied:

"That is the end of it, you will not hear me speak of it again.[89][. . .] I am well aware of what I must do; my offering will be even greater, and one which you cannot refuse."

---

[88] 3171–74 **We accept . . . we remain at your service** *Ço vulum nus, / e nus repeirerum a vus / mult volenters, si mesters est ; / nostre servise vus est prest*: the formality of the first person plural pronoun implies that Giles is also speaking formally for God; this usage is parallel to the royal first person plural (as in the statement traditionally attributed to Queen Victoria: "We are not amused!")

[89] 3229 **you will not hear me speak of it again** *ja meis ne m'en orrez parler*: this line stands alone, without a matching rhyme, marking a lacuna of one line or more.

The Life of Saint Giles

The abbot did not want to prolong his stay. He mounted his horse and bade adieu to the knights and the courtiers. Followed by a large number of people, Charlemagne accompanied Giles for some distance as he set out on his way; when it was time to part company there were many tears as they reluctantly took leave of each other (3223–40).

The abbot continued on his way to his home country, but he could not tolerate a long day's travel because of the great pain given by his wound, which broke open and bled each day, intensifying his suffering. Despite this he rode on until he had reached his abbey, where he was welcomed with great rejoicing. The prior and all the monks came out to greet him affectionately, overjoyed at his return. Giles gave a kiss to each one, asking how they were and enquiring if they lacked for clothing or provisions. Each one replied individually that he had an abundance of both.

"Praise be to God!" the abbot responded. "My lords," he continued, "the king of France, who has placed his hope in your good works, sends you his greetings and assurances of his friendship, and prays that you remember him in your prayers and in your good deeds. And I tell you now that we believe he sincerely loves you. He offered you a rich gift of vestments, gold and silver, and he had the best pieces from his treasury loaded onto a packhorse, but I did not wish to accept them. My refusal sorely upset the king, but he told me in all sincerity that he would come here to see you and would bring you a share of his wealth. You will welcome him as a brother into the community, to share in the benefits of the good works of the abbey" (3241–76).

Giles continued living in the abbey for a long period. He would sit alone in his chapel, away from the bustle of activity of his fellows. He led an ascetic, holy life, eating and drinking little, withdrawing as much as possible from the daily life of others. He slept very little at night, and spent his days chanting psalms and reciting biblical verses. He tenderly lamented and beseeched his Lord:

"Oh Lord, source of true comfort, who destroyed hell through your death: by your power and righteousness you killed the Murderer, because your death and your Passion utterly condemned him. Sweet Lord, true gentle Father, guide me on what I should do with this newly endowed monastery which king Flovent has founded here. As long as he lives I am certain that he will provide for it as best he can within his powers; but I do not know if the king who follows him will love it as much as he does. I suspect that the next king will provide nothing for the monastery, but will instead strip it of its possessions. The good people who have come here to live have given up worldly life. Most of them, I believe, have come here on my account, not because of the good that I have done, but because they hoped that great things would be accomplished here; but of this there has been very little.[90] I will have performed my duties badly if I leave them leader-

---

[90] 3309 **but of this there has been very little** *de ben i ad mut povrement*: lit. "there has been a paucity of good."

less — and if this monastery were not guaranteed, confirmed and dedicated, and its rights and privileges assured, so that the brothers may have lasting peace and so that whatever king may come after me will not take away their rights and privileges, nor their tilled fields or their pastures, their woodlots or their arable lands, their crop revenues or their fisheries, or anything with which the king has endowed them. Otherwise, in my opinion, if I now leave things as they are, all my pain and suffering will not have profited me in the least. I must go to Rome while I am still able to do so on my own, in order to better achieve these ends, for I do not have long to live!" (3277–3329).

Giles summoned the whole convent, and when all the brothers had gathered he explained it all in detail to them:

"My lords," he began, "listen now to the reason I have summoned you. I know for a fact that I do not have long to live. The king founded this abbey, and endowed it with a good portion of his own land and wealth. We can count on the fact that as long as he lives he will not allow anyone to diminish our rights in any fashion. Even so, while he is still in power we should seek guaranteed assurances of our rights. We do not know how long he will live, just as no man can ever know when he will die. I have given this considerable thought: while I still have the physical strength necessary to do so, I must travel to Rome to secure the guarantee of our rights."

The monks discussed this at length, being reluctant to agree that the abbot should go to Rome, but in the end accepted and duly granted him permission to go. What more can I say? When he was ready, he mounted his horse and took several monks with him. After much difficulty and discomfort they arrived in Rome (3330–63).

The pope received Giles with great honours, for he had been told that there was no deceit or treachery in Giles' person, or in the life he led. As a result the pope admired and respected him, and had him eat and drink with him, and Giles slept in the pope's own chamber where they dined and drank together. With great solicitude the pope asked Giles about his way of life, and about his country of origin. The abbot replied that he was Greek, that he was born in Greece and had lived in Provence in a woodland close to the Rhone.

"At first it was a hermitage, but now there is an abbey, newly founded by the good king Flovent, who had it built and attracted people there to establish a fine convent; the monks strictly follow the monastic rule in their service to God Omnipotent. The king richly endowed the convent with gifts from his own wealth and land. I have come here to ask that you consecrate this new foundation and give papal confirmation of our privileges from Rome, so that in future no one will have to fear losing their possessions or the rights that they have been granted."[91]

---

[91] 3395 **losing their possessions or the rights that they have been granted** *de perdre ço k'il eü unt*: lit. "losing that which they have had." This translation expands the literal sense

The pope told him in reply that he would gladly continue the support of the monastery and grant them privileges "in the form in which you choose to have them framed and written down and sealed."

"Lord abbot," the pope continued, "be advised that you will receive aid and support from us as long as we live, but please note that in return we require that we be granted brotherhood in your monastery."

"My lord," responded Giles, who willingly accepted this request, "we grant that you be accepted into the fellowship of our monastery" (3364–3408).

When in this fashion the abbot had satisfactorily addressed his earlier concerns, he asked permission from the pope to return to his own country.

"My lord," he said, "grant me leave for I must return to my home. May our Lord God in his grace bless you for the honour you have shown me."

"Sire, you should not thank me; instead the whole world should give thanks for the hour of your birth. May you be entrusted to God's care. Give our greetings to your brotherhood in the monastery. [. . .] Here are two elaborately carved cypress doors:[92] none like this will ever be made in the future, and there are no two like them anywhere in the world.[93] They are painted, with detailed carvings showing the twelve apostles, and inlaid with much gold and silver. I have long greatly admired them. But I am puzzled as to how I can send them to your monastery. I suspect they will be too much for you to carry, for they are very heavy."

"My lord," answered Giles, "God is all-powerful. If it is his will that we have them, he will bring them to our monastery. Give the doors to us, and God will have them brought to us, without our trying to find a method or means of bringing them that distance."[94]

Listen now, my lords, to the great miracle that God performed for his servant: the abbot took the two doors and, placing them in the Tiber, raised his hand and made the sign of the cross over them, and commended them to God.

"Depart," he commanded, "I order you, in the name of the powerful King of Heaven, to float without stopping, across both fresh water and the sea, until you come to our monastery."

---

to emphasize that they are concerned about guarding both their physical possessions and their legal rights. By establishing that the authority of their rights is directly granted by papal decree, the monastery is freed from intervention by local kings or bishops on their rights of property and choice of abbot.

[92] 3423 **two elaborately carved cypress doors** *Dous mut riches us de ciprés*: although there is no break in the rhyme, the sense of the passage indicates that there is a lacuna in the text: the pope is presenting Giles with a gift to be taken back to the monastery.

[93] Carved cypress doors dating from the fifth century, similar to the ones described here, are still extant in the church of Santa Sabina, Rome. See Richard Delbrueck, "Notes on the Wooden Doors of Santa Sabina," *Art Bulletin* 34 (1952): 139–45.

[94] 3439 **without . . . means** *e nus*[= *ne* + *les*] *querruns engin e art*: lit. "we will not seek a method or means for them."

Be assured the doors did not stop: they went floating down the Tiber, staying side by side. God steered and guided them right to the port next to the monastery.

Giles set out on his way, riding and travelling across country on his route home, until he at last reached the abbey. On all sides, everywhere he turned, people asked him:

"My lord, have you heard? Two doors (there are none like them in all of Christendom) have arrived here in port, without being brought by any mortal man!"

The abbot was very happy when he heard the news, and thanked our Lord:

"O God, glorious king, great is your strength and your righteousness! Your grace cannot be hidden! All is accomplished according to your will. He who serves you is very wise, for you clearly performed a great miracle in answer to my prayers, since you have steered these doors here in such a way that they are untouched and undamaged!" (3409–78).

He had them carried to the church and mounted in the doorframes. They fit the door jambs perfectly, as if they had been made to measure. In this way the building itself testified that it had received confirmation from Rome, from which it derives its authority. The abbot was overjoyed that everything he wished had been accomplished, and that the monastery's rights were now guaranteed. He continued living there with his brethren, spending night and day in prayer, but he had become very weak.

The time was approaching, the day when he would end his labours. His Lord did not wish Giles to remain below on this earth with us: his good deeds will now reap their reward. Our Lord sent for Giles, and informed him, by means of the Holy Spirit, of the day that he would depart this earth.

He knew with certainty the day of his death, when he would leave this world. His illness grew progressively worse, and caused him enormous suffering. He knew full well that he was near death, and he summoned his monks and addressed them compassionately:

"My lords, listen to me. As long as it has been God's will I have lived and dwelt here among you, and have been your master. In the name of God, the most glorious, I beseech you, if there is anyone, of low or high estate, that I have offended, or to whom I have done wrong, may he pardon me out of charity. I can no longer stay with you, for I am nearing my time of death: before this night is over my soul will have left my body. My soul will be rewarded according to the deeds I have done. Be careful, I beg you in the name of our Lord God, that strife does not rise up among you, but take counsel among yourselves regarding whom you will elect from your number as the one to be master over you and have responsibility for the maintenance of the abbey. Do not choose someone on the basis of his noble birth, or his physical attractiveness, or his age. Even a man in the earliest days of his youth can be intent on good deeds; do not refuse a man because of his age, if you know him to be a good man. Be charitable among yourselves, and be attentive to the needs of the poor. I should speak to you at length, and admonish you to do good deeds, but I cannot stay that long with you, and I am losing the power of speech. In God's name I pray that each one of you, individually, perform the last rites for me. As long as I am alive, take care of me; make sure that I am anointed with holy oil, and that I receive confession and communion. Prepare my body with great honour, for by the grace of our Lord this monastery will be sought out by those coming from afar, and I have been informed of this by God. The pilgrims who will come here from distant regions must also be housed and fed" (3479–3552).

When the monks heard Giles say that his death was imminent, they mourned deeply, weeping and sighing. They pulled and tore out their hair, and made great wailing and lamentation on the news of his death, and before nightfall forty-eight monks had fallen prostrate in grief. When they grew tired of weeping, they began to voice their sorrow:

"Master, true pastor, friend and servant of our Lord, we are sad and full of tears at your leaving. Who now will lead us? It is no wonder we are weeping: we will never in the future have a master such as you. Lord, who will now give us advice? Who will comfort us? No one will ever give us such great solace—your death is a source of great sorrow to us!"

They mourned the whole day in this fashion, right until night fell. The monks prepared themselves, and began the service, but they performed it with great difficulty, often interrupted by their own tears. Nonetheless, despite their weeping, they completed it with great dignity (3553–80).

The monks were all seated around Giles' bed. A little before midnight, around the hour when the cock crows, Giles raised himself to a sitting position; he knew that his death was near, that he would not live long. He struggled to move his tongue, his heart was faltering, and his body felt heavy, but his mind was very clear. Raising both hands heavenward, he offered a brief, moving prayer:

"God, omnipotent King, you who became flesh in Mary, in the city of Bethany you raised Lazarus from the dead.[95] You saved the people of Israel from bondage to King Pharaoh when you had them cross the Red Sea without either a boat or a ship.[96] In order to free Susanna you made Daniel speak, saving her from the false accusation of the two wicked priests who had condemned her, and turning the punishment back on them.[97] You likewise rescued Jonah from the stomach of the whale,[98] and you cast out seven devils from the body of Mary

---

[95] 3593–95 **flesh in Mary ... Lazarus from the dead**: cf. Matthew 1:18–25, Luke 1:26–38, John 11:1–44.

[96] 3596–99 **saved the people of Israel ... ship**: cf. Exodus 14:21–31.

[97] 3600–5 **free Susanna ... them**: cf. Daniel 13.

[98] 3606–7 **rescued Jonah from the stomach of the whale**: cf. Jonah 1–2.

Magdalene and turned her aside from her folly, so that she believed fully in you.[99] She came to look for you in the tomb; when she did not find you, she began to cry tenderly, confused and full of sorrow. And at Cana, in Galilee, you turned water into wine at the wedding of Architriclinus.[100] You lived on earth as long as it pleased you, in fulfilment of the will of your dear Father. There you performed many miracles for the deaf, the blind, and the mute, who were all healed by you (3581–3623).

"By your own will you suffered death for us. To redeem your people you permitted your suffering on the cross, and by your own will, under no constraint, you went unwaveringly to your own death. When you drew near to Jerusalem, Lord, you humbled yourself profoundly when you rode in on the back of a donkey. The young Hebrew boys who were in Jerusalem welcomed you with great rejoicing, casting the cloaks they were wearing down onto the street before you, and strewing green olive branches on the streets and pathways, and they cried as in one voice: '*Osanna filio David!*'[101] Blessed be your coming, which we have so long awaited, for all the people who perished because of Adam will be redeemed by the one who comes here!' The Jews who heard this were full of sorrow; they were disturbed that the children sang *Osanna*. They looked for a way to betray you, and by night they came to seize you and led you away, bound as a captive, to be beaten and insulted. They crowned you with thorns, they beat and bludgeoned you. With two thieves you were hung, pierced with nails, and stretched out on a cross. Joseph and Nicodemus took you down from the cross and placed you in the sepulchre. Armed knights and guards did not keep a good watch, the day they lost their Lord, and you were lost forever to the Jews, who, because they did not believe in your Incarnation, your death, and your Passion, are now wretched and disappointed. They have now seen and experienced what was prophesied about them, for since then their descendants have not had a king and they have been exiled into many lands. When it pleased you, you rose up from the tomb where Joseph had placed you. You descended immediately to hell to save your people who were there; you cast out your followers who had been placed there undeservedly. Those who saw you ascend to heaven from the Mount of Olives were right to be amazed, for it was a great miracle to witness. In the flesh you ascended to

---

[99] 3608–15 **cast out seven devils . . . fully in you**: cf. Matthew 28:1–8, Mark 16:9–11, Luke 24:1–11, John 20:11–18.

[100] 3618 **Architriclinus** *Architriclin*: cf. John 2:1–12; *architriclinus*, the Latin common noun designating one who organizes a feast, was thought in the Middle Ages to be the proper name of the groom at the wedding of Cana. Cf. Laurent, *SGilles*, 225, and Mod. Fr. *architriclin*.

[101] 3640 *Osanna filio David*: as in the *Vie*, the translation retains the biblical citation in Latin ("Hosanna to the son of David," cf. Matthew 21:9). For the description of Jesus' entrance into Jerusalem, vv. 3629–48, cf. Matthew 21:1–11, Mark 11:1–10, Luke 19:28–38, John 12:12–16.

heaven, you who created everything out of nothing. There you are, and will be, forever. I beseech you, King of Paradise, that all who come here to seek my help, and who honour this place, will be offered your help, and that their prayers will be granted. You have already granted me this; I have the letter with me which I have kept to this day, both out of love for you and as a witness of your love. It was sent to me by you, I know, while I was celebrating mass at the church of Sainte Croix. But now I must leave it behind, for death obliges me to part with it. Glorious Lord, most high King, receive my soul this day. St. Michael, righteous guide, lead me to my Lord.[102] I have delayed too long, it seems to me, in joining my friends!" (3624–3702).

With these words his prayer ended. His heart faltered, his tongue fell silent, he could no longer speak. He had the whole convent gather together and they knelt before him. He kissed each one, raising his hand to make the sign of the cross on each person, commending all to God. He crossed his hands on his chest, for death was near and his life was drawing to a close. He closed his eyes, his mouth opened, and his soul departed from his body. Many angels were there to receive him, as the Latin record tells us, and the angel St. Michael carried his soul up to heaven (3703–18).

Hear now about a great miracle which is found in our written source. I offer as witness the clerks who wrote it and those who have heard the life of Giles. On the night that Saint Giles died (what I recount here is true) angels were present to receive him, and two monks of this monastery were able to see them. Because of their great religious faith it was revealed to these two witnesses how Giles was honoured. These two monks saw clearly how the angels carried Giles off with great joy, and they remembered most of the melodies and the singing. Giles felt such joy that he could not have asked for more. He who serves faithfully will be served faithfully in return: Giles had served God well, and he was well rewarded; he was crowned in paradise (3719–38).

His body, which has remained here on earth, is treated with the highest honour: it is sealed in a rich reliquary, decorated with much silver and gold.[103] God performs many miracles on his behalf. People come from many countries: pilgrims from elsewhere come to Provence to seek his intercession. Giles is exalted and honoured throughout all Christendom. He well deserves to be honoured, for he was much beloved of Our Lord, and this was shown in the end when he sent his angels to welcome him and to lead him as an heir to his kingdom.

Let us now pray to this beloved of God, whose life we have heard, that he pray to his dear Lord for us, that he, in his mercy, grant that we follow the path by which we may come to him. And may he be grateful to the canon who la-

---

[102] The archangel Michael is invoked here in his traditional role as the guide who greets souls departing the earth and leads them to heaven.

[103] 3742 **much silver and gold** *or e argent ad assez*: this detail is confirmed in the extensive description of the tomb, given in the twelfth-century *Pilgrim's Guide*, 76–77.

boured and struggled to translate this life. He does not wish to keep his identity hidden: Guillaume de Berneville is his name, who out of love for God and Saint Giles undertook this labour and this burden. May his sins be pardoned! May God and the good baron Saint Giles give him his just reward. May Giles lead him in his company to appear before the King of paradise. May those who have this life copied, and those who hear it and have it read, and who listen to it out of their love for God, and who are touched by it in their hearts—may God give them their reward, and may they be freed of their sins when they are at the feet of our Lord, through the prayers of our good Saint Giles (3739–80).

Here I bring my narrative to an end. May it please God not to forget us on the day of final judgement, when we will be in his court; may it please him that we be there, and may he allow us to remain there where his friends wish to be, there where there is joy without end. And may he defend us against the suffering of hell, where there is lamentation day and night. Take care not to go there! For there is found only weeping and wailing. God protect us from entering there! Let all of you here present say Amen!

II.
Simund de Freine

The Passion of Saint George

Passio beati Georgii militis et martiris[1]

A writer who expresses good sense is wise: his work profits many, since writing which demonstrates sound reason benefits all people.[2] Everything contained in this vernacular work will be of great moral benefit to the listener. I wish to tell you of Saint George and describe his martyrdom. He was fierce in the defence of his religion; he would sooner be drawn and quartered than sin against God by believing in Mohammed.[3] He would let himself be drowned rather than recant his faith. He was subjected to pain and suffering but he remained always true, stout of heart, firm, strong and steadfast. Never, even in the face of death, did he scorn his God and his religion, permitting instead that he be put to death (1–20).

To tell the story as it should be told, and to record the events properly, I wish to begin with details of the tyrant who then ruled. He was emperor of Rome, and history records his name as Dacien.[4] More than anyone else in all the world he was cruel, fierce, and evil. He put all his effort and thought into persecuting Christians. He had Christians seized and beaten in order to destroy our religion. His mind was focused only on hating the King of Heaven. There was never a man alive who had such hatred of God (21–36).

---

[1] **Rubric** On the Latin rubric, see above, 26 n. 10.
[2] **1–20** The first letter of each line of the prologue (vv. 1–20) spells out the author's name in the acrostic "SIMUND DE FREINE ME FIST." See above, 27 n. 18.
[3] **11 Mohammed** *Mahon*: the reference to the prophet of Islam (c. 570–632) is anachronistic; see above, 29.
[4] **26 Dacien** *Dacien*: on the use of Dacien, rather than Diocletian, as emperor of Rome, see above, 30.

One day he called together his nobles in order to perpetrate a great persecution for their diversion. The city where he held this council was called Milette. Thirty-two kings attended, along with their marvelling retinues.

"Lords," he said, "hear me, and give me your counsel on how best to proceed. I have called you all here in order to confound the Christians. Whoever confesses to being Christian will be put to death cruelly: I will have his back flayed down to the bone, and then salt put on the wounds. I will have his two eyes plucked out, and he will be ignominiously beheaded. Whoever does not believe in Apollo[5] will be put to death in evil fashion; whoever does not believe in him I will have drawn[6] by horses" (37–56).

Then he showed them the fetters with which he would bind Christians, and demonstrated the tortures to which he would submit the Christian people. Because of their fear of his threats no one there present dared to come forward to uphold God's law. Everyone looked carefully about on all sides, seeking to protect himself, like a hare does when it sees a hound. But George was of noble courage, he would not flinch, come what may: neither for threat of sword or lance would he abandon his belief (57–70).

I told you earlier of the emperor who scorned our law. I will now tell you of the valiant Saint George. To recount the tale as it should be told, I will tell you here of his ancestry, what type of man he was, and how he loved God dearly. Cappadocia is the name of the country where he was born. He was from a very noble family, and was of great goodness from an early age. He was a knight and had set out to earn esteem for his valour. He earned a wide reputation by deeds of arms with lance and shield.[7] He was wealthy, with many possessions, and he wished to use his riches wisely: he wanted to earn income from his possessions and turned his attention to this. He wanted to employ his wealth in order to increase his riches (71–92).

---

[5] 53 **Apollo** *Apolin*: the classical deity, called *Apolin, Apollon* in French, was traditionally considered by the medieval Church to be a devil, and figures in the *Chanson de Roland* as one member of the Saracen Trinity of false gods (along with Tervagant and Mahomet).

[6] 56 **drawn by horses** *De chivaus . . . frai detreire*: a cruel method of inflicting death, in which the victim's arms and legs are tied to horses that are driven in opposite directions to tear the body apart.

[7] 85–86 **He earned a wide reputation** *Que de den fut grant parlance*: the edition prints *Que de Deu fut grant parlance*, but suggests a correction to *de lui* is necessary; the text could be *Que deden* "so that in this" (or alternatively *Que de gen* "so that among people"), with the meaning running on from the previous sentence: "had set out to earn esteem for his valour, with lance and shield, so that in this endeavour he was much talked about," or "so that he was much talked about by the people."

For a long time he thought in this manner; then God caused him to abandon his earlier preoccupations. Once he had accepted this divine teaching, he confessed to himself:

"When I die all this will be worthless. I have been very childish to have desired riches so strongly. Why should I struggle to win what is worthless? Everyone can see clearly that wealth is of no value. The possessions that man amasses are like the moon: the moon is first a crescent, then it waxes full, then it wanes within a fortnight. So it is with riches: they are quickly gained and quickly diminished, now coming, now going. He who loves them too dearly is a fool! (93–112).

"I want to use my wealth in the service of God; I want to exchange it for divine treasure. He who spends his life in God's service spares himself from a terrible gallows. In the end when a person leaves this life, only then does his life begin. He who lives this goodly life was born blessed and has lived happily.[8] He will go off to the joy of paradise, from which he cannot be separated. There he will find glorious bliss and unending joy. Whoever strives for this does good; he will do his utmost to serve God[9] (113–26).

"Whoever does not do this will regret it when it comes to the weighing of his sins: for then he will rue the day of his judgement, unless the judge lies. Whoever is slow to serve God heaps great sin upon himself. Who can afford to take the risk that he will be repentant at the end of his life? It is madness to trust to this, for old sticks do not bend in the wind[10]—you cannot use an old dried-out stalk to bind up a bunch of faggots, you need a young green switch. I will begin without delay to serve God, before I am surprised by death. I will go immediately to the infidel emperor who is using his power to force Christians to renounce their God. I have called him emperor, but it is better to call him degrader, for he degrades the law of God who gave him his empire.[11] I will tell him to cease his

---

[8] 119–20 **was born blessed and has lived happily** *Qui en cele vie vit / Beor fu néz e beor le vit*: the French uses a pun on *vit*, which means both "saw" and "lived."

[9] 125–26 **Whoever strives for this . . . to serve God** *Ben fait qui de ceo se peine, / A Dieu servir mettra peine*: the translation inverts the order of the verses. The sense of these lines foreshadows the physical pains yet to come for the martyr. Matzke emends *mettra* to *mettrai*.

[10] 136 **old stick** *veu verge*: the metaphor of *veu verge* "old stick" and *hard* "binding rod" does not translate easily for the modern reader; the translation expands on the original text to make explicit what would have been quickly understood by a medieval audience acquainted with this rural practice. The meaning is: "It is better to change your life when you are young and flexible rather than waiting until you are old and set in your habits, incapable of changing your evil ways."

[11] 145–48 **I have called him emperor, but it is better to call him degrader** *Jo l'ai nomé emperur, / Meuz pus dire empeirur*: lit. "I could better call him degrader." The author is making an extended play on words, which is lost in translation, opposing *emperur* "emperor" and *empeirur* "one who makes things worse," continuing with *empire* "he makes worse," v. 147, and *empire*, "empire" v. 148.

persecution of Jesus Christ. I will tell him directly that his belief is in error, and that he is being deceived by the devil. I want to teach him my true belief, without fear or trembling; I will show him that he is embarked on madness, that his actions are leading him down the wrong path, and that he will forever suffer for the folly which he is now undertaking!" (127–58).

Such were his thoughts, which he set out at once to put into action; he did not tarry on the way, but came immediately to the emperor. When he stood in front of the emperor he defended the law of Christ, saying:

"Lord emperor, you commit a great wrong when you seize Christians and keep them in fetters. When you worship a statue you offer a great insult to God. It is not right that man worship a block of wood that is mute, deaf and blind, that cannot see or listen, and that cannot itself hear even a single word. It is extremely foolish to worship a tree, carved into a form that remains incapable of hearing.[12] Whatever a carpenter has carved cannot be a god of any worth! Abandon such folly, my lord, and believe no more in such a god. Put behind you this error and believe instead in God who is the Father, the Son, and the Holy Spirit. Whoever does not believe in this fashion will perish on the Day of Judgement!" (159–86).

The emperor, moved by anger, did not let him speak further.

"George," he said, "in my view you are mistaken with respect to my god. You have lied so much about him that I am now very angry with you. If you do not repent, you will regret that you uttered such lies. Because you have told so many lies you will be seized and tied up. You will be bound and tortured, and spared none of my vengeance. Your slander about me has been so extensive that I would be justified in putting you to death for such lies and calumnies. But if you choose instead to accept my beliefs, you will find me most pleasant and agreeable! (187–204).

"I will grant you great honours, fine castles with magnificent towers, gold and silver, and fine silks, to start you on your way in your new life. Change your mistaken belief and worship this image. Make a sacrifice with me and you will gain great joy. You will never win such joy through Jesus, the son of Mary!" (205–14).

George responded in the following fashion, confounding the emperor.

"My lord," he said, "listen to me, you who defend your god. Place your god on a fire, and you can then see his power, if your god can prevent the flame from setting him alight. You can hang me with a vile noose if your god is not slow to carry out such a miracle. One thing I would like to ask: if your god sees with his eyes, he does not hear with his ears; if your god is deaf, is it not a miracle? He has a nose but smells nothing. Many torments attack him, he cannot speak a single word, he cannot even move his lips, nor a foot nor a hand. I do not believe your god is holy. Indeed, sire, you know well, and have many reasons to think this,

---

[12] Psalms 115:4–8, 134:15–17.

that whoever believes in the god in whom you trust is very unwise and a miscreant deluded by false belief" (215–38).

These words grieved the emperor greatly, and he almost collapsed from anger. He responded with a great fury inspired by the devil:

"George, I am right to order that you be thrown in prison! You have embarked on a path of folly which will cause you great suffering. Your madness will bring you much pain and torture. But you should know that I am moved to great pity by the fact that your support of a false religion will bring you death. You know well that my god is true and righteous. All those who accept Apollo and hold him dear have their wishes granted immediately, and they know him to be most agreeable. Christians are beggars because they are unbelievers. They are poor, and lack possessions because their God is powerless! (239–62).

"I can tell you many reasons why you should scorn your law, and I can find many arguments to disprove your foolish statements. According to your own words, you believe your God to be at once Father, Son, and Holy Spirit. This is a bold-faced lie, for a son is born after his father; everyone can plainly see that a father and son cannot be one person. So tell me, then, according to your religion how can God be three in one? When the Jews crucified your God, when they tortured him, where were the other two Gods? They put two thieves with him on the cross: what have you to say of them? Whichever God he was, either one or three, all of them died with him; whichever he was, third or fourth, Pilate did well when he had him scourged. You believe in a hanged man, in a man sold for a silver coin. After this same man was put on the cross, your voice can no longer vaunt him. It is a complete and utter lie to say that God suffered pain and death. Death can never afflict God, nor can man ever be freed from death. It is clear to me that whoever said God suffered death was wrong (263–94).

"Your God was put in a manger. Tell me, then, what he was like: when he was hungry could he eat straw? He was surely a God held in low esteem to be placed before a donkey! Tell me more about this Jesus, about whom you are so confused: tell me the impossible, that he was born of a virgin! Who is such a fool that he accepts that any virgin could give birth, that any woman could bear a child unless she had first been made love to by a man? Those who accept this religion are very sadly deceived. This law is totally false, and my argument clearly negates it. George, since this is now proven, I ask you, in the spirit of friendship, to choose the better belief, and follow the true god" (295–316).

"Indeed, my lord," George responded, "I am willing to believe in this fashion."

This made the emperor happy, and he jumped up with joy. The king then said:

"Dear friend, since you accept this god, with all my heart I wish to embrace you, and to bring you to make your peace with Apollo!" (317–24).

George replied to him saying:

"I will reserve your kiss for later, since I suspect—indeed I know—that I will not at all follow your wishes, for instead I choose to believe in the true God, and I will never renounce him. You believe me to be defeated by your reasoning, but I can tell you truthfully that your words are those of one who understands nothing. Now do not take this as a reason for anger: I want to explain my beliefs to you. If I prove to you that my religion is logical, grant that it be accepted and well established in your country (325–38).

"God is the Father, God is the Son, God is the Holy Spirit. Each One is all Three, I believe, and each One is in himself God. I do not argue that they are three Gods, but One, and he is such that by his great power he is three persons, with one being; a true man and perfect God, Father, Son and Holy Spirit. Father and Son were together one, and all three together remain. The Father was never without the Son, no more than fire is without light, and the Holy Spirit has been since the beginning. Whoever says otherwise is lacking in reason. We hold all Three to be one God, who is both man, God and king (339–56).

"God is man? If such is true, why then was he a mortal man? I will give you a good reason; if you please, hear me out.

"God made Adam and Eve, whose sin causes us much sorrow. When Adam sinned against God, he could not make amends by himself, but it was necessary that it be man who redressed Adam's mistake. Since it could not be Adam, it was necessary that another man be born. Thus God behaved righteously when he became a mortal man on our behalf; He wished to become a man for mankind, because of the sin of the apple. God thought deeply on how he could save the world. To save us all from hell he sent down from heaven his dear Son Jesus Christ who became flesh in the virgin's womb. He was born of the beautiful virgin Mary. She was both virgin and mother through the power of his Father (357–82).

"Did the virgin then bear a child without first having carnal knowledge of a man? Yes. I will tell you a parallel example, in which you will see it clearly with your own eyes. Sunlight, when it shines on glass, passes right through it, yet the glass remains whole, brightly shining and clear. In the same fashion Mary, whose flesh remained unblemished, bore a child; when her womb was carrying God she was none the less a virgin. She bore her child as a virgin, and placed him immediately before a donkey in a manger. He was placed there to show that He was untainted by the sin of pride, so that we might follow his example of humility and poverty.[13] He went among men on foot for thirty years, then suffered death on the cross to redeem our sin (383–404).

"I have here answered you why I believe in a man who was hung on a cross. Jesus Christ suffered death for us, but God did not ever die. Was Jesus then not God? Yes, but he also became a mortal man, and that man suffered pain according to human nature. Insofar as he was God he could not die. Now you have heard, I am confident, all the tenets of my belief. Anyone who wishes to

---

[13] 397–99 **in a manger. He was placed there to show** *en sa creche. / Pur mustrer . . . fu mis*: the translation modifies the punctuation in Matzke's edition, to make a full stop at the end of v. 397 (*manger*), and to make v. 398 a clause in the following sentence.

understand the truth will not question a single word of what I have said. Since God has done so much for man, anyone who does not choose to love our Lord God I hold to be an utter infidel, whose heart is hard and bitter" (405–22).

"George," said the emperor, "I will have you stoned to death! I will have you skinned alive so that you will come to your senses! And if I cannot make you change your mind I will make you die a cruel death!"

Dacien could no longer remain still. He had a wooden horse prepared,[14] which was flat on the base but sharpened to a point on the top, like those wooden poles cut and shaped to make pikes. It was as sharp as a barber's razor. He was placed astride this sharpened point to make him recant. They weighed down his feet with lead and iron to pull down his legs further, and lit a flame underneath him to cause him anguish. His body was pricked all over with needles and covered with poisonous ointment. His skin was severely excoriated to make him submit and admit defeat (423–44).

But listen now to the great miracle that happened. George felt no pain at all! Despite the pain caused by this pointed implement, he remained no less joyful. When Dacien saw this, he was infuriated. He had George taken down from the instrument of torture, and he began to think how he could inflict greater pain on him. He had him led off to a distant site for further torments; there he was brutally beaten, and twenty-four wounds were inflicted on him, into which salt was rubbed in order to drive him mad with pain. His feet were pierced with nails, to increase his pain. Blood streamed from his feet like water flowing from a pipe (445–62).

These torments were cruel, but God was all the more gentle and courteous to him, for I assure you in all truthfulness, his body felt no pain. Even as they inflicted vile torture on George, God made it seem very sweet to him. Then it was ordered that he be thrown into a dungeon, and he was cast into a dark prison surrounded by walls. It was dark and foul and filled with vermin. George was fearful because he remained in utter darkness. Then one night he saw a great light, brighter than anyone had ever seen before. There was so much light it seemed that the sun was shining on him. God in his mercy appeared there, and said to him:

"George, do not be afraid if you are beaten and wounded; you will die three times for my sake, defending my law. Three times, by my power, you will come back to life from death.[15] The fourth time that you die you will remain with me, and I will place you beside me on my right hand in celestial paradise" (463–92).

---

[14] 430 **wooden horse**: this pyramid-shaped instrument with a sharpened point on which the victim is impaled in a seated position, then pulled down onto it by weights, is later known as a Judas cradle.

[15] 485 **Three times** *treis fez*: this would inevitably remind listeners of the New Testament prophecy by Jesus to Peter, that he would deny Christ three times before the cock crows (Matthew 26:34, Luke 22:34, John 13:38). Here, however, George will affirm the power of his God three times, before being taken to heaven after the fourth execution.

Then George rejoiced and feared the emperor no more. He was so glad in his heart he could no longer eat at all, nor sleep in his bed because of his joy at this message. Dacien was enraged at him and wanted to put him to death the next day; he undertook to destroy him, and had him brought the following day (493–502).

[. . .][16] a wheel studded with iron, and on it he had installed sharpened steel nails. Among the nails he had placed six well-sharpened swords of iron. He had it made in such a fashion that when it turned, anyone who was placed on the wheel was wounded continuously, so that blood flowed from everywhere on the body. George was bound on this wheel, and cut to pieces until he was dead; he could not escape, and quickly lost his life (503–17).

Dacien then cried out: "Now it is clear that his God failed him. If he had power at any time he would have come to George's rescue." He had the bones thrown into a large and deep well, so that no one could go there to bring him back to life.

Immediately after this the sky was covered by an enormous cloud, the like of which had never been seen, and before evening fell there was great thunder and lightning. Mountains and valleys were flattened and were not as they had been before; and the earth shook everywhere, and the people were terrified. Then there came a bright light, such as had never before been seen, and God descended from heaven with the archangel Saint Michael. Saint Michael was not slow [. . .][17] through whom God performed a wonderful miracle: over the bones he made the sign of the cross with his hand, and Saint George was made whole again (518–42) [. . .] and George then said to the emperor:[18] "By the great power He has shown on my behalf you can see the truth of my God in whom I believe. Were his power not great, you may know for certain that I would not now be alive and healthy, after having died such a death!" (543–50).

Dacien was much aggrieved when George was raised from the dead. His heart was so filled with anger and rage that he was at a loss for words, but he swore and declared that this man was not Saint George. But all around him there were a thousand people who said it was he; anyone who could see him with his own eyes could not deny that it was George.

"George," he said, "how is it that your body is not harmed by iron? Who has cast this spell which makes you feel no pain?" (551–64).

---

[16] 503 No line rhymes with v. 503 to complete a couplet. The break in rhyme and in sense indicates a lacuna in the manuscript.

[17] 538 **Saint Michael was not slow** *Seint Michel ne fut pas lenz*: the broken rhyme and the incomplete sense suggest a lacuna of at least one line after v. 538.

[18] 543 **George then said to the emperor** *Lores dist a l'emperur:* the sense suggests two or more lines are missing after v. 542, since the subject of the verb in v. 543 is George, not Saint Michael, who is the subject of the verb in v. 542.

"Indeed, emperor," he replied, "it is God the Father who has done this. Your evil has not hit its mark; God has conquered your hatred."

A pagan who heard this began to exult and mock Saint George. He was a well-known nobleman, Magnacius by name:

"George," he shouted, "you who praise your God, listen to me! Fourteen thrones have been carved, all well decorated and fashioned. They are destined for the dignitaries who often sit on them. If your God, on your behalf, can turn them back into fruit-bearing trees, the moment I see the fruit on those trees I will believe immediately in your God!" (565–82).

He who can do good is born blessed: from these thrones Saint George made trees spring forth bearing fruit, and Dacien was defeated. When he saw this, Magnacius was filled with scorn for Apollo. He renounced Apollo and Tervagant immediately, and became a Christian along with many people who had come there. He believed in God along with many others, and more than a hundred were baptized (583–94).

The evil and cruel Dacien was eager to avenge himself. He sent messengers throughout the land seeking good magicians to advise and help him. A very clever one came forward, who seemed very knowledgeable, Anastasius by name.

"I will give you good advice," he said.

He set about immediately to show his skill. In full view of everyone in the square he had an ox cut in half; but such was his skill and artifice that the ox then walked away in one piece. He boasted of his powers and said that Dacien could gouge out both his eyes if he, Anastasius, did not succeed in destroying Saint George, a task which he would undertake most willingly (595–615).

He took an enormous toad, an adder, and a serpent, along with a lizard, and put with them a highly poisonous spider, and crushed their bodies to extract the venom, which he put in a drink.[19] [. . .] He pronounced his enchantment over the brew and brought forth many devils. He then had Saint George drink from it:

"If this goes down your throat without causing you harm, your God is good and faithful" (616–29).

Saint George swallowed the drink, which did not harm him at all. There was no need for an antidote; God had miraculously saved him. Anastasius saw this, and his heart was completely converted to God. He was baptized at once and believed in Jesus Christ.

When Anastasius changed his religion, Dacien took his revenge; he ordered him decapitated, but the angels rejoiced. Angels now descended, singing with great joy, and led him straight up to heaven where the other martyrs dwell; he was taken to heaven above where there is unending bliss (630–47).

Dacien was distraught because the poisoned drink had failed, and since it had done no harm, he looked for another way in which to destroy George. Then

---

[19] 623 **drink** *beivre*: the lack of a rhyme for *beivre* suggests at least one missing line.

he hit on a diabolical and vicious method: he had sixty nails hammered into Saint George's skull and by this cruel torture caused him great suffering, but George had such a pure and good heart, filled with such love of Jesus Christ, that his pain was turned to joy. God again took pity on him in his suffering, and he restored his head to wholeness. God tore out the nails pounded into his head and nowhere on his head was there any sign of a wound (648–67).

Dacien remained furious, his earlier anger in no way abated. He did not wish to make peace with God, and still sought to conquer Saint George. He next committed a monstrously evil act: when George would not recant his religion he had him cut in two pieces with a saw. Inspired by his hatred, Dacien then had a large cauldron of resin set to boil into which the body was cast. When the flesh had completely cooked and fallen off the bones, he had all the liquid drained off, so that not a drop remained. He did this fearing that if anyone could obtain and carry off any part of it, it might be possible to bring the body back to life by some magician's art (668–87).

Saint Michael came immediately and collected what remained of the bones, along with the little bits of the body which had been cast aside. Then Jesus came and placed his blessing on the remains, and by his grace the body was resurrected on the spot. All the people witnessed and knew this miracle. They cried out, saying that the God George worshipped was powerful. All exclaimed with one voice:

"Bless us with the sign of the cross!"

All wished to be baptized and give themselves to God. George was overjoyed, but there was no water available nearby. Since water was needed, he struck the ground with his foot, and by the power of God a fountain of water sprang forth. George took some of this water, blessed it, and baptized the people. There were at least five hundred who came and stood with him before the emperor. Each one declared aloud that Jesus Christ was the true God. They were confirmed in this belief by their witnessing of God's miracle (688–719).

Dacien was filled with rage and shame and tried to deny their story. He declared that it was done not by God, but by magic trickery. His heart was so evil and obdurate that he would not accept the miracle at any cost. He then ordered George to be seized and sent to live with an old woman in a very small hovel. In such a place he would not find happiness, but would perish from shame. As soon as Dacien had declared his plan Saint George was sent there as a prisoner (720–33).

The dwelling to which George came was held up by crucks;[20] nothing else supported it and the least thing could have caused a wall or a beam to fall down on his head or shoulders. When the widow saw her guest she removed the pots

---

[20] 735 **cruck** *furche*: a forked timber, rising from the ground to the roof ridge, supporting the roof beam of a house; this building technique was well-known in Anglo-Saxon England (s.v. cruck[2], crock, *sb.*[5], *OED*).

and tripod from the room to make it clean and tidy. She prepared his room neatly, but it remained empty.

"Welcome, my guest," she said, "you have come to a good hotel! You are lodged here," she continued in jest, "in luxury."

Saint George saw that she was joking, and was grateful to her for this. He asked her for bread; the widow replied:

"There is none; in this house there is not a single grain of wheat with which to make bread."

He responded:

"Who is your god?"

The widow answered:

"You know well that I worship Apollo who is noble, mild, and righteous."

"Widow," he said, "you have no bread because Apollo is powerless. This much is certain: your poverty is due to him."

The widow replied:

"Please be seated, and do not worry. I intend to go out to see if I can find bread; and be assured, if I find some, you will have all you need" (734–69).

When the widow had gone into the street to beg for bread God provided it in such quantity that she had all she could carry. . . . Now, in order to improve her dwelling,[21] God instantly made the house both longer and wider. At once it miraculously became twelve feet higher. The length of the cruck outside was twelve feet taller, and the wood, which had been almost rotten, now was covered in blossoms. Inside the house the table was set on well-made trestles and covered with a beautiful, fine white cloth, with knives, spoons, and salt cellars, and brightly shining serving dishes. There was all the food and drink any Christian could want! (770–90).

The widow who previously had no bread now could have a whole sack full. When she returned to her house she believed Saint George to be God on high, and at once fell down at his feet.

"Woman," he said, "rise up! I assure you that I am not God. Indeed, I am only a mortal man. But it is God who works through me to show you his great power" (791–800).

The widow seized him by the foot, asking for mercy, saying:

"I have a child who is blind and deaf, naked and lame, unable to walk. If you will undertake to cure him and make him healthy, I will have myself and him baptized; I want to renounce Apollo."

George then took her child in his hands and prayed at length to God that he be able to hear and see. His prayer was answered, for the child regained his sight and hearing. George held him and continued praying until he regained his speech. The child still could not walk, but George did not wish to cure him of

---

[21] 774 **to improve her dwelling** *Pur atorner cel ostel*: another line without a matching rhyme, suggesting that a missing line precedes v. 774.

this illness: later on in my narrative you will be told the reason why he reserved this for another time.

The widow did not want to wait, but immediately chose to be baptized. After seeing such a great miracle, she despised Apollo and had herself and her child baptized at once (801–26).

In this manner God wrought a fine miracle, but He now worked a completely new one. A woman came running to Saint George in tears, sighing with sorrow, mournful, dejected and anguished. She threw herself at his feet and with a pleading heart said:

"Lord, please listen to me, you who have the power to help me. This morning I had two oxen, which I used in my work.[22] . . . I now have no other earthly possessions. One of my sons, who is young and foolish, has broken the neck of one of them. Now my land lies waste and I shall soon be in poverty. I regret being alive, for I will now be wretched always. In the name of this God in whom you believe, pray to Him on my behalf that He restore to health my ox by which I earned my living" (827–49).

Saint George was noble, gentle, and kindly to all. When he saw the woman cry he began to pray. After he had prayed for a while, by the grace of God he did a singular thing:

"Woman," he said, "cry no more, but go at once, without delay. Place my staff on your ox, and God will heal it at that very moment."

The woman took his staff, and immediately put it on the ox. Our Lord God restored its health and the next day it showed no signs of injury (850–63).

At that moment Dacien the evil king came out of his palace. When he saw the blossoming cruck timber he was so angry he thought he would die. He asked his people:

"What is in bloom over there?"

And someone replied:

"George has shown great power. That used to be a mean hut, so small that one could hardly enter; now it is a new dwelling, both long and wide, spacious and beautiful. There was a cruck at the gable holding up this hovel. He made it burst into bloom, I believe, so he could later exalt his religion."

Dacien had George summoned:

"George," he said, "do not hide from me by whose power you have done such a miracle. What God is this who looks after you? Who casts a spell such as this by which you fool the people? This cruck in bloom shows clearly that you know a great deal of sorcery" (864–87).

George responded, saying:

---

[22] 839 **I now have no other earthly possessions** . . . *Jo n'oi suz ciel plus estor*: this line is without a matching rhyme, making the couplet incomplete and suggesting that a line (or more) is missing.

"My God is Jesus Christ, who made heaven above and created all things. Him I remember always; He is God, the King of glory, who by his power constrains all your thoughts. When I am filled with his grace I do not fear you in any way. He does whatever I ask; you have seen it with your own eyes. But your god is deaf and hears nothing in any court. He is halt, dumb and blind, and is the devils' plaything. In truth, his nature is such that he could be split apart to make pickets. He could be splintered into pickets for a hedge, and his wounds would never heal" (888–907).

Dacien was already beside himself with rage:

"George," he shouted, "you are raving mad! You would never utter such foolishness if you weren't caught up in a fantasy. Such wickedness grieves me, and my heart is full of sorrow. But it would be a great shame to perpetrate an insult against a madman. When you have regained your proper senses, you will receive great honour from me. Abandon your insults and wickedness, and change your foolish belief. Once you have given up your folly there will be no one more worthy than you. George, if ever you were to accept our religion,[23] I can see that you would know very well how to denigrate and scorn the law of Jesus. But now do just one thing for me, and you will have won me over completely. I tell you this, I swear and promise it to be true: there is no one in all my empire, I tell you this in all honesty, who will be closer to me than you. Believe as I believe, and I will give you a share of my jewels, chosen from among the richest and most beautiful, and you will have fine horses. Be true to my god, believe in Apollo, and you will be happy in the end" (908–39).

Saint George quickly took this advice:

"Send a provost with the order to have the people gather here immediately, for I accept your request to make a sacrifice with them as witnesses."

Dacien was overjoyed at the news, but he would later greatly regret it. He wanted to give George a kiss, but George was not pleased by this sign of acceptance. Dacien truly believed that George was about to do fully what he wanted him to do, but George had something completely different in mind. He would not do Dacien's bidding no matter what the cost, not for anything in the world. Instead, he had spoken with great deceptiveness (940–55).

Then the widow came forward, leading her crippled child who had earlier recovered his voice, hearing, and vision. Sighing dejectedly and with sadness and sorrow, she addressed George directly, saying:

"Why is it that you are now deceived by the devil? Are you willing in the end to abandon God for Apollo? In whom then can God place his trust, if you are willing to deny Him? In a short space of time you have changed your mind for

---

[23] 923 **accept our religion** *tenez nostre lei* MS *tenge vre lei*: Matzke emends both the verb and the poss. adj.; the latter is clearly written *vre*, but *u* and *v* are usually interchangeable, and *u* and *n* are frequently confused in writing, so the emendation is justified by the form of the letter, as well as being required for the sense.

the worse. Give your pledge to God and change your foolish belief. You should not in any way make a sacrifice to Apollo: everyone who knows him is aware that he is just a vile object made of wood!" (956–75).

In his heart George rejoiced at what the widow said, and he gladly took the child from his mother.

"Child," he said, "may Jesus Christ who formed and made us, and who through me has granted you health in three of your faculties, may He now here grant you by his grace complete health."

And instantly God made him able to walk and run about the square.

Then George went up directly to where Apollo was, for he wanted to make evident to the people that anyone who worshipped a devil was foolish. He wanted it to be clear how the people had been tricked. He took a large crowd of two thousand five hundred people with him. It was in order to draw a large crowd that he had promised earlier by deception and cunning to make a sacrifice (976–99).

When George came into the temple Apollo knew that he would be defeated. He who wished to be called a god would willingly have hidden himself. George then uttered his challenge:

"Who is here within?"

Apollo, who hated repentance, did not want to lie:

"Sir," he said, "I ask for your pity. It is I, Apollo, who am within."

George then commanded:

"Come out and show yourself."

Apollo was reluctant and replied with a trembling voice,

"I am willing to show myself, kind sir, voluntarily, when it is absolutely necessary. The best advice is that when you cannot avoid doing something, you should do it willingly" (1000–17).

He came out, since he was obliged to do so, so that the people could look at him. Whoever looked at his head saw that he was an ugly beast. His horrid head, with his hair standing on end, was large and misshapen. His black hair hung down like the tail of a horse. His hairy forehead was like that of a bear, completely deformed. He had two horns on his forehead like those of an ox. His eyebrows were like two fox tails. His eyes were crossed, ill-set and widely spaced: there was at least a palm-span, if not a quarter of an arm's length, between them. His face was very thin, blacker than pitch. Without a word of a lie, no corpse ever had an uglier look than he. His nose was vilely shaped, hanging down like a goshawk's beak, and it spewed forth black smoke like a house ablaze. His mouth was as wide as a hound's, from which came flame and fire, and he gnashed his teeth like a mastiff biting someone. His foul breath smelled like sulfur thrown on flames; his was not at all the sweet mouth that gives a lover's kisses (1018–51).

When George saw his horrible and ferocious appearance he said to him:

"Lord Apollo, why do people bow down to you? Your body is not noble enough to be worshipped!"

Apollo replied:

"I will not lie: I force them to follow me."

George answered:

"You are so false and unfaithful to God that you should indeed be struck down by lightning, you who cast your spells on people. Your magic powder, by which you have made many a fool, comes from Saint Vulture,[24] the devil" (1052–65).

He struck the ground with his foot, making a deep, wide pit into which he threw Apollo in front of all these people. He cast into the abyss the one who had extracted tithes from thousands. And God did even more on behalf of Saint George by knocking down all the idols. Whether they were of wood or stone, not one image remained intact. Now you can understand that it was in this fashion that George intended to carry out the sacrifice which he had earlier promised to make (1066–79).

Anyone who saw Dacien then would have seen that he was beside himself with rage. Only a close friend would have listened to him while he was in this state.[25]

"George," he said, "why have you attracted all my people here to shame me in front of them? I can no longer trust them. But my power is worth little if I cannot avenge my shame. You called my people here, but you were very deceptive. There was no possibility that I could have known the treachery in your heart. Now the deceit hidden in your heart is openly revealed. Do you know, George, what I think? Now that all the traitors are assembled here it is you who should carry their banner because you know the methods of treachery so well. You have acted with polished deceit, just like a bishop's piece in chess. The bishop, when it is put in check, often escapes by taking rooks and pawns by unexpected moves. You have betrayed Apollo, and for this you will come to a bad end. He who dares to betray a god must in turn himself fall. This is a court ruling known throughout the world: no one can be saved from death who has committed treason. You will be completely destroyed, and you have trusted to sorcery, to your own misfortune. I recall well your tricks, for which you will pay with life and limb. The cruck burst into bloom only by your trickery; because of your love for this flowering I will make you die most vilely" (1080–1121).

---

[24] 1064–65 **Saint Vulture** *seint Busart*: the name *Busart* given to the mock saint is chosen to rhyme with the noun *musart* "fool." Saint Trickster or Saint Deception might be a more likely parallel, although the literal translation (*busart* "buzzard, vulture") also prefigures the victimization of these hapless believers.

[25] 1082–83 **Only a close friend would have listened to him while he was in this state** *Mult lui serreit amis chers, / Qui dunc lui prestast deners*: lit. "anyone who would then have lent him money would have been a dear friend." MS: *A qui deners prestast*: Matzke emends to create the rhyme and to complete the allegorical statement, although the sense remains ambiguous. The sense is either, "He would have considered anyone who trusted him while he was in this state to be a dear friend," or "Only a close friend would have trusted him while he was in this state."

Then in his anger he ordered them to prepare an awe-inspiring martyrdom. Large candles were lit and placed on his back. George's soft and tender flesh could not protect itself from the fire; when the flame reached his flesh, his body began to melt. His body vanished, like snow in sunshine. Hot grease flowed from every part of his body. No meat grilled over charcoal ever burned as quickly. When the fat had been rendered from his back and sides, the body caught fire and turned into a cinder. But why should I go into more detail? Suffice it to say that his body was subjected to every indignity. I can sum up in a word: as a result of such torture he died there and then (1122–43).

Now hear what the wicked traitor next did. He had whatever remained of George's body carried to a high plain at the top of a mountain, for he believed that if any part of his body was left, crows would come and quickly eat it. He didn't want any part remaining from which George might be resuscitated.

But God had told George earlier that he would raise him from death three times to teach the people they should have faith in God. And in order to fulfil this prophecy God again brought him back to life. When the people who had been especially sent there with his remains saw this, they all cried out:

"George's God is powerful! The one in whom George believes shows clearly that his faith is right. George's God is good and true." So spoke clerics and laypeople alike (1144–67).

Dacien was filled with grief and anger, and strove harder to defeat George. He prepared a hellish torment for him by heating an iron boot, and when it was red-hot he had George place his foot in it in front of the crowd. George felt pain and suffering in good measure, but the angel of God was close by to protect him, so the fire did not wound him in the least.

Dacien, who wished to defeat Jesus Christ, searched for another, more evil torture. One such involved wild animals: he put George like a criminal among leopards and lions, among serpents and fierce, biting, famished wolves; among savage bears, in the midst of several rapacious wild boars, among dragons and snakes which usually kill humans. In short, he wanted the animals to devour him. He wanted him to suffer death without the comfort of God. He thought at the time that God would be unable to rescue him (1168–97).

Whoever loves and follows God is in return loved by God; when you have God's protection nothing should cause you fear. Here God has shown us this clearly. The lions and leopards all approached him, and then — what a fine and touching miracle — they all bowed down to him. The wolf which was so famished licked his feet, and the bear and wild boar also tried to lick him. And the dragon as well, whose breath was so foul, full of fire and flame, also caressed his feet and legs and hands with his tongue. In this way George escaped unscathed (1198–1215).

When Alexandrine, Dacien's wife and queen, saw this, she was ashamed of herself and ran throughout the city, not hiding her distraught state, and cried out to the pagans:

"Lords, I am a Christian! Even if I should lose my life, I will not abandon my belief in Jesus, the Son of Mary. Jesus Christ is the true God and Apollo a false one. He has been cast down into a pit, and whoever believes in him is lost!"

This caused Dacien exquisite pain.

"Tell me, my queen," he said, "has George inspired this folly in you by his trickery? Are you willing to leave me and renounce your religion for him? What marvel have you witnessed that has so deceived you? Rest assured that you are mad to believe so firmly in his word!" (1216–39).

The queen replied with true and honest heart:

"Sire, you are certainly mistaken, for I know, and you also know at the bottom of your heart, that your religion is false. Anyone who does not deny reason can see in the example of this man George that his God is clement and good and that Apollo is very evil. Because I have seen his power I wish to follow his law; no man's argument will persuade me to abandon this religion. He who is travelling on foot and becomes tired, and wishes to rest a while in a meadow, does not show good sense if he chooses to sit down on a thistle. Your religion is even more of a folly than this, for God has granted that anyone who loves Jesus Christ and abandons the devil will have eternal life. Whoever believes in Him will be saved, this I know and believe firmly.[26] But whoever believes in Apollo will be forever lost!" (1240–65).

The queen was of steadfast faith. She would not waver at any cost in her belief; she wished to follow Saint George, even if her throat were to be slashed. Dacien was amazed and had no idea what he should do. When he couldn't budge her from her convictions he was at a complete loss and said to her:

"My dearly beloved, abandon this madness of yours. My dear, out of your love for me, do not renounce your religion!"

The queen remained firm, considering his argument to be of no value. She did not wish to change her belief, even on pain of execution. When Dacien saw he could not expect any other response from her, he had her seized and dragged off by her hair to be publicly tortured. Because she was filled with God's spirit she willingly bore the pain. God gave her the wisdom to bear it all patiently; she suffered shame, pain, and dishonour all for the love of God. She wished to believe in Jesus Christ, and fervently asked Saint George to baptize her in the name of God so that she would be saved (1266–95).

George stood up immediately and raised his hands towards God.

"God," he said, "celestial King, who deigned to be born a man for us; God, powerful beyond all doubt, who by your strength and power fed five thousand with the five loaves that you gave them, and made twelve baskets full of bread to be left over;[27] Lord, who made the sun, the moon and every star, and who created

---

[26] Cf. John 3:16.

[27] 1301–05 **with the five loaves** ... *De cinc peins*: The miracle of the loaves and fishes (cf. Matthew 14:15–21, John 6:1–14) is included in this statement of Christian doctrine

the darkness of night, and the sun to shine during the day; who made the four winds to blow from the four quarters of the sea; Lord, I ask and pray that your angels come down here to baptize this woman who wishes to renounce the devil" (1296–1315).

After he had prayed a cloud appeared and then came rain which left much water. From the rain which fell he took water in his hands and ran to the queen who had such perfect love for God.

"Be assured," he said, "that God loves me, for he has sent me to baptize you."

He blessed the water immediately with the sign of the cross, and let it fall on her, saying,

"I baptize you,[28] [. . .] in the name of the Holy Spirit I now baptize you."

She thereupon became a Christian and followed the Christian religion (1316–32).

As soon as she was baptized she was led off to be beheaded. But you can be certain that she did not fear martyrdom in the least. She had such comfort from God that death did not daunt her at all. As the sword was raised to execute her, in front of everyone she prayed devoutly, saying:

"God in whom I believe, have pity on me. Jesus Christ, the Son of Mary, since I die for your sake I ask for your mercy that I may see you face to face."

A voice from heaven replied to her on behalf of Jesus Christ:

"Woman, fear not; you will suffer death to gain life. God has told his angels to bring your soul to him."

Then she presented her neck, and said:

"I commend myself to God."

At this word her head was struck off, and God rejoiced greatly. He had her soul raised on high where there is unending joy. Here you see an example of how God returns love to those who have served him. Here you have evident proof: service to God is time well spent! (1333–64).

I have told you here about the queen and her perfect love for God. I want now to tell you more about Dacien. He had George summoned, and told him he wanted to follow his religion, since his God loved him so much that he raised people from the dead.

"George," he said, "several people's bodies are buried just outside here. If you will ask your God to raise them alive out of the earth, and if your God does this for you so that they are alive and speaking, I will believe in Him on the spot, and will hold my god in scorn."

George firmly believed that God would do what he wished, and he responded:

---

summarized in George's prayer.

[28] 1328 **saying, "I baptize you** *E li dist: 'Jo vus baptiz*: this line is not followed by a line with the same rhyme, suggesting a line (or more) has been missed by the scribe.

"My lord, I will willingly ask God to do this, on condition that if those who are dead are brought back to life, you will no longer persecute those who believe in Jesus, son of Mary" (1365–88).

Dacien promised that he would indeed honour this condition. George had the earth removed and the tomb opened. Nothing but ashes was found inside, and he had some of this removed, and holding the ashes in his hand, he prayed to Jesus Christ.

"God omnipotent," he said, "eternal Father, Father, Son and Holy Spirit, almighty God: you, who as the one true God created the world out of the void, and all the elements, earth, water, fire and air. You who by your strength and power make peace and moderation between all things, who joined together rightly and justly the dry with the damp, the hot with the cold. God who by a fine miracle made wine out of water, who by a marvellous miracle saved Daniel from the lion; you, truly, by whom Lazarus was raised from the dead; Jesus Christ the true Saviour, Jesus the Son, and Jesus the Father, Jesus king of humility, Lord full of pity, Jesus sweet and kind, who took flesh and blood and was born of a woman, the blessed virgin Mary, and who then fasted forty days to deliver us from suffering; who finally died to redeem our sin, then rose again from the dead, without your guards noticing it; whom it pleased to descend into purgatory to free souls there, and then went up to heaven; anyone who believes anything other than all this is a fool. Lord God, I ask you to resuscitate these dead!" (1388–1434).

After Saint George had prayed, he could consider himself blessed, for a voice came down to him out of heaven saying that God would do all he asked and more: He did not wish to deny him anything, he could pray to Him with confidence. God accomplished what he had asked: from the tomb he raised up nine women and three children, and five grown men along with them. Those who were resuscitated inspired great pity. They all kneeled before Saint George and asked him earnestly that in God's name he permit that they not return to the place from which they had come. For He knew well and truly that it was a painful dwelling place where they suffered great torment all the days of the week. George put his faith in God and asked for his mercy that they not be led back to where they had been tortured. Then he embraced and comforted one of those who had come back from the dead. He asked him to tell his name and how he died and in which god he had believed, so that he, George, could be certain of who he was and what he had done (1435–64).

"My name is Joel," the man said, "and I have suffered for many years,[29] endured torments over many winters and many summers. I died when I was at the peak of my powers, some two hundred years ago. Lord Apollo was my god, and for this I have suffered tortures beyond description, so great has been my

---

[29] 1466 **I have suffered for many years** *Mult ai eu maint dur noël*: Simund uses the feast of Christmas (*noël*), rhyming with *Joel*, to signal the passage of each year, lit. "I have had many a difficult Christmas."

martyrdom. I was taken to hell, where my body was bound in iron. Satan was eager to make my suffering unbearable. There I felt and experienced the pains which wrack wretched mortals. There I saw putridness and stench, and great misfortunes, and was put in a bath a hundred times colder than ice. When any wretch was in it, the cold made his teeth chatter. Another bath was prepared elsewhere, hotter than any fire that burns. This makes the body so hot that the bowels burst open and fall out. People are taken there by force, to be exposed repeatedly to both heat and cold, where they are alternately freezing with cold and burning with heat.[30] This torment is without end. Beelzebub and Satan laugh, at the expense of these wretches. They continuously go from place to place to make sport of their suffering. Those who have committed adultery endure exquisite pain. Those who have broken their oath or forsworn themselves are put in unending fire. When usurers come there they pay dearly for their money: those who have demanded three coins' interest for four coins lent are beaten continuously. Those who have died in lechery lead a vile existence in hell, for Satan thrusts them into eternal flames. Each one, according to his evil, pays dearly for his vice; the devil inflicts shame on each one, neither count nor king is spared" (1465–1514).

After the man had spoken these words, George at once called for all the others whom God had raised from death, who had long lain buried in the earth but now had been raised from the dead. Each one was baptized and returned to Jesus. Not a single one of them remained on earth after baptism, for each one was taken into paradise and lived there in joy (1515–26).

As this beautiful miracle was happening Dacien remained silent. He paid no more attention to it than he would to a dream: he said it was a deception. He was so evil and debased that he would not believe his own eyes. His heart was three times harder than the stone used for making walls. He would not at any cost choose to love God, so wicked and bitter was his heart. He harboured at all times an anger toward God greater than any tongue can say. He was in such a rage that his face was scarlet; he was so caught up in his fury that his heart almost burst; he was so puffed up with his anger that his belt broke; he was so enraged and infuriated that he fell down from his throne in confusion (1527–46).

"Alas," he cried, "what can I possibly say? George has taken all my empire from me. He has drawn all my people to him, and everyone has already been baptized. I have often tortured him, but although he was tortured yesterday, this does not prevent him from tricking my people into following him today. I can cause him no further suffering by my torments. Yet, for all the pain I might have caused him yesterday, this never prevents him from persuading my people into joining him

---

[30] 1492–93 **where they are alternately freezing with cold and burning with heat** *Sovent unt chaut, sovent freit. / Ore unt freit, ore unt chaut*: the translation freely expands the image to avoid the bald repetition of the literal text: "Often they are hot, often cold. Now they are cold, now they are hot."

today. He knows so much sorcery, and he connives and lies so that foolish people align themselves with this madman and all believe his folly, and the madness continues. If his madness persists, our religion is considered unworthy; if I put up with his resistance my heart is seen as hardened against my own god. I do not want to hold him in prison, for I see that he has learned by his evil to escape from there each time he has been seized. I eagerly wish to make him suffer; he has furiously sought to dishonour me. I want to torture him until his heart is filled with anger. To my shame he is still alive, he who despises my god. He is full of great pride, but I will soon strike him down. I saw yesterday how I will put him to death. His heart is too full of bile, and his words are too filled with honey. He is too cunning and clever, deceiving all and sundry. Anyone who does not follow Apollo is evil and base. He wrongs and shames my god, for which he will soon die by the sword and lance, and there will be no more talk of him. I will have him given such blows and cuts by the sword over all his body that his god will come too late to his rescue. Because I have not taken vengeance on him who has disputed my religion, I have suffered too long, and Apollo has lost too much. But since he does not wish to make peace, tomorrow he will die without fail!" (1548–1600).

Dacien was ready for his evil act.

"Take this vassal, make certain that he is well bound, and guide him to the place where my queen, gone mad, was earlier beheaded."

Immediately a very cruel, wicked, and ferocious attendant came forward and dragged George off by his hair, inflicting great pain. In his mouth he put a bit, such as is used for a colt, and made him leave wearing this horse's bridle; never have I seen anyone led off in this way. He went off with the bit in his mouth, without a halter, like a horse being led by hand. The marvelling multitude ran to the place where he later died; there was not one in five hundred who did not immediately rush to the spot. A large crowd accompanied him, asking for his blessing. Everyone declared and knew well that his God could save them; everyone said in his heart that they would be lost if they kept their former religion (1601–26).

When George arrived finally at the fortress[31] where he would be put to death, he turned to the people and said with great pity:

"My lords, I pray to the God for whom I must here die, who chose to die for us all, and who suffered death because it pleased him to do so. To him I pray that by his grace he make you all Christians, and give you such counsel." [. . .][32]

With a confident and noble heart he looked to heaven above.

---

[31] 1627 **at the fortress** *desqu'al fort*: George is executed on the same spot as Alexandrine. This is the first time it is called a fortress; the Latin sources state it is "outside the city" (*extra civitatem* and *foras civitatem*: Guilcher, *Deux Versions*, 129, 131).

[32] 1637 **and give you such counsel** *E tel conseil vus envie*: the lack of a rhyme for v. 1637 and the break in syntax both suggest a lacuna in the text. Matzke believes the missing line may be: *Par quei tut tens avrez vie*, "By which you will have eternal life."

"God," he said, "King of glory, you have victory over everything. I commend these people to you, and pray that through your grace they may renounce the devil, and see you in heaven" (1627–45).

A voice then said to him:

"George, you will not die again. Accept death willingly. In it you will find comfort. By this death you will win life which death can never take away. You must no longer stay in the world; come at once up to heaven, come quickly on high: for now you shall have life eternal."

Thereupon the executioner raised his sword and struck off his head, beheading Saint George with one blow. Angels came down from heaven with the archangel Michael, singing songs in celestial harmonies of miraculous sweetness. They took his soul and carried it with hymns to heaven above where there is eternal rejoicing. Now he has exchanged his pain for bliss; now he lives in joy, not sorrow. No tongue can describe the ecstasy he has gained from his great martyrdom (1646–71).

The nobles of the city had great compassion for his body. By night they took the body in secret from where it lay. They carried it to the church and anointed it with balm, and it was buried at night in a place where later many have been healed. It is clear that God cherishes George, for miracles happen there often. There many deaf regain their hearing and the lame begin to walk; the mute speak aloud and many blind people see.[33]

But now hear what became of the emperor in the end. At first he thought he had won a victory, but then things turned out differently. That very day he was struck by lightning and burned to a powder. All those who were with him drank from the same cup:[34] they were struck with such a thunderbolt that they died on the spot. The man who placed the bridle on George did so to his own misfortune. He was struck with such a bolt of lightning that his house was destroyed. God thus showed clearly their wrongdoing, for each one died. They were all sent to hell, whereas Saint George went to paradise. Where they are there is no joy, and Saint George is on high, in celestial paradise. May God grant that we all may be there; may He grant us pure joy which never ends, day after day, and blissful eternal life. Amen, amen, let us each say amen (1672–1711).

---

[33] Cf. Matthew 15:31, Luke 7:22.

[34] 1693 **drank from the same cup** *De cel hanap mesme burent*: a metaphor for "suffered the same fate," based, perhaps, on the image of Socrates and the Greek tradition of voluntary execution by drinking from a poisoned cup.

III.
Simon de Walsingham
Monk of St. Edmunds Abbey, Bury

The Life of Saint Faith, Virgin Martyr

My lords, you who believe in God and are confirmed in the faith, unless I lie,[1] you have heard and know it to be true that no living being, either young or old, of high or low estate,[2] shall be saved without a steadfast faith. This is a truth that I fully believe—righteous Faith[3] will save us and bring us to celestial joy (1–10).

For that reason, if you agree,[4] you should all the more willingly hear the life of St. Faith sung and read, and her virtues described, for as you hear more about Faith you will be more steadfast in your faith. Listen to me, then, and I will tell you of St. Faith, a most holy young maiden who was fair of face and even more beautiful in her faith; of her holy life and passion and her saintly conduct; of how her saintly life and holy name were in perfect harmony, complementing each other better than a jewel enhances a ring, for they were wholly one, as she herself said when the tyrant asked her name, as you yourself will hear later in my

---

[1] **3 unless I lie** *si jeo ne ment*: a tag line, more colloquially "truth be told," "without word of a lie." The literal translation is used to show that this is a rhetorical strategy—if you believe that I am telling the truth here, you must also accept what I say about St. Faith.

[2] **6 of high or low estate** *petit ne grant*: this could also mean "a child or fully grown person." The reference to social status would have particular relevance to both the wealthy monks of Bury St. Edmunds Abbey and to the aristocratic members of Campsey convent, where this manuscript was later read at mealtimes.

[3] **9 righteous Faith** *La bone Fei*: the writer is using a play on words—this is both *bone Fei* and *bone fei*, "righteous Faith" and "the right faith." The deliberate play on the double meaning of proper name and theological virtue is used repeatedly in the narrative. Medieval manuscripts normally use lowercase letters for proper names, so the ambiguity of the oral form also remains in the written manuscript. It is the modern editor who disambiguates *Fei* and *fei* for the printed text.

[4] **13 if you agree** *sel* (MS *cel*) *vus vient a pleisir*: another tag line (lit. "if this meets with your pleasure", "if you will").

story, if you pay close attention. But you who are about to listen to my recital, I beseech you in God's name not to blame me if I make mistakes in my French narrative—I know that I am presumptuous in this undertaking, since I am unlearned and inexperienced in translating into the vernacular.[5] I am but a weak sinner who falters night and day, in thought, in deed, and in word, so when I dare to undertake to narrate in any way at all[6] the life of St. Faith, you should rightly hold me to account: but I must be forgiven, for I am doing it out of my devotion to, and in honour of, this young maiden whose beauty is second only to that of the Virgin Mary (11–48).

I will tell you my motive, and explain why I cherish, honour, and especially wish to venerate Faith: on the feast night of her passion (6 October)—which is a solemn veneration of the moment of her liberation from her earthly suffering—I myself was born into my earthly tribulations. On the day her torments ended, my own travails began; on the day she received joy and honour, I was born into a life of pain and suffering; she now lives in rejoicing and gladness, while I live in lamentation and sadness, and the painful struggle of this translation. For this reason, I hope that you, God, will permit her to come to my aid[7] both in this earthly struggle and in this narration which I offer as an act of penance[8] (for there are

---

[5] 37 **since I am unlearned and inexperienced in translating into the vernacular** *Jeo ke ne suy guere lettré*, MS *Ieo ke ne say guer de letre*: the meaning is kept by replacing *saveir guer de letre* with *estre guere lettré*. Baker makes this emendation, which is necessary for the rhyme with *enromancé* "poorly skilled in the vernacular"; on the usual sense of *enromancer* "translate into the vernacular" [i.e. French] see *AND* 233a. In this iteration of the modesty topos Simon seems to be self-deprecating about his education and his skill in French. Or is this an example of (exaggerated) second-language anxiety engendered by social class distinctions, to show deference to his learned superiors? Abbot Samson was trained at the University of Paris, and was renowned for his skill in both French and Latin (see above, 50). Simon himself was not a Master, although five of his fellow monks, including his kinsman Thomas of Walsingham, held this title, according to the chronicle describing the election dispute of 1213–15 at Bury St. Edmunds (R. Thomson, *Chronicle of the Election of Hugh* [Oxford: Clarendon Press, 1974], xxxvi).

[6] 43 **undertake . . . in any way at all** *E en nule manere enprendre*: the phrase is slightly ambiguous and emphasizes the modesty topos.

[7] 63–65 **the painful struggle of this translation. For this reason, I hope that you, God, will permit her to come to my aid** *En cest travailz peines / E pur ceo en espeir deines / K'ele me sucure*: Baker states that the text is corrupt here, and suggests emending vv. 63–64: *En cest travail assez me peine / E pur ceo en espeir ke deine* . . . This translation, however, takes *travailz* v. 63 to mean the work of translation at hand, as well as the more general travails of life, and emends v. 64: *espeir [ke] deines*, with God understood as the 2nd pers. sing. subject.

[8] 66 **this narration which I offer as an act of penance** *cest travail d'espenëie*, MS *ceste trauail depenie*: the scribal form *epenie* shows loss of preconsonantal *s*. Baker proposes the form *espenëie* as deverbal noun from *espeneir* "expiate"; the standard form is *espenissement*; the infinitive has collateral forms *espenir, -einir, -eneir, -ener, -enoir* (cf. *AND* 266a).

many in this world to whom you give abundant help). Through her intercession may she usher me into the eternal joy which she herself received on the very day that I was born into the toil of this earthly life. For these reasons I began writing this work—may God grant that I profit from it (49–74).

Earlier I explained why I should be pardoned any errors in my narrative. I give you now another reason why I have undertaken this task. One of my companions, a worthy man, well versed in learning and with much good sense,[9] a man whose short physical stature is the opposite of his imposing moral strength, especially requested that I, as a compatriot, born and raised in the same region as himself, undertake this translation, for the honour of God and the veneration of Saint Faith, beloved of God (75–87).

And out of my own love for our fellowship[10] I have begun this work. May God grant that it benefit all who will have it in their possession and want to hear it read.[11] Those who have not learned Latin have no choice but to listen to my vernacular rendition. My lords, in the name of God I beg that you not forget my name in the prayers which you offer in supplication to St. Faith. I am Simon of Walsingham, a servant of Saint Mary in Saint Edmunds Abbey.[12]

---

[9] 80 **well-versed in learning and with much good sense** *Grant en science e en resun*: as Jocelin of Brakelond demonstrates (*Chronicle*, ed. and trans. Jane, 62–64), Abbot Samson was both an eloquent and learned monk, and an able administrator who quickly restored the Abbey's ruined finances after his election as abbot. He preferred the active to the contemplative life and held practical common sense in high esteem.

[10] 88–89 **out of my own love for our fellowship I have begun this work** *par amur en compaignie / Ay comencé icest escrit*: the fellowship is that of the monastic order at Bury St. Edmunds. It would also be possible to construe this as "And I, out of love, have begun this work in your company," referring to the work as a public performance before his fellow monks.

[11] 91–93 **all who will have it in their possession and want to hear it read** *A tuz iceus ky l'averunt / E ki entendre en voudrunt*: the use of *averunt* is unexpected in this context (Baker asks if the meaning is *le* [sc. *l'escrit*] *verunt?*); the usual coordinate of *oir* in this context is *lire* (cf. vv. 12–13). But the use of *averunt* "own, have in their possession" here expresses the extension of the power of the textual object. Saints' lives quite commonly promise that simple possession of the text can bring benefits, and texts of lives were themselves sometimes used as apotropaic objects (see J. Wogan-Browne, "Wreaths of Thyme: The Female Translator in Anglo-Norman Hagiography," in *The Medieval Translator* 4, ed. Roger Ellis and Ruth Evans [Binghamton, NY: MRTS, 1994], 45–65, at 48). *Deivent entendre* is also subject to interpretation—it could mean "should," "must," or, as translated: "have no choice but to listen to."

[12] 99–100 **I am Simon . . Abbey** *Symon de Walsingham ai nun / . . . a seint Eadmun*: Bury St. Edmunds was built in honour of Edmund, king of East Anglia, martyred in 869. Benedictine monks replaced the secular priests in the eleventh century and the abbey flourished until the Dissolution. See above, 49–51, for details on Simon, the abbey, and St. Mary's church. Three men from Walsingham, monks Simon and Thomas, along with clerk Stephen, son of Roger of Walsingham, were among those sent to Rome in 1214 by

When you read my name, God grant that you include me in your blessings; pray God, Mother Mary, and St. Faith, beloved of God, that Christ, through her holy intercession, grant that we all may enter the kingdom of the Father. And now I will relate briefly to you the details I have learned from the Latin[13] regarding the passion of St. Faith, and how Jesus took her to himself in heaven (88–110).

In the days when Maximian and the evil Diocletian ruled the city of Rome, they were enemies of God, and served the devil to the best of their ability and obeyed his will,[14] despising Jesus Christ and Christians above all else.[15] At the time of which I speak, there was in the city of Agen a maiden of great renown, the most beautiful in the land, daughter of the most noble family in the country. She was very fair of face, and even more beautiful in her heart. This lovely girl was named Faith, and faith was her strength. Jesus Christ gave her this name when he placed faith in her heart, for by the example of faith he converted several souls to himself, for St. Faith was the first to carry the banner of martyrdom in the city of Agen, of which she is both patron and a jewel (111–36).

Her faith led her to martyrdom and made her despise harsh torture; her strong faith crowned her with martyrdom and led her to God. Armed with all righteousness, blessed St. Faith was young in years but she was maturely wise in her heart. She sought to acquire knowledge rather than worldly goods. She loved chaste virtue more than the finest gold; she valued humility more than riches. She greatly despised all sin and wantonness and dishonourable and shameful acts. The grace of God was upon her, shielding her from all evil, leading her to flee this world in order to love and serve God, inspiring her hatred of earthly pleasures and her disdain for worldly delights. St. Faith, beloved of God, led a

---

St. Edmunds Abbey to seek papal support against King John for the election of Abbot Hugh (Thomson, *Chronicle of the Election of Hugh*, 32–43). There were seventy to eighty monks at the Abbey c. 1207; in 1260 there were 80 monks, 21 chaplains, and 111 servants (see Knowles, *Medieval Religious Houses*, 61).

[13] 108 **learned from the Latin** *ke latin mei aprent:* See above, 51–52.

[14] 115–116 **served ... obeyed** *serverent ... obeierent*: the scribe uses the first conjugation terminations (*-erent*), not the second conjugation endings (*-irent*), perhaps imitating the preceding two lines which have *-erent*; earlier the scribe had used *-irent* where *-erent* is expected (*comencirent* v. 58, in rhyme with *finirent* v. 57), again modelling the second form on the immediately preceding standard form.

[15] 111–18 **In the days when Maximian and the evil Diocletian ruled the city of Rome** *En cel tens ke Maximien/ E li fel Dyoclicien / En la cité de Rome regnerent...*: Diocletian (c. 240–316), emperor 284–305, appointed Maximian as junior emperor in 285, and put him in charge of the western half of the empire. Although both were of equal imperial rank, Diocletian was always dominant. The decrees of Diocletian in 303, requiring that everyone in the Roman empire make sacrifices to the imperial cult, were part of what later was called the Great Persecution of Christians, which continued until 311. See *Encyclopedia of Early Christianity*, ed. Everett Ferguson (New York and London: Garland, 1990), s.v. Diocletian, 263–65.

holy life through vigils and self-denial, along with fasting, acts of charity, and prayer. And Jesus Christ in his mercy repaid her for her suffering: he crowned her with martyrdom and led her into heavenly bliss. Listen closely and I will tell you how this came to pass (137–66).

The emperors whom I named, the two vicious tyrants who hated Christians, torturing and mistreating them, sent into their jurisdiction of Agen a provost, an enemy of God[16] named Dacien, a cruel, ungodly pagan. He was extremely wicked and arrogant, choleric, evil and given to excess; all things righteous inspired his envy, and he detested God above all else. This treacherous man went throughout the land torturing those who believed in God. Guided by the devil, he entered the city of Agen; he was enticed there by the devil who had him completely in his sway[17] (167–84).

After he had arrived in Agen, Dacien attacked the followers of Jesus.[18] He ordered the people to assemble, he said, because he wished to know for certain which ones were honourable, and willing to pray to their gods. He would bestow great favours on those he saw making sacrifices to the gods he wished to honour and hold dear, and he would shower them with his gratitude. But if there was anyone, either young or old,[19] who did not obey him and who did not make sacrifices, but instead called out to Jesus Christ, he would submit him to great torture, and have him cruelly put to death (185–200).

Then the Christians were seized and held captive in chains, and others went into hiding, for they greatly feared his power. This tyrant, this persecutor, had heard much talk of the glorious St. Faith, this precious woman whose beloved

---

[16] 171–72 **sent into their jurisdiction of Agen a provost, an enemy of God** *Enveierent cum lur bailli / Un provost, un Deu enemi* MS *Envuerent en lur bailli / Un provost, un deu enemi*: the translation follows the manuscript reading, rather than "sent as their governor" in Baker's emended text.

[17] 183–84 **he was enticed there by the devil who had him completely in his sway** *A ceo l'eu[s]t le diable entiré / Ki le out del tut en postié*: Baker considers these lines corrupt, and proposes *A ceo leu est le diable entir / Ki l'out del tut en poëstir* "the devil has absolute power in this place, he had him completely in his power." We construe the verbs as pluperfect subjunctive (*l'eu[s]t . . . entiré*), with *s* erased in the manuscript by scribe or corrector, to change it to pluperfect indicative (*l'eut entiré*), and preterite (*le out en postié*). We interpret *entirer* "attract, entice" as a neologism.

[18] 186 **Dacien attacked** *Cel Dacien enveint*: read MS *enueiut*? = *enveiout* (impf. 3 of *envaier* "assail"). Baker proposes *enveint* as a form of *aveint, avint* from *aveindre* (although the senses of this verb given in *AND* do not seem to fit); the sense "assail, attack" is more likely. Cf. the verb *envair, envaier* "assail," and nouns *envaie, envaisement, envaissement* "attack" (*AND* 245a).

[19] 195 **either young or old** *petit u grant*: although this could again be a reference to social status (see note to v. 6, above), here it is more likely to be a foreshadowing of the summoning of the child Faith.

name was known throughout the land.[20] This jewel shone so clearly that he heard others speak of the brilliance that surrounded glorious St. Faith, of the clarity of this precious gem, for her radiant renown shone throughout the country. The tyrant was jealous of this good name, and wished to destroy it, but he could not, for the more he struggled to dampen its radiance, the more clearly her reputation shone forth, as you will hear later if you listen to my story (201–22).

Dacien, of whom I have spoken above, ordered the maiden to be brought, for he wanted to hear in her own words if she was willing to abandon her faith, or if he could in some way, either by threats or by pleading, turn her away from holy faith to embrace evil. But when he ordered her before him for this purpose he acted with great folly (223–32).

When St. Faith was summoned, she was not afraid; she did not hide in fear, but boldly came forth. She bravely presented herself, not at all fearing the tyrant. She placed her trust so firmly in Jesus and in his holy power that she became still and approached him in prayer, so that she had no fear of Dacien or of his threats. In this way she showed the faith which was within her holy name; in this way her name was consonant with her pious devotion. With serenity she called on God's name, and prayed in this fashion:[21]

"Fair Lord, glorious Jesus, you who were born of a holy virgin for our redemption, and suffered death because of your love for us; sweet Lord, glorious Jesus, grant me grace and strength to spread wisdom and knowledge here so that I may confound your enemy, so that those who will hear faith spoken of here may follow my example."

And when she had prayed thus, arming herself with the sign of the holy cross, she came before Dacien who loved neither God nor Christians (233–64).

When the beloved dear one of God came before her judge, the evil man fell silent as his eyes studied her, marvelling at her beauty. Then he began his interrogation:

---

[20] **207–10 glorious St. Faith . . . beloved name was known throughout the land** *De seinte Fey la gloriuse . . . Kar de li clere renumee*, MS *Kar de li chere numee / Luseit par tute la cuntree*, MS *Lur sert par tute la cuntree*: these lines are repeated, vv. 213–216, with variants (e.g. *gemme* 214 for *femme* 208). The correction of vv. 209–210 by Baker is based on this repetition. The MS has a "+" marked in the margin at the end of v. 203 (to mark the need to add a superscript letter for the second vowel in *averser*), and fainter "+" marks at the end of vv. 209, 210, both emended by Baker. It is possible, however, to construe the MS lines, without emendation: "for from her, a beloved renown is provided to them (lit. serves them) throughout the land." The passage is clearly written for stylistic effect, making the proposed *lectio difficilior* plausible.

[21] **250 prayed in this fashion** *En duce manere pria*, MS *E en deu manere pria*: Baker emends to *duce*, but one could also propose *E en teu manere pria*, in which the scribe has only mistaken one letter, a *t* for a *d;* the translation here follows the latter reading.

"Tell me your name, do not keep it secret!"[22]

The beautiful maiden, whom he perceived as terror-stricken,[23] did not withhold her name then. She replied bravely and politely, saying:

"I do not wish to conceal my name from you: Faith is my name, and willingly I dare to pronounce it. There has never been any distinction between my name and my faith. Acts of faith are my deeds, Faith is my name, my name and my deeds are one and the same."[24]

Then Dacien, the vile evil pagan, said to her:

"Now that you have told me your name, I want to know your religion, and your faith and your beliefs as well, without lengthy explanation" (265–86).[25]

God's beloved, St. Faith, who was filled with the Holy Spirit, replied to her enemy, saying:

"I do not seek to hide my faith nor my beliefs. I have been a Christian since childhood; from the time in my infancy when I was baptized in the name of God, I have given myself completely to Jesus who suffered death to save us all, to Jesus Christ the Son of Mary who rules this earth; I give myself to him, I surrender to him, I go to him with devotion" (287–300).[26]

---

[22] 270 **do not keep it secret** *ne festes celé*: this statement is proof that Dacien is acting in bad faith. He has ordered Faith before him precisely because he has already heard her name, renowned throughout the land.

[23] 271–72 **The beautiful maiden, whom he perceived as terror-stricken ... her name** *La bele ke n'ert esbaïe / Sun nun unkes ne celad mie*, MS *La bele ke veit esbaie / Sun nun hu ne celad mie*: the translation follows the MS, rather than Baker's emendation to *unkes*, reading manuscript *hu* (= *ui*) to mean "at that time, on that day."

[24] 279 **acts of faith are my deeds** *Feyz sunt mes fes*: the original has a pun on the plurals of *fey* and *fait* (both phonetically /fez/, or /fes/); the translation could also be "deeds are my (acts of) faith." The source Latin text is much simpler: *Fides nomine et opere vocor* (Baker, 66).

[25] 286 **without lengthy explanation** *sanz demustrance* (lit. "without demonstration, proof, outward manifestation"): *demustrance* is used in legal contexts to mean the statement of a plaintiff's case (see *AND* 156a). Here it seems to suggest that Dacien does not wish a lengthy statement of Faith's beliefs (unless it is seen as a scribal error, and *demustrance* should be emended to *demurance* "delay"). It is possible that *demustrance* is used ironically here, since it is precisely a *demustrance* of her beliefs that Dacien will see in the course of his interrogation.

[26] 300 **I go to him with devotion** *A li auke devotement*: Baker suggests *auke* might be a scribal error, without suggesting what should replace it; *auke* "something, somewhat, to some extent" is at once pronoun adj., and adv. An alternative word might be *auge* (pr. subj. 1 of *aller*), although the subjunctive is slightly unexpected (it could perhaps be seen as expressing a wish, or obligation—"may I go devotedly to him").

When Dacien heard this he was angered and distressed, but nonetheless, with treacherous intention, he replied courteously; he feigned a gracious air,[27] thinking thereby to entice her to obey him, saying to her with a pleasant countenance:

"Oh sweet maiden, you are so fair and comely, I am filled with pity for your beauty, and for this reason I offer you the following advice. Noble and attractive damsel, now when your beauty most becomes you, while you are in the flower of your virginal radiance, abandon this madness, give up your religion which is nothing but folly, and go instead to worship and make sacrifice to saint Diana.[28] You should indeed honour her, for she is the goddess of love; take my advice and worship her, for you are made in her image.[29] If you will do this you will gain great honour; I will bestow on you rich gifts and much honour for the sake of her love; untold wealth will be yours if you will only worship this goddess" (301–30).

St. Faith, the beloved of God, who considered all Decius' promises to be worthless, replied very wisely, saying to him cheerfully:

"I have learned in Holy Scripture, from the wise men of the past through whom God has spoken, who have called out devils in the name of God, that all your gods are devils, and that there is no strength or virtue in them: they have mouths, but cannot speak, hands but cannot work; they have ears yet hear nothing, eyes yet cannot see; they have feet yet cannot walk or move about by themselves.[30] And you counsel me to worship such evil gods?" (331–48).

When the evil tyrant heard this he was made weak with anger; he rolled his eyes in great rage at the maiden he had summoned, saying to her:

"You revile my gods unjustly by saying they are devils, and have no innate powers.[31] I will avenge their shame. If you will not make sacrifices to them, I can assure you of two things: I will make you kneel to me and I will inflict on you great suffering, and after many tortures you will die" (349–62).

---

[27] 306 **feigned** *se fenist*: the MS reading should be corrected to read *se feinst*, pret. 3 of *feindre*.

[28] 320 **saint Diana** *seinte Dyane*: the unexpected use of "saint" (also in the Latin text, *et sanctissimae Dianae sacrifica*) is an example of Dacien's appropriation of Christian terminology. There is also a parallel to Acts 19:24–41.

[29] 324 **you are made in her image** *Kar semblable est a ta nature*: (lit. "she is similar to your nature"). The implication is that her beauty, like that of the goddess Diana, inspires love. In his reference to Saint Diana (v. 320), and to Faith being made in the image of the goddess, Dacien is using Christian terminology in a perverse attempt to persuade Faith to recant her faith.

[30] 341–46 **they have mouths, but cannot speak ... or move about by themselves** *Buches unt, ne pount parler ... Ne par eus memes remuer*: Cf. Ps. 115:5–7; *St. George*, above, 144.

[31] 356 **have no innate powers** *nent de force n'unt*, MS *nent ne unt*: Baker's emendation (*[de force]*, not noted in his edition) is based on v. 340.

The Life of Saint Faith, Virgin Martyr

When St. Faith, God's beloved, filled with divine faith, heard these threats she responded immediately to the tyrant:

"My lord tyrant, rest assured that I do not fear you at all; for the sake of Jesus Christ I will gladly suffer pain and torment, and even death; since he died for me, I must now die for him. Jesus Christ our Lord was born out of love for us, for us he was tortured on the cross, and for our sins he suffered death. For this reason I eagerly desire to suffer death for his holy name" (363–78).

When her adversary heard these words, he was filled with anger. He ordered his men at arms to have a bed of brass brought immediately, a grill he had had constructed to torture the faithful of God. They stripped St. Faith and laid her on this sacrificial altar.

The young virgin was laid out naked on this bed; they who did not worship the church, which is the body of Christ,[32] stretched out her tender limbs on this bed; they put a fire underneath it as they had been commanded to do; on iron pans[33] the cruel soldiers placed burning coals; these wicked enemies of God threw fat on the flames, these evil-doers threw oil on the brushwood in the middle of the flames. Her very delicate, young and tender limbs were extremely weary; the flame made smoke rise up from this blessed virgin, but she bore this suffering and pain nobly, in the name of Jesus our Lord for whom she had a very great love. And he in his holy mercy did not forget her. Endurance and strength were given to her so that she feared nothing; by the pain that she suffered she conquered the devil and his helpers. Words cannot tell or recount the cruelty of her martyrdom, which inspired great pity for her in those who stood nearby. They cried out in a loud voice condemning this cruel judgement; and they declared openly, with tears streaming down their distraught faces:[34]

"Ah, what wickedness! Such evil has never before been seen! Alas,[35] what cruelty, such as has never before been spoken of! Alas! Alas! What great suffering! Never before has greater pain been recounted! Alas, that by a false condemnation this chaste body, this innocent one is so cruelly tortured! What an evil act, what

---

[32] 390 **they who did not worship the church, which is the body of Christ** *Ceus ke les amis Deu [n]'amerent*, MS *Ceus ke les membres deu[n'] aurerent*: the translation follows the manuscript (emending to add the negative particle), rather than Baker, who misreads *auerent* "worshipped" as *amerent* "loved"; *les membres Deu* is a reference to the church, and the translation adds the phrase "which is the body of Christ," implied in the word *membres*. Cf. Romans 12:5; 1 Corinthians 12:12, 20, 27; Colossians 1:18.

[33] 393 **on iron pans** *a croiz de fer*: cf. the Latin *ferreis batillis*. Either standard meaning of *batillum* "fire-pan, fire shovel" would fit in this context, although the French relies on the adj. alone, used as a noun, *croiz = cros, creus* "shallow," to express both "pan" and "shallow."

[34] 420 **distraught faces** *chere amere*, MS *clere amere*: Baker neglects to note the MS form, which he has emended.

[35] 423 **Alas, what cruelty** *Ai quele crueleté*, MS *Al quel cruelete*: the translation emends to *Al[as], quel[e] crueleté*.

a sin, that this maiden, who has never erred and never spoken evil of any living person, is so cruelly tortured! How nobly she endures it for Jesus Christ, the son of Mary! May he now comfort her, and we give ourselves to him henceforth, and consecrate ourselves to him; we now give ourselves to the Son of Mary; our gods are worthless, for they cannot help themselves or be of use to us" (379–442).

My lords, as the Latin text which Lord Benjamin sent me relates,[36] many others became Christians on that day, and believed in our Lord and abandoned their false religion because of St. Faith's example. Because I do not find them recorded in my source text, I cannot give you the names of all those who were martyred and beheaded because of their love for God (443–52).

My lords, at the time that this happened, at the same time that St. Faith was enduring the suffering that I have described to you, for the love of Jesus, her sweet protector, a holy man of great faith and beloved of God, a young nobleman by the name of Caprais, along with several other Christians, left the city, fleeing the pagans and their persecution; and I will tell you why: as the faithful of God they did not wish to witness the sacrifices made to the devil, nor to scorn Him who suffered death for their sins. They chose not to be debased by this act of great treachery, nor did they want their eyes to be defiled by this great act of cruelty. For Jesus himself commanded his disciples, whom he loved, to flee from place to place if they came under pagan persecution.[37] And he himself first showed the wisdom he had taught them when he fled into Egypt to escape Pharaoh. He knew well what the future held, how his followers would be obliged to flee and hide themselves for his love. By his own sweet mercy, he fled the land so that his disciples would not be reproached, so that such an act done later by them would not bring blame, dishonour, or shame. He delayed martyrdom thus a short while to show that there were times and seasons when it is right to flee evil and persecution.[38] Saint Caprais did likewise when he hid in the rocks, in a wide cave in the countryside nearby, from which he could witness what was happening in the city. He looked toward the city and saw the great torments that St. Faith, God's beloved, suffered for the Son of Mary (453–502).

---

[36] 444 **which Lord Benjamin sent me** *Ke m'enveia danz Benjamin*, MS *menua danz B.*: Benjamin's identity is unknown; Baker, 53, suggests he may be from the priory at Horsham St. Faith, while Legge (*ANC*, 10) suggests another Benedictine monk (from Bury?). Since the abbey at Bury had its own chapel to St. Faith, it also likely had Latin foundation texts for the cult of Faith in its large library (see above, 51).

[37] 473–76 **For Jesus himself** *Kar Jesu memes* MS *Kar deu memes*: as Baker notes, the author uses *Deu* occasionally for *Jesu*. On the sentiments expressed, cf. Matthew 10:23: "And when they shall persecute you in this city flee into another."

[38] 489 **martyrdom thus a short while** *Un pou isi de [son] martire*: Baker refers to Matthew 12:14–15 as an example of Christ choosing to avoid persecution ("And the Pharisees going out made a consultation against him, how they might destroy him. But Jesus knowing it retired from thence").

When he saw her, he was moved to pity, and he wept tenderly. He raised his hands to heaven and prayed that God have mercy on St. Faith who endured such great suffering in his name, that he give her strength and courage to conquer the pain of the fire, and that she be given the victory of a martyr's crown.

With tears, Caprais prostrated himself on the ground and prayed that God, in his mercy, show him the power of heaven[39] and make known to him how St. Faith remained steadfast in the flames where she lay. And God, who does not forget his own, heard his prayer: he showed him the power of heaven and gave him divine grace. Caprais, the holy martyr, who would suffer the same torments for the Son of Mary, turned his gaze toward the beloved of God, bound to the grill and enveloped in fearsome flames, and he saw a white dove descend from heaven, such as he had never before looked upon; his eyes had never beheld a dove of such whiteness or such beauty; for he had witnessed no flower in summer or snow on frozen ground of such whiteness, or of such a ravishing colour. It carried a crown of gold, of such richness as he had never before seen. It was ornamented with magnificent precious stones and splendid gems, and it shone more brightly than the summer-day sun at its zenith, the hour when it shines most brightly in the firmament. The dove placed this resplendent crown on the head of the virgin, the martyr who suffered great torments for God, who rewarded her well. In Caprais' vision she was at that moment clothed in an exceedingly white garment, a brightly shining new white robe. Then he saw clearly and understood that Jesus Christ in his mercy had already given her the victory of his eternal glory, that her suffering had passed and her great joy had begun (503–60).

The white dove which descended from heaven, as you have heard, flew around the sainted martyr and comforted her with its sweet flight; with its wings it caressed her and protected her from the flames;[40] by the divine grace of Jesus it extinguished the strength and power of the flames and the gridiron, so that the fire and the torment felt like dewdrops; thus St. Faith the blessed felt neither pain nor suffering, our Lord be praised!

When the blessed Caprais who had seen all the secrets of heaven cast his eyes on the virgin, he beheld her whole and beautiful, for she was not wounded by any of the torments she had endured. She shone forth from this torture like a star in the heavens. Because of the crown Jesus Christ had sent her by his angel, she was very beautiful, and rejoiced greatly, adorned with the star God had sent down to her by his angel from paradise (561–88).

When St. Caprais had seen the glory and the power that Jesus Christ had given to the blessed St. Faith, he did not wish to remain in hiding any longer. He

---

[39] 515 **the power of heaven** *La vertu del ciel*: *vertu* can be either "power" or "miracle, wonder."

[40] 566 **protected her from the flames** *Et de la flamme defendi* MS *Et de la flamme le fendi*: emendation is not needed; the form *fendre* "protect, defend" is also found in the *Saint Brendan* (cf. *AND* 299b).

wanted to embark on the torments that St. Faith, beloved of God, had suffered for the Son of Mary, for he knew that by this means they would enter together into that glory which was theirs.[41] He was certain of this reward, and for this reason did not fear death, nor any other torture, so fervent was he in the love of God. Stepping down from the rock, he struck it with his right hand. Hear, my lords, how much God loved him, see what a miracle he showed through him! He smote the rock with his hand, and pure water gushed from the stone.[42] Immediately a fountain of sweet water flowed forth, clear and refreshing. From the bare rock a spring of sparkling water welled up, continuing to this day, as the writer of the Latin text tells us. Every infirm person who drinks from it recovers good health straightaway, provided that they are faithful believers and truly repentant, through the grace of the martyr who had chosen to seek refuge in the rock (589–620).

St. Caprais the blessed, of whom you have heard me speak, came down from the rock and went straight to the place where St. Faith most righteously suffered great torture for the love of God. There where she had demonstrated the meaning of her name by her holy passion, no one was on guard or paid attention to his arrival until he stood beside the fire over which St. Faith lay on the gridiron. In the hearing of all he cried out and preached in the name of Jesus; he praised aloud the name of Jesus and his strength and power (621–36).

When the tyrant heard him praise aloud the name of Jesus, he had him brought before him and he demanded to know his name, what country he was from, and details of his family and friends. Caprais replied boldly and directly:

"I will tell you about my religion, and then I will tell you my name; I am Christian and was baptized with the name Caprais; I am descended from a noble family, but in my heart I am a son of God, who made me, who created me, who redeemed me with his blood; I am a son and servant of Jesus Christ, who created the whole world" (637–54).

When the tyrant heard these words, he responded with cajoling words and flattery:

"You are extremely handsome and attractive, and I am filled with compassion for your youth and beauty. If you choose to heed my advice many rewards will come your way in the future; emperors will admire you and shower you with riches, and you will live always in the palace among their closest friends" (655–66).

---

[41] 597–98 **they would enter together into that glory that was theirs** *k'il partireit / A cele gloire k'ele aveit*, MS *k'il partire[ie]nt / A cele gloire ke il aveient*: rather than changing both verbs to the 3rd pers. sing., we emend *partire[ie]nt,* keeping this verb in the same person as *aveient*. Including himself in the 3rd pers. plural form, Caprais anticipates his joint martyrdom with Faith.

[42] An allusion to Moses striking the rock to provide water for the people; cf. Exodus 17:6, Numbers 20:2–11.

The blessed Caprais, inspired by the grace of God, and instructed, I believe, by the victory of St. Faith, and by the strength and glory he had seen in her, replied to Dacien as if he feared him not at all:

"In the palace of that emperor who is Lord of this earth, I desire greatly to honour him (for everyone should wish to do so);[43] blessed are his followers who dwell always in his palace. Their great joy will never end, but will last forever.[44] I dedicate myself to this emperor, who is our Lord Jesus, the high king of paradise, who never forsakes his own. I have loved and followed him since childhood; all my hope is placed in him" (667–88).

Then his adversary said to him:

"I had thought to turn you away from your foolish misbelief and convert you to the right way of thinking, and give you possessions and responsibilities, rich lands and cities."[45]

Saint Caprais replied to him, saying:

"I put my trust in Jesus Christ, giver of all things to those who love him, who gives generously to his followers whatever is needed for their salvation. In him I place my trust: he will not fail me. I am certain that at the end of this mortal life he will give me a treasure which will never fail me: that is the joy of paradise which he gives to all his beloved" (689–706).

When Dacien understood the strength of Caprais' convictions, and that he was eloquent and enlightened through his great intelligence, he knew that he would not defeat him in debate, and he remarked to his close friends:[46]

"I do not dare argue longer with him, for I cannot win: I will not conquer him by words, and will be defeated in the struggle."

---

[43] 677 **I desire greatly to honour him** *Ai [MS Al] grant desir de son honur*: Baker emends without comment, and suggests there may be a lacuna here. The Latin is brief: *ita respondit: 'In illius desidero habitare palatio, quem a baptismo dilexi . . .'* (Baker, 74, from *Passio*, VIII).

[44] Cf. Psalm 83:5 [Vulgate].

[45] 691–93 **foolish misbelief . . . the right way of thinking** *mescreance : creance; fez*: these words are used with ironic inversion in the mouth of Dacien: his *mescreance* "foolish misbelief" is the *creance* "true faith" of Caprais, and Dacien uses the pagan sense of *creance* "right way of thinking." Similarly *fez*, which is a pun on the plural of *fey* (*feyz* "acts of faith," as used earlier by Faith), could mean either "legal deeds to property," or "responsibility, permission to perform various acts or deeds." Dacien's proposal is articulated, then, using terms from the Christian faith of Caprais, but with an inverse meaning.

[46] 711–12 **he would not defeat him in debate and he remarked to his close friends** *Par desputer ne li veintra, / A ses privez amis dit a*, MS *Par desputer ne li veinterunt / Puis a lur privez amis distrunt*: the translation follows Baker's emendation; the original text could be translated "he knew that they would not defeat him by debating, and they would admit among themselves privately, 'I do not dare argue longer with him . . .'"

He then gave Caprais over to his soldiers and commanded them to tear apart his tender flesh and torture him mercilessly. They did as he commanded and afflicted him most cruelly (707–22).[47]

The holy martyr, with happy countenance and gentle grace, for the love of God bore the pain and torture joyfully, with a steadfast faith. Not once did he cease to preach and admonish the bystanders, constantly praising the name, strength, and power of Jesus to those who stood around him, who were moved to great pity for him. They cried out with compassion for him, for he was much loved by all. On his behalf they made a great lamentation, crying out through their tears:

"For what crime[48] is this man put to death? By what evil condemnation?[49] Why is this innocent man punished,[50] this saint crowned with all good? Lord! why is he tortured so? Assuredly he is condemned in error, without reason; and the maiden also, by a very evil, deceitful judgement, which today, alas!, alas! causes such suffering!"[51]

All who saw him wept very tenderly on his behalf, because he was so gentle and sweet (723–51).[52]

Caprais appeared like a beautiful angel in his steadfast loyalty, as if God had looked down upon him from heaven; his face remained unchanged while he endured the torment. With a joyful and devoted countenance he bore the pain and suffering inflicted on him by the enemies of God because of their hatred of Jesus' holy name.

Two brothers who watched him marvelled at his strength. The elder was named Primus, the younger was Felicianus. These two were inspired there and then by the sweetness of paradise; they were enflamed with the holy fire which

---

[47] 722 **afflicted him most cruelly** *Mut le peinerent cruelement*, MS *pernerent cruelement*: Baker emends to *peinerent* but *pernerent*, pret. 6 of *prendre* "seize" could be kept, or *prendre* = *reprendre* "chastize, correct"; cf. *AND* 548a.

[48] 737 **crime** *mauveiseté*: another pun. It is both a "crime" imputed to Caprais, and an "evil end" pursued by Dacien.

[49] 739 **evil condemnation** *mauvais jugement*: another double entendre: "erroneous, mistaken judgement" as well as "evil, malicious sentence."

[50] 740 **Why is this innocent man punished** *Pur quei prist [il] cest innocent*: again *prendre* has the sense of *reprendre* "reprove, punish"; cf. note to v.722, above.

[51] 747 **judgement which today . . . causes** *Par assent u a cest jur*: the translation emends to *Par assent u [i] a cest jur* "By the order/consent by which there is this day, which causes this day." This is another example of word-play: *assent* can be either the order of Dacien, or the consent of Faith, with the result that Faith and Caprais can be seen either as victims or as consenting heroes.

[52] 749 **wept very tenderly on his behalf** *Pur li mut tendrement plurerent*: the focus now returns to Caprais only. The rhyme indicates that there are probably at least two lines missing in the text here, since *ameable* v. 751, and *visé* v. 752 both lack rhyming lines.

our Lord Jesus visited[53] on his apostles when the Holy Spirit was sent down upon them. They were ardent in their love of God; they had no fear of the treacherous Dacien nor of any other pagan. For the honour of the Son of Mary they joined the company of Saint Caprais the blessed, who was tortured for Jesus. Into this danger and torment they rushed forth boldly; they were willing to suffer death for him who had deigned to die for them. In this fashion all three were united in the name of the holy Trinity; in this way God was honoured and his holy name glorified; by this means the devil lost his power and strength, and his ally Dacien and all the other pagans were confounded and distressed, conquered, shamed, and reviled (752–92).

Dacien was refuted and thwarted[54] by the incident I have recounted to you about the brothers who so boldly offered themselves up to torture and who had no fear to die for the love of God. He saw that for them suffering death for Jesus was a comfort, and Dacien knew well that he would not change their minds, or turn them away from the law of God.

His body was distorted with anger and rage like a serpent unable to prevent itself from puffing up with venom when it is poised to strike.[55] When Dacien was unable to conquer them by the pain he inflicted on them, he pronounced his formal sentence, ordering that they lead St. Faith, beloved of God, along with her holy company, to the pagan temple, and if they did not make sacrifices to the gods, that they be beheaded on the spot and their bodies thrown to the crows. His orders were carried out without delay (793–818).

St. Faith, beloved of God—this brightly-polished jewel, this pure gold now well refined by the purging fire, and St. Caprais the blessed, along with the two others whose names I told you—these saintly companions were led off to the temple because of their faith in Jesus Christ the son of Mary, and for his holy

---

[53] 767–70 **the holy fire which our Lord Jesus visited . . . sent down upon them** *de [cel] seint fu / Dunt . . . Jhesu / Ses [seinz] apostles enumbra / Quant le seint esprit lur dona*: the verb *enumbrer* is used in religious contexts to describe the conception of Christ by the Holy Spirit, related to Mary in the Annunciation by the angel Gabriel (Luke 1:35). Here, it is used with reference to the descent of the Holy Spirit at Pentecost, although no examples of this latter sense are given in the *AND* (cf. *AND* 245a). This is an early use of the sense "remplir du Saint Esprit"; the sense "overshadow, give shade to, protect" is found in the *Psautier d'Oxford*, Ps. 90:4, and Ps. 139:8 (Baker, 60).

[54] 793 **was refuted** *Dacien ky ert [mut] iré* MS *Dacien ky ert uee*: the translation retains the verb *veer* "contradict, refute, deny; forbid," rather than Baker's emendation to *iré*, "angered."

[55] 803–6 **distorted with anger like a serpent which cannot prevent itself from puffing up with venom when it is poised to strike** *De irë e de maltalent / Se torst cume fet la serpent / Kant del venin li bat al quer / E (si) ne se pot pas desenfler*: this image is not found in the Latin source. There is some ambiguity: is it the snake which cannot back down and return to its normal shape, or Dacien who cannot regain his physical composure, or both?

name they were decapitated when they refused to make sacrifices and worship false gods. After beheading them, the soldiers threw their bodies into the streets. But the Lord God received their souls with great honour on that day, crowning them in heaven with unending glory (819–36).

The Christians in the city hastened stealthily by night, and with tears and heavy sighs reverently recovered the bodies of the glorious martyrs. They carried off their bodies in secret and honoured them with their devotion; they greatly feared that by treachery the wicked and despised pagans would move them, or throw them into deep waters where they would never be found or honoured by Christians. But the Lord God did not wish to permit this, nor to remove from the city of Agen the most precious treasure of his glorious martyrs; he did not wish to deprive the city of those it had nurtured and who were later tortured there, before they received the crown of martyrdom. There in Agen the bodies were placed in the earth, while their souls dwelt in paradise with Jesus Christ our Lord. And their bodies lay for a long time buried in this city where they were martyred, until the great cruelty of the pagans had been quashed (837–66).

When the Lord God, who rules all, gives us his peace through the holy church, he exalts all Christendom. It happened that in the same city a man was consecrated bishop, a worthy man of great renown and of deep religious belief; Lucidius, I believe, was his name.[56] He wished to honour the saints and he had their bodies raised up out of the earth. He had them carried in a procession, with chants and great reverence, into a church he had prepared for their use. He made it the most beautiful church possible, and dedicated it in honour of St. Faith, the holy beloved of the most high king, for whose love she was tortured unto martyrdom. Now her torment has ended and her joy begun. May holy Mary, mother of God, of whom she is now a companion, and God, through her sweetness, grant us, by her love and her saintly prayers, joy in the kingdom of her Father. Amen (867–94).

After the bodies of the saints you have heard about were recovered, the bishop of the city, Lucidius by name, put the body of St. Faith in a beautiful tomb by itself in a suburb of the city, where he had built a rich and magnificent church in honour of the virgin, the blessed St. Faith who is highly honoured in heaven. Then, because of her love for him, Jesus showed his power each day to those who needed his mercy for any illness of body, limbs, or sight, or other ailments they might have. And he raised the dead to life in the name of St. Faith the beloved of God (895–914).

---

[56] 874 **Lucidius ... name** *Lucidius ... out a nun*: as Baker notes, the Latin texts all name him *Dulcidius*, or *Dulcitius*. His episcopacy is dated variously as the early fifth century (*A Dictionary of Christian Biography*, ed. William Smith and Henry Wise ([New York: AMS Press, 1969], 1:910b), or in the first part of the sixth century (Sheingorn, *Book*, 288, n. 10, citing Frances T. Wands, "The Romanesque Architecture and Sculpture of Saint Caprais in Agen," 2 vols. [Ph.D. diss., Yale University, 1982], 18).

Because of the miracles wrought by Jesus Christ for the love of his martyr, great crowds of people from distant lands and foreign countries were to be seen, coming on horseback or on foot to the city of Agen, then much honoured by the blessed St. Faith. But later it was stripped of this honour to give great benefit elsewhere;[57] the great treasure Agen lost served to enrich Conques. I know well that this pleased the martyr, and that it was by her own wish that her relics were carried from Agen and translated to Conques (915–30).

Our Latin text tells us, according to the witness of the author himself, that the church of Conques stood on the north slope of a valley between two mountains, and although it was formerly sacked by pagan enemies of God, it remained standing. In the time of Charles the emperor a renowned hermit, Dado by name, lived a saintly life there in secret, and in response to the hermit's prayers and supplications Charlemagne commanded his son Louis to take charge of the restoration of this holy site and to rebuild the church.[58] Louis so willingly undertook this task that, with the grace of Jesus Christ, he restored the site as new, rebuilding everything formerly destroyed by the pagans. Day by day the site grew more richly appointed and inspired admiration, and as a result a number of people left their worldly life and took their vocation at Conques, and lived there in honesty and devout service. St. Faith the virgin martyr loved the companionship, I believe, of the faithful at Conques. For that reason she wished to be placed there, and honour the site by her presence and the country round about with her miracles and her goodness, as you have often heard. You will hear further details of her miracles when I have more leisure to recount them, but I cannot do so now for I wish to inform you of another matter relating to her good deeds.[59] In short, I will tell you here as concisely as I can the story of how her body was carried from Agen and translated to Conques (931–76).

---

[57] 923–24 **later it was stripped of this honour** *Mes puis esteit par (de) grant valur / Despuiliée de cel honur*: the text is slightly ambiguous: it could mean the theft was done efficaciously, or it could express the idea that the potential for good at Conques trumped the good being done at Agen.

[58] 938–40 **In the time of Charles the emperor a renowned hermit, Dado** *En tens Charles l'empereur...Uns heremite Dado numé*: Baker dates the creation of the monastery by Dado between 790 and 795. Louis I (778–840), "the Pious," was named king of Aquitaine by Charlemagne in 781, when Louis was three years of age; Baker suggests Louis could have participated in the rebuilding between the ages of twelve and seventeen years. Dado left the leadership of the abbey in 801, so the rebuilding was probably completed before that date. See above, 56–57, for further details on Conques.

[59] 968–71 **further details of her miracles . . . I cannot do so now** *E en ses miracles orrez / Quant greigniur leisir averay . . . a autre chose voil entendre*: Simon here seems to promise to translate later more details of miracles (no doubt from the *Liber miraculorum*), but now turns his attention to the *Translatio*, and his text ends without returning to the promised lengthier treatment of miracles.

The history written in Latin tells us that the black-robed monks who lived at this time at Conques were repeatedly admonished, and commanded in their sleep by visions, to translate to their monastery the holy body of which you have heard me speak.[60] They discussed often among themselves how, and by what means, they could attain this treasure and accomplish their dreams. There was among them one brother who was worthy, wise, and very astute,[61] who always behaved prudently and with frank honesty, and who accomplished every task he undertook with great efficiency. He was named Arinisdus, written thus in my Latin source—those among you who have heard these names before, please correct me where I am in error (977–98).

They debated this matter among themselves at length, deciding in the end to send this brother to Agen with a companion (whose name I cannot give you) as spies to discover the means by which they could obtain the body they so desired of the sainted martyr.

The monk set out on his journey in the guise of a shrewd and sly pilgrim. He travelled by horse and on foot until he came to the city of Agen where the holy martyr lay. When he entered the church, he led the monks to believe he wished to join them and live there indefinitely. To make a long story short, because of this clever pretense and because of his prudent behaviour, he was admitted as a conventual member of the congregation. But they did not know why he had come there: had they known, he would not have been received as a member. After he had been welcomed among them, he remained above reproach, for he was humble and obedient to all of both high and low estate, behaving toward everyone with the same humility. Whatever he was asked to do, he did quickly and with good cheer, so that all praised him and lauded his behaviour among themselves.[62]

It thus came to pass,[63] according to God's will—for he saw into this monk's heart and knew his thoughts—that he was assigned the task he most desired:

---

[60] 977 **The history written in Latin** *L'estorie*: the only known Latin source which mentions the monks' visions encouraging them to "transfer" the relics to Conques is the metrical version of the *Translatio*: *Nam Conchacenses monachi, / In somnis saepe moniti, / De transferenda Virgine / Loquebantur creberrime* (AASS, Oct. III, 290, §4.1–4).

[61] 990 **worthy, wise, and very astute** *pruz e sages e cointe esteit*: *cointe* has many nuances, including "cunning, malicious" as well as "quick-witted, astute, shrewd, clever, wise."

[62] 1031–32 **all praised him and lauded his behaviour** *trestuz li preiserent / E de sa porture se loerent*: Simon here anticipates the monks' later discovery that they have been deceived, since the element of self-deception is expressed by *se loerent*, lit. "they complimented themselves" (that they had chosen wisely when they admitted Arinisdus to their community).

[63] 1033 **It thus came to pass, according to God's will** *A vivre issi cum Deu le vout*, MS *Avint issi cum Deu le vout*: the translation follows the sense of the MS (Baker emends, without comment).

namely, the care of the sacristy and the responsibility for guarding the tomb where the holy body lay, the object of his secret intentions (999–1040).

The monk, who was prudent and cautious,[64] spent ten years living in this monastic community, but he never forgot why he had come. He did not tell the others everything he had in mind,[65] remaining always a spy on the lookout for a time and a means of achieving his desire. He worked and schemed until one year he found the right time and opportunity, a day during the feast of Epiphany, when no work is done except what is necessary for the celebration of this feast day and for praising our Lord. After the Mass had been sung, those who had attended went off to their meal, to celebrate the day and take refreshment. But Arinisdus[66] did not return with them, cleverly excusing himself, saying he wished to attend to his duties, to see to the capes and vestments and other furnishings of the church—work which the other monks liked to avoid (1041–68).

While the others were enjoying themselves, Arinisdus was keeping his own watch at the tomb of the martyr, but he could not break it open because it was bound by iron on all sides. He turned his mind to ways in which he could open it, but when he could not do so, he began to break away the marble at the base of the martyr's tomb; he boldly continued until he had created a large hole. With great ingenuity he pulled the martyr's body out through this hole and placed it with due care in a fine wicker container.[67] With the help of Jesus Christ he left the city that night, bearing the much-desired treasure. Travelling all night, he left Agen far behind him (1069–90).

In the morning when all the others had awakened and risen, they went into the church to pray. They noticed that the sacristan was not there, and were very dismayed to discover that their sacristan, guardian of the church, had tricked them. They ran off to check whether he had taken away any part of the treasure entrusted to him, and as they approached the tomb and found it broken open they saw that he had carried off their dear patroness. Had you been there then you would have seen them all weeping, wailing, and lamenting through their

---

[64] 1041 **The monk, who was prudent and cautious** *Li moine, ki ert purveiant*: the adj. *purveiant* also means "foresightful," but the fact that Arisnidus waits ten years before finding his opportunity shows a strong element of caution as well.

[65] 1046 **He did not tell the others everything** *Tut lur avel dist il a tuz*, MS *Tut la ne dist il a tuz*: Baker emends the text, but it is possible to read this line without correction as meaning that Arisnidus simply did not "in that place, tell everything to everyone."

[66] 1061, 1070 **Arinisdus** MS *Arnuldus*: the emendation is based on the Latin text and on this name given earlier, v. 995. The scribe has written clearly *arnuldus*.

[67] 1083–85 **he pulled the martyr's body out through this hole and placed it with due care in a fine wicker container** *Si treit hors le cors al martir / E le mist trestut a son leisir / En* [MS E en] *une bele esceppe mist*: in the *Translatio* the container in which Arinisdus carries off the relics is a "sack" (*pera* in the metrical version, *saculus* in the prose version). Cf. Modern English *skip*, *skep*, from Old English *sceppe*, whence the French form *esc(h)eppe, eskippe* (cf. *AND* 260b).

sobs, as if the whole city had been captured, burned, or flooded! Then the people in the convent, both lay and clerical alike, decided they would send someone in pursuit, for they could think of no other recourse. This they did, but without succeeding, for they took a wrong turn on their way. They thought they were on the road to Conques but instead went straight to Gascony. When they arrived they saw that they had been deceived and had taken the wrong road, so they returned to Agen (1091–1122).

But two others were then sent out who did not go astray. On good swift horses, possessed of both speed and endurance, at a place called Lalbenque[68] they caught up with Arinisdus, resting beneath a tree, but they did not recognize him; it was as if he was unknown to them, even though they had often seen him before. They began to question him, asking if he had seen a man such as they were seeking pass by there, and he replied that not a living soul, not even a pilgrim, had travelled on that road since he had sat beneath the tree; of this he was certain, he said. The men lost heart at this news and returned home to Agen (1123–42).

The people of Agen, now despairing of their plundered treasure, decided that they would keep the theft secret among themselves and not reveal to a single person this shame, this outrage, this great loss and harm done to them by Arinisdus, their sacristan. They would not reveal that he had carried off the body of their dear patroness, the relics of St. Faith which were so powerful, through which they had been honoured and enriched with great blessings[69] (1143–56).

The monks grieved greatly, lamenting and weeping for their treasure, lost through Arinisdus's deception. The latter, however, rejoiced and was happy that he had escaped from them. He travelled until he came to a place he knew called Figeac—I don't know the name or the region, except from my Latin source, which says that King Pepin ordered it to be built. I cannot give you further details of this monastery, except to say that it was a dependent house of Conques, if I am not mistaken (1157–72).[70]

---

[68] 1128 **Lalbenque** *Albenke*: named *Albenca* in Latin, now called Lalbenque, capital of the arrondissement of Cahors, midway between Agen and Conques (cf. Baker, 83, citing Bouillet and Servières, 54).

[69] 1156 **enriched ... blessings** *Enrichiz de grant dignetez*: the meaning of *dignetez* also includes "power, authority, privilege" as well as "blessing."

[70] 1165 **Figeac** *Figultus ... Pipin*: the MS has *figulcus* (or *figultus*), probably a scribal misreading of *figiacus*. Despite the narrator's comment that his Latin source reads *Figulcus*, it is written *Figiacum* in all known Latin sources. Modern Figeac is forty kilometres from Conques. Pepin or Pippin (c. 823–64) succeeded his father as king of Aquitaine in 838. There is an extant royal diploma, datable to 838, bestowing on Conques various gifts and allowing the monastery to remove to a more accessible site at Figeac. On the rivalry between Conques and Figeac, see above, 44. The rivalry between the two foundations was not settled until 1096 (see Sheingorn, *Book*, 6–9).

The Life of Saint Faith, Virgin Martyr

In this place there was a blind man who regained his sight through the power of St. Faith, and because of his own firm faith.[71] This blind man had often been told by the Holy Spirit in visions and dreams that he would recover his sight when the blessed St. Faith was translated to Conques. And it so happened, thanks be to God! As soon as he learned through the Holy Spirit that she had been carried there he went to see the body. At the moment he touched it and held the container in which it was carried, at that instant he recovered his sight, and gave praise to the Son of Mary, and his beloved, St. Faith (1173–92).

Then you should have seen the people coming in throngs and weeping for joy! With tears they kissed the container and gave praise to God and his martyr. You would have seen a great crowd of ill and ailing people, all of whom were healed when they touched the ossuary basket (1193–1200).[72]

Arinisdus did not delay, but hastened on towards Conques, and when he was close, he sent news of his arrival to the people of Conques, who were very elated, I can assure you! They rejoiced in this news of the virgin's arrival, St. Faith the blessed, whom they had so desired. They had the bells rung to summon the clergy, and when all were gathered they set off to meet the body. In a beautiful procession and with great reverence they received it that day, and singing chants they carried it to Conques in great honour. In a beautiful and appropriate setting they placed the blessed body which honours this place, and through which our Lord Jesus showed many a miracle, and continues still each day through his most holy mercy to bless all those who are burdened with illness or sins. Whoever wished to repent and seek the help of the martyr felt himself immediately healed and unburdened of all ills. May the Lord God in his kindness grant us, through the intercession of St. Faith's love, reparation for the sins we now bear. May God forgive us for our sins and protect us from all evil, and permit us to enter his joy through the love of his dear martyr, of whom we have spoken. Amen, amen, let us all say amen (1201–42).

---

[71] 1175–76 **through the power of St. Faith, and because of his own firm faith** *Par les merites seinte Fey / E par la creance k'il out en sey*: the repetition of *par* is no doubt a scribal dittography. Baker emends, dropping the second *par* without comment.

[72] 1188, 1195, 1200 **container . . . ossuary basket** *escheppe* 1188, 1195, *ceppe* 1200: the third time it is used the special nature of this wicker container is expressed by the translation "ossuary basket." The term "skip" is associated with more mundane uses, either in agriculture or the building trades.

IV.
Guillaume Le Clerc de Normandie

The Romance of Mary Magdalene

Here begins the romance of Mary Magdalene in French[1]

After our Lord Jesus Christ, the true Saviour, rose from death and left his followers to go up to heaven to sit on the right hand of God in majesty, the Apostles dispersed and converted people in many lands. Glorious Mary Magdalene, who was filled with the love of God, along with Martha, her sister, and Lazarus, whom Jesus had raised from the dead; and the man born blind[2] whom Jesus had cured, to the amazement of many Jews; and the gracious Marcilla,[3] who uttered the beautiful words of blessing on Jesus and on the womb which bore him and on the breast which succoured him; along with their sixth companion, the esteemed disciple, Maximinus by name,[4] one of the seventy—these six, along with other

---

[1] **Here begins the romance of Mary Magdalene in French** *Ici comence le romanz / De sainte Marie Magdalene*: the opening rubric title is not in P. The title **Romance** (*romanz*) signifies both the Romance language (*romanz*) and the type of narrative (romance). See also the Note on Translations, Manuscripts and Editions, above, 75.

[2] 13 **blind** *ciu*: the word missing in P is found in W. Cf. John 9 which relates the story of the man cured of blindness, and the amazement of the Pharisees.

[3] 16 **gracious Marcilla** *courtoise Ma[r]cilla*: the senses of this word include "noble," "courtly," "handsome," but in this context "gracious" seems closer to the sense intended. In the non-canonical tradition the woman in the crowd (Luke 11:27) is named Marcilla.

[4] 23 **Maximinus** *Maximi[n]us*: here called the "esteemed disciple," he is named in apocryphal texts as the first bishop of Aix. He was reported to have given communion to Mary Magdalene at the moment of her death, on the site of the present village of Saint-Maximin, near Saint-Baume de Provence. According to tradition, the Magdalen lived the last part of her life there, as a hermit in a grotto. The basilica of Saint-Maximin was begun in the late thirteenth century, and reputedly housed the relics of Mary Magdalene which had just been "discovered" on that site. Maximinus' name is used only twice in the *Romance of Mary Magdalene* (vv. 23, 701), and is written in full only once (in P, v. 701; cf. *Maxius* P, v. 23, and *Maximius*, or *Maximins*, in W, vv. 23, 701).

companions who believed in our Lord,[5] took their leave of Saint Peter and, crossing the Grecian sea, landed at Marseille (1–29).[6]

In the city, to their astonishment, they could not find lodgings, and, with little to eat or drink, were obliged to take shelter for the night in the entrance to a temple dedicated to a false god, where people gathered to worship vain idols. At daybreak the following morning these foolish people could be seen coming and going into the temple. Mary Magdalene, with a seemly bearing,[7] began to preach to them, saying that they should leave sin and worship Jesus. She taught them how he came to earth, how he lived, and how he was resurrected and ascended to heaven, and how on Judgement Day he would come to sit in judgement of their lives (30–50).

Many who found her quite beautiful paid attention to her argument, and listened to her quietly, for she spoke most nobly. And it was not surprising that her beautiful crimson lips, which had kissed the feet of God,[8] knew how to speak courteously. She preached so much, I assure you, that a noble ruler of the country, who was governor of the province, came with his beautiful wife to pray to his god at the temple, in the hope that his god would grant that the ruler's wife might conceive and bear him a child; for he had neither daughter nor son, and this made him sad and dejected, full of doubts and sorrow (51–69).

Mary Magdalene stood up and preached to such effect that, in short, the wife of this wealthy man quietly listened to her; later, in secret, she sent to Mary Magdalene and her companions some of her own possessions, by means of a servant whom she trusted completely, without her husband's knowledge. Then very shortly afterwards she saw Mary Magdalene in a vision: Mary admonished her in a clear voice to urge her husband to have pity and compassion on God's saints who lay out of doors because they could not find shelter, and that he should provide for them. But the lady dared not recount the dream to her husband, for she knew him to be cruel. And a second time the vision came to her in the same way

---

[5] 25–26 **along with . . . our Lord** *Ou autre genz qu'il aveient / Ki en nostre Seigneur creient*: W alone has vv. 25–26 which state that the group led by Mary Magdalene was larger than the six people named in this list.

[6] 29 **landed at Marseille** *ariverent a Marceille*: the opening scene (vv. 1–29) relates the apostolic work of Mary Magdalene, who because she gave the news of the resurrection to the Apostles (John 20:1–2) was often called the "Apostle to the Apostles." The Magdalene's journey to Marseille is here placed in the context of the canonical apostolic missions. The injunction to travel to all parts of the earth and preach is evoked by the reference to the "seventy," the group of Jesus' disciples given this commission (cf. Luke 10:1–11, 16–20).

[7] 40 **with a seemly bearing** *od le cors gent*: the Latin text has a more expansive description: *vultu placido, facie serena, lingua diserta, corpore procero, verba salutis* "with a gentle and serene countenance, an eloquent tongue, a tall body and a salutary sermon" (Weiss 86, §115, 6; CCHL 526, §2, 6–7).

[8] Cf. Luke 7:37–38, 45.

as I have told you, and again on the third night the vision appeared to them both, so that both believed that the lady who came to them was filled with splendour, and they were afraid (70–98).

"Are you sleeping, wicked tyrant?" the lady said, "you who have eaten and drunk so much that you have made yourself ill, while God's saints are afflicted in the street, famished and naked? Know that evil has come upon you and your wife, the serpent, because she did not want to tell you or teach you my message. If you do not immediately order that the saints be given help it will go badly for you!" (99–109).

With these words she vanished, and they awakened at once, marvelling in great fear.[9] Then the lady said to her husband:

"My lord, did you hear and see the apparition of this lady?"

"Indeed," he replied, "certainly, and I am amazed and greatly shaken by it. What do you think we should do?"

"My lord," she said, "this is the third time that she has appeared to me and that I have seen her in this fashion. But I was so fearful of incurring your anger that I dared not tell you of it. If you want to follow my advice, let us offer them help,[10] and ask the lady to pray to her God, about whom she preaches every day, that he grant us a child. If the lady were to make it possible that, through her God, we could have a son or daughter to be our heir, then I would gladly support her preaching."

"Wife,"[11] he said, "you have spoken well, and I will have provisions sent to them immediately" (110–38).

The next morning, as soon as day broke, the wealthy man did not delay. He had all the inhabitants of the city assemble, and commanded that they welcome these people and listen often to them. He had a good dwelling place found for them, and he had their every need ministered to, so that they no longer suffered any discomfort. And he and his wife knelt before Mary Magdalene, and prayed that she intercede with her God so that he grant them a son or daughter.

Mary Magdalene did so, and the worthy man who had made this request lay with his wife and had sexual relations with her, and after a short time he made her pregnant (139–56).

When she felt the child move in her, she cried:

---

[9] 111–13 **and they awakened at once, marvelling in great fear** *E cil meintenant s'esveillerent, / Que durement se esmerveillerent, / E si urent mult grant pour*: W has a slightly different reading: *Et cil meintenant s'esveillierent / Ki dormeient: s'esmerveillierent / Et si ourent mut grant pour* "they who had been sleeping awakened; they marvelled and had great fear."

[10] 125 **Let us offer them help** *Faimes lor bien*: the author has earlier used the phrase *lur feist bien faire* 87, and the general sense is "offer physical aid and moral support."

[11] 137 **"Wife," he said** *"Dame," feit il*: the translation follows W; cf. P: *"Par fei," fait il* "By my faith," he said.

"My lord, it is true, I am carrying a live child! Mary Magdalene is most holy, and her God is glorious and more powerful than all others!"

"My lady,"[12] he replied, "you have spoken the truth, and I will go at once to find out about this. I want to go without delay to the Holy Sepulchre to pray. I will go to Jerusalem to see for myself[13] if what she tells us about Jesus is true."

"My lord," she responded, "I will come with you. How can we be separated, one from the other?[14] It is not right,[15] you should not go without me! I must be with you both coming and going, I must sustain you through both good and evil, rise up with you and lie down with you, eat and drink with you, and be with you as my lord while you work and while you rest."[16]

"On the contrary, my lady," he stated, "you will remain here! You will keep safe what we have.[17] The trip would be too difficult for you, the sea is very rough,

---

[12] 163 **My lady** *Dame*: cf. W: *"Certes," feit il,* "'Indeed,' he said."

[13] 165–68 **I want to go without delay to the Holy Sepulchre to pray, I will go to Jerusalem to see for myself** *Ne voil jeo plus demorer / Ke jeo nen auge a[l] sepulcre orer, / Desque en Jherusalem iray / Et par mei meimes enproveray*: these lines, found only in W, make the purpose of the pilgrimage more explicit.

[14] 171–72 **"My lord, . . . the other** *"Sire," fet ele, "jo irrai od vus!/ Coment [nus] departirum nus?*: these lines, missing in W, stress the agony of separation.

[15] 173 **It is not right** *Ceo ne serreit pas bone foi*: cf. W: *"Sire," feit la dame, "par fey"* "My lord," replied his wife, "by my faith."

[16] 175–80 **I must be with you both coming and going, I must sustain you through both good and evil, rise up with you and lie down with you, eat and drink with you, and be with you as my lord while you work and while you rest** *Od vus dei aler et venir, / Les biens e les mals sustenir, / Od vus lever, od vus cuchier, / Od vus beivre, od vous mangier, / E od vus com od mon seignor / Estre al travail e al su[j]or*: the litany of conjugal obligations begins with a restatement of the refusal to be separated, found in the famous biblical scene of Ruth and Naomi (cf. Ruth 1:16). The French text here follows the Latin source closely, but adds the lines referring to good and evil, eating and drinking: *Quod cum matrona attenderet, ait: 'Quid est, domine? Putasne sine me quoquam proficisci? Absit. Te enim recedente recedam, te veniente veniam, te quiescente quiescam'*: "When his wife heard this, she replied: 'What is this, my lord? Did you think to travel anywhere without me? Let it not be so! When you leave, I will leave, when you come back, I will come back, when you rest, I will rest'" (Weiss 100, §115, 27; CCHL 527, §4, 8–11).

[17] 182 **You will keep safe what we have** *Ceo ke nus avum garderez*: this refers both to the child *in utero* and to the ruler's worldly possessions (and power). The latter sense is made very explicit in the Latin text: *et possessionibus nostris curam impendes, ne me absente aliquis nostrae iurisdictionis terminos praesumat exterminare vel aliquid contra potestatem nostram temere usurpare* "and you will take care of our possessions, so that in my absence no one will attempt to diminish my authority or dare to do anything to usurp my power" (Weiss 100, §115, 28; CCHL 527, §4, 12–14).

and you are pregnant with our child. Instead, in your painted chamber[18] I will have you waited upon, and bathed, for you must not do any physical labour."

"My lord," she said, "this cannot be! I will never see the child born if I remain behind without you, for the sake of a bath[19] or any other physical comfort!"

She wept and pleaded so much that her husband granted her wish (157–94).

He came to Mary Magdalene and explained that he wished to go the Sepulchre in Jerusalem and take his wife with him. Whatever he had as possessions, both houses and income, he gave into the Magdalene's care and protection. Then the next day he provided himself with gold and silver coins, for he wanted to begin his voyage at once. And Mary Magdalene graciously[20] gave him the first cross ever worn by a pilgrim. In short, she put a cross on his shoulder as a sign, and she commended him to God and blessed him with the sign of the cross. She marked him with the cross so that the devil could never tempt him, nor make him forsake his pilgrimage (195–214).

When they were prepared they took their leave of the lady who on their behalf had prayed earnestly to God that he bring them back in safety[21] to their own country. Then they entered the ship which was ready in the harbour. As soon as they had a wind from the north the sailors embarked and raised the sail. When they reached the open sea they went straight to Acre by the most direct route that the winds allowed. They sailed without stopping one whole day and the following night. With sails fully set they were joyfully travelling along when great misadventure befell them,[22] for one's fortune on both sea and land often changes quickly. In a few hours a wind arose which smashed and shook the ship. The sea

---

[18] 186 **painted chamber** *chambre depeinte*: the ruler wants his wife to remain in the domestic protective environment of her private bedroom in a manner analogous to that of the child in the womb. Just as the child must be protected, so must his wife remain in the confines of her chamber. The man-made, constructed nature of this room is also in obvious contrast to the dangerous chaos of the natural world of the sea voyage.

[19] 192 **for the sake of a bath** *pur nul baigne*: the translation follows W; cf. P *pur nul gain* "for any profit, gain." The reading of W is more consistent with the rhetorical stance of the speaker, although *gain* does fit with the material possessions mentioned more extensively in the Latin source (cf. note to v. 182).

[20] 205–6 **And Mary Magdalene graciously gave him** *Et la curteise Magdaleine / Li done*: the adj. *curteise* again presents a challenge. As at v. 16, above, the translation opts for the sense of "graciousness" shown in this action of the noble, beautiful Magdalene.

[21] 218–21 **that he bring ... in the harbour** *Ke les remaint en son pais / E les conduie a salveté ... Ke fu apparaile[e] al port:* W lacks vv. 219–20, leaving out the explicit mention of safety, and replacing vv. 220–21 with a single line *En une nief entrent au port,* "they board a ship in the port."

[22] 233–34 **when great misadventure befell them** *Quant aventure lor mult gerre*: lit. "when fortune attacked them greatly." In v. 234 (**For one's fortune on both sea and land** *Ke a la mer e a la tere*) the translation replaces the subject pronoun *Ke* with its antecedent noun, *aventure* v. 233, which here has the sense "fortune."

began to swell, and the gale-force wind to strengthen, as if it would smash everything to pieces, lines, sails, beams and mast. All begged for help from whatever quarter they thought likely. Those who loved Mary Magdalene called out softly in her name, but the storm continued to grow and no one knew what to do. In the midst of this tempest the woman began to go into labour, with such pain that she could not raise her head (215–52).

Queen of Mercy! Who could recount this story and not be moved to tears and heartfelt sorrow? The lady had not yet come to the time when she was expected to give birth. But just such a misfortune has happened often in the past to many a woman, who has found herself in such dire straits either because of her own actions, or due to illness or fear, or a physical injury or some other misadventure, so that she has given birth much before the expected time to a child who would live a long life, just as God had so ordained; for in Him are all our journeys, all our comings and goings in this changeable world.[23] Just as the sea is quickly changing, so is the world and our destiny! (253–71).

Lord! What can this poor exhausted woman do now, who has been placed in such a dangerous situation? For the wind has not abated, but grows stronger; the sea is growing rough, and the storm is doubling in strength! The ship shudders and creaks, and the woman cries out. Sweet Mary Magdalene, what will your pilgrim do?[24] She could have been in her marbled chamber, and have had the help of women who know what to do in such situations. If only the woman could have an hour's rest, and not be wracked by her great anguish. She hears the wind whipping up the sea, and the waves lifting up the ship, and her heart almost fails. If she had had a hundred women with her, not a single one would have been able to lift a hand to help her.

I cannot recount this without being deeply moved, for the woman suffered so much that she weakened and died. And the child was drawn out of his dead mother, who died before he came into the world. With his little mouth he sought comfort from the nipple, but he found nothing which gave him the sustenance to which he was entitled, and he immediately began his plaintive cry (272–303).

It goes without saying that this caused the father great pain, for there was nothing he could do to make the situation better; he could only add his own tears and lamentations to those of his son. If he had not been so strongly confirmed in his faith, and if God had not helped him in this misfortune, he would have fallen

---

[23] 265–69 **a child who would live a long life ... in this changeable world** *Enfant ke longement vivreit ... Parmi cest siecle trespassable*: the statement that a prematurely-born child often lives a long life is perhaps unexpected in this context, but this assertion foreshadows the eventual destiny of this unborn child who is saved by divine intervention. On life surrounded by the presence of God see Acts 17:27–28.

[24] 278–79 **Sweet Mary ... your pilgrim do?** *Duze Magdaleine Marie, / Ke fra vostre pelerine?*: these words, translated as a statement by the narrator, could also be construed as direct speech by the woman in labour.

The Romance of Mary Magdalene

into despair. The pilgrim's cross was of great help to him, as was she who had prayed for him, so that he did not despair. But his heart was filled with sorrow so great that I don't know how to describe it to you.[25] For what could this man possibly do in the face of such grief and pain? (304–19).

The ship was driven along at great speed by the violent storm, causing terror and despair, which showed on the faces of the sailors. One, attempting to make the sailors' case better, recognizing and knowing that the woman's soul had left her body, said:

"The only thing we can do now is to throw the body overboard, for there is no place to keep it here. We will have better weather yet today when the dead woman transported onboard our ship is removed. It has long been proven that the sea cannot support such a cargo, that a dead body must be thrown overboard." Then everyone cried:

"Let's do it now! Let's take the body and remove it, and throw it into the sea!" (320–38).

When the pilgrim heard this, you can be sure that he was upset! Here he suffered pain upon pain, so that all colour drained from his face.

"Sirs," he pleaded, "have pity, for God's sake! I have scarcely had a chance to look at the body from which her soul has departed![26] What if she is not dead? Perhaps she is only unconscious? Such things have often happened![27] Wait awhile to see if she is breathing! Please, can you not wait and allow me to keep her a little time? Spare the child who is still alive, do not kill him! That would be too horrible a crime; you will be murderers if you throw him alive into the water!" (339–56).

As they uttered these words, they noticed a mountain close by, over the bow of the ship. When the pilgrim saw it he called out to the master helmsman:

"Sir, take me from here across to that mountain, and I will give all that you would dare to take from among my riches. Make the ship wait here a little while, until I have buried this body. I will give you a share of my treasures, which will make you wealthy forever" (357–69).[28]

---

[25] 316–17 **But his heart was filled with sorrow so great that I don't know how to describe it to you** *Mes si grant dolur al quer a / Que le ne vus say retraire*: the translation follows W, keeping a first person narrator; cf P: *Mes si grant dolor al quer a / Ke nuls homme nel saureit retraire* "But his heart was filled with sorrow so great that no one could recount it."

[26] 344 **I have scarcely had a chance to look at** *Onckore n'a[i] ge gaires gardé*: cf. W *Uncore n'avés guaires gardé* (ms. *gardeu*) "you have scarcely looked at." Both versions are plausible, stressing that the sailors are acting hastily, either without looking closely at the body themselves, or by not allowing the husband time to inspect the body.

[27] Cf. Matthew 9:24, Mark 5:39, Luke 8:52.

[28] 368 **I will give you a share of my treasures** *Jeo vus partirai mes tresors*: cf. W: *Jeo vus porterai me[s] tresors*, "I will bring you my treasures."

When the helmsman heard this, he had the sail lowered and they moved on more slowly, for he loved and delighted in the thought of his promised reward, which would not be small.[29] They immediately launched the landing boat, which was very safe and well made,[30] loaded them into it, and rowed over to the mountainous island. The pilgrim, who wished to bury his wife, was unable to dig a hole in the earth, for it was too hard and unyielding, but he found by chance a suitable place tucked under a hollowed-out rock. Under this he placed the body of his wife, in her shift and other garments, and beside her breast he placed the child who was still living. He covered them with his cloak. You can be sure that when he had to take his leave of them, he was filled with great sorrow and uttered many sad sighs.

"Oh, gentle Mary Magdalene," he lamented, "it was to my great pain and suffering that ever you came to my country! I was wretched and miserable, dear lady, when I believed you, to my great sorrow. Lady, you committed a great sin when you asked your Lord that my wife might have a child, for by that child she has died. Now both mother and child are dead: my lady,[31] is this not your fault? I entrusted whatever I had to your care when I began this voyage. To you, and to your God, whom you believe to be so powerful, I now commend this body and the child. May you be a help to the soul of my wife who has died in such a cruel misfortune!" (370–412).

After he had thus expressed his grief at length, he went back to his companions, who rowed him out to the ship. They raised the sail, and now that the storm had died down, the ship moved on at full speed.

But I do not wish to proceed further in my story without telling you about the sweet sinner who was a preacher on land, who also became a nurse on the island mountain and, at sea, performed what was required for a nursing infant. They would have had the child swallowed up by the sea if his father had not prayed to Mary Magdalene, through whom God forgave his sins.[32] Glorious Mary Magdalene remained alive and well on land, but her prayer and her worth

---

[29] 370–73 **When the helmsman heard this, he had the sail lowered** *Kant ceo entent li esteremanz, . . . Maintenant fet abeisser le trief*: the translation follows W in which vv. 370, 373 use the third person singular, as opposed to the third person plural in P: *ceo oent les esturmanz* "the helmsmen heard this" . . . *Besserent maintenant le tref,* "they lowered the sail."

[30] 376 **which was very safe and well made** *Que mut est seur [et bon] et bel*: the translation follows W; cf. P: *Ke mult ert riche e bon e bel* "which was very rich and well made."

[31] 404 **my lady, is this not your fault?** *Dame, dun n'est vostre li tort?*: the translation follows W; cf. P: *Vis m'est ke vostre est li tort,* "in my view the fault lies with you."

[32] 426 **They would have allowed the sea to swallow up the child** *De la mer l'eussent fait beivre*: lit. "they would have made him drink the sea." The translation avoids the literal sense by reversing the swallower and the swallowed; the phrase "throw into the drink," while recuperating some of the sense of *beivre la mer*, seems too colloquial.

were such in the sight of God that the infant, who was still living and whose father had commended him to her in good faith, through divine providence found in the mother's lifeless nipple sweet milk, of which the child drank his fill and was comforted. This is a very great miracle indeed, but I know that our Lord can do anything that pleases him. He who made water gush from the desert rock before the eyes of his people can certainly accomplish what I am recounting.[33] He protected the body on the mountainside so that it did not wither or decompose, and the infant was better nourished than if he had had several wet-nurses, for he sought no pleasures other than the breast at which he suckled, which was neither too large nor too small, but suitably full and beautiful. The child was sustained by the breast and slept beneath the cloak, which had a very soft lining. The lady was not touched by the rain or the dew, nor affected by the heat or cold, but lay there on the hard rock. During the long time she remained there no animal attacked her, no bird landed on her, nor was she infested with vermin (413–64).

But I can assure you that when the lady's soul left her body it continued on the pilgrimage that the lady had wished to undertake: her soul remained close to her husband wherever he went, but no one could see it (465–70).

When the violent storm died down and the sea became calm and serene, the ship went directly to Syria. God came to the aid of the pilgrim who sought him, for he led him directly to a good harbour. When he had paid for his passage, he set out immediately. He hadn't travelled far when he met Saint Peter, whose heart was greatly gladdened when he saw the cross the pilgrim was wearing sewn on his right shoulder, for he had never seen another pilgrim wear one. He sought to reassure him, saying,

"Who are you, kind sir?" And the pilgrim began to tell him where he came from, from what country, and what he had come there looking for, and who had given him the cross; he recounted the whole story of his misfortunes and described how he had arrived there (471–96).

"Oh, kind friend," responded Peter, "you had a wise advisor. You have followed good advice, and I welcome you most warmly! I will be your companion, your helper, and your guide. I will lead you to Jerusalem and show you all the country round about, and I will teach you how God came for our salvation. And if your wife is sleeping, Jesus Christ, who died for us, will be able to turn your sorrow into joy and gladness in short order, when he chooses to do so" (497–511).

The noble pilgrim's heart was made lighter when he heard these words, and he rejoiced greatly upon learning that he had truly found Saint Peter. He went with him gladly, obeying all his commandments. Saint Peter instructed him in the faith, and led him to Jerusalem and the Sepulcher where God had lain, to the temple of Solomon, to Bethlehem where Jesus was born, and to the mount of Calvary as well. He also showed him and taught him about the river where he

---

[33] Cf. Exodus 17:6, Numbers 20:7–11.

was baptized. He led him through the whole country, and every day confirmed in him the true faith and true belief. The pilgrim stayed with him for more than two years in this region, until he requested leave to depart, and Saint Peter granted it to him, commanding him to believe as he had taught him (512–35).

When Saint Peter had blessed him and marked him with the sign of the cross, the noble pilgrim took his leave and departed.[34] He went straight to the sea coast, where he sought advice from the sailors as to which ship was going to Marseille. One of them said to him:

"This one, good sir, is all ready to go and has taken on a large cargo."

Then he embarked on the ship after he had agreed upon the fare, and when they had a good south wind the sailors silently slipped out of the harbor and sailed on until they reached the high seas. The mariners travelled on with a strong favourable wind until they came alongside an island mountain, just as the Saviour of the world in his wisdom had provided they should, in order to demonstrate his miracles (536–56).

When the pilgrim saw the mountain, he recognized it at once. He called out to the captain, earnestly pressing him, and sealed the bargain with the large gift he promised him, so that the captain had the landing boat lowered into the sea and the sail dropped. He had him rowed over to the island, just as the pilgrim, who was to give him a large reward, had begged him to do (557–66).

When they came close to the shore, they saw a small[35] child seated on the shingle beach, playing and amusing himself with the pebbles that he found there. When he saw them approaching, he fled back up the mountain as fast as he could to his refuge, for he had not learned anything about humans from seeing other people on the island: he had never before seen a man. As soon as the pilgrim could touch land he jumped out of the boat, asking his companions to wait, and he climbed alone up the mountainside to the place where he had earlier been. He saw clearly where the child had gone, and he went there straightaway and found the child under the cloak, handsome and big for his age. The child was suckling the breast, hiding beneath the sheltering cloak as he had learned to do. The prince saw his wife, whom he had so loved, his fellow pilgrim,[36] completely intact, her face fresh and smiling, and her whole body seemed still alive. Her garments

---

[34] 536–37 **the noble pilgrim departed** *Li franc pelerin s'en repeire*: the translation follows W; cf. P: *Congié ad pris si s'en repaire*, "he took his leave and departed."

[35] 568 **small child** *enfançoné*: translated from W: *Un enfançoné unt veu*; cf. P: *Un enfancet de greinur eage / Virent juer* "they saw an older small child playing."

[36] 590–92: **The prince saw his wife, whom he had so loved, his fellow pilgrim, completely intact, her face fresh and smiling** *Sa femme k'il out tant amé / Veit, la pelerine tut enterrine, / Freche et riante la chier*: the translation follows W. P reads: *Sa muillier, que il out tant amee, / Trova li prodhom tute entiere, / E frecche e rovente la chiere*, "the worthy man found his wife, whom he had loved so much, her body untouched, her face fresh and of good colour."

were fresh and fragrant, as if they had been stored and hung out to air, and they smelled even more sweetly than before. He took the small and very handsome child in his arms, and cried out with tears of joy: "Gentle Mary Magdalene! My lady, may you be honoured![37] And may He, your God, and his power, be blessed and honoured, for He alone should be worshipped, He alone is worthy of glory and praise and victory. Your prayer has protected my child for me. He has been better nourished than if a woman had suckled him and given him all he could eat and drink. Sweet lady, I know and see that God has granted me all this for your sake. Since you have given me this child and kept him here for me, give me back his mother who lies here. I know truly that Jesus Christ is so gentle, so kind, and so powerful that He can do it, my lady, if you chose to ask it of Him! Then there would be no man on earth richer than I would be, and I would serve you always, if we could go back to Marseille together" (567–626).

As soon as he had said these words he looked at his wife and noticed that she was softly breathing; then she opened her eyes and spoke, and with her first words she praised God and Mary Magdalene. When the good man heard her speak, he called out to her:

"My dear, are you alive?"

"Yes!" she replied, "indeed I am![38] I am alive and well, thanks be to God and Mary Magdalene, who received my son at the time of my great suffering when we were on the sea. Ever since, she has watched over me and has led me with you wherever you are. I have always been at your side, and whatever you saw, I saw. When Saint Peter was your guide, Mary Magdalene held me and caused me to see, hear, and know everything, and I can recount it all to you" (627–49). Then she related everything that he had said and done and she told it all in its proper order.

"Oh, my dearly beloved!" he exclaimed. "Our Lord is such that we must never forget Him from now on. It is very good to trust in Him, and if the gentle Magdalene leads us back to our own country, we and all our people must always obey, honour, and serve her. Let us go down to the landing boat awaiting us, and we will shortly be on a fine ship in fair weather. Anyone who does not worship Jesus Christ is foolish, for all other gods are worthless and of no help to their people" (650–68).

After they had spoken in this fashion, they went down to the boat and to the sailors who awaited them and who applied themselves at once to the oars and rowed them back to the ship. Everyone asked the pilgrim news of his wife and child, and he immediately narrated to them the story of their adventures. Then he paid his wife's passage, which he considered money well spent. They unfurled the sail and it caught the wind. The ship began to move, not stopping until it reached Marseille (669–82).

---

[37] 603 **My lady, may you be honoured** *Dame, honuree seies tu*: the translation follows W; cf. P: *Beneuree seies tu*, "May you be blessed."

[38] 636 **indeed I am!** *a estrus*; translated from W; cf. P: *ço estes vus* "is that you?"

The news spread everywhere in the city, and all heard of the prince's return, and that his wife had borne a son, a very handsome child.[39] Shortly after his return,[40] the nobleman came before Mary Magdalene, who rarely had any opposition from people to whom she preached. He came to her as quickly as he could and threw himself down at her feet, praising and thanking her. Before all the assembled people of the land he told his story, then immediately asked for baptism, and Mary Magdalene had him baptized, along with his wife and child. Maximinus baptized them, and because of the miracle that they had just heard, many others who were also there were baptized. And the prince ordered the temple that he had formerly cherished to be torn down. He founded a church on the site, and endowed it with land and incomes, thereby establishing the Christian faith. He remained a good Christian ever after, and his wife was righteous and saintly, sincere in her love for God. Their son grew up and loved God, and welcomed Christians, and in this fashion and by these means, as William tells us, Mary Magdalene and her companions converted the country to God, who reigns, now and forever, and whose kingdom is without end. May we all go to Him straightaway when we die, to live in glory with the King Victorious. Amen (683–724).

---

[39] 687 **a very handsome child** *mult bel enfant de sun age*: lit. "a very handsome child for his age."

[40] 688 **Shortly after his return** *Einz k'il feist lung estage*: lit. "before he had stayed there for a long time."

Appendix

1. Guillaume de Berneville, *La Vie de saint Gilles*

i. Storm at Sea, followed by Clear Sailing (vv. 771–95, 876–912)

Fleeing Athens in secret, Giles arrives at the seashore, and prays for a ship to carry him across the sea. In the distance he sees a vessel struggling in a storm, and prays for the safety of the sailors. Later Giles joins the merchants on the ship and they set off for Provence, sailing in bright sunshine with a fair wind.

	Il est assis, car mult fu las;	fol. 118 rb
772	prie Dieu e seint Nicholas	
	k'il lui tramete alkun veissel,	
	buce u kenar, nef u batel,	
	ki utre l'en poüst porter.	
776	Il esgardat en haute mer,	
	e vit une nef periller	
	e a turmente dechascer,	
	e repuneit entre les undes	
780	ki erent grandes e parfundes,	
	kar la mer ert mult hericee,	fol. 118 va
	undeie e brait cum esragee.	
	La nef veit par la mer walcrant,	
784	la tempeste la veit menant,	
	kar mult par fet leide turmente,	
	esclaire e tone e plot e vente.	
	Tant de la mer tant del grant vent	
788	pur poi ke cele nef ne fent!	
	L'unde la porte contre munt,	
	l'autre la treit vers le parfunt,	
	l'une la peint, l'autre la bute,	
792	pur poi k'ele ne desront tute!	
	Gires veit la nef periller	
	e la mer braire e engrosser:	
	des mariners out grant pité.	

[...]

876	Le jur fud bel, le solail cler,	fol. 119 rb
	la mer fud paisible e le vent:	
	a la nef vunt ignelement;	
	lez sunt del bel tens ke il unt.	
880	Traient lur ancres, si s'en vunt.	
	A plein se astent d'eschiper,	
	kar mult coveitent le passer.	
	Bons fud li venz e la mer quieie:	
884	ne lur estoet muver lur greie,	
	ne n'i out la nuit lof cloé,	
	estuïnc trait ne tref gardé,	
	ne n'i out halé bagordinge,	
888	ne escote ne scolaringe,	
	ne fud mester de boesline:	
	tute fud queie la marine;	
	ne lur estut pas estricher,	
892	ne tendre tref ne helenger.	
	Fort ert l'estai e li hobent	fol. 119 va
	ki fermé furent vers le vent,	
	e d'autre part, devers le bort,	
896	sunt li nodraz e li bras fort;	
	bones utanges out el tref,	
	meillurs n'estot a nule nef;	
	bons fud li tref e la nef fort,	
900	e unt bon vent ki tost les port.	
	Tute noit current a la lune,	
	le tref windé tresk'a la hune:	
	ne lur estut muver funain	
904	trestuite nuit ne l'endemain.	
	Lur aire vunt od la mer pleine,	
	kar issi veit cil ke Deus aime.	
	Gires se dort, car mult fud las,	
	od l'esterman lez le windas.	

Commentary

The *Vie de s. Gilles* is written in octosyllabic couplets, the narrative form most commonly used in medieval French. Guillaume de Berneville's mastery of the verse form can be seen in his supple syntax and varied rhythms, for in addition to the most frequent division of the line into two halves of four syllables, Guillaume also uses rhythms of 1+3+4, 2+6, 3+5, and so on (see, for example, vv. 777,

788, 792, 793, 829 [all 2+6]; vv. 772, 775, 783, 901 [all 3+5]; vv. 778, 780, 789, 881 [all 5+3]). His use of rhyme is unstilted and unpretentious. The passage excerpted here is famous for the range of Guillaume's maritime lexicon, clear evidence of his detailed knowledge of seafaring. But it is more than just an exercise in lexical virtuosity: the affective quality of the detailed shipcraft, and the depth of Guillaume's attention to the "gear and tackle and trim" (as Gerard Manley Hopkins has it)[1] of human craftmanship, ingenuity and skill make this both one of the most detailed and at the same time one of the most affecting versions of the ship at sea topos—a universal metaphor of human life as a journey toward an unknown future. Guillaume expresses both the negative and positive potentialities in the metaphor, showing first the dangers (the merchant sailors as hapless victims of the storm), and then the triumphs of life (the well-built ship and the professional skills of the sailors).

Guillaume integrates this metaphor into the narrative structure: Giles has just abandoned his wealth and his social position to travel incognito through the wilderness landscape, to begin his search for spiritual enlightenment. The isolated seashore is the first real obstacle in his literal (and metaphorical) path, and the sea crossing is the next stage in his divinely ordained trajectory. Guillaume combines an extravagantly rich vocabulary (deploying and expanding the stock of nautical terms used in other medieval texts) [2] along with a carefully constructed interplay of social and religious relationships. The relationships among Giles, the merchant sailors, and the island hermit are all created by, or are functions of, this maritime adventure in which they are fortuitously (i.e. by God's grace) brought together for their mutual benefit and safety.

The extracts discussed here are limited to the two continuous passages with detailed seafaring images, but the larger narrative details underline the symbolic significance of these descriptions. The interdependence of the religious and worldly is already evident in this episode: the foundering ship which must come to shore is a providential answer to Giles' prayer, just as the merchants, upon reaching land, recognize that Giles' prayers have saved them. Both recognize that they need each other to complete their journeys (Giles to cross the sea seeking spiritual enlightenment, the merchants to return home in safety bearing their merchandise). They are also complementary in another fashion: Giles has just rejected his worldly wealth (and his *familia* are concerned about his lack of proper clothing and food), but he now joins forces with merchants carrying luxurious eastern fabrics and the richest foods and spices, in a tacit agreement that he

---

[1] "And áll trades, their gear and tackle and trim"; see "Pied Beauty," in *Poems of Gerard Manley Hopkins*, ed. W. H. Gardner and N. H. MacKenzie, 4th ed. (Oxford: Oxford University Press, 1967).

[2] See Joël Grisward, "A propos du thème descriptif de la tempête chez Wace et chez Thomas d'Angleterre," in *Mélanges de langue et de littérature du Moyen Age et de la Renaissance offerts à Jean Frappier* (Geneva: Droz, 1970), 1:375–89.

needs the strengths of the worldly merchants to accomplish his spiritual ends. The merchants, for their part, inform themselves of Giles' past and future goals, and insist on freely helping him in thanks for his (past and future) aid in gaining providential help against the vagaries of misfortune.

In the first seafaring episode Guillaume concentrates on the dangers of storms at sea. Double or multiple terms qualify most of the actions or objects depicted: thus Giles prays to both God and St. Nicholas (patron of sailors), hoping for a vessel (naming four types, two specific, two general: *buce u kenar, nef u batel*; see Note to v. 774). The description of the storm and ship uses verbs of sound and motion, while verbs of seeing connect Giles to the scene: he "looked" (*esguardat*, v. 776), and "saw" (*vit*, v. 777); and at the end of the scene the act of seeing is repeated (*Gires veit la nef,* v. 793). The verbs *periller* "be in peril, in danger of sinking" (vv. 777, 793) and *dechascer* "be driven, run before the wind" (v. 778) give a broad view of the motion of the ship, while in closer focus Guillaume uses the verbs *repuneit* "was hidden, disappeared" (v. 779), *veit . . . walcrant* "was drifting, moving uncontrollably" (v. 783), *veit menant* "pushed along" (at the whim of the storm, v. 784). The sea has both movement and sound: it "makes waves" (*undeie*, v. 782), which are "high, with deep troughs" (*grandes e parfundes*, v. 780); it becomes animate, "roaring like a wild beast" (*brait cum esragee*, v. 782; *braire e engrosser,* "roar and become turbulent" v. 794), while its roughness is like a bristling pelt, "with hairs standing on end" (*hericee*, v. 781). The "storm" (*turmente*, vv. 778, 785; *tempeste*, v. 784) is "fierce" (ugly, *leide*, v. 785), created by four meteorological events: "lightning, thunder, rain, and wind," all expressed by verbs in a single verse (*esclaire e tone e plot e vente*, v. 786).

It is the combination of "agitated sea and strong winds" which nearly sinks the ship (*Tant de la mer tant del grant vent*, v. 787). The push and pull of the waves, from crest to trough, expressed by the repetition of *l'unde / l'autre* ("one wave / another wave," vv. 789–90), *l'une / l'autre*, "this one / that one" v. 791) and the four verbs *porte* ("thrusts up," v. 789), *treit* ("pitches down," v. 790), *peint* ("pushes up," v. 791), *bute* ("drops down," v. 791), is reminiscent of the description of the eternal torment of Judas, battered by the waves while he is chained to a rock in the sea in the *Voyage de Saint Brendan*.[3] Although Giles is moved to pity for the sailors, the storm is viewed only from a distance, and the audience does not experience the fear of those on board ship (in contrast to the storm scene written by Guillaume le Clerc de Normandie, discussed in Appendix 4 below).

---

[3] Benedeit, *Le Voyage de Saint Brendan*, ed. Short and Merrilees: *Undes de mer le ferent fort, / Pur quei n'ad fin la süe mort. / Le une le fert, pur poi ne funt; / Le altre detriers jetet l'amunt. / Peril devant, peril desus, / Peril detriers, peril dejus:* "The waves of the sea struck him forcefully, so that his death was endless. One wave strikes him and he almost sinks to the depths, the next one crashes into him and sends him back up to the top. He faces peril in front of him, above him, behind and below him" (vv. 1229–34).

The narrative (not included in our extract) following this passage recounts the sailors meeting Giles, and establishes their mutual interdependence, noted above. After they have agreed to set out on the next stage of their journeys together, the smooth beginning of their voyage is described in detail. The richness of technical terms is an expression of the beneficence of divine guidance; it is also an expression of sheer delight in human ingenuity and craftsmanship. The list of skilled manoeuvres that can be used to take advantage of, or protect from, winds and currents as the vessel navigates the unknown are concrete reminders of what can be gained by teamwork and human inventiveness. Mutual help and cooperation between the religious pilgrim Giles and the worldly travellers is encapsulated in the image of the sleepers on deck at the end of this passage.

The divine direction of their joint enterprise is also signalled before they complete their voyage by Giles' fortuitous encounter with the island hermit, which directly follows the second part of our extract. This meeting is parallel to the merchant's first interaction with Giles, and provides an exemplary image of asceticism and solitude, literally as an island apart from society, a place with no disputes or quarrels. The image of the island hermit is similar to Brendan and his monks' island encounters with holy men, and is a positive counterpart to the Brendanesque image of the perils of the sea seen in Judas' torment noted above.

In depicting the ship's swift and smooth passage across the sea Guillaume again uses double terms: the day was "fine" (*bel*, vv. 876, 879), the sky "clear" (*cler*, v. 876), both sea and wind are "calm" (*paisible*, v. 877, then *bons* and *quieie*, vv. 883, 890). In this section Guillaume's lexical virtuosity is more evident, for in the space of thirty-four lines he uses some twenty-six technical nautical terms, often including both an object and an action connected to it.[4] He is able to include many of these terms by stating a series of actions the sailors had no need to perform (since the weather was so fine), a technique that makes his list easily expandable.[5]

---

[4] See Robin Ward, *The World of the Medieval Shipmaster: Law, Business and the Sea c. 1350–c. 1450* (Rochester: Boydell Press, 2009), chap. 7: "The Shipmaster at Sea—Seamanship," 157–78, for discussion of nautical terms found in non-literary sources. For the use of French (which borrows nautical terms from many sources) by all sailors plying their trade between the Continent and Britain, see Maryanne Kowaleski, "The French of England: A Maritime *lingua franca?*" in *Language and Culture in Medieval Britain: The French of England c. 1100–c. 1500*, ed. Jocelyn Wogan-Browne (York: York Medieval Press, 2009), 103–17. Cf. also Robert Gruss, *Petit Dictionnaire de marine*, 3rd ed. (Paris: Société d'éditions géographiques, maritimes et coloniales, 1952), with 430 illustrations.

[5] See *Wace's Roman de Brut, A History of the British: Text and Translation*, by Judith Weiss (Exeter: Exeter University Press, 1999), 282 for a translation of Wace's description of Arthur crossing the English Channel (*Roman de Brut*, vv. 11193–238). See also Note to v. 885, above.

In the following list of technical expressions from this passage, I give the infinitive form of the relevant verb. All these terms are expressions of human skill and ingenuity in the face of whatever challenges the sea (or life) may present: *traire ancre*, "weigh anchor," v. 880; *eschiper*, "load, equip (a ship for sailing), embark," v. 881; *muver lur greie*, "change their tack, adjust their rigging (to change point of sail)," etc.; cf. *muver funain*, v. 903), v. 884; *clouer lof*, "fix, fasten, tie fast the luff (windward edge of sail)," v. 885; *traire estuïnc*, "lower the stunsail" (cf. ModF *bonnette*, a second supplementary sail, of lighter weight than the main sail, and added to the same spar, to increase the volume of sail), v. 886; *garder tref*, "watch, trim the sail," v. 886; *haler bagordinge*, "man, pull on the halliards," or ropes for taking in the sail (rolling or bunching it up to take it out of the wind), v. 887; *haler escote*, "pull on the sheets" (ropes to hold the bottom corner of the sail against the wind), v. 888; *haler scolaringe*, "tighten or pull on the *scolaringe*" (a word of unknown meaning: possibly a grommet on the sail for the sheet; or something connected to ModF *ralingue*, the reinforcement made of rope sewn along the windward edge of a sail), v. 888; *boesline*, "line, rope attached to the bow" (attaching the windward edge of the sail to the bow, holding the sail against the wind), v. 889; *estricher*, "strike, or take in, sail" (pull sail up to the yardarm, or spar, to reduce the surface catching the wind), v. 891; *tendre tref*, "add, pull out more sail" (to catch the wind), v. 892; *helenger*, "tie the rudder (?)" (word of unknown origin; see Note to v. 891), v. 892; *estai*, "stay, rigging" (which braces the mast from movement forward or backward), v. 893; *fermer li hobent vers le vent*, "tighten (against the wind) the rigging" (guy-lines which brace the mast from the sides and from the back), v. 893; *nodraz*, "rigging knots(?)," (word of unknown meaning; *noeuds droits?* some sort of knot?), v. 896; *bras*, "braces" (ropes attached to the end of the yard, or spar, holding the sail, used to orient the sail by changing the angle of the spar on the horizontal plane), v. 896; *utanges*, "runner-ties" (on sails, or spars, ropes running through block and tackle pulleys, used to hoist whatever is attached to them), v. 897; *tref*, "sail," vv. 897, 899, 902; *nef*, "ship," vv, 898, 899; *winder le tref*, "haul up the sail," v. 902; *la hune*, "the crow's nest," v. 902; *muver funain*, "change, adjust the rigging" (*funain* <FUNIS rope, sheet, line), v. 903; *esterman*, "helmsman," v. 908; *windas*, "capstan, windlass" (used to raise the anchor), v. 908.

Throughout this detailed technical passage Guillaume's rapid rhythm mimics the quick passage of the ship across the sea. The series of nine lines (seven beginning with *ne*) which list the sailing manoeuvres that were not necessary (vv. 884–92) are balanced by a series of eight lines which state the positive qualities of the ship ("there was no better," "sails were sturdy and the ship stout," etc., vv. 893–900). The serenity of the voyage (and its technical expertise) is captured by the image of Giles falling asleep between the helmsman and the capstan, and by the statement "he whom God loves travels thus" (v. 906).[6] Divine providence smiles on this crew which joins together worldly merchants and a spiritual pilgrim, both aware of their need for mutual support.

ii. The Miracle of the Eucharist (vv. 2976–3015)

Giles is celebrating Mass at the Church of the Holy Cross in Orleans. During the *Secreta* of the Mass he offers a private prayer to God while holding the host. His address to the host includes a statement of the doctrine of transubstantiation.

2976	El segrei u li abbes fu	fol. 138 ra
	e le cors Nostre Seignur tint,	
	de Charlemeine li sovint;	
	al cors pïement se demente:	
2980	"A! Deu," feit il, "verrai entente,	
	Reis ki fus senz comencement	
	e seras senz definement,	
	tut tens fus e tut tens seras,	
2984	e establis e comandas	
	ke tis cors fud sacrefïez	
	pur raançun de nos pechez,	
	mult est grant merveille de tei	
2988	e de tun cors ke jo ci vei:	
	tu es enter el cel la sus,	
	e nus avum tun cors ça jus;	
	Sire, tu es e la e ci,	
2992	pur quant n'es pas en dous parti:	fol. 138 rb
	un seul Deu es en deïté.	
	Establi as e comandé	
	beiver tun sanc, ta char manger,	
2996	e tut dis est tis cors enter;	
	unkes ne pot amenuser	
	ne pur user ne pur manger:	
	totes ures est enterrin.	
3000	Le ten regner n'avra ja fin.	
	Ki dignement ne te receit,	
	sa mort manjue e sa mort beit,	

---

[6] This scene recalls that of Jesus sleeping on the boat on Galilee, awakened by his disciples frightened by a sudden storm; cf. Matthew 8:23–27, Mark 4:35–41, Luke 8:22–25.

```
             jol sei e crei certainement.
3004    Tei pri jo, Pere omnipotent,
             de Charlemein' aez pité,
             ki pur tei ad tant travaillé,
             tant regnes pris par poüsté,
3008    pur eschaucer crestïenté.
             Ne regarder a sa folie!
             Jesu, le fiz sainte Marie,
             conseillez mei quei jo ferai,
3012    quel penitance lui durrai,
             quant il ne volt le feit gehir;
             meis, s'il te pleist, nel deis suffrir
             ke dïable ait de lui saisine."
```

Commentary

Throughout the *Vie* Giles offers prayers for people who have asked him to intercede on their behalf. The prayer during the Eucharist is offered by Giles on behalf of both himself and Charlemagne. Placed at the heart of the extended episode dealing with Charlemagne's sin and confession, Giles' prayer becomes a focal point for several narrative threads: it accords with the church's new insistence on the importance of penance and the necessity of confession; it effectively demonstrates the indispensability of priestly sacramental status in this process, and the fact that even the mightiest secular king of medieval Europe, Charlemagne, the Holy Roman Emperor, must submit to the church's authority. The subordination of secular power to God's power was an intense concern of the church in the twelfth century: the conflict between Henry II and Archbishop Thomas Becket, culminating in Becket's assassination in his cathedral at Canterbury in 1170, is a dramatic case in point. This episode deals with an equally well-known (although only legendary) royal sin, connected to Charlemagne and Roland, protagonists in the French foundational epic, the *Chanson de Roland*. According to the legend Roland was born of an incestuous relationship between Charlemagne and his sister. In this Eucharist scene, the *Vie de s. Gilles* demonstrates that even the most exemplary secular powers must in the end submit to divine power.[7] The narrative also effectively asserts the centrality of confession (and explicates its function in the sacrament of communion) in the (spiritual) lives of the rich and famous.

The prayer cited in our extract is addressed to Christ by Giles while he is holding the sanctified Host, which, according to doctrine, has become *essentially*

---

[7] The legendary sin does not figure in the *Chanson de Roland*, where Roland is the nephew of Charlemagne. The sin is a later accretion to the legend; see above, 131 n. 87.

the body of Christ.[8] Giles is speaking at the point in the service called the *Secreta* (*El segrei u li abbes fu*, v. 2976), when the priest utters a private prayer, usually asking that his own sins be forgiven and that he be worthy of performing the sacrament of the Eucharist.

This sacrament is at the heart of Christian life, for in it the faithful mystically participate in the Passion, eating and drinking the body and blood of Christ (in the eucharistic bread and wine), and so confirming their membership in the Church, also seen as the body of Christ. To partake of the sacrament of the Eucharist without having first confessed one's sins and asked for forgiveness was condemned by doctrine as an abuse, explicitly mentioned by Giles ("whoever does not sincerely receive you [through communion] eats and drinks his own death [cf. 1 Corinthians 11:29]; this I believe and know to be true," vv. 3001–3). It is this abuse that Giles wishes to persuade Charlemagne to avoid by making his confession.

This prayer exemplifies Guillaume's subtle didacticism, for its doctrinal and theological content is particularly relevant, both with respect to Charlemagne's sin and to the debate on the nature of the Eucharist and the doctrine of transubstantiation begun in the mid-eleventh century. Lanfranc of Bec (later archbishop of Canterbury) supported doctrines of the Real Presence and of Transubstantiation, established at the Roman councils of 1059 and 1079. He argued vigorously against Berengarius of Tours, who had maintained that the communion host and wine were only sacramentally, not physically, the body and blood of Christ.[9]

Giles himself has imitated Christ's Passion through the ascetic cultivation of his wound which remains unhealed and untreated ("I seek instead the suffering of my body," *le cors voil jo ke seit doilant*, v. 2151). As a result his prayer spoken directly to the body of Christ (held in his hand in front of the altar) is strengthened by his own suffering, offered as a sacrifice for the remission of his own sins.

The prayer proceeds by a series of theological constants: first, God is invoked as source of all knowledge (v. 2980), eternal, without beginning or end (vv. 2981–83); Christ's Passion for the redemption of humanity's sins (vv. 2985–86) was "ordained and established" (*establis e comandas*, v. 2984) by God. The same two verbs are used to state that the Eucharist is divinely instituted (*Establi as e comandé*, v. 2994), and the sacrament is the explicitly physical act of eating and

---

[8] The term was part of the doctrine of transubstantiation, discussed below. This doctrine argued that the communion bread, or host, was in essence the body of Christ. As a result Giles is both holding the body of Christ and addressing a prayer to Christ in heaven.

[9] See *Lanfranc of Canterbury, On the Body and Blood of the Lord, and Guitmund of Aversa, On the Truth of the Body and Blood of Christ in the Eucharist*, trans. Mark G. Vaillancourt, The Fathers of the Church: Medieval Continuation 10 (Washington, DC: Catholic University of America Press, 2009); see also Macy, *Treasures from the Storeroom*.

drinking ("drink your blood, eat your flesh," *beiver tun sanc, ta char manger,* v. 2995).[10]

Speaking directly to Christ, Giles expresses wonder and reverence at the mystery of the Eucharist, using predominantly the second person singular form of address for verbs, pronouns, and possessive adjectives: *merveille de tei* (v. 2987), *tun cors* (vv. 2988, 2990), *tis cors* (vv. 2983, 2996), *tun sanc, ta char* (v. 2995), etc. (only two verbs are in the second person plural, *aez pité* 3005, *conseillez mei* 3011, and there are no second person plural pronouns). This near complete use of second person singular forms creates a stylistic effect of particular intimacy between Giles and Christ, since it stands out from the routinely mixed use of second person plural and singular forms in medieval French.

Through Giles, Guillaume expresses in the vernacular eucharistic theology's standard tenets in a way both succinct and comprehensible: the doctrine of the Real Presence (Christ is both here and in Heaven, vv. 2989–91), and the indivisible Body (vv. 2992–93), and the view that the chewing and drinking of the Eucharist's elements do not diminish the body of Christ ("yet forever your body remains whole, it can never be diminished even when it is consumed and eaten, for it forever remains whole," vv. 2996–99).[11]

In the intimacy of the *secreta* of the Mass, Giles begins and ends his prayer with reference to Charlemagne. After evoking the mystery of the Eucharist, Giles asks for pity from God the Father for Charlemagne because he has been a military champion of Christianity (*tant regnes pris,* v. 3007), and asks the advice of Jesus, son of Mary, on the appropriate penance to give when the king will not confess. "But please," he begs (as he holds the body of Christ in the Host), "do not let the devil take him!" (vv. 3014–15).

Giles' prayer during the sacrament is witnessed by Charlemagne (suitably attired as king), who arrives after the Mass has begun (vv. 2961–68). The following scene, when an angel descends with a heavenly letter of absolution, is introduced with a line which mirrors exactly the beginning of the prayer scene (*El segrei u li abbes fu,* v. 2976), drawing to our attention that this scene is a direct response to

---

[10] Cf. John 6:53–56.

[11] Guitmund of Aversa, a student of Lanfranc, writing about 1075, states the doctrine as follows (which Vaillancourt characterizes as standard eucharistic theology): "We are also able to say that he is as much in one little portion of the Host as he is in the whole Host. [. . .] Thus the whole Host is the body of Christ in such a way that each and every separate particle is the whole body of Christ. Three separate particles are not three bodies, but only one body. [. . .] Therefore, they must not now be called many particles, but rather, one Host, intact and undivided, even though it seems to be divided by priestly ministry, because of the great mystery, as I have said, which must be celebrated in this way. In a like manner, if the Host seems to be broken by the teeth or in some other way, we understand it to be unbroken, because we believe that the whole body is contained in each single part" (*Lanfranc* [. . .] *and Guitmund of Aversa,* trans. Vaillancourt, 15).

Giles: *Al secrei u li abbes fu / est un angele a lui descendu, / en sa main porte un bref petit* ("While the abbot was performing the *secreta*, an angel came down to him, bearing in his hand a small letter," vv. 3019–21).

The scene of the double Eucharist miracle (both the sacramental mystery and the heavenly letter) is central to the *Vie*, allying Guillaume's subtle and cogent dramatization of doctrine with the other central mystery of the narrative, the unconfessed sin of Charlemagne. This, though absolved, remains unspoken in the text. The late eleventh-century eucharistic crisis was connected with the larger reform movement in the church (which also included the establishment of regular canons under the Augustinian rule, mentioned earlier, above 10). One of the reformers' major aims was to rid the clergy of the sins of simony and concubinage, so that they would be worthy to perform the sacrament of the Eucharist.[12] Giles' appointment as abbot is specifically noted as being without simony (v. 2247), and Guillaume's use of eucharistic theology demonstrates an Augustinian understanding of the importance of clerical purity in the administration of the sacraments to the laity.

iii. Spirited Conversation (vv. 3112–46)

After celebrating Mass, and receiving the letter containing the description of Charlemagne's unspoken sin, Giles speaks to the king at length, urging him to confess. In response to a rhetorical question posed by Giles, Charlemagne interjects a response, leading to the following lively dialogue.

3112	Feble sen as e fol pensé,	fol. 139 rb
	ke tun mesfeit ne vols gehir.	
	Quides tu vers Deu ren covrir?	
	Ço ne poz tu faire vers mei.	
3116	–Vers vus? Si puis. –Nenal, par fei!	
	–Ne puis? Pur quei? –Car jol sai bien.	
	–Ço ne sout unkes crestïen.	
	–Jo sui crestïens e sil sai.	
3120	–Ne l'os creire. –Jol musterai.	
	–Vus, comment le poez saveir?	
	–Ço guarde tu? –Nel puis veer.	
	–Pur quant jol sai. –E vus coment?	

---

[12] Simony was the purchase of ecclesiastical office. See Morris, *The Papal Monarchy*, 99–101: "The church and clergy must be freed from practices which made them ritually impure. Simony and clerical marriage were often discussed not as obstacles to pastoral service, but in terms of physical corruption. [. . .] It was a terrible impurity for the priest to go from a woman's bed to handle the body of the Lord on the altar." This also led to the emphasis on the doctrine of the physical presence of Christ in the bread and wine.

3124	–Il m'est tut dit. –N'en quid neënt.	
	–Nel quides tu? –Jo nun, par fei.	
	–Tant est maiur folie! –De quei?	
	–Pur ço ke te covent gehir.	
3128	–Ço ne serra tresk'al murir.	
	–Dunc ert trop tart. –Jo ne puis meis.	
	–Si poz. –Coment? –Fai tei confés.	
	–Certes nu frai a mun vivant.	
3132	–Mult par es ore nun savant,	fol. 139 va
	ke le quidez vers Deu celer,	
	a mei nel poz tu resconcer.	
	–Par les seinz Deu, merveilles oi!	
3136	–Ore ne te chaut, suffre un poi,	
	si purras ben sempres oïr.	
	–Je ne vus os pas dementir,	
	mes si uns altres le diseit,	
3140	jo dirraie k'il mentireit.	
	–E coment si jol vu disaie?	
	–Dunc ne di jo ke nel crereie.	
	–Crerras le tu si jol vus di?	
3144	–Oïl, ço sachez ben de fi."	
	Atant a treit avant le bref,	
	si l'ad leü de chef en chef.	

Commentary

Guillaume creates several lively passages in direct speech, either in extended monologues, such as the eucharistic prayer discussed above, or dramatic dialogues, in which the characters interact directly, without the narrative voice's intervention. The following is an example of this latter style (another notable example is the dialogue between Giles and the Guest Master, vv. 2427–62).

In this scene the dialogue is launched when Charlemagne interrupts to respond to a rhetorical question used by Giles in his *bref sermon endreit de sa confessïun* ("short talk to him about confession," v. 3092). Charlemagne knows from Giles' changed demeanour after the Mass that the abbot has heard good news, so the king leads him by the hand to a bench where they can talk. Giles begins to counsel Charlemagne, developing the theme that death always comes unexpectedly, and that Charlemagne risks damnation if he does not confess his sin. The first lines of this extract summarize Giles' argument: your unwillingness to confess is "foolishness and unreasonable," "do you think you can hide anything from God?" (vv. 3112–14). Then Giles asserts dismissively: "You can't even hide it from me," *Ço ne poz tu faire vers mei* (v. 3115), and the key terms *ço* ("this"), *poz* (and other reflexes of the verb *poeir* "be able"), and *mei* (and the other personal pronouns "I, me, you"), along with reflexes of the verbs *saveir* ("know"), *creire* ("believe"), *mustrer* ("show"), *(re)garder* ("look"), *veer* ("see"), are bandied back and forth in the dramatic exchange over the next twenty-nine lines, in the complete absence of the narrative voice. The exchange is punctuated by negative particles, and the interrogative and exclamative pronouns *ço* ("this"), *coment* ("how, what"), *quei* ("what, why").

The change of speaker is often at the half-line (nine times), and once there are three changes of speaker within one line (v. 3130). Eleven times the change in speaker occurs with each new line, and only three times is a single reply two or three lines long. In this rapid rhythm, questions, denials, and assertions follow on each other naturally, often with the verb being repeated, either in denial or assertion, in response to a question.

The first interjection by Charlemagne, for example, questions the assertion *vers mei* ("from me," v. 3115) by Giles, with *Vers vus?* ("From you," v. 3116), then asserts: *Si puis* ("Yes, I can," v. 3116), which is countered by the denial *Nenal, par fei!* ("By my faith, no, you can't!" v. 3116). The verbal gymnastics often rely on sarcasm: in response to Giles' assertion that he knows Charlemagne's sin ("I know it well," *jol sai bien,* v. 3117), Charlemagne declares that no Christian knows it, drawing the response: "I'm Christian and I know it!" (v. 3119). The petulance shown by Charlemagne is startlingly small-minded in contrast to the elegant expression of courtly manners displayed by both men in earlier scenes and at the beginning of this conversation. Perhaps Giles allows the tone to escalate, to show Charlemagne that his refusal to confess is both stubborn and childish. This heated exchange can only be seen as both comic and awe-inspiring by the audience, unaccustomed to overhearing such an intimate confession of obstinacy from a great king. Although Charlemagne does not speak his hidden sin, this dramatic dialogue is a confession of a different order, since it exposes his obdurate refusal to do so as the childish weakness that it is.

The scene is so thoroughly dramatized that no stage directions are needed for the audience to know what Giles is holding when he asks Charlemagne "'Ço guarde tu?'" ("Do you see this?" v. 3122), referring to the letter sent by an angel. Charlemagne, however, responds that he "cannot see it" (*Nel puis veer,* v. 3122), and his lack of seeing and understanding is amplified in the crescendo of their verbal joust. Giles eventually begins to dampen down the conflict, offering a conciliatory response: *Ore ne te chaut, suffre un poi, / si purras ben sempres oïr* ("Don't let this upset you . . . ," vv. 3136–37), and they gradually return to more courtly behaviour. The scene ends with the quick statement: "With that Giles brought out the letter and read it to the king from top to bottom" (vv. 3145–46). We can imagine the two friends returning to a state of being seated courteously and peaceably on the bench as Giles reads the details of Charlemagne's sin, which Guillaume still keeps hidden from the audience.

2. Simund de Freine, *La Vie de saint Georges* (vv. 1527–1600)

Dacien Explores His Own Anger

Incredulous at yet another miracle effected by George, Dacien reflects on the failure of his previous attempts to break George's faith, and on the impossible position in which he finds himself. Whipping himself into a renewed fury of rage and frustration, he vows that this time he will destroy his opponent: "tomorrow he will die without fail!"

	Quant cil bel miracle vint,	fol.116 vb
1528	Dacïen nul plet n'en tint.	
	Plus n'en tint plet que de songe;	
	Diseit que ceo fu mensonge.	
	Tant fu fel e de mal eire	
1532	Que ses oilz ne voleit creire;	
	Treis tant out le quer plus dur	
	Que pere qui seit mis en mur.	
	Deu ne vout pur ren amer,	
1536	Tant out fel quer e amer;	
	Vers lui portat tut tens ire	
	Plus que lange ne poet dire.	
	En tel ire fu ja mis	
1540	Que tut vermeil fu li vis;	
	D'ire fu itant grevez,	
	Pres lui fu le quer crevez.	
	Iré fu a desmesure,	
1544	D'ire rumpi sa ceinture.	
	Tant iré fu e cunfus,	
	De son trone chaï jus.	
	"Las," fait il, "que purrei dire;	
1548	George me tout mon empire.	
	Tut atreit a lui ma gent,	
	Chescun ja baptesme prent.	
	Sovent le faz tormenter;	
1552	Mes tut fust tormenté er,	
	Ja pur ceo ne larrat hui	
	Enginner ma gent a lui;	
	Par torment nel pus grever.	fol. 117 ra
1556	Mes, gref torment li feisse er,	
	Ja pur ceo ne lairait hui	
	Ma gent aresner a lui;	

	Il set tant d'enchantement,
1560	E tant chace e tant ment
	Que le fol a fol se lie,
	E creit chescun sa folie.
	Si sa folur longes dure
1564	Nostre lei est tenue dure.
	Si jo sun durer endur
	Vers mon deu le quer ai dur.
	Nel voil tenir en prison,
1568	Car vei que par mesprison
	D'iloc venir ad apris
	Tante feiz cum l'om l'ad pris.
	Faire li voil tant martire;
1572	A me honir ad tant ire
	Voil que tant seit tormenté
	Dunt avrat le quer iré.
	A hontage de mei vit,
1576	Qui mon deu ad en despit.
	Mult est plein de grant orgoil,
	Mes abatre tost le voil.
	La manere purvi er
1580	Coment jol frai devïer.
	Trop ad plein le quer de fel
	E trop set sa lange mel;
	Trop set de engin e art,
1584	Le terz enginner e le quart.
	Trop est fel e de put lin
	Qui ne creit en Apolin.
	A mon deu fait honte e tort,
1588	Dunt il avrat tost la mort
	Par espee e par lance,
	Que de lui n'ert mes parlance.
	Doner lui frai de l'espee
1592	E teus coups e tel colee
	Que son deu pur tut son cors
	Tard lui vendrat a socors.
	Trop ai longement sosfert,
1596	A Apolin trop i pert
	Que de lui n'ai pris vengance
	Qui ad troblé ma creance.
	Mes quant il ne vout la peis
1600	Demain murra sanz releis."

Commentary

In this passage the narrator introduces (vv. 1527–46) Dacien's final introspective monologue (vv. 1547–1600). With this monologue, Simund poetically voices Dacien's ultimate intellectual defeat, making it much more meaningful than the purely physical destruction of the emperor and his agents by divine vengeance at the end of the Latin legend.

The probable Latin source text for this passage is found, as Matzke notes, in the Y family of manuscripts, which alone places the scene of Joel's resuscitation after that of Empress Alexandria's death, and which also includes the detail of Dacien's belt and the subsequent dramatic fall from his throne.[13] The Latin text is much less detailed than Simund's reworking:

> Audiens autem hec Dacianus imperator tremefactus est ita ut zona, qua cingebatur, rumperetur pro nimio timore. Genua autem ei tremebant, ita ut caderet de trono suo et voce magna clamavit: "Ve, michi misero, quoniam periit regnum meum. Omnem autem populum meum convertit Georgius et tradidit domino suo. Quod si adhuc vixerit, me ipsum igne cremabit. Quia hoc die septem anni sunt, quod eum tormentis affligo. Illius autem virtus aderescit. Unde ergo jubeo mitti frenum in ore suo et duci foras civitatem, ubi Alexandria regina interfecta est et in ipso eodem loco jubemus decollari."[14]

> (Upon hearing this the emperor Dacianus trembled such that the belt that girded his body was broken by his exceedingly great fear. His knees were shaking so much that he fell off his throne and cried out in a loud voice: "Woe is me! my kingdom has vanished. George has converted all my people and handed them over to his Lord. If he lives that long, he will burn me myself with fire. Today marks seven years that I have submitted him to torture, yet his strength never falters. Therefore I now decree that a bridle be placed in his mouth and that he be led outside the city to where queen Alexandria was put to death, and we order that he there be beheaded.")

In developing this scene Simund shows, as he has throughout the life, that language itself is on George's side. In contrast to George, Dacien's perverse volition is misaligned in its understanding of God's universe, and his emotions and reason can be expressed only in incomplete and self-thwarting ways.

As the passage opens, Dacien has just witnessed the resuscitated Joel and his companions ascending to heaven, and is struck dumb by this miracle. Simund expresses this by juxtaposing the semantically irreconcilable terms *nul*

---

[13] Matzke, *Oeuvres de Simund de Freine*, lxxxvi–lxxxvii. Paris BnF MS latin 5256 is a typical manuscript in this family. For a transcription, see Guilcher, *Deux Versions*, 125–31.

[14] Guilcher, *Deux Versions*, 131.

plet n'en tint ("he remained silent," v. 1528) and *diseit* ("said," v. 1530). The phrase *tenir plet* is in fact polysemic and can also mean "to plead a case, in law." It therefore carries the added idea of Dacien's intellectual defeat—his metaphorical loss of a court case. Then, repeated, but inverted in the next line (*Plus n'en tint plet que de songe*, v. 1529), the phrase offers yet a third meaning: "he paid no more attention to it than to a dream." The rhyme *songe* "dream" : *mensonge* "lie" (vv. 1529–30), although extremely frequent in medieval French poetry, nonetheless emphasizes that it is his speech which is a lie, since it conflicts with what his eyes have seen; two verses later the narrator says that "he would not believe his own eyes" (v. 1532).

Simund also introduces courtly love terms, as he had done earlier in the third kiss scene (vv. 1048–51, noted above, 36–38). Puns based on expressions of love are frequent in courtly literature (in *Cligès*, for example, Chrétien de Troyes puns on the "pains of love"—*mal d'amer*—and "seasickness"—*mal de mer*), and the use of courtly language in hagiography is also well known.[15] In vv. 1533–41 there are many images of the heart, and puns on love and its opposites, and Simund uses this vocabulary to reveal the tyrant as lacking a proper relationship to God. Dacien's heart is evoked repeatedly: it is "three times harder than stone" (vv. 1533–34), "wicked and bitter" (v. 1536), and "almost burst" (vv. 1541–42). Dacien's bitterness and unwillingness to love God are stressed by the rhyme which links *amer* "to love" and *amer* "bitter" (vv. 1535–36), as in the pun also used by Chrétien (*Cligés*, vv. 541–46). By adapting these well-known courtly terms to the negative portrayal of Dacien, Simund gives added emotional depth to the tyrant's character, making him much less of a stock figure.

Wordplay linking *dire* ("to say") and *d'ire* ("of anger") signals Dacien's inarticulacy in this passage. Dacien's inability to vent his fury is made explicit in *Plus que lange ne poet dire* "greater than any tongue can say" (v. 1538): this tag phrase (very common in medieval French hagiography)[16] is made effective by the pun linking its final rhyme word *dire* ("say," v. 1538), with the repeated opening words *D'ire* ("with anger" three verses later, vv. 1541, 1544), along with both *ire* "fury" (v. 1539), and *iré* "infuriated" (vv. 1543, 1545).

---

[15] In Clemence's *Life of S. Catherine*, for example, the tyrant's regret (vv. 2165–2230) is expressed in courtly love terms reminiscent of *Tristan*: see Wogan-Browne and Burgess, *Virgin Lives*, 76, note 75, for a bibliography on this topic; see also Wogan-Browne, *Saints' Lives*, 223–45. The language of *fin' amur* is used by the nuns of Barking to express *agape*, rather than *eros*: see D. Russell, "'Sun num n'i vult dire': Identity Matters at Barking Abbey," forthcoming in *Authorship and Authority: Barking Abbey and its Texts*, ed. D. Bussell and J. Brown.

[16] The phrase is a paraphrastic allusion to 1 Corinthians 2:9; it is used, for example, in the *Life of S. Faith*, vv. 413–414, in Clemence's *Life of St. Catherine*, vv. 1790–93, and in the *Vie s. Osith*, vv. 1680–82 (see the Campsey Project, http://margot.uwaterloo.ca).

Dacien's frustration and anger are seen in his (*lit.*) "completely scarlet face" (in the alliterative *tut vermeil fu li vis*, v. 1540), and his heart almost bursting (v. 1542) from rage. The scene then expands to, and ends with, the comic depiction of Dacien breaking his belt with fury, and falling off his throne: *Iré fu a desmesure, / D'ire rumpi sa ceinture. / Tant iré fu e cunfus / De son trone chaï jus:* (*lit.*) "He was infuriated beyond reason, and in his fury burst his belt; he was so enraged and beside himself that he fell down from his throne in confusion" (vv. 1543–46). Simund has replaced the "fear and trembling" found in the Latin source with his development of "anger and frustration" linked to the passage's theme of language strangulated and frustrated.

This verbally complex and visually comic image is immediately followed by Dacien's long introspective monologue, beginning yet again with the theme of speech: "*Las," fait il, "que purrei* **dire**; */ George me tout mon empire*": 'Alas,' he cried, 'what can I possibly **say**? George has taken all my empire from me.'" The words are again freighted with meaning: George has taken away both Dacien's empire (removing his power as emperor over his kingdom, and the allegiance of his subjects, including his queen), and his *empire* in the sense of Dacien's ability to make things worse (*empirer*), a theme which was evoked in George's first monologue by the same pun (vv. 145–48, noted above, 36).

Dacien's monologue repeatedly uses words containing the same syllable, -*ment*, as in *ma gent* "my people," *torment* "torture," *enchantement* "sorcery, magic spells," *ment* "he lies"; spread over vv. 1549–60, these constitute a series of interior rhymes. Dacien knows he has lost his power over his people, his torture of other people is ineffective, and so he accuses George of sorcery and lies. A virtuoso play on the words *dur* "hard" and *durer* "last, endure," extended over four verses, emphasizes George's endurance and Dacien's lack of forebearance:

Si sa folur longes **dure**
Nostre lei est tenue **dure**.
Si jo sun **durer endur**
Vers mon deu le quer ai **dur**. (vv. 1563–66)

"If his madness persists, our religion is considered unworthy; if I put up with his resistance my heart is seen as hardened against my god."

The play on like sounds is almost a chiasmus in *sun durer endur*.

Dacien's self-awareness, including his sense of impending loss, is shown in his attempt to inflict on George the same mental torture and anger that he himself feels: *Voil que tant seit tormenté, / Dunt avrat le quer iré*, "I want to torture him until his heart is filled with anger" (vv. 1571–72). He wants George to suffer the same loss of reputation that he himself has suffered from George: *Que de lui n'ert mes parlance*, "so there will be no more talk of him," (v. 1590). It will be noted that the greatest harm that Dacien can imagine to inflict on George is that the saint cease to be even the *object* of speech.

In this final monologue, Simund gives Dacien's character much more depth and subtlety than is found in his Latin source, as we can see in his sustained development of key words and images to interiorize Dacien's emotions, and his awareness of futility in his attempts to destroy George.

Simon of Walsingham, *La Vie sainte Foy*

i. First Interrogation of St Faith by Dacien (vv. 265–300)

When Faith is brought before the proconsul to be interrogated her beauty astounds Dacien. Faith responds with sophisticated wordplay on the subject of her name and her faith.

	Quant la Deu amye e sa drue	fol. 149 va
	Devant le juge esteit venue,	
	Li fel se tout, si l'esguarda,	
268	De sa beuté se merveillia;	
	Puis si ad dit e demandé:	
	"Di mei tun nun, ne festes celé."	
	La bele ke veit esbaie,	
272	Sun nun hu[nc] ne celad mie,	
	Cele respundi hardyement,	
	Si li dit curteysement:	
	"Ne vus voil mun nun celer,	
276	Fey ay a nun, bien le os numer;	
	Ne aveit unkes destaunce	
	Entre mun nun e ma creaunce;	
	Feyz sunt mes fes, Fey est mun nun,	
280	Mun nun, mes fes, si sunt tuz un."	
	Dunc li diseit Dacien,	
	Ly felun puant paen:	
	"Kant mei as conté tun nun,	
284	Saver voil ta religiun,	
	E ta fei e ta creance	
	Voil saver sanz demustrance."	
	Seinte Fey la Deu amie,	
288	Ke del Seint Espirit ert replenie,	
	Respundi a l'adverser	
	E li dist: "Ne quer celer	
	Ne ma fei ne ma creance,	

292	Crestien sui de enfaunce;
	Puis ke fui de funz levee,
	E en le nun Deu baptizee,
	A Jhesu del tut me rendi
296	Ke pur nus tuz la mort suffri,
	A Jhesu Crist le fiz Marie
	Ke cele terre ad en baillie; fol. 149 vb
	A li me doinz, a li me rend
300	A li auke devotement."

Commentary

The opening description of Faith (*la Deu amye e sa drue*, "the beloved dear one of God" v. 265) uses the vocabulary of courtly lovers (*amye, drue*), and this makes believable the description of her judge as struck dumb when he gazes on her beauty (vv. 267–68). The theme of the male gaze is introduced by *esguarda*, "his eyes studied her" (v. 267), and by *La bele ke veit esbaie*, "the beautiful maiden whom he perceived as terror-stricken" (v. 271). The theme of the male gaze will be repeated in the twice-told torture scene, and repeated with variation in the account of Faith's translation, when the pursuers from Agen fail to recognize Arinisdus sitting beneath a tree, although they knew him well.

Dacien's first words to Faith demand that she tell him her name, and not hide it (vv. 269–70)—beginning the litany in which Faith repeatedly tells him her name (with puns on Faith and faith, *Fey ay a nun, bien le os numer; / Ne aveit unkes destaunce / Entre mun nun e ma creaunce; / Feyz sunt mes fes, Fey est mun nun, / Mun nun, mes fes, si sunt tuz un*: "Faith is my name, and willingly I dare to pronounce it. There has never been any distinction between my name and my faith. Acts of faith are my deeds, Faith is my name, my name and my deeds are one and the same," vv. 276–80).

Faith and the narrator assert repeatedly that she does not wish to hide her name (vv. 272, 275, 290). But although he now knows her name, Dacien fails to fully understand her response and demands to know her faith, and her religion (vv. 283–86).

Dacien, described as her *juge* "judge" (v. 266), is also "an evil man" (*fel*, v. 267), a "vile evil pagan" (*felun puant paen*, v. 282), and her "enemy" (*adverser*, v. 289, a term also used to denote Satan). Although Dacien is attracted physically to Faith, she remains "the beloved of God" (*la Deu amye*, v. 287), to whom she gives herself body and soul (*A Jhesu del tut me rendi*, "I have given myself completely to Jesus," v. 295). She ends her speech with a parallel syntactic triplet, emphasizing Faith's gift of her virginity to God rather than to Dacien: *A li me doinz, a li me rend, / A li auke devotement*, "I give myself to him, I surrender to him, I go to him with devotion" (vv. 299–300).

ii. Faith on Her Bed of Torture (vv. 379–412, 523–96)

The details of Faith's torture on the bed of brass emphasize her physical vulnerability and the presence of the male gaze: Caprais' vision of her suffering adds further and different signification to the scene.

	Quant ceo oy cel adverser	fol. 150 rb
380	En li nent out ke cur[u]cer.	
	A ses serjanz ad comandé	
	Ke un lit de areim fut tost porté,	
	Un greil ke il out fet aturner	
384	Pur les amis Deu tormenter;	
	Seinte Fei unt despolié	
	E sur cel etuel cuchié.	
	La pucele tute nue	
388	Fu sur cel lit estendue;	
	Ses tendre membres estenderent,	
	Ceus ke les membres Deu [n']aurerent;	
	Par desuz mistrent le feu	
392	Issi cum comandé lur fu;	
	A croiz de fer tisuns ardanz	
	I mistrent li crueus serjanz;	
	Gresse en la flamme geterent	
396	Iceus feluns ke Deu ne amerent;	
	Gresse geterent en cretuns	
	Enz en la flamme ceus feluns.	fol. 150 va
	Par de li, iceus jeuenes e tendris,	
400	Ke tant furent las ses membris,	
	De la flamme ert fumee,	
	De icele pucele bonuree;	
	Mes ele suffri bonement	
404	Icele peine, icel torment;	
	E en le nun Jhesu nostre seigniur	
	Ver ki out mut grant amur	
	E il par sa seinte merci	
408	Ne le mist pas en ubli;	
	Suffrance e vertu li dona	
	Dunt nule rien s'emaia;	
	Par les peines ke ele suffri	
412	Le dieble e les seens venqui.	

[The crowd of spectators exclaim and lament at the unusual cruelty of the martyrdom, and many convert. Meanwhile, Caprais and a few other Christians, following the precedent of Christ's flight into Egypt when pursued by Herod, have gone to the hills above Agen. From a distance Caprais witnesses Faith's martyrdom and in prayer asks God to show him how the young girl endured her torture (vv. 413–522).]

      Capraisse li seint martir,
      Ke memes les peines suffrir
      Deveit pur le fiz Marie,
526   Esguarda vers le Deu amie
      Ke en greil esteit liee
      De orible flamme environe[e],
      Si vit descendre del ciel
530   Un blanc columbe, unke ne vit tel,
      Unckes si blanc ne si tres bel
      Ne vit mes des oiz de columbel;
      Kar nul flur de estee,
534   Ne neif sur la gelee
      Ne vit mes de tele blanchur
      Nul si dilitable colur.
      Une corone de or porta,
538   Dunc tant riche ne esguarda;
      De riches peres preciuses
      De gemmes tres deliciuses
      Ert la corune aurné
542   Si dona greigniur clarté
      Ke ne fet li soleil en esté
      Al jur quant est plus haut levé,
      A l'ure quant il meuz resplent,
546   [E] est plus cler del firmament.
      Icele corone tres bele
      Mist au chief de la pucele
      De cele martir ke tant suffri
550   Pur Deu ke bien li meri;
      Vestue le veit a cel[e] ure
      De une tres blanche vesture
      De noe, vesture blanche e clere
554   Lusant de grant manere;
      Dunt il vit bien e entendi
      Ke Jhesu Crist par sa merci
      Li aveit ja doné victoire
558   En sa pardurable gloire,
      Ke se[s] peines furent passés
      E les granz joies comencés.

Appendix

	Le blanche columbe ke descendi	
562	De cel cum vus avez oy,	
	Entur la seinte martir volat	fol. 151vb
	E de son duz voil li confortat;	
	De ses eles la blandi	
566	E de la flamme le fendi;	
	E par la seinte grace Jhesu	
	Esteint la force e la vertu	
	Del flamme e del greil	
570	E del fu e del peril	
	Cum ceo fet de une rosee;	
	Dunt seinte Fey la bonuree	
	Ne senti peine ne dolur;	
574	Loé seit nostre Seigniur	
	Qant Capraisse li bonurez	
	Ki de cel vit les secrez	
	Esguarda vers la pucele	
578	Si la vit en terre bele,	
	Ki de rien esteit blecé	
	De turment k'ele out enduré;	
	Ausi luseit en cel turment	
582	Cum fet esteile en firmament;	
	De la corone ke Jhesu Crist	
	Par son angele li tramist	
	Esteit tres bele e certes lee,	
586	E de cel estoile afublee	
	Ke Dampnedeu li out tramis	
	Par son angele de parais	
	Quant seint Capraisse out veu	
590	La gloire et la vertu	
	Ke Jhesu Crist aveit donee	
	A seinte Fei la bonuree,	
	Ne voleit plus lung tapir,	
594	As peines voleit partir	
	Ke seinte Fey la Deu amie	
	Soffri pur le fiz Marie.	

Rejected readings: 538 esguarga 539 peris

Commentary

The *Vie sainte Fey* intensifies the erotic inflection (present to some extent in the Latin source) of the torture scene (vv. 381–412): the nubile young girl Faith is stripped naked (vv. 385, 387), with her tender limbs (vv. 389, 399–400) stretched out and tied to the four corners of a brass bed (vv. 386–88), leaving her exposed fully to the flames beneath the bed (and to the gaze of spectators).[17] In this scene, she is potentially the object of multiple desires: of the narrating voice itself, of Dacien, whose authority is being questioned, and of Caprais, Faith's Christian companion. Around the central witnesses are further figures also invested in Faith's torture: her converts Felicianus and Primus; the clerical male writer of the Latin *passio;* Simon, the vernacular author; the Life's patron, Abbot Samson; and the monks at Bury St Edmunds for whom Simon writes.[18] Yet, for all the voyeuristic potential of this scene, it would be difficult to argue that its point is simply the scopic and erotic possession of a young girl as a passive object. Dacien does not have the brass bed made specially for Faith, but already has it in his armoury of instruments for torturing the faithful at large (vv. 383–84). When Faith is placed on the bed, her "tender limbs" (*tendre membres*, v. 389) are immediately related to the church as the body of Christ (*les membres Deu*, v. 340). Stoking the flames with grease (vv. 395, 397), the torturers are like so many demons labouring in the fires of hell as Faith overcomes the devil (v. 412). The audience of spectators underscore the exceptional cruelty of the torture in their lament (vv. 421–42, not given here), and themselves witness to the power of Faith's role in the scene by converting (vv. 442–53, not given here).

Simon follows the Latin source in presenting the torture scene a second time, replayed in even more detail through the eyes of Caprais (vv. 523–96 above). But as Jocelyn Wogan-Browne notes, in this scene Caprais is "as much visionary witness as voyeur."[19] Simon thus moves beyond the first level of erotically inflected fantasy to invest the saint with metaphorical gem-like permanence and brilliance. Caprais perceives the flesh of Faith crowned in gold and jewels, and clothed in radiant white garments, so that her virginal body is transformed into a brightly shining jewel.[20] As Caprais sees Faith's mortal body transmuted amid the flames into her eternal identity, metaphors of snow, flowers, brilliant sunshine, dew, and stars (533, 534, 543–44, 571, 582) give the scene extraordi-

---

[17] See Emma Campbell, "Sacrificial Spectacle and Interpassive Vision in the Anglo-Norman Life of Saint Faith," in *Troubled Vision: Gender, Sexuality, and Sight in Medieval Text and Image*, ed. eadem and Robert Mills (New York: Palgrave, 2004), 97–115.

[18] On the sexualization of violence in hagiography, see Gaunt, *Gender and Genre*, chap. 4, "Saints, Sex and Community: Hagiography," 180–233; Kay, "The Sublime Body," 3–20.

[19] Wogan-Browne, *Saints' Lives*, 71–72.

[20] See Wogan-Browne, *Saints' Lives*, 71–72 for an analysis of the verbs of perception used in this scene.

nary sensory intensity; but it is the intensity of directly perceiving the divine. The narrative places Caprais' ability to see God's dove/angel crowning and enrobing Faith under the category of God's "secrets" (*secrez*, v. 576). This privileged vision of Faith's victory in paradise is also a prefiguration of the jewelled reliquary at Conques, which would have been known by reputation to Simon and his audience, and which is alluded to in the Prologue (vv. 25–26), as also in the poem's recurrent image of Faith as a brightly shining gem, or refined gold (vv. 136, 147, 211–20, 819–22). The double scene of Faith's martyrdom suggests that eroticism is here a mode of entry into a compelling spectacle, and that its object is the erotics of the treasure, in heaven and on earth, that Faith signifies for her devotional communities.

4. Guillaume le Clerc de Normandie, *Le Romanz de Marie Magdalene*

Storm at Sea and Premature Birth (vv. 231–308)

With the instruction and blessing of Mary Magdalene, the prince of Marseille and his wife have embarked on a ship to make their pilgrimage to Jerusalem. The sea voyage is proceeding smoothly and swiftly when a sudden storm arises. Because of the sea's violent turbulence the prince's wife goes into labour prematurely. The mother dies in childbirth, and the father adds his tears to the crying of the motherless newborn.

	A mult grant joie s'en aloent	fol. 68 vb
232	E a plaine veile sigloent,	
	Quant aventure lor mult gerre,	
	Ke a la mer e a la tere	
	Se change e remue sovent.	
236	A poi d'ore venta un vent	
	Ki fist la nef croistre e branler.	
	La mer comenza a emfler,	
	E les gros venz a esforcier	
240	Com s'il volsist tut depescier:	
	Cordes, e veil, e tref, e mast.	
	N'i out nul que ne reclamast	
	Tel aie com il quidout	
244	Ki la mester aver li pout.	
	La Magdaleine i fu nomee	
	De cels ki l'aveient amee,	
	E reclamee ducement.	
248	Mes tut adés crut le torment,	

   Ke nuls ne se sout conseiller.
   La prist la dame a travailler
   Del son ventre en cele tempeste,
252 Si qu'ele ne pout lever la teste.
    Reine de misericorde!
   Ki est cil ki cest pas recorde
   Ki del quer ne suspire e plure?
256 Encore n'iert pas la dame a l'ore
   A son droit terme parvenue,
   Mes aventure est avenue
   A meinte femme meinte foiz,
260 Ke ele esteit en tel destroiz
   Ke avoit bien devant son jor,
   Par maladie ou par pour,   fol. 69 ra
   Par talent ou par bleceure,
264 Ou ja par aucun' aventure,
   Enfant ke longement vivreit
   Si com Deus purveu aveit
   En qui tutes veies sont
268 De cels qui venent e qui vont
   Parmi cest siecle trespassable.
   Si com la mer est changable,
   Change li mondes e trespasse.
272 Mes Deus! ke fra ore la lasse,
   Que est posee en si fort cas?
   Kar li venz ne s'abesse pas
   En ses forz, e la mer s'atruble,
276 E la tormente crest a duble:
   La mer croist, e la femme crie.
   Duze Magdaleine Marie,
   Ke f[e]ra vostre pelerine,
280 Ki en bele chambre marbrine
   Peust estre, e aie avoir
   De femmes ki deveient savoir
   De tel afaire e de tel chose?
284 Se la dame une ore repose
   Ke ele ne sent la grant angoisse,
   Ele ot le vent que la mer froisse,
   E la wage que les nefs soz lieve,
288 Si que por poi ne fent ou crieve.
   Si cent femmes od lui eust,
   Ja une sole ne peust
   La main lever por li aider!

292	Jeo ne puis ci entor plaider	
	Ke jeo n'ai le quer esmeu,	
	Kar tel mal ad la dame eu	fol. 69 rb
	Qu'ele morut e espira.	
296	E li emfes hors se tira	
	De sa mere, ke ainz fu morte	
	Ke il fust bien hors de la porte.	
	Od sa buche[tte] vet querant	
300	Alcun solaz de la traiant,	
	Mes il ne trove ke li rende	
	Sa dreiture ne sa merende.	
	Lors comenza son lai de plor.	
304	Se li pere en ad dolor,	
	Ceo ne fet mie a demander!	
	Kar il ne lui pot amender	
	Nule chose de son afaire,	
	Od lui estuet crier e braire.	

Rejected readings: 243 quidouot   267 vies   268 vivent e qui ont   276 la mer t.   286 out   300 creant   304 pierres

Commentary

The central storm in the *Romanz* is a contrast to the Magdalen's earlier uneventful sea passage (recounted in two lines: *La mer de Grece trespasserent / E ariverent a Marseille*, "(*lit.*) they crossed the Grecian sea and arrived at Marseille," vv. 28–29). For the Prince of Marseille and his wife, the perils en route are many, and are expanded from the Latin source. Guillaume's use of nautical terms, although much less virtuosic than the passage in the *Vie de s. Gilles*, is similarly technical in its description of the ship and the work of the sailors: "the sailors embarked and raised sail" (*Eskiperent li marinier / E firent les veiles drescier*, vv. 223–24); they reach "open sea" (*palacre*, v. 225); they travel at full sail (*a pleine veil sigloent*, v. 232). A distinction is made between the ship (*nef*, vv. 366, 415, 418, 474, etc.) and the landing tender (*batel*, v. 375, 662, 670); the sailors (*li marinier*, v. 223) include the master helmsman (*maistre esturmant*, v. 361, 370), and the captain (*le maistre marinier*, v. 559); the terminology is varied to describe when the sail is both raised (*firent les veiles drescier*, v. 224; *haucierent le tref*, v. 416), and lowered (*baissier fait maintenant le tref*, v. 373; *a fait le sigle abaissier*, v. 563). The sea after the storm is calm and serene (*la mer fu serie e queie*, v. 473).

The rhymes in this passage, which are occasionally rich or leonine, are typical of Guillaume's style (e.g. *mast : reclamast*, vv. 241–42, *tempeste : teste*, vv. 251–52; *misericorde : recorde*, vv. 253–54; *parvenue : avenue*, vv. 257–58; *truble : duble*,

vv. 275–76; *pelerine : marbrine*, vv. 279–80; *avoir : savoir*, vv. 281–82; *eust : peust*, vv. 289–90; *rende : marende*, vv. 301–2).

The description of the storm's effect on the sea and the ship is specific and dramatic: the sudden onset of the wind is expressed by the alliteration in *A poi d'ore venta un vent*, v. 236; the effect on the ship is seen in two verbs, *croistre* (smash, shatter, break open), *branler* (shake, shudder), v. 237. Sea and wind are graphically depicted: the gale winds (*gros venz*, v. 239) grow in strength (*esforcier*, v. 239), causing great swells in the sea (*La mer comenza a emfler*, v. 238), as if the sea wishes to tear the ship apart, lines and sail, beams and mast (*Com s'il volsist tut depescier : / Cordes e veile, tref e mast*, vv. 241–42). Later Guillaume remarks that the wind has not abated (*ne s'abesse pas / En ses forz*, vv. 274–75), the sea is agitated with crashing waves (*s'atruble*, v. 275; *la mere croist*, v. 277); pounded by the wind *(le vent que la mer froisse*, v. 286), it tosses the ships about *(la wage que les nefs soz lieve*, v. 287).

The narrator also heightens the emotional force of the scene by adding repeated expressions of his own pity at what he is recounting: *Reine de misericorde! / Ki est cil ki cest pas recorde / Ki del quer ne suspire e plure?*: "Queen of Mercy! Who could recount this story and not be moved to tears and heartfelt sorrow?" (vv. 253–55). *Mes Deus! ke fra ore la lasse, / Que est posee en si fort cas?*: "Lord! What can this poor exhausted woman do now, who has been placed in such a dangerous situation?" (vv. 272–73). *Jeo ne puis ci entor plaider / Ke jeo n'ai le quer esmeu*: "I cannot recount this without being deeply moved" (vv. 292–93).

The entreaty to Mary Magdalene, which evokes the cossetted birthing scene earlier rejected by the prince's wife, could be words of the woman in labour herself, or more likely, her thoughts indirectly stated by the narrator: *Duze Magdaleine Marie / Ke f[e]ra vostre pelerine, / Ki en bele chambre marbrine / Peust estre, e aie avoir / De femmes ki deveient savoir / De tel afaire e de tel chose?*: "Sweet Mary Magdalene, what will your pilgrim do? She could have been in her marbled chamber and had the help of women who know what to do in such situations" (vv. 278–83).

The narrator also expands on the theme of premature births, vv. 256–71, in which he uses a number of parallel structures (*Mes aventure est avenue / A meinte femme meinte foiz*, vv. 258–59; *Par maladie ou par pour, / Par talent ou par bleceure, / Ou ja par aucun' aventure*, vv. 262–64) to place this particular crisis in the context of other premature births which have turned out well with God's blessing. But this one ends in the death of the mother, and the narrator again extends the details beyond his Latin source: *E li emfes hors se tira / De sa mere, ke ainz fu morte / Ke il fust bien hors de la porte*: "And the child was drawn out of his dead mother, who died before he came into the world" (vv. 296–98). In Guillaume's version, the father, who remains helpless in front of his dead wife and newborn son, "can only add his own tears and lamentations to those of his son" (*Od lui estuet crier e braire*, v. 308). Guillaume's care in rendering this scene is eloquent testimony to his ability, as noted above (71), to make hagiography reach out to laypeople and vividly to enter their concerns.

Index of Proper Names

The double numbers following entries refer to the French verse text. The first number in bold identifies the individual texts (**1**= *Vie S. Gilles*, **2**= *Vie S. Georges*, **3**= *Vie S. Fey*, **4**=*Romanz de Marie Magdaleine*). The text reference number in bold is followed immediately by a full stop and the line number within each text; subsequent line numbers from the same text, separated by a comma, follow this first reference; a semi-colon separates the references to each separate text. Thus the numerical references following "Adam" (**1**.2128, 3645; **2**.361, 363, 368) indicate that the name occurs in the *Vie S. Gilles*, at lines 2128, 3645, and in the *Vie S. Georges* at lines 361, 363, 368. Proper names that are used extensively are followed by a sample list of line references only, followed by *etc.*; all other references are exhaustive. An asterisk indicates that the name is discussed in a note. Line references to names inserted in the translation for clarity (replacing possibly ambiguous pronouns) are enclosed in square brackets.

Acre (city in Palestine) **4**.226
Adam, the first man **1**.2128, 3645; **2**.361, 363, [366], 368
Advent, liturgical season leading up to Christmas **1**.1565
Agen (*Agen, Agenne*), city in SW France **3**.120, 135, [171], 182, 185, 852, [859], 920, [925], 929, 975, 1001, 1010, 1090, 1122, 1141, 1143
Alexandrine, queen, wife of Dacien **2**.1216
Anastasius, a magician **2**.603, [614], 634, [638]
Apollo (*Apolin*), pagan god **2**.53*, 256, 324, 588, 589, 758, 761, 808, 824, 938, 965, 973, 989, 1001, 1006, 1009, 1012, 1054, 1058, 1069, 1106, 1227, 1249, 1264, 1471, 1586, 1596
Architriclinus, bridegroom at wedding attended by Jesus at Cana **1**.3618*
Arinisdus, monk **3**.995, 1061, 1070, 1127, 1149, 1160, 1201
Arles, city in France **1**.1068*, [1070]
Athens **1**.23, 1987
Aurelius, archdeacon serving Caesarius, bishop of Arles **1**.1185, [1188, 1203, 1207, 1215]
Balthasar, one of the three Wise Men **1**.2114*
Baratrum, name for hell **1**.220*
Beelzebub, a devil **2**.1495
Benjamin, monk (librarian?) **3**.444*
Bethany, city near Bethlehem **1**.3594*

Bethlehem **1.**2111; **4.**523
Blois, city on the Loire River in France **1.**1167*
Bretons, inhabitants of Brittany **1.**2850
Burgundy **1.**1544
Caesarius, bishop of Arles (470–542) **1.**1063*
Calvary, site of crucifixion of Jesus **4.**524
Cana, town in Galilee **1.**3616
Cappadocia, native country of George **2.**79
Caprais, martyr, companion of Faith **3.**460, 493, [513], 523, [551], 575, 589, 621, [643], 648, 667, 695, [708], [717], [753], 777, 823
Charlemagne, Charles (*Charlemeines*,*Charles*, *Charlun*), emperor of France (742–814) **1.**1547, 2326*, [2349], 2377, [2381], 2421, 2473, 2541, 2700, 2717, 2855, [2874], [2903], 2906, 2978, 3005, 3057, 3084, 3147*, 3195, 3202, 3237; **3.**938*, 943
Christian **1.**822, 3118, 3119; **2.**30, 31, 46, 47, 58, 60, 143, 167, etc.; **3.**118, 169, 201, 264, 292, etc.; **4.**[709], 710, 714
Christmas (*Noël*) **1.**1565, 1571; **2.**1466*
Conques (*Cunckes, Cunkes, Cunches*), city in France **3.**926, 930, [933], 958, [962], 976, 979, 1117, 1172, 1182, 1202, 1205, 1219
Dacien, provost of Diocletian, called emperor in the *Life of George* **2.**26*, [429], 449, 499, 518, 551, 586, 595, 612, 639, 648, 668, [676], 720, [732], 865, [880], 908, 946, 950, [953], 1080, 1168, 1180, [1217], 1230, 1270, [1282], 1367, 1389, 1528, 1601; **3.**173, 186, 223, 243, 263, 281, 301, 673, 707, 773, 789, 793, [801], [804]
Dado, hermit, founder of monastery at Conques **3.**940*
Daniel, biblical prophet **1.**3601; **2.**1412
David, biblical king **1.**3640*
Denis, Saint, basilica and town on outskirts of Paris, named after patron saint of France (and by metonymy, France) **1.**2421, 2473, 2612
Diana (*Dyane*), goddess of the hunt **3.**320*
Diocletian, Roman emperor **3.**112*
Edmund, saint, patron of Bury St. Edmunds **3.**100*
Egypt **3.**479
Epiphany (*Thiphane*), feast of (6 January), associated in the West with the visit of the Magi **3.**1053
Eve (biblical) **2.**361
Faith (*Fey*) **3.**9*, 13, 15, 18, 42, [51], 87, 97, 104, 109, 127, 133, 141, 157, 207*, 213, 233, 276, 279, 287, 305, 331, 363, 385, 448, 454, 501, 507, 516, 572, 592, 595, 625, 632, 670, 811, 819, 883, 899, 905, 914, 922, 961, 1153, 1175, 1181, 1192, 1209, [1234]
Felicianus, martyr companion of Primus and Caprais **3.**764
Figeac (*Figultus*), town near Conques **3.**1165*

Index of Proper Names 229

Flovent, king of Septimania (Toulouse, Gascony, Provence and Burgundy) **1.**1542*, 1548, 1568, 1821, [2334], [3296], 3383
France (both the *Ile de France*, the region around Paris, and the larger empire of France) **1.**1546, [1549], 2326, [2338], 2376, 2436, 2541, 2568, 2578, 2612, 2619, 2961, 3259
French **1.**1299, 2850; **3.**35; **4.**rubric*
Galilee **1.**3616
Gascony (*Gaskoin, Gascoine, Gasgoine, Wascoinie*), region in SW France **1.**1066, 1543, 2315; **3.**1118
Gaspar, one of the three Wise Men **1.**2113*
George, soldier and martyr **2.**7, 67, 74, 189, 215, 243, 313, 325, etc.
Giles, hermit, abbot, saint (*Gire, Gires*) **1.**18, 24, 41, [44], [46], 55, 88, etc.
God (*Deu(s), Dampnedeu, Dé*) **1.**34, 36, 37, 49, 52, 73, 78, 94, 97, etc.; **2.**10, 19, 36, 64, 78, 422, 862, etc.; **3.**1, 34, [64], 74, 86, 87, 90, 95, etc.; **4.**10, 14, 57, 87, 102, [129], [133], 151, 161, 210, 217, etc.
Grecian (sea), **4.**28
Greece **1.**28, 491, 823, 1986, 2148, 3377
Greek (nationality) **1.**18, 22, 823, 853, 1299, 3377
Guillaume de Berneville, author of the *Vie de s. Gilles* **1.**1039, 3765
Hebrew (*Ebreu petit vallatun*), boys **1.**3632
Israel **1.**3597
Jerusalem **1.**2112, 3629, 3633; **4.**167, [197], 503, 520
Jesus (Christ) **1.**[2815], 3010; **2.**150, 214, 301, 377, 407, 409, 637, 658, 692, 717, etc.; **3.**110, 118, 129, 161, 186, 198, 239, 251, 255, etc.; **4.**2, 12, [14], 18, 43, 169, 508, [523], 618, 666
Jews (*Judeu, Jués, Gieu*) **1.**186, 2121, 3646, 3663; **2.**275; **4.**15
Joel, resuscitated pagan **2.**1465
Joseph, of Aramathea (biblical) **1.**3657, [3671]
Judas, disciple of Jesus **1.**2805
Julian, saint **1.**2500*
Lalbenque, city near Cahors **3.**1128*
Lazarus (*Lasdres, Lazarus*), raised from the dead by Jesus **1.**3595; **2.**1414; **4.**11
Louis, "the pious," son of Charlemagne **3.**945*, 949
Lucidius, bishop of Agen **3.**874*, 898
Magnacius, magician **2.**572, 587
Martha, sister of Mary Magdalene **4.**11
Mary Magdalene **1.**3608; **4.**9, 40, 40, 70, [77], 81, [82], 149, 153, 160, 195, [201], 205, 245, 278, 393, [427], 429, 602, 632, 638, 646, 657, 689, 698, 718
Mary, BVM, mother of Jesus **1.**408, 478, 3010, 3593; **2.**214, 380, 391, 1225, 1345, 1388, 1422; **3.**48, 100, 103, 297, 435, 439, 502, 525, 596, 775, 826, 889, 1191
Marcilla, name given by tradition to the woman mentioned in Luke 11:27, **4.**16*

Marseille **1.**1040, 1045, 1059; **4.**29, 540, [625], 682
Martin, saint **1.**359*, 1456
Maximian, Roman emperor **3.**111*
Maximinus, companion of Mary Magdalene **4.**23*, 701
Melchior, one of the three Wise Men **1.**2114*
Michael, archangel **1.**3699*, 3717; **2.**537, 538, 688, 1661
Milette, city where Dacien tortures George **2.**39
Mohammed (*Mahon*), the prophet **2.**11*
Montpellier, city in France **1.**1229, 1568, 1644, 1748, 2364, 3226
Mount of Olives, biblical **1.**3678
Nicholas, patron saint of sailors **1.**772
Nicodemus, disciple of Jesus (cf. John 19:39–40) **1.**3657
Nîmes (*cité de Nesmals*), city in France **1.**1755
Normans **1.**2850
Orleans, city in France **1.**2477, 2615, 2618, 2622, 2907
Pelagia, mother of Giles **1.**27
Pepin, king of Aquitaine **3.**1168*
Peter, disciple of Jesus, saint **1.**2235, 2808, 2813; **4.**27, 482, 497, 516, 519, 533, [536], 645
Pharaoh, biblical king of Egypt (cf. Ex. 13:17–31) **1.**3596; **3.**480
Pilate (biblical) **2.**284
Provence, southern province of France **1.**844, 1066, 1228, 1544, 2314, 2315, 2324, 2355, 3167, 3378, 3745
Rhone (*Rodne*), river **1.**1227, 1229, 1242, 1562, 2332, 3379
Roland, nephew of Charlemagne and protagonist of the *Chanson de Roland* **1.**2894*
Rome **1.**557, 827, 866, 2323, 3326, 3351, 3355, 3363, 3393, 3485; **2.**25; **3.**113
Roncesval, mountain pass in the Pyrenees **1.**2893*
Rouen, penny (coin) **1.**2201*
Russia **1.**848*
Satan **1.**2946; **2.**1477, 1495, 1509
Saviour (Christ) **2.**1415; **4.**2, 554
Septimania, province of southern Gaul, between the Rhône, the Pyrenees, and the Massif Central **1.**1786
Simon (*Symon*), of Walsingham **3.**99*
Solomon, king **4.**522
Spirit, Holy **1.**3499; **2.**184, 268, 340, 348, 353, etc.; **3.**288, 770, 1179, 1185
Susanna, and the elders (cf. Dan. 13:1–63)**1.**3600
Syria (*Sulie*) **4.**475
Tervagant, pagan deity **2.**589
Theocrita, widow, host of Giles in Arles **1.**1077, 1085, 1112, 1157, 1194
Theodorus, father of Giles **1.**25
Tiber (*Teivre*), river passing through Rome **1.**3444, 3453

Index of Proper Names 231

Toulouse, region in SW France **1.**1543
Trinity, the Christian triune deity (God the Father, the Son, and the Holy Spirit) **3.**784
Veredemius, hermit **1.**1284*, 1293, 1358, [1427], [1432]. [1445]. [1453]
Vulture (*Busart*), saint (= the devil) **2.**1064*
Walsingham, *see* Simon
William, Guillaume Le Clerc de Normandie **4.**716; and see Note on Translations, Manuscripts, and Editions, 75.